MEDIEVAL NAPLES

A DOCUMENTARY HISTORY
400–1400

MEDIEVAL NAPLES

A DOCUMENTARY HISTORY
400–1400

BY

RONALD G. MUSTO

ITALICA PRESS
NEW YORK
2013

A Documentary History of Naples Series
Medieval Naples, 400–1400

ITALICA PRESS, INC.
595 Main Street
New York, New York 10044
inquiries@italicapress.com

Library of Congress Cataloging-in-Publication Data

Medieval Naples, a documentary history : historical texts, 400–1400 / edited by Ronald G. Musto.
  pages cm. -- (A documentary history of Naples)
Includes bibliographical references and index.
ISBN 978-1-59910-247-4 (hardcover : alkaline paper) -- ISBN 978-1-59910-248-1 (paperback : alkaline paper) -- ISBN 978-1-59910-246-7 (e-book)
1. Naples (Italy) -- History--To 1503--Sources. I. Musto, Ronald G.
DG847.M43 2012
945'.731--dc23
        2012035039

Cover art: Sta. Chiara, facade. Photo: Italica Press.

FOR A COMPLETE LIST OF ITALICA PRESS TITLES
VISIT OUR WEB SITE AT:
WWW.ITALICAPRESS.COM

CONTENTS

CONTENTS

■

ILLUSTRATIONS

ABBREVIATIONS

ASN	Archivio di Stato di Napoli
ASPN	*Archivio Storico per le Province Napoletane*
BN	Naples, Biblioteca Nazionale
Bruzelius & Tronzo	Bruzelius, Caroline, and William Tronzo. *Medieval Naples: An Architectural & Urban History 400–1400*. New York: Italica Press, 2011
Carratelli	Carratelli, Giovanni Pugliese, ed. *Storia e civiltà della Campania*. Vol. 2: *Il Medioevo*. Naples: Electa, 1992
La Rocca	La Rocca, Cristina. *Italy in the Early Middle Ages 476–1000*. Oxford: Oxford University Press, 2002
L'état Angevin	*L'état Angevin: Pouvoir, culture et société entre XIIIe et XIVe siècle. Actes du colloque international organisé par l'American Academy in Rome (Rome–Naples, 7–11 novembre 1995).* Collection de l'École française de Rome 245; Nuovi studi storici 45. Rome: École française de Rome & ISIME, 1998
Musca	Musca, Giosuè. *La cultura angioina: Civiltà del Mezzogiorno.* Milan: Silvano Editoriale, 1985
Napoli: La città e il mare	Giampaola, Daniela, Vittoria Carsana, and Beatrice Roncella, eds. *Napoli: La città e il mare. Piazza Bovio: Tra Romani e Bizantini.* Naples: Electa, 2010
PL	Migne, J.-P. *Patrologiae Cursus Completus: Series Latina.* Paris: Migne et al., 1844–1902
RIS	*Rerum Italicarum Scriptores.* Ludovico Antonio Muratori, ed. Milan: Societas Palatina, 1727–29
SN	*Storia di Napoli.* Ernesto Pontieri, ed. 11 vols. Naples: Società Editrice Storia di Napoli, 1967–78

■

PREFACE

We are pleased to present *Medieval Naples, 400–1400* as part of Italica Press's *Documentary History of Naples*. The publication process of this volume has been highly collaborative. Four authors have been involved in its planning, discussion and implementation since its inception over a decade ago. Caroline Bruzelius and William Tronzo have contributed a previous volume, *Medieval Naples: An Architectural & Urban History, 400–1400* (New York: Italica Press, 2011). In this volume Eileen Gardiner has collected and edited literary and hagiographic texts and contributed sections on literacy and the book. Ronald G. Musto provides texts and introductions to its religious, political and socio-economic history.

This combination of disciplinary approaches and perspectives on the same historical data is especially important for the history of medieval Naples, an area of great richness and complexity and yet one little known outside of Italy and among European specialists. In North America it remains an emerging field and one requiring an ever-expanding circle of studies and forms of publication, from the most specialized to more general approaches.

In that spirit the following book is intended as a general, though rigorous, introduction to the broad sweep of Naples' development in the Middle Ages. This is the first comprehensive English-language collection of sources to treat the history of the city from late antiquity to the beginnings of the Renaissance for general readers, students or scholars unfamiliar with the history of the city and the types of sources available for further research. Readings cover the historical, economic, literary, artistic, religious and cultural life from the fall of Rome through the Byzantine, ducal (Lombard), Norman, Hohenstaufen and Angevin periods. Narrative sources predominate both to provide a historical framework and to convey the flavor of a range of medieval writing. Special emphasis is given to the Angevin period, first because of this editor's special competence and interest, second because of its relative wealth of source materials and third because of the period's recent interest to Anglophone scholars. The collection ends with the death of Queen Giovanna I and ascendency of the Durazzan line of Angevins, which roughly coincides with the beginning of the Renaissance.

Among the primary sources presented here in English translation — many for the first time — are chronicles and histories; archival materials including accounts, tax, financial, legal and commercial records; contracts, wills, notarial and legislative documents; poetry, romances, biographies, letters, travelers' accounts and legends; liturgical and hagiographic texts; as well as examples of manuscript production. Texts are numbered consecutively and arranged by period and then chronologically. Each is preceded by an introduction contextualizing the reading and providing source bibliography.

A new introduction offers a comprehensive survey, with a discussion of the historiography and of important research and interpretive issues. These include the material development of the medieval city from late antiquity through the end of the Angevin period, the condition and use of the available primary sources and archaeological evidence, with particular attention given to the wide variety of recent excavations and of archival materials. It also treats the question of the ruralization and recovery of Naples' urban core through the little known ducal period — with some discussion of the city's changing population — the question of Naples' importance as a commercial and political capital, its developing economic and material base and the issue of its relationship to its hinterland on the one hand and to broader Mediterranean contexts on the other. The introduction also surveys the changes in Naples' urban plan, its walls and fortifications, its port and its commercial and residential development, examining the archival evidence for the survival of the city's less important architectural remains. For the later Middle Ages, I include Naples' intellectual life and trace the complex historiography of what I term the "black legend of the Angevins" and its continued impact on perceptions of Naples and the Italian South.

This print edition is an expanded and revised version of the book first presented online and then as an e-book for the Kindle. The digital edition takes full advantage of online capabilities: hyperlinking to complete bibliographical information on WorldCat, to Italica Press's image galleries, video and sound, architecture, sculpture and paintings, maps, drawings and engravings, ground plans and elevations, digital archives and manuscript collections, online reference works and images, and to Italica's online bibliographies and Interactive Map of Medieval Naples.

My thanks Prof. Joseph D. Alchermes of Connecticut College; Dottoressa Daniela Giampaolo of the Ministero per i Beni e le Attività Culturali, Soprintendenza Speciale per i Beni Archeologici di Napoli e Pompei; and Dottori Antonio Carpenito, Rita Ligouri and Antonio Di Maio of the Attività Tecniche di Supporto di Napoli. We are thankful to Dottoressa Orsola Foglia of the Soprintendenza per i Beni Architettonici Paesaggistici, Storici, Artistici ed Etnoantropologici di Napoli e Provincia. Arch. Dott. Foglia's splendid restoration of, and preservation work on, S. Giovanni Maggiore makes clear the need for Naples' medieval monuments to be better known, studied and published both in Italy and here in North America.

At the American Academy in Rome I would like to thank Professor Christopher S. Celenza, Director; Marina Lella, Executive Assistant to the Director; Pina Pasquantonio, Assistant Director for Operations; and Cristina Puglisi, Deputy Director, for their gracious hospitality during several successive stays in preparation for this volume.

Many of the following texts are our original translations; but I would also like to thank those whose work we have excerpted, trust that we have done so within the bounds of fair use, and hope that we will call further attention to these important works.

Finally, I would like to express thanks to co-authors Caroline Bruzelius, Eileen Gardiner and William Tronzo for sharing their work and insights as this series developed over two decades from a newly imagined idea to a complex and fully realized series of books, web sites and other digital resources.

■

Ronald G. Musto, Series Editor
A Documentary History of Naples
New York City, January 2013

Fig. 1. S. Giorgio Maggiore, ambulatory. Photo: Italica Press.

INTRODUCTION:
BETWEEN ROME AND ARAGON.
NAPLES 400–1400

Naples' transformation from a mid-sized seaport of the Roman Empire to a regional and then national capital has been the subject of constant study over the past century. This is due both to its present condition as the most problematic of Italian cities and to its history as Italy's most splendid and wealthy historic capital. This introduction provides general background to the urban and artistic development of the city of Naples and its immediate environs from the end of the Roman Empire to the end of the Angevin period and its reincorporation into another empire with the Aragonese conquest. It is meant both to provide a general context and reference for the readings that will follow in subsequent chapters and to offer a continuous narrative that supplements the frames in those chapters. It will therefore briefly survey the political history of Naples and Campania from the fifth to the fifteenth century, make note of important urbanist, architectural, and artistic monuments and influences from these years, and provide a historiographical introduction.

Much of this material is derived, revised and updated from previous work,[1] but the intervening two decades have seen a marked increase in the quantity and the methodological sophistication of approaches to the history of southern Italy in the Middle Ages. This historiography has traditionally been based on a range of sources — archaeological, material and written. While new archaeological discoveries have been made and published in recent years attendant to the extension of Naples' *Metropolitana*,[2] the textual evidence remains much the

---

1. See Enrico Bacco, C. d'Engenio Caracciolo, Eileen Gardiner, Caroline A. Bruzelius, and Ronald G. Musto, *Naples: An Early Guide* (New York: Italica Press, 1991), xiii–lxii, esp. xxvii–xxxviii. For bibliography since then, see *Medieval Naples: A Documentary History, 400–1400*, http://www.italicapress.com/index286.html.

2. See William Tronzo, "Naples in the Early Middle Ages," in Caroline

same as it was in the nineteenth century, although modern and online editions are making these sources more accessible and reliable. Meanwhile, a generation of archival reconstruction under Riccardo Filangieri and his associates have now reclaimed much of the Angevin archives destroyed in World War II.[3]

While the early centuries of Naples' medieval development have been well studied in Italy and on the Continent,[4] until recently the era from c.400 to c.1400 was largely ignored by Anglophone scholarship, with the exception of the Norman period in southern Italy. This, on the other hand, has been well studied in the Anglophone world for almost a century, and in America ever since Charles Homer Haskins included it in his *The Normans in European History*[5] as part of the progressive

---

Bruzelius and William Tronzo, *Medieval Naples: An Architectural & Urban History 400–1400* (New York: Italica Press, 2011), 1–47.

3.   Ninety percent of the Neapolitan archives for these periods were destroyed in the war. See Riccardo Filangieri, "Report on the Destruction by the Germans, September 30, 1943, of the Depository of Priceless Historical Records of the Naples State Archives," *American Archivist* 7 (1944): 252–55; and E.M. Jamison, "Documents from the Angevin Registers of Naples: Charles I," *Papers of the British School at Rome* 17 (1949): 87–89. For a description of the life of the city in 1943 and 1944 see Norman Lewis, *Naples '44* (New York: Pantheon, 1978). Many Angevin records have, fortunately, been reconstructed from previously published or transcribed papers. See Jole Mazzoleni, *Le fonti documentarie e bibliografiche dal secolo x al secolo xx conservate presso l'Archivio di Stato di Napoli* (Naples: ASN, 1974), 31–52. Most of the Hohenstaufen records had already been published by German historians of the nineteenth century; and many Aragonese records were brought to Barcelona in the fifteenth century. For the remarkable progress of the reconstruction of the Angevin archives in recent years, see Riccardo Filangieri, Stefano Palmieri, Maria L. Storch, et al., *I registri della cancelleria angioina* (Naples: Accademia Pontaniana, 1950–2006 to date.) See also Bibliography, http://www.italicapress.com/index346.html, especially Supplemental Bibliographies: The Angevins.

4.   The *Storia di Napoli* synthesized research through the 1960s and, even though superseded in many aspects by new research, remains a fundamental starting point. See *Storia di Napoli*, Ernesto Pontieri, ed., 11 vols. (Naples: Società Editrice Storia di Napoli, 1967–78).

5.   Boston: Houghton Mifflin, 1915, with subsequent reprints. Haskins' only significant Anglophone source was E. Jamison, "The Norman Administration of Apulia and Capua," *Papers of the British School at Rome* 6 (1913): 211–481.

achievements of this northern people "as founders and organizers of states and contributors to European culture."[6] This
northern perspective has remained crucial to the historiography. Long studied among Anglophone scholars for its links
to the Normans of the North, the *Mezzogiorno*, or South of
Italy, has often been seen as one lost to historical memory
since late antiquity and brought back into the light of historiography only occasionally under the influence of the North.
This understanding was also crucial to German scholars of
the medieval imperial period due to the vital importance of
the South and of Sicily to the history of the Hohenstaufen
dynasty and its impact on the German lands themselves.
This outlook, with some modifications under the impact of
Mediterranean studies[7] and broader cultural criticism,[8] has

---

6.   Page vii. Or again (p. 13), "The men who subdued England and Sicily...
warriors and adventurers in untamed lands and upon uncharted seas, they were
organizers of states and rulers of people." In short, these northerners were active
agents, creating and organizing untamed nature and passive human objects,
bringing them into conscious history. For further evidence of this attitude, see
Henry Adams, *Mont-Saint-Michel and Chartres* [1905] (New York: Doubleday
Anchor, 1959), 1–4. "Normans were everywhere in 1066 and everywhere in the
lead of their age."

7.   The bibliography, though recent, is large and growing. See especially the
dozens of volumes in Brill's Medieval Mediterranean series, as well as new groups
like the Mediterranean Studies Association or the University of California's
Mediterranean Seminar. The foundational studies remain Fernand Braudel, *The
Mediterranean and the Mediterranean World in the Age of Philip II*, Siân Reynold,
trans. 2 vols. (New York: Harper & Row, 1972–73); and Peregrine Horden and
Nicholas Purcell, *The Corrupting Sea: A Study of Mediterranean History* (Oxford:
Blackwell, 2000).

8.   See Robert Lumley and Jonathan Morris, eds., *The New History of the
Italian South: The Mezzogiorno Revisited* (Exeter: University of Exeter Press,
1997); Jane Schneider, *Italy's "Southern Question": Orientalism in One Country*
(Berkeley: University of California Press, 1998); John A. Davis, "The South,
the Risorgimento, and the Origins of the 'Southern Problem'," in John A.
Davis, ed., *Gramsci and Italy's Passive Revolution* (London: Croom Helm, 1979);
idem, "Casting off the 'Southern Problem': Or the Peculiarities of the South
Reconsidered," in Schneider, op. cit., 205–24; Nelson Moe, *The View from Vesuvius:
Italian Culture and the Southern Question*, Studies in the History of Society and
Culture 46 (Berkeley: University of California Press, 2002); Francesco Senatore,

continued among Anglophone scholars of political, religious and cultural history into the twenty-first century. In more recent years the Angevin period has received increasing attention from Anglophone, especially American, historians and art historians.

On the other hand, it is difficult to disentangle the history of Naples itself during this period as a distinct political, religious and cultural center from that of the Campania or of the broader Mezzogiorno. This is due to several factors: the nature of our primary sources, which are often general narratives of the South and its rulers; the nature of specific archival collections,[9] which have driven many individual urban case-studies; the aforementioned interests of previous historiography on an almost teleological development leading up to the Normans and the origins of the Angevin Regno; and finally the paucity of significant physical remains within the city of Naples for the centuries between the fall of Rome and the Angevins.

"The Kingdom of Naples," in Andrea Gamberini and Isabella Lazzarini, eds., *The Italian Renaissance State* (New York: Cambridge University Press, 2012), 30–49, esp. 45–49; and my analysis in the forthcoming "Introduction: Naples in Myth and History," in *Artistic Centers of the Italian Renaissance: Naples*, Marcia B. Hall, ed. (New York: Cambridge University Press). For the broader issues of the South, see Supplemental Bibliographies, "Introduction and Multiperiod Works," http://www.italicapress.com/index346.html.

9. For Naples these have now been digitized by the Unione Accademia Nazionale as the *Archivio della Latinità Italiano del Medioevo* (ALIM) and are available at http://www.uan.it/Notarili/alimnot.nsf/RPD. The sources include both the archives of Cava de' Tirreni in the *Codex Diplomaticus Cavensis* and those edited and published in the *Regii Neapolitani Archivi Monumenta* (1845). Other archives and case studies are cited, for example, by Patricia Skinner, "The Tyrrhenian Coastal Cities under the Normans," in Graham A. Loud with A.J. Metcalfe, eds., *The Society of Norman Italy*, The Medieval Mediterranean 38 (Leiden: Brill, 2002), 75–96. Amedeo Feniello, *Napoli: Società ed economia (902–1137)* (Rome: Istituto Storico Italiano per il Medio Evo, 2011; hereafter Feniello, *Napoli*), 22–30, provides an excellent overview of the sources for the later ducal period. My special thanks and appreciation to Prof. Feniello for making his digital manuscript available to me prior to publication. With this work Prof. Feniello brings the study of the extant archival evidence for Naples during this period to a new level of expertise and analysis.

Much of what we say below therefore will synthesize secondary interpretation of Naples and of analogous urban developments, which sometimes have direct bearing on this city. It will also cite studies of the fragmentary remains of Naples' historical and archaeological record. In recent years the latter has been amplified as new digs begin to fill out the picture of urban life and development over the Byzantine and ducal periods. In addition, new urban improvement projects, such as the extension of the *Metropolitana* transit system, make it possible to uncover and study previously unknown remains from late antiquity and the early medieval period.[10]

LATE ROMAN AND BYZANTINE NAPLES (325–568)

The Bay of Naples was one of the earliest regions of Europe to feel the impact of Christianity. St. Paul first set foot in Italy at Pozzuoli on his way to trial in Rome and supposedly found Christians already there (Acts 28:14). Naples itself soon became a leading center of Christian culture and art, as its many catacombs bear witness. These trends have been summarized and analyzed recently by William Tronzo.[11] At the same time the city and its bay remained a favorite resort of the Roman elite, and the basic patterns of Roman life remained unchanged through the late empire. Naples itself remained a city of culture, while neighboring Pozzuoli continued to be the chief commercial port of the region, serving

---

10. For a general introduction to the historiographical issues see, for example, Cristina La Rocca, *Italy in the Early Middle Ages 476–1000* (Oxford: Oxford University Press, 2002), "Introduction," 1–10; Sauro Gelichi, "The Cities," in La Rocca, 168–88. Paul Arthur has both synthesized and brought this question forward for the early Middle Ages in his *Naples: From Roman Town to City-State* (London: British School at Rome, 2002). For a discussion of the recent Piazza Bovio *Metropolitana* digs, see the exhibition catalog: Daniela Giampaola, Vittoria Carsana, and Beatrice Roncella, eds., *Napoli: La città e il mare. Piazza Bovio: Tra Romani e Bizantini* (Naples: Electa, 2010); for other excavations see Arthur, *Naples*, 153–58.

11. See Tronzo, "Naples in the Early Middle Ages," in Bruzelius & Tronzo, 12–24. See also Giovanni Vitolo, *Le città campane fra tarda antichità e alto medioevo* (Salerno: Laveglia, 2005).

both the Campania and Rome. Neighboring Baiae (Baia) and Misenum across the bay retained their positions respectively as imperial resort and chief naval base.

In 410 the Visigoth Alaric, fresh from his sack of Rome, passed through Campania on his way south. Gaiseric and his Vandals soon followed in 455. Yet the first "barbarian invasions" changed the face of Italy very little.[12] Aside from toppling and displacing already teetering regimes and ruling elites, their numbers were small,[13] and their destructive waves merely passed through the peninsula. By the sixth century, however, the Goths, a Germanic tribe from north and west of the Black Sea, had come to stay. It does also appear from the archaeological evidence that the basic unit of ancient life — the *civitas* — began to recede in late antiquity and the early Middle Ages. Many settlements in the old agricultural heartlands either disappeared or were moved to more secure hilltop sites, much shrunken from their ancient size.

---

12. The impact of the migration of these new peoples is still hotly debated among historians and archaeologists. See, for example, a review and analysis of the recent historiography in Chris Wickham, *The Inheritance of Rome: A History of Europe from 400 to 1000* (New York: Viking, 2009), 1–12 et passim; and the review of the recent historiography by Andrew Gillett in *The Medieval Review* 07.10.12 (https://scholarworks.iu.edu/dspace/bitstream/handle/2022/6332/07.10.12. html). The notion of the transformative nature of the event, alternately termed "barbarian invasions" by Mediterranean scholars or the "migrations" of peoples by northern Europeans, has recently been the subject of a comparative historiographical review by Norman Etherington, "Barbarians Ancient and Modern," *American Historical Review* 116.1 (Feb. 2011): 31–57. For the latest major work see Peter Heather, *Empires and Barbarians: The Fall of Rome and the Birth of Europe* (New York: Oxford University Press, 2010); its recent review by Walter Goffart in *The Medieval Review* 10.08.06 (https://scholarworks.iu.edu/dspace/bitstream/handle/2022/9050/10.08.06.html); and, for a very recent overview, Ralph W. Mathisen and Danuta Shanzer, "Introduction," in *Romans, Barbarians, and the Transformation of the Roman World: Cultural Interaction and the Creation of Identity in Late Antiquity* (Farnham, Surrey: Ashgate, 2011), 1–11.

13. Wickham, *Inheritance of Rome*, 101, notes that the consensus now accepts about 100,000 total population for ruling groups like the Vandals and Ostrogoths, including about 20,000 to 25,000 adult males. Walter Pohl, "Invasions and Ethnic Identity," in La Rocca, 11–33 at 18–19, proposes a Gothic fighting force of about 30,000, and an overall migration of about 100,000 Goths into an Italy whose population still numbered several millions.

Yet students of the period have still not reached a consensus as to whether this was because of military threat, general lawlessness, or dramatic changes to the human and natural ecology of Campania.[14] Chris Wickham attempts to synthesize this disparity of view by making the important distinction between the cultural continuity of the Roman population, especially the elite — their sense that they still lived within the ancient world that they had inherited, a mentality fully borne out in the narrative sources — and the far more limited means at their disposal to implement this continuity, a "simplification," borne out by the archaeological and artistic remains of the period.[15]

Naples itself seems to have escaped the general decline for the period. In fact, along with many other urban centers along the Mediterranean littoral, it appears to have gathered some increasing importance. This was due to some degree to migration from the countryside for the greater security of the city, to Naples' increased importance as a trading emporium to the eastern Mediterranean, and to its role as a military entrepôt for imperial expeditions. But the change was gradual and few remains were available to document this shift until the recent archaeological discoveries at such sites as Piazza Bovio. Here evidence suggests the almost continuous, if uneven, use of the littoral beyond the ancient walls both for a port and for small-scale manufacturing.[16]

Amphorae collected at both the Piazza Bovio and Piazza Nicolo Amore digs indicate that Naples remained in close commercial connection with North Africa for grains,[17] with

---

14. See, for example the following essays in La Rocca: Chris Wickham, "Rural Economy and Society," 118–43; Riccardo Francovich, "Changing Structures of Settlements," 144–67; and Sauro Gelichi, "The Cities," 168–88.

15. Wickham, *Inheritance of Rome*, 9; idem, *Early Medieval Italy: Central Power and Local Society 400-1000* (Ann Arbor: University of Michigan Press, 1989), 78, 147–52; Francovich, "Changing Structures," 151–53.

16. See the following essays in *Napoli: La città e il mare*: Daniela Giampaola, "Il paesaggio costiero di Neapolis tra Greci e Bizantini," 17–26; Mariella Gentile, "La fortificazione bizantina," 51–56, esp. 51; Stefania Febbraro, "Il quartiere artigianale e la necropoli," 57–61; and Beatrice Roncella, "I magazini," 63–68.

17. See Vittoria Carsana and Valeria d'Amico, "Piazza Bovio. Produzioni

the Aegean and the Levant for wines and small luxury items, including fine cloth, as well as with Egypt into the seventh century. The discovery of several stages of building remains at Piazza Bovio demonstrates the continuous use of the area for the manufacture of glass and mosaics,[18] iron and some fine metal work[19] that at least partially served the city's political and religious elites.

The extension of the walls by Valentinian III in the 440s and by Belisarius and Narses in the mid-sixth century enclosed a large new area around S. Giovanni Maggiore.[20] Later, the once stately monumental complex bordering the ancient harbor — including the triumphal arch of the Severan period[21] and possibly the stadium complex to the southeast, were disassembled, their fragments reincorporated into the fabric of Byzantine defense towers facing the waterfront during the sixth or seventh century.[22]

---

e consumi in età bizantina: La ceramica dalla metà del VI al X secolo," in *Napoli: La città e il mare*, 69–80. Wickham, *Inheritance of Rome*, 41, asserts that the Vandal occupation of North Africa destroyed this link and was the true prime mover of Rome's decline.

18. See Franca del Vecchio, "I vetri: Il ciclo della produzione e i manufatti," in *Napoli: La città e il mare*, 81–85.

19. See Francesca Sogliani, "I metalli: Testimonianze dell'officina tardoantica e altomedievale," in *Napoli: La città e il mare*, 87–89.

20. Arthur, *Naples*, 35. For the church, see also Gennaro Borrelli, *La basilica di S. Giovanni Maggiore* (Naples: Officine Grafiche "Glaux," 1967); and the CD-ROM edited by Orsola Foglia (Naples: Soprintendenza per i Beni Architettonici, n.d.). For the Italica Press web gallery, see http://www.flickr.com/photos/80499896@N05/sets/72157630149610864.

21. See Daniela Giampaola, "Introduzione allo scavo e alla mostra," in *Napoli: La città e il mare*, 11–16 at 12; and Giuliana Cavalieri Manasse and Henner von Hesberg, "Dalle decorazioni architettoniche ai monumenti romani," in *Napoli: La città e il mare*, 27–50.

22. Mariella Gentile, "La fortificazione bizantina," in *Napoli: La città e il mare*, 51–56.

DUCAL NAPLES (568–1139)[23]

The city, like most of Italy, fell under the control of Theodoric (493–526) and his Ostrogoths until the Byzantine emperor Justinian (527–65) launched the reconquest of southern and central Italy under Belisarius.[24] A brilliant general, Belisarius took the city in 536 — after a vain siege by land and sea for months — by bringing an advanced guard in through a broken aqueduct. Belisarius' successes were his very downfall, and a jealous Justinian soon replaced him with Narses.

Amid raging war, depredation and starvation across Italy, and in the face of a Persian invasion of the Byzantine Empire, court intrigue at Constantinople finally neutralized Narses' efforts to consolidate Byzantine gains in Italy. The new Gothic king, Totila (541–52), recaptured Naples in 543; and despite Belisarius' return to Italy and then Narses' reappointment in 548, the city of Naples remained under Gothic control through the remainder of the Gothic Wars. Then, just as suddenly as the Romans from Constantinople had taken southern Italy, they lost it to a new invasion: this time by the Lombards, a people originally from what is now eastern Germany, under King Alboin in 568.[25]

With the assassination of Alboin in 572 (arranged by the Byzantines) and then of his successor Cleph in 574/75, the Lombards in Italy decided to divide their possessions among thirty-six Lombard dukes. Much of their early history in the South was taken up with carving out these new duchies. The wars that

---

23. For complete bibliography, see Vera von Falkenhausen, "La Campania tra Goti e Bizantini," in Giovanni Pugliese Carratelli, ed., *Storia e civiltà della Campania: Il Medioevo* (Naples: Electa, 1992), 7–35; Bruno Figliuolo, "Longobardi e Normanni," in Carratelli, *Il Medioevo*, 37–86; Musto, *Naples Bibliography,* 25–28; and Supplemental Bibliographies, "Ducal Naples," http://www.italicapress.com/index346.html.

24. For these events, see Reading 7; and SN 1:82-117. Eleanor Shipley Duckett, *Gateway to the Middle Ages: Italy* (Ann Arbor: University of Michigan Press, 1961), 1–57, is still useful. For the early history of southern Italy and Naples, see SN 1:118–518; and Wickham, *Early Medieval Italy,* 9–27.

25. For a useful synthesis see Neil Christie, *The Lombards: The Ancient Longobards* (Oxford: Blackwell, 1995), esp. 69–108.

created them devastated most of the South's old diocesan *civitates* — the Roman imperial administrative towns and now the seats of Christian bishops — and urban life declined in all but the most prosperous agricultural or coastal areas. Although the chronology of this process is still uncertain, most of the old rural settlements of Campania disappeared as their populations shriveled or sought refuge in fortified hill towns or *castra*. By the beginning of the seventh century ancient rural patterns had disappeared in the South, and no new social forms had yet replaced them.[26]

By this time Naples was almost alone of the Byzantine areas of Italy in its independence from the Lombards and its continuous tradition of civic life. While Lombard dukes began actively influencing the city's affairs by the eighth century, Naples retained its Roman and, beneath that, its Greek language, character and culture. It was nominally, and at times directly, under a Byzantine *strategos*; it retained vestiges of a senatorial class and kept its *curia*, or ruling council, into the tenth century. It retained and fostered a unique class of administrators, trained in the Romano-Byzantine tradition, reflecting a clearly identifiable, highly structured scribal culture for its official and other pubic documents from at least the early eigth century.[27] Political life resembled that of late imperial Rome or Constantinople, and political parties formed around the election to its bishop's throne.

If that late Roman institution had collapsed in northern Italy under the Lombards and did not survive their conversion from Arianism to Catholicism, in Naples the bishop held his active role in the civic administration. The city retained its status as a *civitas* and as the seat of that bishop. This seat centered around the duomo (cathedral) dedicated first to the Savior, then to Sta. Restituta, and around the adjacent bishop's palace.[28] Even

---

26. See Claudio Azzara, "Ecclesiastical Institutions," in La Rocca, 85–101, esp. 85–87; Barbara M. Kreutz, *Before the Normans: Southern Italy in the Ninth and Tenth Centuries* (Philadelphia: University of Pennsylvania Press, 1996), 3.

27. See Jean-Marie Martin, "Les documents de Naples, Amalfi, Gaète (IXe–XIIe siècles: Ecriture, diplomatique, notariat," in Jean-Marie Martin, Annick Peters-Custot and Vivien Prigent, eds., *L'heritage Byzantine en Italie (VIIIe–XIIe siècle.* 1: *La frabrique documentaire.* Collection de L'École Française de Rome 449 (Rome: École Française de Rome, 2011), 51–85, esp. 51–72.

28. See Bruzelius & Tronzo, 24–41. The city became an archbishopric in 990

though the bishops of Naples could not match those of Rome in the shear economic clout they held through their ownership of land both inside and outside the city, they remained among the largest landholders in a society where land meant wealth and political power. By the ninth century this power had become hereditary among a small handful of families, one or two of whom controlled the office of duke as well. Some individuals, in fact, actually held both offices at once.[29]

The Byzantine duchy's public landholdings, the *publicum*, gradually became the private holdings of the ducal family and later dynasty of the Sergians: the basis of their economic and political power.[30] Authority on all levels gradually shifted from a public office to a privatized contract between strong protectors and weaker clients: an ancient Mediterranean relationship increasingly influenced by the customs of the Lombards, Franks and Germans. Nevertheless, despite all incursions of new peoples, Naples remained Mediterranean in its culture and outlook: diverse and inclusive like all the surviving trading centers of late antiquity. As Barbara Kreutz has noted, "fluidity" would remain a hallmark of Naples and the South through the ducal period.[31]

While Naples seems to have escaped the general fate of most urban centers of Italy, especially of the South, with the fall of Rome, its population undoubtedly declined through the depredations, mass displacements and population changes of the Gothic Wars. Paul Arthur[32] has recently estimated its population to be about 20,000 by the end of the sixth century, and large areas of the city inside the walls were already deserted by the time of Belisarius' siege in 536/37. We remain uncertain of the extent

---

under Sergius I. See Arthur, *Naples*, 168; Cilento, "La chiesa," SN 2.2:721–22. See the Italica Press web gallery: http://www.flickr.com/photos/80499896@N05/sets/72157630149817080.

29. See Wickham, *Early Medieval Italy*, 78; Arthur, *Naples*, 167–68; and Luigi Andrea Berto, "*Utilius est veritatem proferre*. A Difficult Memory to Manage: Narrating the Relationships between Bishops and Dukes in Early Medieval Naples," *Viator* 39.2 (2008): 49–63..

30. See Reading 23.

31. *Before the Normans*, xxx.

32. *Naples*, 21–25 et passim. See Readings 8–9.

of the early medieval walls,[33] but we do know that the city was one of the few to retain its ancient defenses, its Roman aqueduct, its forum and (converted) temples. As many of the older public buildings — e.g., the stadium and hippodrome — fell into disuse, their places were taken by new Christian institutions: over thirty monastic houses spreading upon the remains of the Roman city and outside its walls.[34] In addition to these were the seven major *diaconiae* constructed under the late empire for the distribution of food and other necessities to the city's poor. Never large buildings in scale, they were concentrated in the area between the old forum, new cathedral complex and the praetorium, the most densely populated section of the city in the early Middle Ages into the ducal period.[35] In the later Middle Ages and especially in the Baroque period, these *diaconiae* were either completely reconstructed or, like so many of Naples' smaller or "private" early medieval churches, have since disappeared. On the other hand, our sources tell us that the immense imperial remains around the baths of Baiae and at Pozzuoli survived well into the 860s[36] when Emperor Louis II and Empress Engelberga visited them. So did the amphitheater at the prospering port of

33. See Bartolomeo Capasso, *Napoli Greco-Romano* (Naples: Società Napoletana di Storia Patria, 1905; repr., Naples: Berisio, 1987), map; idem, *Topografia della città di Napoli nell' xi secolo* (Naples: 1895; repr., Bologna: Arnaldo Forni, 2005); Mario Napoli, "La città," SN 2.2: "La cinta urbana," 739–52; Lucio Santoro, *Le mura di Napoli* (Rome: Istituto Italiano dei Castelli, 1984); Cesare De Seta, *Napoli fra Rinascimento e Illuminismo* (Naples: Electa, 1997), esp. 17; and Arthur, *Naples*, 35–37. Recent research, occasioned by construction excavations on Naples' new *Metropolitana* subway branch, has unearthed evidence of the medieval walls that may change the dating on the southeast expansion of the city around Piazza del Mercato to the late Hohenstaufen, rather than the early Angevin, period. Evidence remains inconclusive to date. See also Musto, Interactive Map: http://www.italicapress.com/index287.html.

34. Cilento, "La chiesa," 655–68; Venditti, "L'architettura," 836.

35. Cilento, 669–70; Venditti, "L'architettura," 832–36; Arthur, *Naples*, 68–69, 162. See also Musto, Interactive Map: http://www.italicapress.com/index287.html.

36. See Jean-Marie Martin, "Les bains dans l'Italie méridionale au Moyen Âge (VIIe–XIIIe siècle)," In *Bains curatifs et bains hygeniques en Italie de l'Antiquité au Moyen Âge*, Marie Guérin-Beauvois and Jean-Marie Martin, eds. Collection de École Française de Rome 383 (Rome: École Française de Rome, 2007), 53–78.

Pozzuoli. Numerous other remains dotted the landscape in the Campi Flegrei and further on in Campania, providing ancient artistic examples, spolia for construction and decoration and even adaptive habitation for the surviving population.

It has long been assumed that the South retained its Greek culture uninterrupted from antiquity, but more recent studies have traced the de-Hellenization of the region during Roman antiquity and the resettlement of Greek communities only with the Byzantine reconquest under Justinian I. Greek influence in the South remained limited to seaports and to scattered Basilian monastic settlements in the interior from the tenth century on. Naples appears alone in its continued Greco-Latin culture, but this too was only the preserve of the urban elite who even distinguished themselves by signing their Latin names in Greek characters.[37] By the mid-ninth century, this tentative new southern culture was shaken by a series of civil wars among the Lombard princes and by the growth of Frankish power under Charlemagne and his heirs, then allied with the Roman popes against the Lombards. Charlemagne had been successful in subjugating the Lombards of the North and of Spoleto to his empire, but those of Benevento and the South continued to elude Carolingian power through the ninth century. Louis II had some successes in retaining southern Italy for the Carolingian Empire, but long supply lines, the nature of his proto-feudal levies and internecine Carolingian struggles made him unable to unravel the complex tangle of interwoven self-interest and aggressive expansionism of all the competing forces there. Byzantines, the Lombards of Benevento, Salerno and Capua, Amalfi and Naples all vied for momentary supremacy and pursued opportunistic polices against their neighbors, making the South one of the more unstable regions of an already unstable Europe.

Equally important was the rise of the Muslim threat. Just as the southern Italian Christians were rarely united, so too must one note that the Muslims of the Mediterranean never presented a monolithic or united front toward Christendom in either

---

37. On the Basilian monasteries, see Kreutz, 10–11. On this use of Greek characters, almost exclusively Neapolitan, see von Falkenhausen, "La Campania," 26. See also Reading 23, and Figs. 61–62.

military or trade and diplomatic policy,[38] despite their stereotypical portrayal in the *chansons de geste*[39] and more recent propaganda. The Muslim world was as varied in its culture and often as conflicted in its policy as the Christian West. Expanding out from North Africa, by the 840s Muslims were already raiding the coasts of southern Italy. By 843 they had established a foothold in Bari at the invitation of the Lombard Radelchi I of Benevento; and between 840 and 880 they held most of the southern heel. By the 880s Muslims had conquered almost all of Sicily.

The policy of Naples contributed to the rise of the Muslim presence. In 812 a slave-raiding party of Mauri[40] had taken Ischia across the Bay of Naples. In 835, however, the Neapolitans invited a band of Aghlabid Arab and Berber mercenaries from North Africa — then unemployed from the conquest of Byzantine Sicily — to aid them in a campaign against the Lombard Sicard of Benevento. Their intervention produced the standoff that was commemorated in 836 in the *Pactum Sicardi* among Benevento and Capua, Naples, Sorrento and Amalfi: one of the most important trade and political treaties of the early Middle Ages in Italy.[41]

---

38. For a recent analysis see Catherine Holmes, "Treaties between Byzantium and the Islamic World," in Philip de Souza and John France, eds., *War and Peace in Ancient and Medieval History* (Cambridge: Cambridge University Press, 2008), 141–57.

39. See, for example, the introductions to Joan M. Ferrante, trans., *Guillaume d'Orange: Four Twelfth-Century Epics* (New York: Columbia University Press, 1974); and Michael A.H. Newth, trans., *Fierabras and Floripas: A French Epic Allegory* (New York: Italica Press, 2010). For a recent overview see Suzanne Conklin Akbari, *Idols in the East: European Representations of Islam and the Orient, 1100-1450* (Ithaca: Cornell University Press, 2009).

40. While "Saracen" was an ancient Roman and early Christian term for inhabitants of the Levant, then distinct from Arabs, by this period the term had come to be synonymous with Muslims and appears frequently in the *chansons de geste,* for example. On the Western perception of the Saracen, see John V. Tolan, *Saracens: Islam in the Medieval European Imagination* (New York: Columbia University Press, 2002). The sources use various terms, *Mauri* (Spanish Ommayids), *Agareni Libicos* (Libyan children of Hagar, Berbers?), *Hismaelitas Hispanos* (Spanish Ishmaelites), which reflect the diversity of origin of the Muslims. See Kreutz, 49–50. On the Muslim presence see Alex Metcalfe, *The Muslims of Medieval Italy* (Edinburgh: Edinburgh University Press, 2009).

41. See below, Reading 18.

In 842 a Neapolitan fleet was present alongside the Arab–Berber army that seized the important Byzantine stronghold of Messina in Sicily. That same year, on the other hand, Duke Sergius I of Naples allied with Gaeta, Amalfi and Sorrento to drive the Muslims from Ponza in the Bay of Naples and followed this up with a naval victory over a Muslim fleet off ancient Paestum.

North African Muslims continued to play a important role in the military campaigns of Neapolitans against Capuans, against Salernitans and against Beneventans in an ever-shifting balance of interest and power. At the same time and more importantly, however, they began to become major trading partners for the newly expanding mercantile cities of Amalfi, and then of Naples. Athanasius II, bishop–duke (876–98), even invited Muslim mercenaries into Naples as part of his military forces, despite repeated pleas and threats by the papacy either to expel them or to face excommunication. Athanasius tolerated and promoted Muslim settlement as close as the foot of Mt. Vesuvius (in 880). In 880/81 therefore Pope John VIII followed through and excommunicated both Amalfi and Naples and its duchy for their Muslim alliances. Athanasius quickly moved to abandon the Muslims and form a new alliance with the resurgent Byzantine Empire, then in the process of reconquering the South.

Through the later ninth century this ever-changing political situation was exacerbated by the continuous presence of Muslim raiders throughout Campania and the South and as far north as Farfa, Spoleto and Rome. The sack of Rome itself in 846 sent shock waves throughout Christendom and would become a mythic event in Western medieval literature. Muslim forces took Taranto in 838 and Bari in 847, founding an emirate there that would last until its reconquest by Emperor Louis II in 871. That same year they laid siege in force to Salerno. They failed to take the city but scoured the countryside for its wealth and depopulated it through massacre and slaving raids. Even the great monastic centers of Volturno (881) and Montecassino (883) were razed to the ground. By 884 Naples and Salerno had allied to drive Muslim mercenaries and raiders from Campania, but those expelled soon established a major base at the Garigliano River,[42] just off the via Appia and via Domitiana, south and east of Gaeta, effectively controlling northern Campania and blocking, or taxing, trade and communication from Naples to Rome and the north.

Further south, by 892 the Byzantines had been so successful in their reconquest of both Muslim and Lombard territories that they were able by establish the new *theme* or imperial province of "Lombardia." But events took a more drastic turn in 902. In that year the Aghlabid emir Ibrahim II (875–902) decided on a policy of outright conquest of the South and sent an immense North African army to take Taormina in Sicily. He then moved on into Calabria, working his way up the peninsula, destroying cities and massacring or enslaving their populations. The situation had now changed from a fluid system in which Naples could easily find its way amid a shifting balance into a far larger strategic threat: its absorption into the Aghlabid Emirate. That year, therefore, fearing immanent Muslim conquest, the Neapolitans abandoned and largely destroyed the *castrum Lucullanum* and the buildings on the Megaride island, lest they become a strategic base for Ibrahim. The monks of S. Severino there took up new quarters within the walled city near the praetorium. With the emir's sudden death later in 902, however, and the reemergence of Byzantine power in the South, the papacy was able to forge an alliance among the regional powers, including Naples, to surround, besiege and then destroy the Muslim base at the Garigliano in 915. From that point on the history of Campania was largely one of political and military hostility to the Muslim world, oversimplified by nineteenth-century historians as a prelude to the Crusades.

---

42.   In the still easily defendable ruins of the amphitheater of ancient Minturnae. See Figliuolo, "Longobardi e Normanni," 42. Not all reuse of antiquity was for artistic display: many ancient amphitheaters served such defensive purposes. Lucca, Rome, and Capua offer other examples. The odeon in Naples was gradually converted to a neighborhood of shops, storerooms and residences, now marked by the curve of via Pisanelli (dell'Anticaglia). See Musto, Interactive Map: http://www.italicapress.com/index287.html. On the other hand, Naples' amphitheater and stadium, outside the ancient walls and thus indefensible, were probably gradually dismantled for building materials. See Arthur, *Naples*, 41.

The ninth century also saw Naples lose whatever nominal ascendancy it had over its regional seaport rivals. Amalfi, Salerno and Gaeta were quickly becoming major international trading centers and — with brief republican interludes — the capitals of their own dynasties, which matched the creation of Naples' own dynasty under Sergius I in 840. There is some speculation that the city's commercial life declined following the sharp curtailment of Muslim raids and the virtual end of the slave trade, from which Naples had continued to reap huge profit since late antiquity.[43] Recent research, however, appears to confirm the city's continuing prominence. With a general improvement in material conditions in Campania throughout the tenth century, Naples retained its vital trade.[44] It continued to export the products of its hinterland: wine; luxury foodstuffs like figs, pomegranates, olive oil and cereals; linen from the mills along the Sebeto River and the shoreline[45]; ironwork, especially weapons (swords were a favorite export to Muslim lands); and slaves (primarily from Christian Lombard lands). Its imports included the gold exchanged for these goods,[46] luxury cloths like silk and fine woolens, church furnishings and hangings from the Muslim Levant, liturgical objects and books from Byzantine Greece or devotional objects like the statuettes of the Madonna and saints manufactured for the export trade in the Muslim East, and papyri from Muslim Egypt for a reading culture that had changed little since late antiquity. In a regional

---

43. See von Falkenhausen, "La Campania," 22: "Napoli medievale non fu una città di mare ne di commercio marittimo"; or Kreutz, 87, who states that "there is virtually no mention of Neapolitan shipping" for this period.

44. See Feniello, *Napoli*, 163–223 and his citations.

45. See Arthur, *Naples*, 109–33.

46. Up until 935 the Byzantine *solidus* was the official coinage of the city and duchy. By 987 the Muslim *tarì* or *tareni* of Sicily replaced the *solidus*, which then became only a unit of exchange (4 *tarì* = 1 *solidus*). In 1060 the Amalfitan *tarì* became the official currency. See Arthur, *Naples*, 133–43; and Feniello, *Napoli*, 202–4, citing J.-M. Martin, "Economia naturale ed economia monetaria nell'Italia meridionale longobarda e bizantina (secoli VI–XI)," in *Storia d'Italia. Annali 6: Economia naturale, economia monetaria*, Ruggiero Romano and Ugo Tucci, eds. (Turin: G. Einaudi, 1983), 181–219. On currency, see also below, Readings 41, 61, 64; and Figs. 48–49.

Mediterranean economy craft, quality and profit knew no religious or ideological boundaries.

URBANISM AND THE ARTS, 600–1100

The position and development of the arts during the ducal period is difficult to summarize briefly. The Lombards of Benevento and Salerno shared a southern Italian interest in proclaiming cultural allegiance to ancient Rome, and much of the building and art of the Mezzogiorno, and of Campania itself, attests to this continued influence: the late imperial plan of Sta. Sophia in Benevento or the use of spolia at Salerno (from Pozzuoli), Carinola, and S. Agata dei Goti, for example.[47] Muslim influence remained apparent in many luxury imported good — textiles, ceramics, leather goods, metalwork — and in some sculptural and decorative motifs.

In Naples itself, traces of these influences are more difficult to identity outside of the major late ancient basilicas. As Paul Arthur has noted, the five major ancient basilicas could easily serve Naples' remaining population for most liturgical events over the course of the year.[48] William Tronzo[49] and Caroline Bruzelius[50] also demonstrate that few large-scale building remains survived the ducal period. We do know from narrative evidence that Bishop Athanasius I (849–72) oversaw an ambitious rebuilding and decoration plan for many of Naples' churches, as well as of hospices (*xenodochia*) for travelers and pilgrims. One of his first projects was to restore the chapel of S. Gennaro in the cathedral and the decorations of the Stefania.[51] Athanasius was also apparently responsible for establishing a

---

47. See Dorothy F. Glass, *Romanesque Sculpture in Campania: Patrons, Programs, and Style* (University Park: The Pennsylvania State University Press, 1991), 21, 41–42, 126–29.

48. *Naples*, 66–68, 79–81. These were S. Giorgio Maggiore, Sta. Maria Maggiore, S. Giovanni Maggiore, S. Lorenzo Maggiore and Sta. Restituta.

49. "Naples in the Early Middle Ages," in Bruzelius & Tronzo, esp. 41–46.

50. "Naples in the High and Late Middle Ages," in Bruzelius & Tronzo, 49–112, esp. 49–62.

51. See Tronzo, "Naples in the Early Middle Ages," in Bruzelius & Tronzo 24–32; and Reading 20.

new house for the monks of S. Gennaro extra Moenia.[52] But few such traces survive for the tenth and eleventh centuries aside from numerous chartulary records of property exchanges and their detailed references to property lines, the presence of courtyards, gardens and other transferred items.[53]

In the late tenth century the city enjoyed a period of cultural flourishing that saw the foundation of Duke Giovanni III's and Duchess Theodora's library.[54] This was stocked both locally, by the continuing production of many illuminated manuscripts at the scriptoria within Naples, in neighboring Cava de' Tirreni and in Campania, and internationally, with the import of manuscripts from Constantinople.[55] Giovanni and Theodora commissioned Latin translations of such works as *The History of Alexander the Great*, which owes its subsequent European fame to their patronage. Their library also contained works by Josephus, Livy, Pseudo-Dionysius the Areopagite, perhaps by Theophanes, and of biblical texts. Naples also seems to have been a center of the production of one of the most famous of southern Italian book traditions: the Exultet rolls,[56] lavishly

---

52. For the Italica Press web gallery, see http://www.flickr.com/photos/80499896@N05/sets/72157630152526498.

53. The important and justly famous *Codex Diplomaticus Cavensis* has now been digitized by the Unione Accademia Nazionale as the *Archivio della Latinità Italiano del Medioevo* (ALIM) and is available at http://www.uan.it/Notarili/alimnot.nsf/RPD. The sources include both the archives of Cava de' Tirreni in the *Codex Diplomaticus Cavensis* and those edited and published in the *Regii Neapolitani Archivi Monumenta* (1845). See also above p. xx n. 9.

54. For Giovanni III and Theodora see Giovanni Italo Cassandro, "Il ducato bizantino," SN 2.1:1–408 at 162–68; Nicola Cilento, "La cultura e gli inizi del studio," SN 2.1:521–640, esp. 591–92; Arthur, *Naples*, 19–20, 26; Massimo Oldoni, "La cultura latina," in Carratelli, 295–400, at 305; Arsenio Frugoni, "La biblioteca di Giovanni III duca di Napoli (dal prologo dall'arciprete Leone al "Romanzo di Alesandro," *Annali della Scuola speciale per archivisti e bibliotecari dell'Universita di Roma* 9 (1969): 161–71. See also below, Readings 21–22.

55. On Greek culture in Campania in general, see Guglielmo Cavallo, "La cultura greca: Itinerari e segni," in Carratelli, 277–92.

56. See Thomas Forrest Kelly, *The Exultet in Southern Italy* (New York: Oxford University Press, 1996). On the images and their iconography, see Myrtilla Avery, *The Exultet Rolls of South Italy*, 2 vols. (Princeton: Princeton University Press, 1936).

illustrated parchment scrolls, datable from the tenth into the fourteenth centuries,[57] used for the Holy Saturday candle-lighting liturgy and derived from both Beneventan and Gallo-Roman traditions. Naples took its place here among many other more important centers, including Benevento, Gaeta, Montecassino, Capua, Salerno and elsewhere in the South. While the only known Neapolitan example dates from c.1150, a fourteenth-century text describing the liturgy in Naples notes that its ceremony dates "from ancient times."[58]

While the Exultet rolls are witness to elaborate liturgies generally presided over by a bishop in a cathedral,[59] within Naples itself such churches as the now derelict Sta. Maria ad Plateam (Sta. Maria in Piazza) testify to a multiplicity of tiny buildings, the "private churches" serving very local communities within the city walls. Between the greater basilicas of the Constantinian era and the large building projects under the Angevins, this seems to have been the normal mode of religious architecture in Naples and to have matched the low population levels and the scarcity of surplus capital required to justify and sustain large-scale construction.[60] Despite its ability to maintain its militia, its Byzantine administrative apparatus,[61] its independence and self-governance with some moments of regional power and importance, from c.600 to c.900, Naples appears to have been a much-shrunken

---

Vol. 2 is a portfolio of b&w plates. See also Guglielmo Cavallo, Giulia Orofino and Oronzo Pecere, eds., *Exultet: Rotoli liturgici del medioevo meridionale* (Rome: Istituto Poligrafico e Zecca dello Stato, 1994); also on CD-ROM (Cassino: Università degli studi di Cassino. Ministero per i beni e le attività culturali, 1999). Some images are available online at: http://medieval.library.nd.edu/facsimiles/exultet.html.

57. Kelly, *Exultet*, 212–62.

58. Vatican City, BAV, MS Vat. Lat. 3784A. On the roll itself see Kelly, *Exultet*, 249–50. For the testimony of Archbishop Giovanni Colonna (1334–42), see idem, 140–41. For the Naples MS, see Fig. 19. For the text, see Reading 30.

59. See Kelly, *Exultet*, 191–211. Kreutz, 142, adheres to the theory that the rolls were used in smaller, more intimate ecclesiastical settings, and this would in fact have fit many of Naples' smaller churches. The lavishness of the rolls, however, does point to the more special and pontifical uses that Kelly stresses.

60. Feniello, *Napoli*, 52–61 et passim, has recently analyzed nearly thirty small *chiese private* attached to noble families and neighborhoods.

61. See Feniello, *Napoli*, 67–78.

city-state. Within its ancient walls and atop its tufa platform, much of the city still lay deserted, littered with garbage dumps and in-fill, derelict buildings, squats, garden plots, vineyards and orchards. Evidence of such "ruralization" in Naples includes the digs at Carminiello ai Mannesi, via S. Paolo and Sta. Patrizia.[62]

The same small scale apparently applied to building lots and housing. As in Rome, Naples saw a proliferation of small spaces, carved out of the larger classical remains of the city or newly built from its reused materials. This scale is attested to in many charters and deeds of exchange now collected both in print and in online archives[63] and recently studied and analyzed by Amedeo Feniello.[64] Unlike Rome's later extended *domus-torre* complexes[65] — the *fortilizia* of its powerful baronial clans — Naples' more concentrated family groups congregated in *domus* complexes that included courtyards and gardens and extended beyond the building lines of single structures[66] but never became urban fortress islands, like Rome's Monte Giordano.

By contrast, a good number of documents studied and transcribed by Capasso and his successors also speak of what was apparently an impressive ducal *palatium*.[67] Originally perhaps the praetorium, it was situated at the Monterone de Pretorio, on the hill of S. Marcellino, near the site of the University of Naples, directly to the east of via Mezzocannone. The steep cliff face still exists beneath S. Marcellino, marked now by the

---

62. On the city's fortifications see Jean-Marie Martin, "Les fortifications de Naples (Ve–XIIIe siècle)," in *Castrum* 8. *Le château et la ville: Espaces et réseaux (VIe–XIIIe siècle)*, Patrice Cressier, ed. (Madrid: Velásquez, 2008), 299–310. On the excavations, see Arthur, *Naples*, 52–56; and Gelichi, "The Cities," esp. 172–82. A useful parallel can be found in the development of the Crypta Balbi in Rome. See Ministero per i Beni e le Attività Culturali. Soprintendenza Archeologica di Roma, *Museo Nazionale Romano: Crypta Balbi* (Rome: Electa, 2000).

63. See nn. 9 and 53 above for ALIM.

64. For Feniello's analysis of the documentary evidence see *Napoli*, 22–30. For a brief survey of urban and religious life, see Giovanni Liccardo, *Vita quotidiana a Napoli prima del medioevo* (Naples: Edizioni Scentifiche Cuzzolin, 1999).

65. See Ronald G. Musto, *Apocalypse in Rome: Cola di Rienzo and the Politics of the New Age* (Berkeley: University of California Press, 2003), 85–90 et passim.

66. See Feniello, *Napoli*, 45–52; Gelichi, "The Cities," 183–86.

67. Arthur, *Naples*, 41–42.

Rampa S. Marcellino as it descends to via Portanova. Arthur and others have discussed descriptions of a palace with an elegant portico overlooking the steep tufa platform that descended down to the harbor and bay. Here the dukes both resided and administered the city and duchy. Close by stood the mint, its location commemorated in the toponym, *"ad monetam."* No traces of either building have been uncovered to date, however.

Another site that rose to prominence in Naples was the ancient *castrum Lucullanum* and the monasteries on the Megaride island. Founded in 482 with a pious bequest by the lady Barbara (or Barbaria) to house a mausoleum for the remains of St. Severinus of Noricum, the house of S. Severino[68] grew next to the *castellum* built around the remains of the villa of Lucullus. There has, however, been substantial discussion as to the actual location of this *castellum* and the later religious houses. Nicola Cilento[69] notes that there were several villas, in addition to that of Lucullus, in the vicinity and that these may have been transformed into several of the early medieval monasteries founded there. That established by followers of St. Severinus of Noricum seems to have been the forerunner of the ninth-century monastery "del Salvatore" or *in insula maris.* This monastery was noted, like Cassiodorus' Vivarium, for its scriptorium, which hosted Dionysius Exiguus and had close ties to Hadrian, abbot of Nisida, later companion to Augustine of Canterbury and ultimately his successor as archbishop of Canterbury. The scriptorium also had a direct impact on Lindisfarne and its famous Gospels book.[70]

Mario Napoli[71] argues that the actual *castrum Lucullanum* rose atop the hill of Pizzofalcone, adjacent to the Megaride island, and that on the island are the remains of both the

---

68. Reading 2. See von Falkenhausen, "La Campania," 9; Gianfranco Fiaccadori, "Il Cristianesimo: Dalle origini alle invasioni barbariche," in Carratelli, 145–70, at 164–68. For Gregory the Great's testimony of multiple religious houses on the site see below, Reading 11, at p. 38.

69. "La chiesa di Napoli nell'alto medioevo," SN 2.2:641–735 at 658–59.

70. Cilento, "La chiesa," 659; Arthur, *Naples,* 70; von Falkenhausen, "La Campania," 9–10.

71. "La città," SN 2.2:737–72 at 764, 768–69.

hermitage of St. Severinus and the monastery of S. Salvatore. Arnaldo Venditti[72] concurs with Napoli and contends, following Capasso, that the *castrum Lucullanum* was more like an *oppidum*, or fortified town, covering most of Pizzofalcone and extending as far as the present Castel Nuovo. Venditti argues that S. Salvatore rose on the Megaride island from at least the seventh century and presents a tentative reconstruction plan of the site.[73] Paul Arthur[74] synthesizes these findings and notes that the topography of the area has, indeed, shifted over the centuries: both the island and the hill of Pizzofalcone changing size and shape considerably. The original villa of Lucullus may, in fact, have spanned both island and hillside. Amedeo Feniello[75] agrees with this reconstruction. The Byzantine and later ducal *castrum* appears to have risen atop the crest of Pizzofalcone, while the seventh-century monastery of S. Salvatore did rise on the island atop the foundations of the hermitage of S. Severino, founded c.492. Excavations carried out on the site in 1924/25 had already discovered a series of caves or cells and a rectangular hall, most likely a refectory, supported by the twelve reused Roman columns still visible on the lower levels of the castle. (See Frontispiece and Fig. 3.)

As Feniello has recently demonstrated, after 900 the situation within Naples appears to have changed rapidly for the better. Population growth, a commensurate increase in land buying and selling, the clearance and improvement of vast tracts of land around the city and into the neighboring countryside[76] saw a simultaneous accumulation of excess capital that both fueled and in part derived from this expansion and resulted in a concentration of wealth into the hands of the urban

---

72. "L'architettura dell'alto medioevo," SN 2.2:773–876, at 836–40.

73. Page 840.

74. *Naples*, 69–71.

75. Feniello, *Napoli*, 7–8.

76. See Arthur, *Naples*, 83–108; Feniello, *Napoli*, 84–161, esp. 103–61; and idem, "Mercato della terra a Napoli nel XII secolo," in *Puer Apuliae: Mélanges offerts à Jean-Marie Martin*, E. Cuozzo, V. Déroche, A. Peters-Custot, V. Prigent, eds, Centre de recherche d'histoire et civilisation de Byzance, Monographies 30 (Paris: CRHCB, 2008).

monasteries.[77] This wealth came to the monasteries primarily in the form of pious donations, part of a European-wide phenomenon at the time. Yet this begs certain questions. From where did the donors themselves derive this new wealth that they so generously shared with the urban religious? And in what types of urban projects was this new capital accumulation expended? Did, for example, Naples see a new wave of construction away from Feniello's myriad small "private churches"[78] to more large-scale building as capital accumulation and flow increased? Was there an appreciable increase in the production or import of luxury goods and other consumable materials? Aside from the noticeable development of the countryside with expanded cereal acreage, vineyards, orchards, mills and other rural building, irrigation and drainage projects,[79] did the Neapolitans direct their capital to urban improvements that would parallel the sudden increase in church building as reported by Ralph Glaber around the year 1000,[80] for example?

By 1100 it is apparent that the flow of capital into Naples had begun to rise dramatically, both from its rural economy and from its international trade. While Feniello has been able to trace a consolidation of ownership away from individual families and toward churches and larger monastic establishments through either bequest or outright purchase, the necessary accumulations of capital required for these consolidations resulted in no large-scale building other than that of the expansion of these monastic complexes. Thus from the tenth to the mid-twelfth century, into the early Norman period, we can trace

---

77.   Feniello, *Napoli*, 139–57. SS. Severino e Sossio alone accounted for 53% of all bequests recorded by Feniello, followed by SS. Sergio e Bacco with 17%. Women's houses, such as that at S. Gregorio Armeno, were further enriched by the accumulation of dowries for each entering nun in the form of direct payments or property holdings.

78.   Feniello, *Napoli*, 52–61, who counts about thirty ranging from monastic to family chapels.

79.   As detailed by Feniello, *Napoli*, 111–19. See also Eleonora Ferraro, "I mulini ad acqua del monastero del SS. Sergio e Bacco tra X e XIII secolo," *Schola Salernitana* 7–8 (2003): 27–38; and Reading 23.

80.   Still useful is Henri Focillon, *The Year 1000* (New York: Harper & Row, 1969).

new building programs or expansions at a good number of Neapolitan churches and monasteries.[81] These include the new fresco cycles at S. Gennaro extra Moenia (10th–11th c.), the reconstruction at S. Giovanni Maggiore (c.992–1003), the merging and expansion of S. Gregorio Armeno (1009), the expansion of the church at S. Paolo Maggiore (991)[82] and its monastery (1186), the foundation of SS. Sergio e Bacco (10th century) and its expansion in 1127 with its merger with S. Sebastiano, the founding of SS. Severino e Sossio in 902 and its uninterrupted expansion thenceforth, the expansion of Sta. Maria Donnaregina after its conversion from Basilian to Benedictine rule in the tenth century and its renovation in 1062, and the first notices of Sta. Maria Donnaromita c.1025.

THE NORMANS (1139–94)[83]

The internecine wars among the Lombards continued into the tenth century despite the occasional presence of the Carolingian and later Salian German emperors in the South. In 965 the Byzantine Empire had surrendered its last foothold on Sicily to the Arab Fatimid Caliphate. For the next fifty years Muslims, Greeks and Lombards vied for control of southern Italy, often seeking the alliance and employment of their former enemies in constantly shifting balances. By the year 1000, these had combined with the continued incursions of Muslims and the sporadic Byzantine control of Apulia, Basilicata and Calabria to create a nearly anarchic political vacuum in the Mezzogiorno.

A new element was soon added to this mix. As the story goes, at Monte Gargano on Apulia's Adriatic shore, Meles, a Lombard warlord from Apulia in revolt against the Greeks, hired on as mercenaries some northmen returning from pilgrimage to

---

81. For locations and references see Arthur, *Naples*, esp. 69–81; and Musto, Interactive Map: http://www.italicapress.com/index287.html.

82. For the Italica Press web gallery, see http://www.flickr.com/photos/80499896@N05/sets/72157630150918068.

83. For complete bibliography, see Musto *Naples Bibliography*, 28–30; and Supplemental Bibliographies, "The Normans," http://www.italicapress.com/index346.html.

Jerusalem. According to another almost-legendary source, their compatriots were also responsible for saving Salerno from Muslim conquest that same year. These "Normans,"[84] as they had long been known in England and France, were the descendants of the Viking conquerors of much of England, Ireland and the French region of Normandy, which still bears their name. More Norman mercenaries were soon arriving in the South in numbers substantial enough to make a military and political impact but never large enough to create the ethnographical changes long attributed to them. The 2,000 to 2,500 Normans that Oldfield cites[85] created a new political elite in the Mezzogiorno but did little to change the complexion of its ethnic mix.

Seeing opportunities opening before them, in 1030 the Normans seized the castle at Aversa, just northwest of Naples, and quickly established their first principality there. By that year the most famous of these Norman clans, the Hauteville, were

---

84. For the Norman period in southern Italy, see Bibliography, plus Supplemental Bibliography: The Normans. Of particular use are John Julius Norwich, *The Kingdom in the Sun, 1130–1194* (London: Longman, 1970); Donald Matthew, *The Norman Kingdom of Sicily* (Cambridge: Cambridge University Press, 1992); Kreutz, 150–58; Paul Oldfield, *City and Community in Norman Italy* (Cambridge: Cambridge University Press, 2009); the numerous articles and important books of G.A. Loud, including *Church and Society in the Norman Principality of Capua, 1058–1197* (Oxford: Clarendon Press, 1985); *Conquerors and Churchmen in Norman Italy* (Aldershot: Ashgate, 1999); *The Age of Robert Guiscard: Southern Italy and the Norman Conquest* (New York: Longman, 2000); with A.J. Metcalfe, *The Society of Norman Italy*; idem, *The Latin Church in Norman Italy* (Cambridge: Cambridge University Press, 2007); and *Roger II and the Creation of the Kingdom of Sicily* (Manchester: Manchster University Press, 2012). See also Skinner, "Tyrrhenian Coastal Cities; and Glass, *Romanesque Sculpture*. Still useful for Naples itself, if now superceded by a generation of international scholarship on Campania and the South, is the *Storia di Napoli*, including Michele Fuiano, "Napoli Normanna e Sveva," SN 2.1:409–520; Mario Napoli, "La città," SN 2.2:737–72; Mario Rotili, "Arti figurativi e arti minori: Nell'età normanna e sveva," SN 2.2:933–86. Of value for architecture and other arts, not least for its illustrations, plans and bibliographies to individual sites and monuments, is Mario D'Onofrio and Valentino Pace, *Italica Romanica: La Campania* (Milan: Jaca Book, 1981).

85. *City and Community,* 23. For the prosopographical sources, see Vera von Falkenhausen, "The South Italian Sources," *Proceedings of the British Academy* 132 (2007): 95–121.

already surveying their political chances in the South. In 1046 Drogo was named count of Apulia by the German emperor Henry II; in 1057 a younger half-brother, Robert Guiscard (the "cunning"), had turned from banditry and raiding in the hills of Calabria into duke of Apulia, the conquest of which he completed in 1071 with the capture of Bari. Meanwhile, Robert's younger brother, Roger, has begun the conquest of Calabria and already had his eyes on Muslim Sicily.

From their footholds in the toe and heel, the Normans gradually consolidated their territories from Byzantines, Lombards and Italian coastal towns and began pushing northward, exerting considerable control over both Latin and Greek churches in their territories. In June 1053, therefore, Pope Leo IX led a papal army against them only to be defeated and captured at Civitate. The price of his ransom was the eventual recognition of the Hauteville Guiscard as "duke" of Apulia and Calabria by Pope Nicholas II in 1059. In return the pope was recognized as feudal liege-lord of the Hauteville lands, an event that would change the face of Neapolitan history again and again. The Norman prince Richard of Capua attempted to conquer Naples in 1077, but after a protracted and unsuccessful siege, he settled for the Neapolitans' acceptance of a nominal protectorate. By 1084, with their freeing of Pope Gregory VII from German emperor Henry IV's siege of the Vatican and their own sack of Rome (the worst damage that city had suffered to that point), the Normans had become the recognized rulers of Italy as far north as the Tiber.

When Robert Guiscard died in 1085, his real heir was not his son Roger Borsa, duke of Apulia, but his younger brother, Roger of Calabria. Once he had consolidated Calabria, this Roger crossed to Messina in 1061 and by 1091 had conquered all of Sicily from the Muslims and began forming a state much like another Norman conqueror, William, had done in England. With its capital at Palermo, Norman Sicily became an amalgam of Muslim, Greek, Latin and Norman cultures and institutions. While Norman Sicily has long been seen as a bridge linking the French, Norman and English worlds of the North with the cultures of the Mediterranean,[86] more recent historiography has

---

86. As, for example, in Haskins, *The Normans in European History*, 192–250. Haskins, 219, declares that after the Hellenistic period, the only noteworthy

tended to downplay the "Anglo-Norman" nature of this Italian political culture and to emphasize its place within a constantly shifting and independently evolving southern Italian scene.

Always a small political elite among a complex of Mediterranean cultures and local interests,[87] the Normans could exert considerable leverage on pre-existing structures, but they could not ultimately dictate a uniformity on the diversity of cultural modes that characterized the South. They could standardize administrative offices and practices to an extent but never eliminate local "liberties" and customs. Instead, the Normans seem to have concentrated on guaranteeing the loyalty of their feudatory bonds across the countryside and on recognizing pre-existing structures in the cities. They appointed their own royal chamberlains and other officials, imposed taxes and control of coinage, dealt harshly with revolt (destroying more than a few southern cities) and constructed their royal fortresses on the perimeters of many major centers. But by and large they respected local freedoms and the ability of urban "*cives*," however defined, to control day-to-day administration of justice, commerce and general urban life. No Norman quarters grew up in any of the southern Italian cities, where Greek, Jewish, Genoese, Pisan or Amalfitan quarters were a commonplace.[88] If the mutilated archival records accurately reflect realities on the ground, the Normans also played little role in property ownership or exchange in Naples or other Campanian cities.[89] They did not, as the previous consensus claimed,[90]

---

achievements in the South were due to the infusion of northerners: the Normans and Hohenstaufen.

87. As Oldfield has noted, *City and Community,* 23–24. See also G.A. Loud, "How 'Norman' was the Norman Conquest of Southern Italy?" *Nottingham Medieval Studies* 25 (1981): 13–35.

88. Oldfield, 24; and Annick Peters-Custot, *Les Grecs de l'Italie méridionale post-byzantine (IXe-XIVe siècle): Une acculturation en douceur* (Rome: École Française de Rome, 2009), esp. 225–343; Loud, "How 'Norman'?"

89. Despite the triumphalist tone of the pro-Norman narrative sources, the archives tell a different story: of the virtual Norman absence from Campanian urban centers. See Skinner, "Tyrrhenian Coastal Cities."

90. See, for example, John K. Hyde, *Society and Politics in Medieval Italy: The*

irrevocably disrupt urban life and its attendant self-governing structures.[91]

Roger II (1130–54) had forced the title "king" of Sicily from Antipope Anacletus II[92] and was crowned in Palermo on Christmas Day 1130. Roger had already seized his cousins' inheritances in Apulia and Calabria and had formed his new kingdom on both sides of the Straits of Messina. By 1129–30 the rapidly changing fortunes of the duchy of Naples saw a *societas* or commune of its citizens — the first in the South — emerge from among the *nobiles* of the city when Duke Sergius VII recognized its authority in the famous *Pactum* or *Promissio* of 1130.[93] After years of withstanding Norman siege, rural devastation and naval blockade, Sergius capitulated to Roger II in order to save the city further hardship; but ironically, allied with the Normans during their siege of Capua, he was killed in 1137. For the next three years the city was governed by the *societas* of nobles,[94] whose local organizations would form the basis of the later medieval *seggi* of the city.

In 1139 Naples fell to the Normans after a lengthy siege that left many dead of starvation and much destruction of the

---

Evolution of the Civil Life, 1000–1350 (New York: St. Martin's Press, 1973), 9; Kreutz, 157; or Giovanni Tabacco, *The Struggle for Power in Medieval Italy: Structures of Political Rule* (Cambridge: Cambridge University Press, 1989), 6–7.

91. See the recent corrective view in Oldfield, 2–6, 53–54, 263–65; and Skinner, "Tyrrhenian Coastal Cities," especially 95–96.

92. On Roger see Hibert Houben, *Roger II of Sicily: A Ruler Between East and West*, trans. G.A. Loud and D. Milburn (Cambridge: Cambridge University Press, 2002). Anacletus II's privilege to Roger II, authorizing the creation of the kingdom of Sicily, dated 27 September 1130, is translated in Loud, *Roger II*, 304–6. See below, Reading 27. See also Loud, "The Papacy and the Rulers of Southern Italy, 1058–1198," in *The Society of Norman Italy*, 151–84.

93. Oldfield, 263–64. For this document, the *Pactum* of Sergius VII, see Reading 26; and Capasso, *Monumenta* 2.2:157–58. For analysis, see Giovanni Cassandro, "La '*promissio*' del duca Sergio e la '*societas napoletana*'," *Archivio Storico Italiano* 1.3–4 (1942). For the political events, see M. Fuiano, *Napoli nel Medioevo (secoli XI–XIII)* (Naples: Libreria Scientifica, 1972); Cassandro, "Il Ducato," SN 2.1:337–52.

94. Oldfield, 186, notes the prominence of this social group in Naples during the twelfth century.

walls and urban fabric, especially in the southern port section and inside the eastern walls. In August 1139 the city formally submitted to Roger II at Benevento; and in September 1140 Roger took physical possession of the fallen city in a ceremony attended by the city's aristocracy at the *castellum del Salvatore* on the Megaride island.[95]

By 1154 the Norman *Regno*, as the kingdom would soon be called, controlled all the territory from Malta to Terracina, south of Rome, to the central mountain borders of Tivoli and Rieti, and to Ascoli on the Adriatic coast. The Norman kings retained their capital at Palermo but had established Salerno very early on as their mainland capital and base, largely with the willing cooperation of the Salernitans themselves.[96]

URBANISM AND THE ARTS, 1100–1200

By the beginning of the twelfth century, Naples boasted a circuit of walls of about 4.5 kilometers,[97] legendary for their invincibility. But with a population of only 25,000 to 30,000, the city was small by its ancient standards.[98]

---

95. See *Chronicle of Falco of Benevento* in Loud, *Roger II*, 245–46; and Reading 28.

96. See Oldfield, 58–59, 66–70.

97. When Roger II took the city he measured the walls at 2363 paces (4460 meters). See the *Chronicle of Falco of Benevento*, in Loud, *Roger II*, 246. Capasso's estimate of the walls at the end of antiquity was 4470 meters. See Napoli, "La città," 743.

98. For comparison, by 1250 Paris and Florence had populations of about 50,000; London, 25,000; Venice 100,000; Genoa and Milan 50,000 to 100,000; and Palermo, 50,000. Rome was little more than a small town, especially after the Norman sack. Medieval urban populations for this period are extremely difficult to determine. No exact census existed; figures, which vary widely from historian to historian, are based on such items as number of hearths, average estimated size of households, tax rolls, army and fleet sizes, building plots, extent of city walls, etc. For some estimates see Daniel Waley and Trevor Dean, *The Italian City Republics*, 4th ed. (Harlow: Longman, 2010), 19–22; John H. Mundy and Peter Riesenberg, *The Medieval Town* (New York: Van Nostrand, 1958), 30; Fritz Rörig, *The Medieval Town* (Berkeley: University of California Press, 1967), 111–21; Oldfield, 165–69. David Nicholas, *Urban Europe, 1100–1700* (New York: Palgrave Macmillan, 2003), presents figures beginning c.1300 but does note (p. 5) that by 1100 Italy south of Rome "had the largest concentration of large cities in Europe."

Yet Naples' absorption into the Norman state eventually brought it unforeseen benefits. Given their international ties throughout Europe and their long-time ambitions — both in Byzantine territory and in the new Crusader states — the Normans decided to strengthen Naples and enhance its commercial status. How was this reflected in the physical structure and contours of the city and its culture?

The Normans left their mark on Naples' urban form in several ways. After the Sicilian uprising of 1156, King William I refortified the old *castrum Lucullanum* or *castellum del Salvatore* (now the Castel dell'Ovo[99]), called "La Normandia," which was to become one of their major fortifications on the bay. William then ordered the building of the Castel Capuano[100] on the site of an old Byzantine *castrum* on the *Campus Neapolis*, the plain at the city's eastern end.[101] In this the Normans repeated a similar pattern from Capua, for example, where they had replaced the *sacrum palatium* of the Capuan princes with their "*castrum lapidum*."[102] Their new castles on the fringes of Naples now replaced the *palatium* of the dukes as the administrative center and probable military praetorium. The Normans thus controlled access to the sea and to the hinterland, both to protect the city from external attack and to guarantee their rule under their *baiulo* or *compalazzo* ("count of the city") and as a fief of the principality of Capua. For the most part, however, as elsewhere in the South, the Neapolitans appear to have governed the city, administered justice and minted their own coinage under their own college of consuls. In addition Neapolitan merchants enjoyed the freedom of the realm from tariffs and duties.[103]

With all of southern Italy united, the contentious wars between Lombard princes and city-states over, trade once again

---

99. See the Italica Press web gallery: http://www.flickr.com/photos/80499896@N05/sets/72157630153362290.

100. See the Italica Press web gallery: http://www.flickr.com/photos/80499896@N05/sets/72157630808244632.

101. See Napoli, "La città," 744.

102. See Oldfield, 39–41.

103. See Giovanni Vitolo, "L'età svevo-angioina," in Carratelli, 87–136, at 90.

flowed uninterrupted both from the interior and along the coast. Naples began to enjoy a period of steady growth. By the end of the twelfth century, the city's population had grown to about 40,000. It became a nexus of trade between southern France, Spain, North Africa and Sicily; and from the Byzantine and Crusader states. In 1191, the royal claimant Tancred of Lecce recognized this preeminence by granting Naples' merchants the "liberty" of movement, without toll or tax, through all Norman lands and seas.[104] With this regional hegemony Naples soon also attracted trade emporiums from Amalfi, Ravello and Scala in the section called the Scalesia.[105] By the thirteenth century, the Genoese had also established their own trade emporium there. The location and nature of the medieval port of Naples has long been a matter of some discussion: whether or not Narses extended the walls down to the ancient port area — the *portus de Arcina* or *de illu Arcina* — and whether the medieval port, the *portus Bulpanum* or *Vulpulum*, was built upon this ancient port or was independent of it.[106] Here again recent research is giving us a far better idea of the extent of the port area during this period.[107]

This internationalism was not confined to trade alone, however. The Norman kingdom became a leading cultural light of Europe. With their centrally controlled state, stable political

104. See Norwich, 374–76. For these privileges under the Hohenstaufen and Angevins, see Reading 61, esp. 222–24.

105. See Oldfield, 217–18; Norwich, 376–77.

106. See Napoli, "La città," 770–72; Arthur, *Naples*, 33–34, both building on the research of Capasso, *Napoli Greco-Romana*, 1–4, and insert map; idem, *Topografia*, 174–86; and Musto, Interactive Map, http://www.italicapress.com/index287.html.

107. See Amedeo Feniello, "Contributo alla storia della 'Iunctura civitatis' (secc. X–XIII)," in *Ricerche sul medioevo napoletano: Aspetti e momenti della vita economica e sociale a Napoli tra X e XV secolo*, A. Leone, ed. (Naples: Athena, 1996). Recent excavations for the Piazza Bovio station of the *Metropolitana* have unearthed what appear to be the remnants of the port's fortification system. See the exhibition catalog of the digs: *Napoli: La città e il mare*; Mario Del Treppo, "La marina napoletana nel medioevo: Porti, navi, equipaggi," in *La fabbrica delle navi: Storia della cantieristica nel Mezzogiorno d'Italia*, A. Fratta, ed. (Naples: Electa, 1990), 40; and T. Colletta, *Napoli città portuale e mercantile: La città bassa, il porto e il mercato dall'VIII al XVII secolo* (Rome: Kappa, 2006), 49.

and economic life and vast new-found resources, the Normans chose the wisest policy for governing a diverse and culturally rich kingdom: they assimilated themselves, accepted local rights, laws and privileges, tolerated local religions and practices — whether Latin, Greek, Muslim or Jewish — adapted Byzantine and Muslim administrative practices where long established, brought the best talents of each culture to serve as their advisors and administrators, and issued laws simultaneously in Arabic, Greek and Latin.

The Normans attempted to transplant much of their own feudal social structure to the rural South, creating fiefs as in the North, but here again they were experienced enough administrators to allow a good deal of local autonomy and custom.[108] They governed their kingdom from a central royal court *(curia regis)* with chancellor, chamberlain, justiciar and later constable and seneschal, much as in England and Normandy. They added a grand admiral and a protonotary-logothete, or head of the secretariat, borrowing here from the Greeks. They also appointed provincial chamberlains, justiciars and curias from among either the Norman feudal class or the native Muslims, Greeks or Italians. Christians, Greeks, Saracens and black Africans alike all served in their royal armies. Norman financial administration converted the Arabic *diwan* into the Italian *duana,* a record that carefully tallied the extent and value of all holdings in the kingdom: a move parallel to William the Conqueror's Domesday Book.[109]

Culturally the Normans blended the Beneventan[110] Latin heritage of the South, based on Montecassino, which had long and strong ties directly to Naples, with the Greek learning of Apulia, Basilicata and Calabria and the Muslim culture of Sicily. The last had been tied to the Islamic and Greco-Roman civilizations of Damascus, Baghdad and Alexandria under the Abbasid

---

108. The old view of Norman hegemony has been tempered in recent years by local studies. See, for example, Peters-Custot, *Les Grecs de l'Italie méridionale,* esp. 225–343.

109. For a recent summation of the evidence, see Oldfield, 82–123.

110. See Kreutz, 140–44; and Graham A. Loud, *Montecassino and Benevento in the Middle Ages: Essays in South Italian Church History* (Aldershot: Ashgate, 2000).

Caliphate since the ninth century. Scholars from France and England seeking to recapture the wisdom of the East and of the Western classics flocked to their colleagues in the South. At Palermo or Salerno one could meet and learn from people who could actually read the Greek and Arab philosophers and scientists in the original, who could provide manuscripts of works by Galen, Plato, Aristotle or Ptolemy. By 1050 there was founded the first and oldest university in the Western world, the medical school of Salerno, less than a day's journey from Naples. Here students from all over Europe came to study the works of Galen and Hippocrates with scholars who knew them in the original Greek.[111] Naples and its Campanian neighbors had continued to live by Roman law, but this became codified under the increasing influence of the new university of Bologna and its revival of ancient imperial codes.

As noted above, it has long been another commonplace of analysis that the Normans transplanted a "northern" Romanesque culture and imposed this upon the Mezzogiorno: an importation from Normandy or more closely from Provence and northern Italian models. Dorothy Glass has convincingly demonstrated, however, that the arts in Campania during this period were not derivative of the North[112] and, in fact, can be shown to exhibit a set of autonomous characteristics that clearly define them as an original Campanian regional style. These include the conscious reuse of ancient spolia (as from Pozzuoli, and most certainly at Naples), the employment of ancient models for new art and the retention of local Lombard traditions, even if often crude by late eleventh- and twelfth-century standards.[113]

---

111. See Paul Oskar Kristeller, "La scuola medica di Salerno secondo ricerche e scoperte recenti," *Quaderni del Centro studi e documentazione della Scuola Medica Salernitana* 5 (Salerno: Scuola Medica Salernitane, 1980), 138–94; Nancy G. Siraisi, *Medieval and Early Renaissance Medicine: An Introduction to Knowledge and Practice* (Chicago: University of Chicago Press, 1990), esp. 13–14, 48–60; Oldfield, 169–83; and Maria Pasca, ed., *La scuola medica salernitana: Storia, immagini, manoscritti dall'XI al XIII secolo*, Soprintendenza per I Beni Ambienti Architettonici, Artistici e Storici di Salerno e Avellino (Naples: Electa, 2005).

112. *Romanesque Sculpture*, especially her conclusions, 223–24.

113. *Romanesque Sculpture*, 21–26, 224.

Perhaps most important to the developing style of Naples and its duchy was the influence of Montecassino under Abbot Desiderius and his immediate circle and successors. The abbey's new basilica was consecrated on October 1, 1071 in the presence of Pope Alexander II and many of the South's most important ecclesiastical and lay leaders, including Archbishop Giovanni II and Duke Sergius V of Naples. The event marked a political and a cultural watershed, for Montecassino's influence became widespread throughout Campania for the next generation.[114] Thereafter the ascendency of the Normans throughout the South opened Campania and Naples not to the North but to the influence of Monreale and Sicily. This is most evident in the Norman cathedral at Salerno[115] and in what Glass calls the "Ravello-Caserta Vecchia school" that included Amalfi, Capua and Sessa Aurunca.[116] While no major ecclesiastical building survives from this period in Naples, the influence of this Ravello–Caserta Vecchia school emerges in a series of carved marble panels in the duomo, now in the chapel of Sta. Maria del Principio of Sta. Restituta, probably dating from the early thirteenth century, perhaps the 1220s. The narrative cycles of Joseph, Samson, other warrior heroes and of S. Gennaro have antecedents in S. Marco in Venice, the baptistry in Florence and S. Paolo fuori le Mura in Rome but owe most of their unique style directly to Sessa Aurunca.[117]

Architecturally, the only other major monuments from this Romanesque period extant in Naples are the campanile of Sta. Maria Maggiore, known as the Pietrasanta,[118] and the triple-aisled church of S. Giovanni a Mare, which Bruzelius dates to the eleventh century, with additions through the fifteenth century.[119] The

---

114. Glass, *Romanesque Sculpture*, 20–21.

115. Glass, *Romanesque Sculpture*, 65–68.

116. Glass, *Romanesque Sculpture*, 90–116, 125–42.

117. Glass, *Romanesque Sculpture*, 143–201; D'Onofrio and Pace, 338–40; Rotili, "Arti figurativi," SN 2.2:936–42, with several illustrations.

118. See Tronzo, "Naples in the Early Middle Ages," in Bruzelius & Tronzo, 44–45. See also the Italica web gallery: http://www.flickr.com/photos/80499896@N05/sets/72157630150746808.

119. D'Onofrio and Pace, 341; Venditti, "L'architettura," 843–44. According to

absence of large-scale building is curious, but it does not seem to have been based on a relative lack of material means. According to Skinner,[120] the city offered a "wealthy prize" for the Normans, and that wealth only increased over the period. As opposed to the construction of large fortifications, the continuation of small-scale ecclesiastical building may, in fact, have been due less to lack of means and more to a cultural practice that lent itself to smaller congregations and more intimate liturgical settings. This might account for the dozens of references to the many small churches, scattered through every corner of the city, in the archival records edited by Capasso, calendared by Arthur[121] and analyzed by Feniello.[122] Like the *diaconiae* already mentioned, their small scale and local functions were eventually superseded by the Angevins' large-scale construction campaigns or later completely altered or destroyed during the Baroque remodeling of the city's liturgical landscape.

THE HOHENSTAUFEN (1194–1266)[123]

The Hauteville dynasty ruled the kingdom of Sicily for the next two generations. By the end of the reign of William II (the Good, 1166–89), the Normans had ties to the most illustrious royal families of Europe; and they took advantage of the system of marriage alliances to insure their status and position in Europe and the Mediterranean. William married the daughter of Henry II of England and in January 1186 finalized the marriage of his aunt Constance, Roger II's daughter, to the German emperor Henry VI, son of Frederick I Barbarossa, Hohenstaufen. It was a marriage born as much out of dynastic prestige as out

---

Bruzelius, "Naples in the High and Late Middle Ages," Bruzelius & Tronzo, 55–57, its first attestation is from a document of 1186. See also the Italica web gallery: http://www.flickr.com/photos/80499896@N05/sets/72157630169072410.

120. Skinner, "Tyrrhenian Coastal Cities," 80. This has recently been confirmed by Feniello, *Napoli*, 119–57.

121. *Naples*, 159–62.

122. *Napoli*, 46–53, with references to Capasso, *Monumenta* and *Regesta*.

123. For complete bibliography, see Musto, *Naples Bibliography*, 30–31; and Supplemental Bibliographies, "The Hohenstaufen," http://www.italicapress.com/index346.html. For a good survey see Vitolo, "L'età svevo-angioina," esp. 87–114.

of the desire to form an alliance that would benefit both against their real and potential enemy: the pope and his anti-imperial (Guelf) allies in the cities of central and northern Italy.

William was making plans to lead the Third Crusade when he died suddenly, and childless, in Palermo on November 18, 1189. His claims to the throne were immediately assumed by Emperor Henry VI Hohenstaufen, the husband of William's declared heir, his aunt Constance. While William had made the Norman barons swear their fealty to Constance,[124] the Neapolitans joined many other southern Italians in siding with William's nephew, Tancred of Lecce, against the Hohenstaufen claim. As noted above, Tancred had offered Naples substantial concessions and recognized what appear to have been already existing rights to a consular government, its own mint, courts, trade and financial controls.[125] In April 1191, Naples fought off a three-month siege by Emperor Henry VI; but with Tancred's death, the city finally surrendered to Henry VI on August 23, 1194. In revenge for Naples' resistance, imperial troops under Chancellor Conrad of Querfurt entirely destroyed the walls of the city.[126] Little is known of Naples' government after 1194, but it appears that it retained some form of collegial government that replaced its fallen consuls.[127]

On Henry's death in Sicily in September 1197, Naples therefore allied with Otto IV of Brunswick, the German Welf (Guelf) opponent of Henry's son and heir, Frederick II Hohenstaufen.[128] With Frederick's apparent diplomatic victory in the South, however, Naples accepted his suzerainty but continued to assert

124. For these events, see Norwich, 345–92.

125. See Oldfield, 125 and n. 11; Vitolo, "L'età svevo-angioina," 87–93.

126. See Richard of San Germano, *Chronicle*. For G.A. Loud's translation of the text, see Reading 35. For Conrad's letter describing the act and his description of Naples and its environs c.1196, see below Reading 37.

127. Oldfield, 147–48; and Vitolo, "L'età svevo-angioina," 96–105.

128. For more specific works on Frederick II, see Musto, *Naples Bibliography*, 30–31; John Larner, *Italy in the Age of Dante and Petrarch, 1216–1380*, Longman History of Italy 2 (London: Longman, 1980), 16–37; David Abulafia, *Frederick II: A Medieval Emperor* (New York: Viking Penguin, 1988); Oldfield, 124–62. For more recent bibliography see Supplemental Bibliographies: The Hohenstaufen, http://www.italicapress.com/index346.html.

its own civil autonomy, rebelling in 1211 on the arrival of Otto IV in the South and earning the condemnation of the city's archbishop and its interdict by Pope Innocent III until the city submitted to Frederick again in 1213. Its political governance, like that of most southern Italian cities under both Normans and Hohenstaufen, remained active and independent despite ultimate royal control. Naples, unlike many southern cities, retained its fluid ruling class, one not restricted to the traditional *nobiles* or the new *milites* introduced under the Normans.[129]

Frederick II, *stupor mundi*, the "wonder of the world" (1215–50), was barely three when he came to the Sicilian throne. His mother Constance therefore acted as his regent in the South and educated him in Sicily under the protection of the papacy, which since the first Norman investiture was the theoretical overlord of the kingdom. As Holy Roman Emperor, crowned in Rome on November 22, 1220, Frederick ruled an empire that encompassed both Germany and northern Italy, including their free republican city-states, the communes. As king of Sicily, Frederick claimed the right of rule over all of southern Italy, except for the papal state. He therefore had many enemies: the German princes, the northern Italian towns, the feudal barons of the kingdom of Sicily, and many within Naples itself. Frederick immediately made himself the enemy of the pope by refusing to abdicate the Regno once he had been crowned emperor.

By 1223, Frederick had consolidated his control over all the kingdom of Sicily. By 1231, despite papal condemnation and invasion, baronial revolt and his absences in Germany and on crusade, he had established peace and economic prosperity all over the Regno. He encouraged agriculture and trade; lowered or eliminated trade duties; coined a stable currency; held annual trade fairs; built bridges, roads and new towns; passed new and uniform laws[130]; and subordinated feudal rights to a central administration. In 1232 and 1240, Frederick summoned two representatives from each major town to parliaments to solidify

---

129. Oldfield, 192–93.

130. On Frederick's legislation, see James M. Powell, ed. and trans., *The Liber Augustalis: Or, Constitutions of Melfi, Promulgated by the Emperor Frederick II for the Kingdom of Sicily in 1231* (Syracuse, NY: Syracuse University Press, 1971).

royal rule and to check the power of local barons. The kingdom had become the wealthiest and most civilized in Christendom. Frederick's court became a new center of philosophy, science, law and art. The emperor also fostered the very first appearance of Italian literature: the Sicilian School of poets.[131]

While Frederick retained his capital at Palermo, he preferred the climate of Pozzuoli and the Bay of Naples' closeness to his northern borders with the papal state. The emperor thus came to favor Naples. He rebuilt its walls, expanded its commercial activity as a balance to the power of Pisa; and, in an attempt to seize the ideological and religious agenda from the papacy, in 1224 he issued the charter for the *studium generale*, the University, or *studio*, of Naples.[132] Among the university's students and later faculty was Thomas Aquinas,[133] the most influential philosopher of the Middle Ages. Frederick not only hoped to further the cultural life of the kingdom but also needed to cancel the influence of the University of Bologna and its pro-papal school of law and theology; he also wanted to break the papacy's monopoly on issuing university charters and to create a class of home-grown and trained bureaucrats for his kingdom. The emperor established the university as a public school, open to all, yet he also forbade his subjects from studying anywhere else for advanced degrees and placed it directly under his royal chancellor. While this brought great cultural activity and prosperity to Naples, it also tied the school to the emperor's political fortunes. Given the Hohenstaufens' iron hand with the city, their efficient and heavy taxation spent on constant and fruitless wars and their eventual revocation of many of the city's privileges, these fortunes were fragile within Naples' walls; and Frederick's dynasty would not survive to make Naples the capital of a new Italian empire.

---

131. See Reading 40.

132. See the document of foundation below, Reading 39. For

133. See below, Reading 44.

THE ANGEVINS (1266–1442)

The history of Angevin Naples[134] is one of disaster deferred, as is that of all of Europe in the early fourteenth century. No political entity — whether city, duchy, emerging nation or church organization — was immune from the calamities that would mark the period. Nor, when historians of the trecento look closely at the history of the kingdom of Naples itself, can they ignore the long-term, deeply structural forces that ran throughout the Angevin period into the reigns of Robert of Anjou and his granddaughter Giovanna I and that ultimately came to a head under the pressure of these pan-European forces of disintegration. As Caroline Bruzelius has recently observed,[135] the reputation of the South for its vast wealth and power may have been overestimated even in the time of Charles I of Anjou, and "the perpetual state of economic crisis of the Angevin court" may have been the result of factors independent of its rulers' personalities and talents.

The Angevin period has been one of the most studied — and long one of the most misinterpreted — in Neapolitan history, its historiography dominated by what I term "the black legend" of the Angevins.[136] According to this historiography, Neapolitan history in the trecento and quattrocento followed an ineluctable arc of rise and decline — in itself a questionable enough framework for the historian — but additionally one based not on normal historical factors but on the personal virtues or vices of its rulers. That legend follows a well-known narrative.

Summoned by an angry Pope Urban IV to wrest the crown of Naples from the excommunicated Hohenstaufen, Prince Charles

---

134. For complete bibliography see Bibliography, http://www.italicapress.com/index346.html, especially Supplemental Bibliographies: The Angevins.

135. Caroline Bruzelius, *The Stones of Naples: Church Building in Angevin Italy, 1266–1343* (New Haven: Yale University Press, 2004), 3 col. 2, invoking Abulafia.

136. Ronald G. Musto, "Review of Paola Vitolo, *La chiesa della Regina: L'Incoronata di Napoli, Giovanna I d'Angiò e Roberto di Oderisio.* Rome: Viella, 2008," *Renaissance Quarterly* 62 (Spring 2009): 200–201. Alessandro Barbero had already spoken of a general "myth" of the Angevins in his "Il mito angioino nella cultura italiana e provenzale fra duecento e trecento," in *Robert d'Angio fra guelfismo e umanesimo,* Biblioteca Storica Subalpina. Deputazione Subalpina di Storia Patria 201.80 (Turin: Palazzo Carignano, 1983), 389–450.

of Anjou conquered Naples and executed the surviving heirs of Frederick II without pity or justice. His throne and that of his heirs was thus based on usurpation and blood. But Charles and then his son Charles II ruled well and firmly, gradually replacing the heterodox and heterogeneous court and regional culture of the Hohenstaufens with the new, orthodox and forward-looking culture of the French court. Thus the new Gothic architecture, the chivalric romance literature that their dynasty favored, the vigorous crusading culture of the emerging French nation, and the religiously sanctioned bloodline *(beata stirps)*[137] of St. Louis remade Naples and the South in the image of the emerging great kingdoms of the North: France and (Angevin) England.[138]

The process of nation and culture building was a long and slow one, but it was one of continual forward motion and ascent, culminating in the reign of Robert of Anjou, called "the Wise" even in his own time. Robert was the richest, most competent, cultured and just ruler of Naples, Italy and probably of Europe at the time. Robert brought Naples to the center of European (i.e., French) culture and surrounded himself with the best artists, intellectuals, jurists, architects and religious leaders that Europe had then to offer. As a ruler he brought Naples to the apogee of wealth and influence and made his kingdom a model of late medieval rule. He also personified the

---

137. See Jean Dunbabin, *Charles I of Anjou: Power, Kingship and State-Making in Thirteenth-Century Europe* (London and New York: Longman, 1998), 9–20, esp. 18; idem, *The French in the Kingdom of Sicily, 1266–1305* (Cambridge: Cambridge University Press, 2011), esp. 189–98; Adrian S. Hoch, "*Beata Stirps,* Royal Patronage and the Identification of the Sainted Rulers in the St. Elizabeth Chapel at Assisi," *Art History* 15.3 (1992): 279–95; and Tanja Michalsky, "Die Repräsentation einer *Beata Stirps*: Darstellung und Ausdruck an den Grabmonumenten der Anjous," in Andrea von Huelsen Esch, Otto Gerhard Oexle, eds., *Die Repräsentation der Gruppen: Texte – Bilder – Objekte* (Göttingen: Vandenhoeck & Ruprecht, 1998), 187–224. On Charles' claims to legitimacy see Claude Carozzi, "La victoire de Bénévent et la légitimité de Charles d'Anjou," in *Guerre, pouvoir et noblesse au Moyen Âge: Mélanges en l'honneur de Philippe Contamine,* Jacques Paviot and Jacques Verger, eds. (Paris: Presses de l'Université de Paris, 2000), 139–45.

138. This has yet again been argued by Jean Dunabbin in *Charles I of Anjou,* esp. 3–8, 181–224. More recently, however, in *The French in the Kingdom of Sicily,* e.g., 1–9, Dunbabin argues for influence in both directions in order to demonstrate European-wide cultural and political spheres.

high moral and ethical standards so prized in a medieval ruler and, according to this historiography, made his court a center of probity. So thorough and conscious was his notion of state-craft that some modern historians have seen him as among the first Renaissance (or proto-Renaissance) rulers of Italy.[139]

But his brilliant career and the upward trajectory that he had plotted were marred both by the blood stain of the Angevins' original usurpation and by the continued stigma of illegitimacy that dogged the dynasty. Robert himself, according to this consensus view, was so conscious of his brother Charles Martel of Hungary's prior claims to the throne that he deliberately set out to legitimize his rule by creating a persona of the wise and rational ruler that essentially made him a modern political figure. But the Angevin ascendancy was tragically cut short by the premature death of Robert's only surviving son, Charles of Calabria, in November 1328, and then by the inability — or refusal — of Robert's second wife, Queen Sancia of Majorca,[140] to bear an heir. Thus the steady progress of the Angevin dynasty toward a modern, rational state was halted just at the threshold of ultimate success. Sancia has been held largely responsible for this failure based on her allegedly obscurantist Franciscan religiosity, a spiritual inclination that these interpretations claim was not at all shared by her rational, more modern, husband Robert.

---

139. Among the most forceful statements see Dunbabin, *Charles I of Anjou,* 8, 203–24; Samantha Kelly, *The New Solomon: Robert of Naples (1309–1343) and Fourteenth-Century Kingship* (Leiden: E.J. Brill, 2003); idem, "Royal Patronage and Royal Propaganda in Angevin Naples: Santa Maria Donna Regina in Context," in Janis Elliott and Cordelia Warr, *The Church of Santa Maria Donna Regina* (Burlington, VT: Ashgate, 2004), 27–43; Darleen Pryds, *The King Embodies the Word: Robert d'Anjou and the Politics of Preaching,* Studies in the History of Christian Thought 93 (Leiden: Brill, 2000); restated more recently by Cathleen A. Fleck in *The Clement Bible at the Medieval Courts of Naples and Avignon: A Story of Papal Power, Royal Prestige, and Patronage* (Farnham, Surrey: Ashgate, 2010); and idem, "Patronage, Art, and the Anjou Bible in Angevin Naples (1266–1352)," in Lieve Watteeuw and Jan Ven der Stock, eds., *The Anjou Bible: A Royal Manuscript Revealed, Naples 1340* (Leuven: Peeters, 2010), 37–51.

140. See Ronald G. Musto, "Queen Sancia of Naples (1286–1345) and the Spiritual Franciscans," in *Women of the Medieval World: Essays in Honor of John H. Mundy,* Julius Kirshner and Suzanne F. Wemple, eds. (New York: Blackwell, 1985), 179–214.

The result of this dynastic break was a discontinuity in historical progress: the most important of several abrupt period changes. According to the standard historiography, the inheritance and the reign of Giovanna I (1343-82)[141] marked a sudden and irrevocable break in the fortunes of the Angevin dynasty into decline and collapse. All the blood-soaked guilt that had founded the dynasty, and that its male rulers had long repressed, now suddenly emerged again during Giovanna I's reign. Irrationality and perversity at the court itself were matched by growing lawlessness and immorality among the people of Naples and by a selfish disregard for the common good by the kingdom's nobility.

As Naples under the male Angevins had been seen as rational and characterized with a vocabulary that speaks of masculine virtues, now — according to this narrative — under Giovanna I Naples took on the attributes of the feminine. A certain fickleness and unfaithfulness, personified by the queen, permeated the entire body politic. Giovanna I quickly brought murder, disloyalty, secretiveness and irrationality to moral and public life, while her betrayals, political incompetence and indecisive paralysis brought collapse to the crown and the kingdom as a whole. One can trace the sudden and dramatic shift in trecento appraisals of Naples in such writers as the Villani, Domenico da Gravina and most especially Petrarch.[142]

---

141. For reliable accounts, see Emile G. Léonard, *Histoire de Jeanne I, reine de Naples, comtesse de Provence (1343-1382): Mémoires et documents historiques*, 3 vols. (Monaco: Imprimerie de Monaco, 1932-37); idem, *Les Angevins de Naples* (Paris: Presses universitaires de France, 1954); Mario Gaglione, *Donne e potere a Napoli: Le sovrane angioine. Consorti, vicarie e regnanti (1266-1442)* (Catanzaro: Rubbertino Editore for l'Alto Patrocinio dell'Università degli Studi di Napoli Federico II, 2009), 175-292; and Elizabeth Casteen, "Sex and Politics in Naples: The Regnant Queenship of Johanna I of Naples, 1343-1382," *Journal of the Historical Society* 11 (June 2011): 183-210. Nancy Goldstone, *The Lady Queen: The Notorious Reign of Joanna I* (New York: Walker & Company, 2009) relies on the long-distorted historiography.

142. I am currently working on a study of trecento historiography in South that will include more detailed analysis of this issue. See also my forthcoming introduction, "Naples in Myth and History," in Hall, *Artistic Centers of the Italian Renaissance: Naples*.

Until very recently nearly all cultural histories of Angevin Naples, including treatments of its artistic, intellectual and political life, stopped at 1343, the year of Robert's death. All else of medieval Naples, beginning with Giovanna I's reign, has been seen as a tragic and perverse afterword to an era of brilliance and reason. According to this historiography, Naples would have to wait until the emergence of the Aragonese dynasty and the final eradication of the last Angevins to witness the Renaissance in the Regno and city. But even with this revival, Naples and the South would forever remain fallen from grace: no longer the richest, strongest emerging state of Europe but a strange and vengeful land, full of mystery, corruption, lust and violence, a culture maimed and thwarted at home, only periodically resuscitated but inevitably altered through foreign force and spirit. As the head was corrupted, so did corruption flow like a polluted stream through the whole body politic, the land and its people.

Unlike a similar dynastic history — that of the Plantagenets of England and their heirs among the houses of Lancaster, York and Tudor — the story of the Angevins and of Naples never achieved the high level of noble tragedy that the same tale of conflicting bloodline and inheritance, treachery, usurpation, illegitimacy and murder did among the English royal line. Perhaps this is because Naples never found its Shakespeare and his history plays to ennoble the trajectory of dynastic crisis into the stuff of individual and national rebirth. According to the accepted historiography, the England that emerged from these troubles in the literary and political imagination of the late sixteenth century — John of Gaunt's "blessed plot" — was a land and nation made wiser and more mature by its travails. By the same period, however, Naples and the South were already marked, like their master Spain, as a land of depravity and corruption: Naples' time of troubles had brought it nothing but a reputation for decline and damnation. Late medieval England has since been framed by the history play, the south of Italy by the Jacobean theater of cruelty[143] and the Gothic novel of the

---

143. The plot of Shakespeare's *The Tempest* is set into motion by the cruelty and deceptions of the Neapolitan royal house. The play premises these events, without elaboration, as almost natural elements of Neapolitan politics. But the

eighteenth and nineteenth centuries.[144] Plotting and duplicity, mysterious dwarfs, sensuous African slaves, hooded monks, illicit passions, illegitimate children and usurpers, whispers among the ruins, hatred, revenge and murder, the ominous rumblings of Vesuvius, all set against the sunny days and outwardly smiling demeanors of the southern Italian took hold of the popular imagination of northern Europe. The black legend of the Angevins had been born.

■

In 1250 Frederick II died after a lingering illness. His enemies immediately regrouped all over Italy to undo his work and to seek revenge.[145] In 1251 Naples rose and, giving its ultimate fealty to the pope in Rome, it reformed the *societas* or commune that had existed briefly at the end of the ducal period and into the Norman kingdom. In the absence of Frederick's son, King Conrad IV, fighting for his inheritance in Germany, Frederick's natural son Manfred became *balio*, or regent, for both the Regno[146] and the Hohenstaufen holdings in Germany.

---

prime example remains Webster's *Duchess of Malfi* [Amalfi] of 1612/13. Artaud's theory of a theater of cruelty has been applied to the later Middle Ages by Jody Enders, *The Medieval Theater of Cruelty: Rhetoric, Memory, Violence* (Ithaca: Cornell University Press, 1999); and Mitchell B. Merback, *The Thief, the Cross, and the Wheel: Pain and the Spectacle of Punishment in Medieval and Renaissance Europe* (Chicago: University of Chicago Press, 1999), among others.

144. The decadence of the Italian South became a hallmark of works as diverse as Horace Walpole's *Castle of Otranto* of 1764, Ann Radcliffe's *The Italian* of 1797, Madame de Staël's *Corinne, or Italy* of 1807 and Alexandre Dumas' *Jeanne de Naples* of 1839–41.

145. For the following narrative, see David Abulafia, *The Western Mediterranean Kingdoms, 1200–1500: The Struggle for Dominion* (London: Longman, 1997), 57–81, 133–71; Carlo De Frede, "Da Carlo I d'Angio à Giovanna I (1263–1382)," in SN 3:1–333; Dunbabin, *French in the Kingdom of Sicily*; Norman Housley, *The Italian Crusades: The Papal-Angevin Alliance and the Crusades against Christian Lay Powers, 1254–1343* (New York: Oxford University Press, 1982); Giovanni Vitolo and Giuseppe Galasso, *Storia del Mezzogiorno* 4. *Il regno dagli Angioini ai Borboni* (Roma: Editalia, 1994).

146. See Enrico Pispisa, *Il regno di Manfredi: Proposte di interpretazione* (Messina: Sicania, 1991).

Pope Innocent IV meanwhile hoped to finally crush the Hohenstaufens in both Germany and Italy and searched for candidates among Europe's royal families to replace them. Conrad was able to reach the South of Italy in time, however, and to consolidate his hold there.

Innocent IV therefore sought a candidate willing to depose the Hohenstaufen heirs by force of arms. Henry III of England backed an invasion force with cash; and with Conrad IV's death in 1254, shortly after his capturing Naples, Innocent entered the Regno with his young charge Conrad V (Conradin) as a figurehead for his plans to annex the kingdom to the papal state. By the time the pope had entered Naples, however, Manfred was able to rally the Hohenstaufen forces; Conradin had defected to him; and in 1258 Manfred had himself crowned king of Sicily.

The Italian wars between Guelfs and Ghibellines, as the imperial faction was called, and the papal crusades against the Hohenstaufen continued to embroil the entire peninsula. Finally, with the accession of King Louis IX's ex-chancellor as Pope Clement IV in 1265, the ambitions of one of the original papal candidates for Frederick II's throne reemerged. Charles, duke of Anjou, Louis' younger brother, had also been count of Provence since 1246. While he had at first refused the pope's offer, under mounting pressure, perhaps from his brother Louis, he now saw a means of uniting papal hostility, French resources and his own ambitions to create an empire in the Mediterranean. He accepted the papal offer to lead a crusade against Manfred. On February 26, 1266 at Benevento Charles' army crushed that of Manfred, who fell trying to rally his German forces after his Saracens and Italians had fled. Charles of Anjou entered Naples on March 7. Soon thereafter, however, Conradin, now a youth of 15, assembled an invasion force of Germans and Ghibellines and entered the kingdom in August 1268. At Tagliacozzo Charles destroyed his army, mercilessly massacring the captives. Conradin was brought to Naples, where on the site of the Campo Moricino (the present Piazza del Mercato) he and his chief lieutenants were publicly beheaded, an act that shocked all of Europe and founded the Angevin dynasty.[147]

---

147. See below, Readings 42–43.

INTRODUCTION

To efface the memory of the Hohenstaufen, Charles of Anjou, now King Charles I (1265–85),[148] soon moved his capital,[149] court and royal administration[150] from Palermo to Naples and made the city a center of royal display and ritual. His decision was prophetic. On March 30, 1282, a conspiracy designed to end Angevin ambitions throughout the Mediterranean,[151] and to take revenge for Conradin and Manfred, erupted into the

---

148. For special studies of Charles I see Dunbabin, *Charles I of Anjou*; Michele Fuiano, *Carlo I d'Angio in Italia: Studi e ricerche* (Naples: Liguori, 1974); Peter Herde, *Karl I von Anjou* (Stuttgart: Kohlhammer, 1979).

149. "*Napoli capitale*" has been the title of any number of important studies of the city; and the term itself is laden with value: an assertion among Italian writers from the late nineteenth through the twentieth century. A search of WorldCat in September 2012 returned 45 books published since 1849 with this formula in their title. Perhaps the best known is Giuseppe Galasso, *Napoli capitale: Identità politica e identità cittadina. Studi e ricerche 1266–1860* (Naples: Electa, 1998). For the late medieval period, see Pierluigi Leone de Castris, "Napoli, capitale del Mezzogiorno angioina: L'arte e la corte," in Giosuè Musca, *La cultura angioina: Civiltà del Mezzogiorno* (Milan: Silvano Editoriale, 1985), 127–99. The concept is most recently explored in several of the essays in the forthcoming Hall, *Artistic Centers of the Italian Renaissance: Naples.*

150. For recent research on the court and administration, see Dunbabin, *French in the Kingdom of Sicily*, 155–88, 235–59; Andreas Kiesewetter, "La cancelleria angioina," in *L'état Angevin: pouvoir, culture et société entre XIIIe et XIVe siècle: Actes du colloque international organisé par l'American Academy in Rome (Rome-Naples, 7–11 novembre 1995)*, Collection de l'École Française de Rome 245, Nuovi studi storici 45 (Rome: École Française de Rome & ISIME, 1998), 360-415; Jole Mazzoleni, "Les archives des Angevins de Naples," in *Marseille et ses rois de Naples: La diagonale angevine, 1265–1382* (Marseille: Archives municipales, EdSud, 1988), 25–29; Stefano Palmieri, *La cancelleria del regno di Sicilia in età angioina* (Naples: Accademia Pontaniana, 2006); Giuliana Vitale, *Élite burocratica e famiglia: Dinamiche nobiliari e processi di costruzione statale nella Napoli angioino-aragonese* (Naples: Liguori, 2003). For the reconstruction of the Angevin archives in recent years see Filangieri et al., *I registri della cancelleria angioina*; and Bibliography, http://www.italicapress.com/index346.html, especially Supplemental Bibliographies: The Angevins.

151. See Gian Luca Borghese, *Carlo I d'Angiò e il Mediterraneo: Politica, diplomazia e commercio internazionale prima dei Vespri* (Rome: Ecole Française de Rome, 2008).

revolt ever since known as the Sicilian Vespers.[152] This brought the Byzantine emperor, the king of Aragon (now married to the Hohenstaufen heiress), and former Hohenstaufen officials together to wrest Sicily from the Angevins. The twenty-year War of the Vespers that followed saw the capture and imprisonment of the future Charles II (1285–1309) by the Aragonese and the eventual Aragonese control of Sicily. By the time of Charles I's death in 1285, his great Mediterranean empire had been shattered, and his kingdom had been reduced to the Italian Mezzogiorno.

Despite this loss — more likely, precisely because of it — the Angevin period was one of international influence, prosperity, artistic,[153] cultural[154] and religious[155] leadership for Naples itself. Charles I built upon Hohenstaufen advances in administration and justice and maintained a solid currency and foreign exchange. Yet his heavy taxation brought many parts of the Regno to desperation and was a leading cause of the Sicilian Vespers.[156] His political policies often worked counter to his economic goals, and he restricted urban liberties and self-government throughout his reign.[157]

---

152. Lawrence V. Mott, *Sea Power in the Medieval Mediterranean: The Catalan-Aragonese Fleet in the War of the Sicilian Vespers*, New Perspectives on Maritime History and Nautical Archaeology (Gainesville: University Press of Florida, 2003); Steven Runciman, *The Sicilian Vespers: A History of the Mediterranean World in the Thirteenth Century* (Cambridge: Cambridge University Press, 1958); and Dunbabin, *Charles I of Anjou*, 99–113.

153. See Bruzelius, *Stones of Naples*; and Bruzelius & Tronzo, *Medieval Naples*.

154. Good introductions include Musca et al., *La cultura angioina*; Francesco Sabatini, *Napoli angioina: Cultura e società* (Naples: Edizioni scientifiche italiane 1975); and Stefano Asperti, *Carlo I d'Angiò e i trovatori: Componenti "provenzali" e angioine nella tradizione manoscritta della lirica trobadorica* (Ravenna: Longo, 1995).

155. For religious trends during this period, see De Frede, "Da Carlo I"; Musto, "Queen Sancia of Naples," 179–214; idem, "Franciscan Joachimism at the Court of Naples, 1309–1345: A New Appraisal," *Archivum Franciscanum Historicum* 90 (1997): 419–86; Roberto Paciocco, "Angioini e 'spirituali': I differenti piani cronologici e tematici di un problema," in *L'état Angevin*, 253–87.

156. See especially Dunbabin, *Charles I of Anjou*, 57–64, 155–65.

157. Dunbabin, *Charles I of Anjou*, 45–47, 65–66.

The War of the Vespers and its aftermath, and the Angevins' possessions in Anjou, Provence and Piedmont, realigned Naples more toward the northern Mediterranean and created an immediate surge in commercial activity and in the city's population. Merchants from Catalonia, Marseilles[158] and Florence founded trade emporiums next to the old Scalesia; bankers and investors soon filled the new section of the city to the southwest of the late Roman imperial walls; while to the east and south, along the waterfront, rose a new manufacturing district around the Campo Moricino (Piazza del Mercato), a move that seems to have already been planned in the Norman or Hohenstaufen periods. To expand the defenses of the city Charles I added a "new castle," the Castel Nuovo,[159] which soon became the royal residence, and he dredged a new harbor and built the tower on the Molo S. Vincenzo. Charles II built the castle of Belforte,[160] later expanded to the Castel S. Elmo, next to the Certosa of S. Martino,[161] which was begun in 1325 under his successor. Population estimates for the city during the Angevin period range anywhere from 25,000 to 100,000 out of a total population for the Regno of between 2 and 2.5 million.[162]

---

158. On the Provençal connection, see Isabelle Bonnot, ed., *Marseille et ses rois de Naples: La diagonale angevine, 1265–1382* (Marseille: Archives municipales, EdSud, 1988).

159. See C.P. Leone De Castris, *Castel Nuovo: Il Museo Civico* (Naples: E. de Rosa, 1990); Marcello Orefice, *Il vecchio Maschio degli Angioini: Tra fantasie e storiche realtà. La rivisitazione di un castello definitivamente perduto* (Naples: Edizioni scientifiche italiane, 2008). See also the Italica Press web gallery: http://www.flickr.com/photos/80499896@N05/sets/72157630165392752.

160. See the Italica Press web gallery: http://www.flickr.com/photos/80499896@N05/sets/72157630808796440.

161. See the Italica Press web gallery: http://www.flickr.com/photos/80499896@N05/sets/72157630152166968.

162. See De Seta, *Napoli fra Rinascimento e Illuminismo*, 85; P. Egidi, "Ricerche sulla populazione dell'Italia meridionale nei secoli XIII e XIV," *Miscellanea di studi storici in onore di Giovanni Sforza*, Paolo Boselli, ed. (Turin: Baroni, 1920), 731–50; Dunbabin, *Charles I of Anjou*, 156; and Harry A. Miskimin, *The Economy of Early Renaissance Europe, 1300–1460* (London and New York: Cambridge University Press, 1978), 73. Oldfield, *City and Community*, 165–66, indicates that Naples'

Charles II's son, Robert of Anjou, the Wise (c.1278–1343), and his second queen, Sancia of Majorca (1286–1345), made Naples a capital of European culture and nurtured some of the earliest figures of the Italian Renaissance.[163] The court of Naples became a meeting place of scholars from Italy, France, Catalonia and Provence; of theologians from Paris and northern Italy; of dissident and heterodox reformers; of writers, poets and artists. The king gained and promoted a European-wide reputation for learning, and he was noted by Dante for his deep, if prolix, sermonizing.[164] Petrarch recounts Robert's keen interest in the city's classical heritage and legends[165]; while Boccaccio paints a lively picture of the city's sophisticated culture, social mores and personalities.[166]

---

population was within this 100,000 range at about 1300. By contrast at this date Venice, Genoa and Milan numbered 100,000 to 150,000; Florence 50,000 to 100,000; London between 80,000 and 100,000; Paris 200,000; Ghent between 60,000 and 80,000; Granada 100,000 and Barcelona 50,000. See William C. Jordan, *The Great Famine: Northern Europe in the Early Fourteenth Century* (Princeton: Princeton University Press, 1996), 128–31; and Nicholas, *Urban Europe*, 13–21. On 28–33, Nicholas provides a corrective to the estimates of Josiah C. Russell, *Medieval Regions and Their Cities* (Bloomington: Indiana University Press, 1972).

163. See De Frede, "Da Carlo I"; Musto, "Queen Sancia of Naples"; and idem, "Franciscan Joachimism"; Welbore St. Claire Baddeley, *Robert the Wise and His Heirs 1278–1352* (London: W. Heinemann, 1897); Romolo Caggese, *Roberto d'Angiò e i suoi tempi*, 2 vols. (Florence: Bemporad e Figlu, 1922–30; reprint Bologna: Il Mulino, 2001); Paul M. Clogan, "Italian Humanism in the Court of King Robert of Anjou," *Acta Conventus Neo-Latini Bariensis: Proceedings of the Ninth International Congress of Neo-Latin Studies, Bari, 29 August to 3 September 1994*, Medieval & Renaissance Texts & Studies 184, Rhoda Schnur, et al., eds. (Tempe, AZ: MRTS, 1998), 189–98.

164. See *Paradiso* VIII.82–83; Pryds; Kelly, *New Solomon*, 1–2; Musto, "Franciscan Joachimism," 456–73. Dante by contrast placed Charles I in Purgatorio VII:64-136.

165. For example, in his *Itinerarium ad sepulchrum domini nostri Yeshu Christi*, trans. by Theodore J. Cachey, Jr. as *Petrarch's Guide to the Holy Land* (Notre Dame: University of Notre Dame Press, 2002), pars. 10–10.1; or in his letter to Robert of 30 April 1341, *Familiares* IV.7, in Francesco Petrarch, *Letters on Familiar Matters (Rerum Familiarium Libri)*, Aldo S. Bernardo, trans., 3 vols. (Albany: State University of New York, and Baltimore: Johns Hopkins University Press, 1975–85; repr., New York: Italica Press, 2005), 1:193–95.

166. See his *Decameron* II.5; his *Fiammetta*; and his *Amorosa Visione*, 12, 42.

During Robert's reign, the kingdom and city of Naples also became a focal point of Italian-wide politics. Robert tried five times to regain Sicily, by then the kingdom of Trinacria, with an immense war fleet based on the Arsenal, which was built between 1301 and 1307 next to the Castel Nuovo. He extended his influence over Rome, sending his own brother John of Gravina to lead an expedition to prevent Lewis of Bavaria's imperial coronation there in 1328. He was at times overlord or protector of Florence, sending his son Charles of Calabria as his deputy to rule the city and maintain his interests in Tuscany. Despite his and Sancia's defiance of Pope John XXII over the dissident Spiritual Franciscans and his challenge to the pope's orthodoxy in the controversy over the Beatific Vision, the king remained the upholder of Guelf interests in Italy for the papacy. Yet his war efforts and his feudal census payments to the papacy — the price for Charles I's conquest — exerted tremendous pressures on the kingdom and the city by way of taxes and in the concessions that Robert was forced to grant the already independent-minded barons. By the mid-fourteenth century there were 3,455 fiefs of the lower nobility in the kingdom, not including the great barons or the patricians of the cities. Most of these nobles were so poor that their desire for livable holdings created a constant menace to central authority, to the maintenance of law and order and to their own impoverished rural populations.[167] In addition to this, many Neapolitan barons straddled both sides of the permeable borders of the Regno and papal states, shifting their feudal allegiances as convenience or higher political purpose dictated.

Nevertheless, throughout Robert and Sancia's reign the city of Naples continued to grow. As Bruzelius has demonstrated,[168]

---

167. See, for example, Larner, 47–48; Luigi de Rosa, "Land and Sea Transport and Economic Depression in the Kingdom of Naples from the Fourteenth to the Eighteenth Century," *The Journal of European Economic History* 25.2 (1996): 339–68; Jean-Marie Martin, "Fiscalité et économie étatique dans le royaume angevin de Sicile à la fin du XIIIe siècle," in *L'état Angevin*, 601–48; Giovanni Vitolo, "Il Regno Angioino," in *Storia del Mezzogiorno*, vol. 4: *Il Regno dagli Angioini ai Borboni*, G. Galasso and R. Romeo, eds. (Rome: Edizioni del Sole-Rizzoli, 1986), 1:9–86.

168. *Stones*, 133–53.

their reign saw many new ecclesiastical buildings — including the construction of Sta. Chiara as a focus of their Franciscan spirituality and their court ceremonial[169] — as well as the expansion of the city's residential quarters, including those of the new Largo delle Corregge between the Castel Nuovo and the old city walls with its Angevin royal palaces and other mansions of the high nobility (now being excavated), its public buildings and gardens, and those of Chiaia on the slopes of Pizzofalcone. Robert's expansion of the state bureaucracy was made possible by his alliance with the new nobility of the cloth, raised from the bourgeois and lower nobility. This paralleled the influx into the city of many other noble households and their attendant followers and provisioners — as well as of foreign and other Italian merchants and bankers.

Naples' population reached new heights just before 1350, cresting to 100,000, along with Venice, Milan and Florence. Paris and Constantinople, the largest cities in Europe, each held about 200,000.[170] There is no way to accurately estimate the rural population seeking both work and security that flocked into the city, but increased taxation and other levies, as well as the growing insecurity of the hinterlands under the impact of increased baronial lawlessness, would indicate that Naples absorbed many such folk into its walls.

The city had reached its medieval limit. In a November 1343 visit to Naples, Petrarch had already witnessed the disastrous tidal storm that destroyed many buildings around the harbor and sank its shipping.[171] Then, in October 1347, the Black Death (bubonic plague) arrived from the Crimea aboard a ship to Messina. It reached Naples along the trade routes within a few weeks. Within two months, according to one estimate, it killed 63,000 in and around the city.[172]

---

169. See Readings 58–59. For the church, see Bruzelius & Tronzo, *Medieval Naples*, 98–106; and the Italica Press web gallery: http://www.flickr.com/photos/80499896@N05/sets/72157630151262510.

170. See n. 162 above.

171. Petrarch, *Familiares* V.5, Bernardo, 1:243–47 and Reading 70 below.

172. Philip Ziegler, *The Black Death* (Harmondsworth: Penguin Books, 1970), 52. For contemporary narrative accounts see Rosemary Horrox, ed.,

It returned in 1362, 1382, 1399 and 1411. By the end of the fourteenth century one estimate puts Naples' population at 36,000.[173] Drastic population declines, in places of up to two-thirds, short-falls in agricultural output, famine,[174] great inflation and decreases in the tax base all contributed to slow the pace of recovery and exasperated the already growing economic failures, social disorder and political confusion that characterize the early Renaissance in Italy and the late fourteenth century throughout much of Europe.

While Robert and Sancia were able to stem the tide of disorder, there successors were not as lucky. Robert's son, Charles, duke of Calabria, had died in 1328; upon Robert's death in 1343, therefore, no direct male heir was available, though the Angevins' family ties with the throne of Hungary offered some possibilities. In accordance with King Robert's will and testament,[175] Queen Sancia became regent and head of the governing council for Charles' elder daughter, who came to the throne as Giovanna I (1343–82).

Historians have not been kind to Naples' Angevin queens, neither Sancia nor the two Giovannas. Giovanna I soon was beset by challenges to her throne and personal safety, first from among her Angevin cousins of the houses of Taranto and Durazzo — the heirs of Robert's younger brothers — and then by the family of her cousin and husband Andrew of Hungary, the younger brother of King Lewis of Hungary, himself the heir of Robert's elder brother, Charles Martel of Hungary. With Andrew's gruesome murder at the palace of Aversa on September 18, 1345 by unknown assailants, suspicions were

---

The Black Death (Manchester: Manchester University Press, 1994). For a recent summary of the historical research and scientific evidence, see Lester K. Little, "Review Article: Plague Historians in Lab Coats," *Past & Present* 213 (Nov. 2012): 267–90. Petrarch also noted the effect of the plague on the city. See below, Reading 63.

173. De Seta, *Napoli fra Rinascimento e Illuminismo*, 118.

174. Jordan, *Great Famine*, 182–88, notes that recovery from the famine may have actually improved the condition of many rural inhabitants in the North by the early 1340s.

175. See Reading 65 below.

immediately turned upon Giovanna.[176] Despite attempts by Pope Clement VI to protect her and her throne, Giovanna was challenged by a violent civil revolt at home fostered by her Neapolitan cousins, and then by the invasion of the kingdom by Lewis of Hungary, seeking both revenge for Andrew and the Neapolitan throne for himself.

Forced into exile in January 1348, Giovanna travelled to her Angevin possessions in Provence and in March arrived at Avignon, which she sold to the pope in exchange for funds to reconquer the Regno from the Hungarians, for the dispensation she needed to marry her cousin, Louis of Taranto, and for the exoneration of charges Lewis of Hungary had leveled against her for Andrew's murder.[177] In July 1348 Giovanna and Taranto returned to retake the kingdom. Naples itself soon fell to Giovanna and her lieutenants, but Louis of Taranto needed years to reconquer the rest of the Regno from the Hungarians and from the roving bands of mercenary companies that they brought with them.[178] The couple celebrated final victory with new nuptials on Pentecost Day (May 23) 1352 and a new coronation by papal legates on May 27. But Taranto himself soon turned on the queen and only his death in May 1362 saved the kingdom from further royal wars. One of Louis's unfortunate legacies was to rekindle the vicious personal rumors against the queen in an effort to discredit her and seize power.

Giovanna I then married Jaime IV, titular king of Majorca, on September 26, 1363; but this prince proved both ineffectual on the battlefield and unbalanced at home, and his swift decline and death in battle in 1375 left the queen with no male protector. She therefore married Duke Otto of Brunswick later that year. Giovanna took the side of Clement VII and the French line of popes, based at Avignon, during the Great Schism (1378–1417) against Urban VI, former

---

176. See Readings 74–76 below.

177. See Reading 77 below.

178. See Guido Guerri dall'Oro, "Les mercenaires dans les campagnes napolitaines de Louis le Grand, roi de Hongrie, 1347–1350," in *Mercenaries and Paid Men: The Mercenary Identity in the Middle Ages,* ed. John France (Leiden, Brill, 2008), 61–88.

archbishop of Bari and now Roman pope. Urban opposed Giovanna's marriage to Otto and her allegiance to Avignon and therefore excommunicated the queen and raised up as her rival Robert of Anjou's grandnephew Charles III of Durazzo, who seized the throne on 1381 and had her murdered in 1382.[179] By that time, however, Giovanna had adopted Duke Louis I of Anjou as her heir. He, however, died in 1384. Charles then went off to assert the Angevin claim to the crown of Hungary and was murdered there in 1386. Louis II of Anjou then invaded the Regno; but Charles' young son, Ladislaus, finally managed to retain the throne by allying with the Roman papacy in 1399.

The noble families of Naples exploited this royal weakness by seizing the government of the city and dividing it into five district councils or *seggi (sedie)*, each controlled by its own faction.[180] By 1386 they felt strong enough to elect six nobles and two *popolani*, as the non-noble merchant class was called, as a city government and to wrest concessions from the young King Ladislaus.[181] Forced to reconquer almost the entire Regno from Louis II of Anjou, Ladislaus and his mother, Margaret of Durazzo, eventually turned back baronial revolt, rival Angevin and Roman papal threats and reestablished the rule of the Durazzan line. Ladislaus then began a career of aggressive expansion against both the papal states and the Tuscan city-states that would involve much of Italy and beyond in an ever widening balance of power. By the time of his death Ladislaus was recognized as protector of the papal states and overlord of much of Tuscany and central Italy. But his power came along with a reputation for unscrupulous violence and aggression.

---

179. See George Peyronnet, " I Durazzo e Renato d'Angiò, 1381–1442," SN 3:335–436 at 337–58; and Reading 82.

180. See De Frede, "Da Carlo I," 292–308; Denys Hay and John Law, *Italy in the Age of the Renaissance, 1380–1530* (London: Longman, 1989), 30–31; and Peyronnet, "I Durazzo," 369–85, 397–400. For Robert of Anjou's policy toward urban factions, see the document from 1338/39 in Trevor Dean, trans. and ed., *The Towns of Italy in the Later Middle Ages: Selected Sources Translated and Annotated* (Manchester: Manchester University Press, 2000), 166–68.

181. On Ladislaus see Peyronnet, " I Durazzo," 359–88.

Upon Ladislaus' death in 1414, possibly by poison, his younger sister, Giovanna II (1414–35), came to power. Her tomb monument to Ladislaus in the church of S. Giovanni a Carbonara[182] is testimony to the high level and originality of Neapolitan arts at the time. Yet history has been even less kind to this Giovanna.[183] According to the accepted historiography, she attempted to stave off the growing power of the Neapolitan barons by forming marriage and love alliances with useful men. Her husbands were William, duke of Austria, and the brutal James de la Marche. Among her reputed lovers were Grand Seneschal Giovanni Caracciolo and the condottiere captains Braccio di Fortibraccio Perugino, Filippo Maria Sforza, Francesco Sforza and Piccinino, whose great companies of mercenaries brought murder, rape, arson and torture throughout the kingdom and peninsula. In 1421 she adopted Alfonso V, king of Aragon and Sicily since 1416, but quickly disowned him and drove him out in 1423, turning instead to her French cousin, Louis III of Anjou (d.1434), and then to his brother, the romantic, and ill-fated, René of Anjou.[184]

When Giovanna II died in 1435, claims to the kingdom were divided between the house of Anjou, through dynastic lineage and the adoptive claims of Duke René, and the house of Aragon, through Alfonso's adoption in 1421. Aragon had been a major Mediterranean power since it had consolidated its own kingdom in the eleventh century and then conquered

182. See Italica web gallery: http://www.flickr.com/photos/80499896@N05/sets/72157630164220128, images 12–20.

183. Peyronnet, "I Durazzo," 389–412. A reassessment of Giovanna II's reign and reputation — similar to that now underway for Sancia of Majorca and Giovanna I — may yield equally fruitful results.

184. See Richard Albert Lecoy de la Marche, *Le roi René: Sa vie, son administration, ses travaux artistiques et littéraires d'après les documents inédits des archives de France et d'Italie* (Paris: Firmin-Didot, 1875); Peyronnet, "I Durazzo," 413–26; Margaret Lucille Kekewich, *The Good King: René of Anjou and Fifteenth Century Europe* (Houndmills, Basingstoke: Palgrave Macmillan, 2008); and Franz Unterkircher, ed., *King René's Book of Love: Le Cueur d'Amours Espris* (New York: G. Braziller, 1975). For the city, see Amedeo Feniello, "Napoli al tempo di Renato d'Angiò," BISEAMI 112 (2010): 273–95.

Catalonia with Barcelona, the Balearics, Sardinia, portions of Greece and Sicily. René, held prisoner until 1438 by the duke of Burgundy, could not match Alfonso's initiative or resources. In 1442, after Alfonso had been laying siege to Naples for weeks, a Neapolitan showed him the very same aqueduct used by Belisarius to enter Naples 900 years before. On June 6, Alfonso took the city. After years of war, René abandoned the kingdom. Despite Neapolitan loyalty to René and the Angevins and their disgust at the "barbaric" Catalans, Alfonso, the Magnanimous, followed up his conquest by showering mercy and favors upon the Neapolitans and began a reign that would make Naples a major center of the Renaissance.[185] As Alfonso I of Naples (1442–58), he built new piazzas and fountains,[186] repaired walls and streets, palaces and religious institutions. The famed *Tavola Strozzi*,[187] now at the Museo di S. Martino, accurately reflects the beauty and importance of the city in 1464.

LITERATE CULTURES IN NAPLES

The complex culture of Naples stems from the rich mixture of people and their languages, a Mediterranean character that was part of the city from the time of its founding under the Greeks. Throughout the Middle Ages, Naples' literary culture reflected the changing dynamic between Mediterranean influence, the cultures of its Italian hinterland (especially of the Lombards) and northern European developments. During the ducal period, from as early as the eighth century to as late as the early

---

185. The best treatments in English remain George L. Hersey, *The Aragonese Arch at Naples, 1443–1475* (New Haven: Yale University Press, 1973); and Jerry H. Bentley, *Politics and Culture in Renaissance Naples* (Princeton: Princeton University Press, 1987). See also Senatore, "Kingdom of Naples." A full introduction to Renaissance Naples will soon appear in Hall, *Artistic Centers: Naples.*

186. See also Amedeo Feniello, "Gli interventi sanitari dei secoli XIV e XV," in *Napoli nel Medioevo. La Città del Mezzogiorno Medievale* 4 (2007): 123–35.

187. See below, pp. 346–47; De Seta, *Napoli fra Rinascimento e Illuminismo*, 11–53; L. Di Mauro, *La Tavola Strozzi* (Naples: E. De Rosa, 1992); Giulio Pane, *La Tavola Strozzi tra Napoli e Firenze: Un'immagine della città nel quattrocento* (Naples: Grimaldi & C. Editori, 2009).

eleventh century, Greek inscriptions were used in the area as well as Latin inscriptions using Greek characters. The monasteries, for both men and women, maintained their ties to Greek culture, and probably were bilingual houses. Under the Normans, "no one vernacular prevailed, and even in court circles there is no evidence for the cultivation of any vernacular literature until the appearance of the poets associated with Frederick II, who used the vernacular in the so-called 'Sicilian' form...." Translation was an important part of the culture, and "the Greeks in particular appear to have skillfully translated Greek works into Latin."[188] Many translations were based on the work of people who knew Greek, but then were finished by others with a greater familiarity with the Neapolitan milieu. John the Deacon records the gift by Bishop Athanasius I (850–72) of three codices by Flavius Josephus to an existing episcopal library.[189]

Benevento was a center of translation activity and cultural production from the eighth century; and its influence reached the duchy of Naples in numerous ways. Under Arechis II, the duke of Benevento from 759 to 774, and prince from 774 to 787, Paul the Deacon[190] composed his *Historia Romana*, a popular work in the Middle Ages, dedicated to Arechi and his wife Adeperga. Probably at Montecassino he later wrote the *Historia Langobardorum*. He also translated numerous other works.

Within Naples itself, Giovanni III (d.968/69) enlarged the library and translation program in honor of his wife Theodora, also a patron of literary culture.[191] Together they had commissioned the archpriest Leo to travel to Constantinople to obtain Greek manuscripts. He returned with such works as the *Chronographia* of Theophanes, the *Antiquities of the Jews* by Flavius Josephus, *De Prodigiis* by Livy, the writings of Pseudo-Dionysius the Areopagite and the *Historia Alexandri Magni*. Leo also completed a Latin translation of *Barlaam e Joasaf* and *Miraculum a S. Michaele in Chonis patratum*. Later, Giovanni Amalfitano, a monk of

---

188. Matthew, *Norman Kingdom of Sicily,* 113.

189. Reading 20 at p. 68.

190. See Readings 13, 17.

191. See p. xxxv n. 54 above and Readings 21–22 below.

the eleventh century, translated several identified works from Greek: the *Passio di Sta. Irene*, the *Sermo de obitu beati Nicolai* and the *Liber de miraculis*.

Book production was an important part of life in Naples, which drew on two world-famous scriptoria, Montecassino to the northeast and Cava de' Tirreni on the Amalfi coast. Within Naples, a famous scriptorium was long part of the monastery of S. Severino, founded by Eugippius in 492 on the Megaride island on the site of the present Castel dell'Ovo. As noted above, the scriptorium had a direct impact in bringing Eastern Mediterranean motifs to the books produced as far north as Lindisfarne.[192]

The Norman and Hohenstaufen contributed to the city's literary culture in poetry, the *chansons de geste*, in legal and philosophical thought[193] and in manuscript production as a center of the Exultet rolls.[194] Under the Angevins, French language and culture joined the mix, and others from the Italian peninsula engaged with the culture of Naples, even as its own language began to emerge in written form. Patronage of non-Neapolitan artists and writers was a long-standing practice in Angevin Naples. Charles I had a complex relationship with poets and writers.[195] Charles II supported the first performance of Adam de La Halle's *Jeu de Robin et Marion*, for example.[196] With the reign of Robert of Anjou, a new level of literary patronage emerged as the court hosted such figures as Petrarch[197] and Boccaccio,[198] whose writings reflect culture and politics in the Angevin Regno, as well as pan-Italian developments. Lavish bibles, such as the Anjou Bible,[199] became a hallmark of Angevin court patronage, while a large corpus of chivalrous

---

192. Page xxxviii.

193. See below, Readings 31, 34, 40.

194. Reading 30.

195. See, for example, Asperti, *Carlo I d'Angiò*.

196. Reading 47.

197. Readings 69–70, 72

198. Readings 73, 78, 81.

199. For the Anjou Bible, see Figs. 30, 39, 43, 50–51.

romances reached the literate classes and may have influenced Neapolitan historiography during the period.[200]

Chapter 6, Literate Cultures,[201] presents a brief visual essay of Neapolitan inscriptions, charters and manuscript books from the seventh through the fourteenth century. In addition, selections from the hagiography, poetry, romances and drama are also interspersed throughout the following collection. This evidence reinforces the documents presented here to reflect the great diversity of language and form of Neapolitan literate cultures.

■

---

200. See below, Readings 76–77 at pp. 276–80 and nn. 157, 162–63.

201. Pages 303–14 below.

CHAPTER 1:
LATE ROMAN AND BYZANTINE NAPLES

1. THE LAST ROMAN EMPEROR OF THE WEST DEPOSED AND EXILED TO NAPLES, 476 CE

Fig. 2. Golden solidus of Romulus Augustulus. Wikimedia.

The Roman Empire is traditionally (and not so accurately) considered to have ended in 476 CE with the deposition of the titular emperor Romulus Augustulus by the Gothic king Odoacer.[1] It is fitting that we begin the history of medieval Naples with this event, since Naples itself was the scene of the last emperor's final days. The event is described in Jordanes, *Getica*. Jordanes was himself a Goth and a *notarius*, or secretary, to Gunthigis Baza, an Ostrogoth military commander of a small client state on the Roman frontier in Moesia, in modern Bulgaria. Jordanes was asked to write a summary of a multi-volume history of the Goths (now lost) by Cassiodorus. He composed this abridgement, the *Getica sive De origine actibusque Gothorum*, c.551. The history takes the Goths from their mythological origins to the later stages of the Gothic Wars against the Byzantine general Belisarius.

Note that in Jordanes' account, the Villa Lucullana (Castel dell'Ovo) is already being referred to as a "castle" or fortress. Our selection is taken from Jordanes, *Getica sive De*

---

1. For a survey of the period, see Introduction, pp. xxi–xxiv.

origine actibusque Gothorum (The Origin and Deeds of the Goths)
trans. by Charles C. Mierow (Princeton: Princeton University
Press, 1908). Online version curated by J. Vanderspoel at
http://www.harbornet.com/folks/theedrich/Goths/Goths1.
htm. Accessed 12/16/12.

XLV.240. When Eurich, as we have already said, beheld these
great and various changes, he seized the city of Arverna, where
the Roman general Ecdicius was at that time in command.
He was a senator of most renowned family and the son of
Avitus, a recent emperor who had usurped the reign for a few
days — for Avitus held the rule for a few days before Olybrius,
and then withdrew of his own accord to Placentia [Piacenza],
where he was ordained bishop. His son Ecdicius strove for a
long time with the Visigoths, but had not the power to prevail.
So he left the country and (what was more important) the city
of Arverna to the enemy and betook himself to safer regions.

241. When the Emperor Nepos heard of this, he ordered
Ecdicius to leave Gaul and come to him, appointing Orestes
in his stead as master of the soldiers. This Orestes thereupon
received the army, set out from Rome against the enemy and
came to Ravenna. Here he tarried while he made his son
Romulus Augustulus emperor. When Nepos learned of this,
he fled to Dalmatia and died there, deprived of his throne, in
the very place where Glycerius, who was formerly emperor,
held at that time the bishopric of Salona.

XLVI. 242. Now when Augustulus had been appointed emperor by his father Orestes in Ravenna, it was not long before
Odoacer, king of the Torcilingi, invaded Italy, as leader of the
Sciri, the Heruli and allies of various races. He put Orestes
to death, drove his son Augustulus from the throne and
condemned him to the punishment of exile in the Castle of
Lucullus in [Naples] Campania.

243. Thus the Western Empire of the Roman race, which
Octavianus Augustus, the first of the Augusti, began to govern
in the seven hundred and ninth year from the founding of the
city, perished with this Augustulus in the five hundred and
twenty-second year from the beginning of the rule of his predecessors and those before them, and from this time onward

kings of the Goths held Rome and Italy. Meanwhile Odoacer, king of nations, subdued all Italy and then at the very outset of his reign slew Count Bracila at Ravenna that he might inspire a fear of himself among the Romans. He strengthened his kingdom and held it for almost thirteen years, even until the appearance of Theodoric, of whom we shall speak hereafter.

2. SEVERINUS OF NORICUM IS BURIED IN NAPLES, 482

The Villa of Lucullus (Villa Lucullana) was a busy place in the late fifth century. St. Severinus was the apostle of Noricum, a Christian missionary on the Danube border during the Rugians' invasion. Noricum is near Eiferingen, at the foot of Mount Kalenberg, not far from Vienna. Severinus was born either in southern Italy or in North Africa. After the death of Attila he trav-

Fig. 3. S. Severino, Castel dell'Ovo. Photo: Italica Press.

eled through the territory along the Danube preaching Christianity and converting many. He died in 482, and his body was taken to Italy and buried at Naples.[2]

Paul the Deacon relates the transfer of the saint's remains in his *History of the Lombards*. In a certain sense, Severinus' "translation" brought the wildness of the collapsing Roman frontiers back to the heart of the empire: a reminder — both politically and spiritually — that the marginal will, as often as not, become central. Severinus' body remained at the Villa Lucullana until 902 when, fearing conquest by the Saracens, the Neapolitans destroyed the *castrum* and the monastery of S. Salvatore on the Megaride island, and the monks moved

---

2.   From Foulke, *History of the Lombards,* 32 n. 2.

inside the walls of Naples, to the present site of the monastery of SS. Severino e Sossio. Emperor Valentinian III had fortified the Villa Lucullana c.440, and during the Lombard (ducal) period the *castellum* began to take the shape of the present Castel dell'Ovo.

Our selection is taken from the *History of the Langobards (Historia Langobardorum)*, trans. by William Dudley Foulke (Philadelphia: University of Pennsylvania Press, 1907), 31–32.

Book I.19. In these times the fuel of great enmities was consumed between Odoacer who was ruling in Italy now for some years, and Feletheus, who is also called Feva, king of the Rugii. This Feletheus dwelt in those days on the further shore of the Danube, which the Danube itself separates from the territories of Noricum. In these territories of the Noricans at that time was the monastery of the blessed Severinus, who, endowed with the sanctity of every abstinence, was already renowned for his many virtues, and though he dwelt in these places up to the end of his life. Now, however, Neapolis [Naples] keeps his remains.

When Eugippius (d. after 533) brought the remains of St. Severinus of Noricum to Naples after the saint's death in 492, he founded the monastery of S. Severino at the site of the Villa Lucullana. His *Vita* of S. Severinus takes up the narrative. Our text is taken from the *Memorandum [Life] of St. Severinus* at http://www.tertullian.org/fathers/severinus_02_text.htm. Accessed 11/30/2012.

46. Barbaria, a lady of rank, venerated St. Severinus with pious devotion. She and her late husband had known him well by reputation and through correspondence. When, after the death of the saint, she heard that his body had with great labor been brought into Italy, and up to that time had not been committed to earth, she invited by frequent letters our venerable priest Marcianus, and also the whole brotherhood. Then with the authorization of Saint Gelasius, pontiff of the Roman see, and received by the people of Naples with reverent obsequies, the body was laid to rest by the hands of

St. Victor the bishop in the Lucullan castle, in a mausoleum, which Barbaria had built.

3. STA. RESTITUTA FOUNDED, c.500

The Villa Lucullana, or *castrum Lucullanum*, is named in yet another document, this from c.540, the *Liber Pontificalis (The Book of Pontiffs)* a collection of lives of the Roman popes from St. Peter up to Stephen V (d.891). The existing work is composed of several compilations, the first of which included the following selection for the pontificate of Pope Sylvester I (314–35).

Composed some time around 540, the *Liber* is less a series of complete biographies than a collection of available documents of all types: lives *(vitae)* and deeds *(actae)*, as well as records of liturgical developments, clerical appointments and inventories of church objects and treasures. It does include some complete biographies and records notable building projects both within Rome and in lands closely associated with the papacy, including Naples.

Here the author records the popular tradition of Constantine's founding of the cathedral of Sta. Restituta. While there is little evidence of the emperor's active role here, a basilica built atop the site of the temple of Apollo certainly dates from the fourth century. William Tronzo notes that, "according to the *Chronicon episcoporum*, at the end of the fifth or beginning of the sixth century Bishop Stephan I (499–504) built a church dedicated to Christ: *'fecit basilicam ad nomen Salvatoris, copulatum cum episcopio'* ('he built a basilica in the name of the Savior, connected to the bishop's palace')."[3]

Aside from Constantine's original foundation, this brief report records the rich endowment of the church, measured in costly liturgical and service items, the attribution to Constantine of a major aqueduct into the city that will play a large part in its later history, his construction of a forum, most likely that in the area around the present S. Paolo Maggiore and S. Lorenzo Maggiore, his assignment to the cathedral of incomes of neighboring rural estates, measured

---

3.   Bruzelius & Tronzo, 31.

in *solidi*,[4] and finally another early reference to "the island" of Megara, the site of the "fort," *castrum Lucullanum*.

Our selection is taken from *The Book of Pontiffs (Liber Pontificalis): The Ancient Biographies of the First Ninety Roman Bishops to AD 715*, Raymond David, ed., rev. 3rd ed. (Liverpool: Liverpool University Press, 2010), 25.

Then the emperor Constantine built the basilica in the city of Naples, to which he presented the following: 2 silver patens each weighing 25 lb; 2 silver *scyphi* each weighing 10 lb; 15 service chalices each weighing 2 lb; 2 silver *amae* each weighing 15 lb; 20 silver lights each weighing 8 lb; 20 bronze lights each weighing 10 lb; and he built an aqueduct 8 miles long; he also built a forum in the same city; and presented the following gift: the property Macari, revenue 150 *solidi*; the property Cimbriana, revenue 105 *solidi*; the property Sclina, revenue 108 *solidi*; the property Afilas, revenue 140 *solidi*; the property Nymfulas, revenue 90 *solidi*; the property 'the Island' with the fort [i.e., *castrum Lucullanum*], revenue 80 *solidi*.

4. CASSIODORUS, *VARIAE*, c.530

Cassiodorus (Flavius Magnus Aurelius Cassiodorus Senator, c.490–c.585) was born at Scylletium, near Catanzaro in Calabria. He began his career as councilor to his father, the governor of Sicily, and soon earned a reputation as a legal expert. During his working life, as quaestor c.507–11, as a consul in 514, then in 523 as *magister officiorum* under Theodoric, replacing the disgraced Boethius. He retained this post under the regency for Theodoric's successor, Athalaric. Around 537/38, Cassiodorus left Italy for

---

4.   The standard coinage of late Rome, first struck by Diocletian in 301 and in currency through the 10th century. On coinage, see Philip Grierson and Mark Blackburn, *Medieval European Coinage, with a Catalogue of the Coins in the Fitzwilliam Museum, Cambridge*, 1: *The Early Middle Ages (5th–10th Centuries)* (Cambridge: Cambridge University Press, 1986); Alessia Rovelli, "Coins and Trade in Early Medieval Italy," *Early Medieval Europe* 17 (2009): 45–76; Richard Reece, "Coins and the Late Roman Economy," in *Theory and Practice in Late Antique Archaeology*, Luke Lavan and William Bowden, eds. (Leiden: Brill, 2003), 139–70; and below, Readings 41, 53, 64.

Constantinople where he remained almost two decades, concentrating on religious questions. On his retirement he founded the monastery of Vivarium on his family estates off the coast of Calabria at Squillace.[5]

Fig. 4. Cassiodorus (Ezra): Florence, Bibliotheca Medicea-Laurenziana, MS Laurenziano Amiatino 1. Based on sixth-century Codex Grandior.

The *Variae epistolae* were composed in 537 from his work on Theodoric's state papers. They obviously refer to a time previous to Belisarius' conquest of Naples in 536. The text has been edited several times, and the standard edition is Theodor Mommsen, *Cassiodori Senatoris Variae*.[6] It has been translated into English by Thomas Hodgkin, *The Letters of Cassiodorus*[7]; and more recently by S.J.B. Barnish.[8] The Hodgkin edition is also available on Project Gutenberg.[9] Our selection is taken from Book VI in this online edition.

While we might expect a rosy picture of a new assignment for a court official, in this case of *comes* or "count," Cassiodorus' letter 23 does highlight several important features of sixth-century Naples under the Goths. The city is delightfully situated and remains prosperous, populous and important enough to hold the court of a royal and imperial praetorium. In addition, Naples itself controls a territory that extends some distance inland and

5.   The standard treatment of his life and work is James J. O'Donnell, *Cassiodorus* (Berkeley: University of California Press, 1979).

6.   *Monumenta Germaniae Historica. Auctorum Antiquissimorum* 12 (Berlin: Weidmann, 1894).

7.   *The Letters of Cassiodorus, Being a Condensed Translation of the* Variae Epistolae *of Magnus Aurelius Cassiodorus Senator* (London: H. Frowde, 1886; repr., 2006)

8.   *Cassiodorus: Variae* (Liverpool: University Press, 1992).

9.   At http://www.gutenberg.org/ebooks/18590. Accessed 12/28/12.

along the coast, vague evidence of the extent of the Byzantine county and later independent duchy. Letter 24 offers indirect evidence of the existence of a prosperous agrarian elite and of the independent governance of the city under its council.

Book VI.23. Formula of the count of Naples. (*Comitiva Neapolitana*).

As the sun sends forth his rays so we send out our servants to the various cities of our dominions, to adorn them with the splendor of their retinue and to facilitate the untying of the knots of the law by the multitude of jurisconsults who follow in their train. Thus we sow a liberal crop of official salaries and reap our harvest in the tranquility of our subjects. For this Indiction we send you as count to weigh the causes of the people of Naples. It is a populous city, and one abounding in delights by sea and land. You may lead there a most delicious life, if your cup be not mixed with bitterness by the criticisms of the citizens on your judgments. You will sit on a jeweled tribunal, and the praetorium will be filled with your officers; but you will also be surrounded by a multitude of fastidious spectators, who assuredly, in their conversation, will judge the judge. See then that you walk warily. Your power extends for a certain distance along the coast, and both the buyer and seller have to pay you tribute. We give you the chance of earning the applause of a vast audience: do you so act that your sovereign may take pleasure in multiplying his gifts.

VI.24. Formula addressed to the gentlemen-farmers (or the titled cultivators) and common councilmen of the city of Naples [and surrounding district] *(Honorati possessores et curiales civitatis Neapolitanae)*.

You pay us tribute, but we have conferred honors upon you. We are now sending you a *comes* [the one appointed in the previous formula], but he will be a terror only to the evil-disposed. Do you live according to reason, since you are reasonable beings, and then the laws may take holiday. Your quietness is our highest joy.

5. EUGIPPIUS AND HAGIOGRAPHY, c.533

Hagiography was an important element of the literature and the liturgy of Naples and of the integration of the Latin and Byzantine calendars. In addition to translating saints' lives from the Greek, Neapolitan scholars also wrote them. The following are examples from a variety of documents:

Vita Mariae Aegyptiacae, trans. by Paul the Deacon of Naples

Poenitentie Theophili, trans. by Paul the Deacon of Naples

Passio Arethae, trans. by Bishop Athanasius II

Passio Eustratati, by Guarimpotus grammaticus, trans. by Bishop Athanasius II

Passio Alexandrini

Sermo in reditu reliquiarium sancti Iohannis Chrysostomi, by Cosma il Vestitore, trans by Guarimpotus grammaticus

Passio SS. Quadraginta Sebastenorum, by John the Deacon (9–10th c.), abbot of S. Severino

Vita Nicolai, by John the Deacon

Peter the Subdeacon, 10th c. translator[10]

Vita Basilii by Pseudo-Anfilochius, trans. by Orso based on a translation of Nicola

Passio Anastasii Persae, trans. by Gregorius Clericus at the request of Abbot Athansius, also with help of a certain Nicola

Passio Theodori, trans. by Bonitus

Passio Blasii, trans. by Bonitus

Passio Abibi

Miraculum di Eufemia

Miraculum sancti Cosma e Damiano, by Cicunione (10th c.)

Passio de S. Mercurio

Vita S. Gregorii Nazianzani.

Eugippius also composed an anthology of the works of Augustine, which was popular throughout the Middle Ages, as well as a lost monastic rule, derived from the Rule of Augustine. His *Memorandum [Life] of St. Severinus*, excerpted in Reading 2 above, is full of Severinus' remarkable deeds, including his rescue of one of his servants (chapter 10).

---

10. See Edoardo D'Angelo, "Petrus Neapolitanus Subdiac.," in Paolo Chiesa and Lucia Castaldi, eds., *La trasmissione dei testi Latini del Medioevo. Medieval Latin Texts and Their Transmisson.* TE.TRA. 1 (Florence: SISMEL, 2004), 349–63.

There was a janitor at the monastery church, Maurus by name, whom St. Severinus had redeemed from the hands of the barbarians. One day the man of God warned him, saying, "Take heed to-day not to go away anywhere: otherwise you shall be in imminent peril." But the janitor, contrary to the warning of the great father, and persuaded by a layman, went out at midday to gather fruit at the second milestone from Favianis. Presently he and the layman were made captives by barbarians and carried across the Danube. In that hour the man of God, reading in his cell, suddenly closed the book, and said, "Quick. Find Maurus!" When the janitor was nowhere found, Severinus crossed the streams of the Danube in all haste and hurried after the robbers, whom the people called Scamarae. Stricken with awe by his reverend presence, they humbly restored the captives whom they had taken.

This *Vita* closes with an early description of Neapolitan street life during the procession bringing St. Severinus' remains to the Villa Lucullana[11]:

46. At this solemnity many afflicted by divers diseases, whom it would be tedious to enumerate, were instantly healed. Among them was a venerable handmaid of God, Processa by name, a citizen of Naples, who suffered from a severe and troublesome sickness. Invited by the virtues of the holy corpse, she hastened to meet it on the way; and when she approached the vehicle in which the venerable body was borne, immediately she was free from sickness in all her members.

Also at that time a blind man, Laudicius, was startled when he heard the unexpected clamor of the people singing psalms, and anxiously asked his household what it was. When they replied that the body of a certain St. Severinus was passing, he was moved by the spirit and asked that he be led to the window, from which one possessed of sight could behold afar off the multitude singing psalms and the carriage bearing the sacred body. And when he leaned forth from the window and prayed, straightway he saw and pointed out his acquaintances

---

11. See Reading 2 above.

and neighbors one by one. Thereupon all who heard him wept for joy and returned thanks to God.

Marinus too, precentor of the holy church at Naples, could not recover his health after a terrible sickness and suffered from a constant headache. In faith he leaned his head against the carriage and immediately lifted it up free from pain. In memory of this benefit, he always came on the anniversary of the saint's burial and rendered to God thanks and the sacrifice of a vow.

I have related three of the numberless miracles, which were wrought on the arrival of the saint through his mediation and virtues. Let it suffice, though many know of more.

A monastery, built at the same place to the memory of the blessed man, still endures. By his merits many possessed with devils have received and do receive healing through the effective grace of God; to whom is honor and glory for ever and ever. Amen.

Illustrious minister of Christ, thou hast the memoir. From it make by thy editorial care a profitable work.

Fig. 5. Roman statue of Mercurius at the Baths at Baiae. Wikimedia. Photo: Kleuske.

6. ON THE BATHS AT BAIAE AND THE BAY OF NAPLES, c.534

Naples has always been synonymous with its bay, and since antiquity Pozzuoli, Baiae and Misenum were seen as integral parts of its natural and human geography. The imperial bath complex at Baiae was among the chief attractions of the region.[12] By the end of the fourth century CE, Baiae had fallen from importance for much of the Roman elite. Yet, as this text shows, it continued to be a well-known

---

12. See John H. D'Arms, *Romans on the Bay of Naples: A Social and Cultural Study of the Villas and Their Owners from 150 B.C. to A.D. 400,* Loeb Classical Monographs (Cambridge: Harvard University Press, 1970), esp. 139–42.

retreat at the end of the Gothic period. It remained so into the later Middle Ages, and Petrarch recounts his own visit to the site in 1343.[13]

Cassiodorus' letter dates from before 534, the year of Athalaric's death, and is written to an unknown holder of the office of *primiscrinius*, chief scribe or chancellor, who served under the prefect of the city of Rome. Was this delightful description first-hand, via Cassiodorus' classical sources, or through some other account? Cassiodorus may well have used Naples as a port back and forth to Constantinople, but we appear to have no record of him on the bay. Vacation pay and leaving the office for extended periods have, it seems, been perennial concerns of administrators.

VARIAE IX.6. TO <BLANK>, PRIMISCRINIUS ON BEHALF OF KING ATHALARIC

You complain that your health is failing under the long pressure of your work and that you fear, if you absent yourself, you may lose the emoluments of your office. At the same time you ask leave to visit the Baths of Baiae. Go then with a mind perfectly at rest as to your emoluments, which we will keep safe for you. Seek the sun, seek the pure air and smiling shore of that lovely bay, thickly set with harbours and dotted with noble islands — that bay in which Nature displays all her marvels and invites man to explore her secrets. There is the Lake of Avernus, with its splendid supply of oysters. There are long piers [of Nisida] jutting out into the sea; and the most delightful fishing in the world is to be had in the fish-ponds — open to the sky — on either side of them. There are warm baths [of Pozzuoli], heated not by brick-work flues and smoky balls of fire, but by Nature herself. The pure air supplies the steam and softly stimulates perspiration, and the health-giving work is so much the better done as Nature is above Art. Let the Coralli [in Moesia, on the shore of the Euxine] boast their wonderful sea, let the pearl fisheries of India vaunt themselves. In our judgment Baiae, for its powers of bestowing pleasure and health, surpasses them all. Go then to Baiae to bathe, and have no fear about the emoluments.

---

13. See below, Reading 69.

7. BELISARIUS CONQUERS NAPLES FROM THE GOTHS, 536

Fig. 6. Belisarius and Justinian I. Mosaic. Ravenna, S. Vitale. Wikimedia. Photo: Bender235.

The events related in the following selection are among the most famous in the history of Naples and of the early medieval world. They appear in Procopius's *History of the Wars*, books V and VI, *The Gothic Wars*.

Procopius of Caesarea was born in Caesarea in Byzantine Palestine.[14] He probably received a conventional education for a member of his provincial elite, may have attended law school, and became a rhetor. In 527, the first year of Emperor Justinian I's reign, he became the *adsessor* (legal adviser) for Flavius Belisarius (c.500–565), the newly appointed imperial chief military commander. Procopius and his informants were eyewitnesses to most of what he narrates. He was in Belisarius' entourage until the general was defeated at the battle of Callinicum against the Sassanid Persians in 531 and recalled to Constantinople. In 533, Procopius accompanied Belisarius in his conquest of the Vandal kingdom in North Africa and took part in the capture of Carthage. Procopius remained in North Africa with Belisarius' successor Solomon when Belisarius returned to Constantinople. He rejoined Belisarius for his campaign against the Ostrogoth kingdom in Italy and was in Rome during the Gothic siege of 537/38. In 540 Procopius was present at Belisarius' entry into the Gothic capital, Ravenna, after which his relationship with the general seems to have cooled. When Belisarius was sent back to Italy in 544, Procopius appears to have no longer been on the commander's staff. He died c.554.

---

14. See J.A.S. Evans, *Procopius* (New York: Twayne, 1972); Averil Cameron, *Procopius and the Sixth Century* (Berkeley: University of California Press, 1985); and Anthony Kaldellis, *Procopius of Caesarea: Tyranny, History, and Philosophy at the End of Antiquity* (Philadelphia: University of Pennsylvania Press, 2004).

Belisarius successfully defeated the Goths after years of long struggle, siege and the destruction of capitals like Naples and Rome and the depopulation of the Campanian countryside through war, massacre, famine and disease. Belisarius himself was soon to be recalled to Constantinople due to the machinations of his political enemies and Justinian's jealousy and was replaced by Narses, under whose command the Byzantines consolidated their gains only to see them disappear with the onslaught of a new barbarian people: the Lombards.

In addition to its fascinating narrative and dramatic speeches, the *History* provides evidence of several important elements of early medieval Naples, including the extent of its walls and fortifications; the aqueduct and its vast cisterns, first built by the ancient Greek settlers of Neapolis; its diverse population — Latins, Greeks, Goths, Middle Easterners, Jews, North Africans — their differing loyalties and their economic and strategic interests in the Middle East and the Italian hinterlands, in the Byzantine orbit and in Rome itself. Procopius' main focus remains on the moral dilemmas of shifting loyalties in late antiquity, but he also provides ample indication of the already pronounced physical decay of Naples, including the deserted, squatter section of the city where the aqueduct opened up. The "Romans" under Belisarius are, of course, the Byzantines.

Our text is excerpted from Procopius, *History of the Wars,* vol. 3, books V–VI.15, H.B. Dewing, trans., Loeb Classical Library (Cambridge: Harvard University Press, 1919), 69–107.

Book V.8. And Belisarius, leaving guards in Syracuse and Panormus [Palermo], crossed with the rest of the army from Messana to Rhegium (where the myths of the poets say Scylla and Charybdis were), and every day the people of that region kept coming over to him. For since their towns had from of old been without walls, they had no means at all of guarding them, and because of their hostility toward the Goths they were, as was natural, greatly dissatisfied with their present government. And Ebrimous came over to Belisarius as a deserter from the Goths, together with all his followers; this man was the son-in-law of Theodatus, being married to Theodenanthe, his daughter. And he was straightway sent to the emperor and received many gifts of honor and in particular attained the patrician dignity. And the army of Belisarius marched from Rhegium through Bruttium and Lucania, and the fleet of ships accompanied it, sailing close to the mainland. But when they reached Campania, they came upon a city on the sea, Naples by name, that was strong not only because of the nature of its site, but also because it contained a numerous garrison of Goths. And Belisarius commanded the ships to anchor in the harbor, which was beyond the range of missiles, while he himself made his camp near the city. He then first took possession by surrender of the fort that is in the suburb, and afterwards permitted the inhabitants of the city at their own request to send some of their notables into his camp, in order that they might tell what their wish was and, after receiving his reply, report to the populace. Straightway, therefore, the Neapolitans sent Stephanus. And he, upon coming before Belisarius, spoke as follows:

"You are not acting justly, O general, in taking the field against men who are Romans and have done no wrong, who inhabit but a small city and have over us a guard of barbarians as masters, so that it does not even lie in our power, if we desire to do so, to oppose them. But it so happens that even these guards had to leave their wives and children, and their most precious possessions in the hands of Theodatus before they came to keep guard over us. Therefore, if they treat with you at all, they will plainly be betraying, not the city, but themselves. And if one must speak the truth with no concealment, you have not counseled to your advantage, either, in coming against us. For if you capture Rome, Naples will be subject to you without any further trouble, whereas if you are repulsed from there, it is probable that you will not be able to hold even this city securely. Consequently the time you spend on this siege will be spent to no purpose."

So spoke Stephanus. And Belisarius replied as follows:

"Whether we have acted wisely or foolishly in coming here is not a question that we propose to submit to the Neapolitans.

But we desire that you first weigh carefully such matters as are appropriate to your deliberations and then act solely in accordance with your own interests. Receive into your city, therefore, the emperor's army, which has come to secure your freedom and that of the other Italians, and do not choose the course that will bring upon you the most grievous misfortunes. For those who, in order to rid themselves of slavery or any other shameful thing, go into war, such men, if they fare well in the struggle, have double good fortune, because along with their victory they have also acquired freedom from their troubles, and if defeated they gain some consolation for themselves, in that, they have not of their own free will chosen to follow the worse fortune. But as for those who have the opportunity to be free without fighting, but yet enter into a struggle in order to make their condition of slavery permanent, such men, even if it so happens that they conquer, have failed in the most vital point, and if in the battle they fare less happily than they wished, they will have, along with their general ill-fortune, also the calamity of defeat. As for the Neapolitans, then, let these words suffice. But as for these Goths who are present, we give them the choice, either to array themselves hereafter on our side under the great emperor, or to go to their homes altogether immune from harm. Because, if both you and they, disregarding all these considerations, dare to raise arms against us, it will be necessary for us also, if God so wills, to treat whomever we meet as an enemy. If, however, it is the will of the Neapolitans to choose the cause of the emperor and thus to be rid of so cruel a slavery, I take it upon myself, giving you pledges, to promise that you will receive at our hands those benefits that the Sicilians lately hoped for, and with regard to which they were unable to say that we had sworn falsely."

Such was the message that Belisarius bade Stephanus take back to the people. But privately he promised him large rewards if he should inspire the Neapolitans with good-will toward the emperor. And Stephanus, upon coming into the city, reported the words of Belisarius and expressed his own opinion that it was inexpedient to fight against the emperor. And he was assisted in his efforts by Antiochus, a man of Syria, but long resident in Naples for the purpose of carrying on a shipping business, who had a great reputation there for wisdom and justice.

But there were two men, Pastor and Asclepiodotus, trained speakers and very notable men among the Neapolitans, who were exceedingly friendly toward the Goths, and quite unwilling to have any change made in the present state of affairs. These two men, planning how they might block the negotiations, induced the multitude to demand many serious concessions and to try to force Belisarius to promise on oath that they should forthwith obtain what they asked for. And after writing down in a document such demands as nobody would have supposed that Belisarius would accept, they gave it to Stephanus. And he, returning to the emperor's army, showed the writing to the general and enquired of him whether he was willing to carry out all the proposals that the Neapolitans made and to take an oath concerning them. And Belisarius promised that they should all be fulfilled for them and so sent him back. Now when the Neapolitans heard this, they were in favor of accepting the general's assurances at once and began to urge that the emperor's army be received into the city with all speed. For he declared that nothing unpleasant would befall them, if the case of the Sicilians was sufficient evidence for anyone to judge by, since, as he pointed out, it had only recently been their lot, after they had exchanged their barbarian tyrants for the sovereignty of Justinian, to be, not only free men, but also immune from all difficulties. And swayed by great excitement they were about to go to the gates with the purpose of throwing them open. And though the Goths were not pleased with what they were doing, still, since they were unable to prevent it, they stood out of the way.

But Pastor and Asclepiodotus called together the people and all the Goths in one place and spoke as follows:

"It is not at all unnatural that the populace of a city should abandon themselves and their own safety, especially if, without consulting any of their notables, they make an independent decision regarding their all. But it is necessary for us, who are on the very point of perishing together with you, to offer as a last contribution to the fatherland this advice. We see, then, fellow citizens, that you are intent upon betraying both

17

yourselves and the city to Belisarius, who promises to confer many benefits upon you and to swear the most solemn oaths in confirmation of his promises. Now if he is able to promise you this also, that to him will come the victory in the war, no one could deny that the course you are taking is to your advantage. For it is great folly not to gratify every whim of him who is to become master. But if this outcome lies in uncertainty, and no man in the world is competent to guarantee the decision of fortune, consider what sort of misfortunes your haste is seeking to attain. For if the Goths overcome their adversaries in the war, they will punish you as enemies and as having done them the foulest wrong. For you are resorting to this act of treason, not under constraint of necessity, but out of deliberate cowardice. So that even to Belisarius, if he wins the victory over his enemies, we shall perhaps appear faithless and betrayers of our rulers, and having proved ourselves deserters, we shall in all probability have a guard set over us permanently by the emperor. For though he who has found a traitor is pleased at the moment of victory by the service rendered, yet afterwards, moved by suspicion based upon the traitor's past, he hates and fears his benefactor, since he himself has in his own possession the evidences of the other's faithlessness. If, however, we show ourselves faithful to the Goths at the present time, manfully submitting to the danger, they will give us great rewards in case they win the mastery over the enemy, and Belisarius, if it should so happen that he is the victor, will be prone to forgive. For loyalty that fails is punished by no man unless he be lacking in understanding. But what has happened to you that you are in terror of being besieged by the enemy, you who have no lack of provisions, have not been deprived by blockade of any of the necessities of life, and hence may sit at home, confident in the fortifications and in your garrison [of Goths] here? And in our opinion even Belisarius would not have consented to this agreement with us if he had any hope of capturing the city by force. And yet if what he desired were what is just and what will be to our advantage, he ought not to be trying to frighten the Neapolitans or to establish his own power by means of an act of injustice on our part toward the Goths; but he should do battle with Theodatus and the Goths, so that without danger to us or treason on our part the city might come into the power of the victors."

When they had finished speaking, Pastor and Asclepiodotus brought forward the Jews, who promised that the city should be in want of none of the necessities, and the Goths on their part promised that they would guard the circuit-wall safely. And the Neapolitans, moved by these arguments, bade Belisarius depart thence with all speed. He, however, began the siege. And he made many attempts upon the circuit-wall, but was always repulsed, losing many of his soldiers, and especially those who laid some claim to valor. For the wall of Naples was inaccessible, on one side by reason of the sea, and on the other because of some difficult country, and those who planned to attack it could gain entrance at no point, not only because of its general situation, but also because the ground sloped steeply. However, Belisarius cut the aqueduct that brought water into the city; but he did not in this way seriously disturb the Neapolitans, since there were wells inside the circuit-wall that sufficed for their needs and kept them from feeling too keenly the loss of the aqueduct.

9. So the besieged, without the knowledge of the enemy, sent to Theodatus in Rome begging him to come to their help with all speed. But Theodatus was not making the least preparation for war, being by nature unmanly, as has been said before. [III.1] And they say that something else happened to him, which terrified him exceedingly and reduced him to still greater anxiety.

I, for my part, do not credit this report, but even so it shall be told. Theodatus even before this time had been prone to make enquiries of those who professed to foretell the future, and on the present occasion he was at a loss what to do in the situation that confronted him — a state that more than anything else is accustomed to drive men to seek prophecies; so he enquired of one of the Hebrews, who had a great reputation for prophecy, what sort of an outcome the present war would have. The Hebrew commanded him to confine three groups of ten swine each in three huts, and after giving them respectively the names of Goths, Romans and the soldiers of the emperor, to wait quietly for a certain number of days. And Theodatus did as he was told. And when the appointed day had come, they both went into the huts and looked at the swine; and they found that of those which had been given the name of Goths all save two were dead, whereas all except a few were living of those which had received the name of the emperor's soldiers; and as for those which had been called Romans, it so happened that, although the hair of all of them had fallen out, yet about half of them survived. When Theodatus beheld this and divined the outcome of the war, a great fear, they say, came upon him, since he knew well that it would certainly be the fate of the Romans to die to half their number and be deprived of their possessions, but that the Goths would be defeated and their race reduced to a few, and that to the emperor would come, with the loss of but a few of his soldiers, the victory in the war. And for this reason, they say, Theodatus felt no impulse to enter into a struggle with Belisarius. As for this story, then, let each one express his views according to the belief or disbelief that he feels regarding it.

But Belisarius, as he besieged the Neapolitans both by land and by sea, was beginning to be vexed. For he was coming to think that they would never yield to him, and, furthermore, he could not hope that the city would be captured, since he was finding that the difficulty of its position was proving to be a very serious obstacle. And the loss of the time that was being spent there distressed him, for he was making his calculations so as to avoid being compelled to go against Theodatus and Rome in the winter season. Indeed he had already even given orders to the army to pack up, his intention being to depart from there as quickly as possible.

But while he was in the greatest perplexity, it came to pass that he met with the following good fortune. One of the Isaurians was seized with the desire to observe the construction of the aqueduct and to discover in what manner it provided the supply of water to the city. So he entered it at a place far distant from the city, where Belisarius had broken it open, and proceeded to walk along it, finding no difficulty, since the water had stopped running because the aqueduct had been broken open. But when he reached a point near the circuit-wall, he came upon a large rock, not placed there by the hand of man, but a part of the natural formation of the place. And those who had built the aqueduct many years before, after they had attached the masonry to this rock, proceeded to make a tunnel from that point on, not sufficiently large, however, for a man to pass through, but large enough to furnish a passage for the water.

And for this reason it came about that the channel of the aqueduct was not everywhere of the same breadth, but one was confronted by a narrow place at that rock, impassable for a man, especially if he wore armor or carried a shield. And when the Isaurian observed this, it seemed to him not impossible for the army to penetrate into the city, if they should make the tunnel at that point broader by a little. But since he himself was a humble person, and never had come into conversation with any of the commanders, he brought the matter before Paucaris, an Isaurian, who had distinguished himself among the guards of Belisarius. So Paucaris immediately reported the whole matter to the general.

And Belisarius, being pleased by the report, took new courage, and by promising to reward the man with great sums of money induced him to attempt the undertaking, and commanded him to associate with himself some of the Isaurians and cut out a passage in the rock as quickly as possible, taking care to allow no one to become aware of what they were doing. Paucaris then selected some Isaurians who were thoroughly suitable for the work and secretly got inside the aqueduct with them. And coming to the place where the rock caused the passage to be narrow, they began their work, not cutting the rock with picks or mattocks, lest by their blows they should reveal to the enemy what they were doing, but scraping it very persistently with sharp instruments of iron. And in a short time the work was done, so that a man wearing a corselet and carrying a shield was able to go through at that point.

But when all his arrangements were at length in complete readiness, the thought occurred to Belisarius that if he should by act of war make his entry into Naples with the army, the result would be that lives would be lost and that all the other things would happen that usually attend the capture of a city by an enemy. And straightway summoning Stephanus, he spoke as follows:

"Many times have I witnessed the capture of cities, and I am well acquainted with what takes place at such a time. For they slay all the men of every age, and as for the women, though they beg to die, they are not granted the boon of death, but are carried off for outrage and are made to suffer treatment that is abominable and most pitiable. And the children, who are thus deprived of their proper maintenance and education, are forced to be slaves, and that, too, of the men who are the most odious of all those on whose hands they see the blood of their fathers. And this is not all, my dear Stephanus, for I make no mention of the conflagration that destroys all the property and blots out the beauty of the city. When I see, as in the mirror of the cities that have been captured in times past, this city of Naples falling victim to such a fate, I am moved to pity both it and you its inhabitants. For such means have now been perfected by me against the city that its capture is inevitable. But I pray that an ancient city, which has for ages been inhabited by both Christians and Romans, may not meet with such a fortune, especially at my hands as commander of Roman troops, not least because in my army are a multitude of barbarians, who have lost brothers or relatives before the wall of this town; for the fury of these men I should be unable to control, if they should capture the city by act of war. While, therefore, it is still within your power to choose and to put into effect what will be to your advantage, adopt the better course and escape misfortune; for when it falls upon you, as it probably will, you will not justly blame fortune but your own judgment."

With these words Belisarius dismissed Stephanus. And he went before the people of Naples weeping and reporting with bitter lamentations all that he had heard Belisarius say. But they, since it was not fated that the Neapolitans should become subjects of the emperor without chastisement, neither became afraid nor did they decide to yield to Belisarius.

10. Then at length Belisarius, on his part, made his preparations to enter the city as follows. Selecting at nightfall about four hundred men and appointing as commander over them

Magnus, who led a detachment of cavalry, and Ennes, the leader of the Isaurians, he commanded them all to put on their corselets, take in hand their shields and swords and remain quiet until he himself should give the signal. And he summoned Bessas and gave him orders to stay with him, for he wished to consult with him concerning a certain matter pertaining to the army. And when it was well on in the night, he explained to Magnus and Ennes the task before them, pointed out the place where he had previously broken open the aqueduct and ordered them to lead the four hundred men into the city, taking lights with them And he sent with them two men skilled in the use of the trumpet, so that as soon as they should get inside the circuit-wall, they might be able both to throw the city into confusion and to notify their own men what they were doing. And he himself was holding in readiness a very great number of ladders that had been constructed previously.

So these men entered the aqueduct and were proceeding toward the city, while he with Bessas and Photius remained at his post and with their help was attending to all details. And he also sent to the camp, commanding the men to remain awake and to keep their arms in their hands. At the same time he kept near him a large force — men whom he considered most courageous. Now of the men who were on their way to the city above half became terrified at the danger and turned back. And since Magnus could not persuade them to follow him, although he urged them again and again, he returned with them to the general. And Belisarius, after reviling these men, selected two hundred of the troops at hand and ordered them to go with Magnus. And Photius also, wishing to lead them, leaped into the channel of the aqueduct, but Belisarius prevented him. Then those who were fleeing from the danger, put to shame by the railings of the general and of Photius, took heart to face it once more and followed with the others. And Belisarius, fearing lest their operations should be perceived by some of the enemy, who were maintaining a guard on the tower that happened to be nearest to the aqueduct, went to that place and commanded Bessas to carry on a conversation in the Gothic tongue with the barbarians there, his purpose being to prevent any clanging of the weapons from being audible to them.

And so Bessas shouted to them in a loud voice, urging the Goths to yield to Belisarius and promising that they should have many rewards. But they jeered at him, indulging in many insults directed at both Belisarius and the emperor. Belisarius and Bessas, then, were thus occupied.

Now the aqueduct of Naples is not only covered until it reaches the wall, but remains covered as it extends to a great distance inside the city, being carried on a high arch of baked brick. Consequently, when the men under the command of Magnus and Ennes had got inside the fortifications, they were one and all unable even to conjecture where in the world they were. Furthermore, they could not leave the aqueduct at any point until the foremost of them came to a place where the aqueduct chanced to be without a roof and where stood a building that had entirely fallen into neglect. Inside this building a certain woman had her dwelling, living alone with utter poverty as her only companion; and an olive tree had grown out over the aqueduct.

So when these men saw the sky and perceived that they were in the midst of the city, they began to plan how they might get out, but they had no means of leaving the aqueduct either with or without their arms. For the structure happened to be very high at that point and, besides, offered no means of climbing to the top. But as the soldiers were in a state of great perplexity and were beginning to crowd each other greatly as they collected there (for already, as the men in the rear kept coming up, a great throng was beginning to gather), the thought occurred to one of them to make trial of the ascent. He immediately therefore laid down his arms, and forcing his way up with hands and feet, reached the woman's house. And seeing her there, he threatened to kill her unless she should remain silent. And she was terror-stricken and remained speechless. He then fastened to the trunk of the olive tree a strong strap, and threw the other end of it into the aqueduct.

So the soldiers, laying hold of it one at a time, managed with difficulty to make the ascent. And after all had come up and a fourth part of the night still remained, they proceeded toward the wall; and they slew the garrison of two of the towers before the men in them had an inkling of the trouble. These towers were on the northern portion of the circuit-wall, where Belisarius was stationed with Bessas and Photius, anxiously awaiting the progress of events. So while the trumpeters were summoning the army to the wall, Belisarius was placing the ladders against the fortifications and commanding the soldiers to mount them. But it so happened that not one of the ladders reached as far as the parapet. For since the workmen had not made them in sight of the wall, they had not been able to arrive at the proper measure. For this reason they bound two together, and it was only by using both of them for the ascent that the soldiers got above the level of the parapet. Such was the progress of these events where Belisarius was engaged.

But on the side of the circuit-wall that faces the sea, where the forces on guard were not barbarians, but Jews, the soldiers were unable either to use the ladders or to scale the wall. For the Jews had already given offence to their enemy by having opposed their efforts to capture the city without a fight, and for this reason they had no hope if they should fall into their hands; so they kept fighting stubbornly, although they could see that the city had already been captured, and held out beyond all expectation against the assaults of their opponents. But when day came and some of those who had mounted the wall marched against them, then at last they also, now that they were being shot at from behind, took to flight, and Naples was captured by storm.

By this time the gates were thrown open and the whole Roman army came in. But those who were stationed about the gates that fronted the east, since, as it happened, they had no ladders at hand, set fire to these gates, which were altogether unguarded; for that part of the wall had been deserted, the guards having taken to flight. And then a great slaughter took place; for all of them were possessed with fury, especially those who had chanced to have a brother or other relative slain in the fighting at the wall. And they kept killing all whom they encountered, sparing neither old nor young, and dashing into the houses they made slaves of the women and children and secured the valuables as plunder; and in this the Massagetae outdid all the rest, for they did not even withhold their hand from the sanctuaries, but slew many of those who had taken refuge in them, until Belisarius, visiting every part of the city, put a stop to this, and calling all together, spoke as follows:

"Inasmuch as God has given us the victory and has permitted us to attain the greatest height of glory, by putting under our hand a city that has never been captured before, it behooves us on our part to show ourselves not unworthy of His grace, but by our humane treatment of the vanquished, to make it plain that we have conquered these men justly. Do not, therefore, hate the Neapolitans with a boundless hatred, and do not allow your hostility toward them to continue beyond the limits of the war. For when men have been vanquished, their victors never hate them any longer. And by killing them you will not be ridding yourselves of enemies for the future, but you will be suffering a loss through the death of your subjects. Therefore, do these men no further harm, nor continue to give way wholly to anger. For it is a disgrace to prevail over the enemy and then to show yourselves vanquished by passion. So let all the possessions of these men suffice for you as the rewards of your valor, but let their wives, together with the children, be given back to the men. And let the conquered learn by experience what kind of friends they have forfeited by reason of foolish counsel."

After speaking thus, Belisarius released to the Neapolitans their women and children and the slaves, one and all, no insult having been experienced by them, and he reconciled the soldiers to the citizens. And thus it came to pass for the Neapolitans that on that day they both became captives and regained their liberty, and that they recovered the most precious of their possessions. For those of them who happened to have gold or anything else of value had previously concealed it by burying it in the earth, and in this way they succeeded in hiding from the enemy the fact that in getting back their houses they were recovering their money also. And the siege, which had lasted about twenty days, ended thus. As for the Goths who were captured in the city — not less than eight hundred in number — Belisarius put them under guard and kept them from all harm, holding them in no less honor than his own soldiers.

And Pastor, who had been leading the people upon a course of folly, as has been previously set forth by me, upon seeing the city captured, fell into a fit of apoplexy and died suddenly, though he had neither been ill before nor suffered any harm from anyone. But Asclepiodotus, who was engaged in this intrigue with him, came before Belisarius with those of the notables who survived. And Stephanus mocked and reviled him with these words:

"See, O basest of all men, what evils you have brought to your fatherland by selling the safety of the citizens for loyalty to the Goths. And furthermore, if things had gone well for the barbarians, you would have claimed the right to be yourself a hireling in their service and to bring to court on the charge of trying to betray the city to the Romans each one of us who have given the better counsel. But now that the emperor has captured the city, and we have been saved by the uprightness of this man, and you even so have had the hardihood recklessly to come into the presence of the general as if you had done no harm to the Neapolitans or to the emperor's army, you will meet with the punishment you deserve."

Such were the words that Stephanus, who was deeply grieved by the misfortune of the city, hurled against Asclepiodotus. And Asclepiodotus replied to him as follows:

"Quite unwittingly, noble sir, you have been heaping praise upon us, when you reproach us for our loyalty to the Goths. For no one could ever be loyal to his masters when they are in danger, except it be by firm conviction. As for me, then, the victors will have in me as true a guardian of the state as they lately found in me an enemy, since he whom nature has endowed with the quality of fidelity does not change his conviction when he changes his fortune. But you, should their fortunes not continue to prosper as before, would readily listen to the overtures of their assailants. For he who has the disease of inconstancy of mind no sooner takes fright than he denies his pledge to those most dear."

Such were the words of Asclepiodotus. But the populace of the Neapolitans, when they saw him returning from Belisarius, gathered in a body and began to charge him with responsibility for all that had befallen them. And they did not leave him until they had killed him and torn his body into small pieces. After that they came to the house of Pastor, seeking for the man. And when the servants insisted that Pastor was dead, they were quite unwilling to believe them until they were shown the man's body. And the Neapolitans impaled him in the outskirts of the town. Then they begged Belisarius to pardon them for what they had done while moved with just anger, and receiving his forgiveness, they dispersed. Such was the fate of the Neapolitans.

8. THE SACK OF NAPLES, 537

The *Liber Pontificalis* offers a slightly more gruesome, if more succinct, version of the same events. The motivation of the writer may well have been to highlight the cruelty of the Byzantines during a period when the papacy sought to assert its independence from the old empire. Procopius, on the other hand, was an official in Belisarius' army and had a clear-cut interest in stressing the perfidy of the Neapolitans themselves and the Greek's comparative leniency. Our selection is taken from David, *The Book of Pontiffs*, 52–53.

60. [Pope] Silverius (536–37) ... 1. But two months later the tyrant Theodahad was snuffed out by God's will, and Vitiges was raised up as king. 2. He immediately traveled to Ravenna and forcibly took Queen Amalasuntha's daughter as his wife. The lord emperor Justinian Augustus was infuriated <when he heard> that Theodahad had killed a queen who had entrusted herself to him and sent the patrician Belisarius with an army to free all of Italy from occupation by the Goths. When the patrician arrived he spent some time in the district of Sicily.

3. But hearing that the Goths had made themselves a king against Justinian's wish, he came to the district of Campania close to Naples and with his army embarked on a siege of that city, since its citizens refused to open up to him. Then the patrician gained entry to the city by fighting. Driven by fury he killed both the Goths and all the Neapolitan citizens and embarked on a sack from which he did not even spare the churches, such a sack that he killed husbands by the sword in their wives' presence and eliminated the captured sons and wives of nobles. No one was spared, not *sacerdotes* [priests], not God's servants, not virgin nuns.

9. NAPLES REPOPULATED BY REFUGEES OF THE GOTHIC WARS, 537/38

Whatever the discrepancy in the sources for the siege and sack of Naples, the city must have been depopulated enough to accommodate a large number of refugees. Here Procopius relates two episodes: Belisarius' decision to transfer the noncombatant population from Rome during its siege by the Goths in 537 and his forced relocation of defeated Goths from the mid-Tiber valley. The Roman refugees travelled both by land down the via Appia and by sea from Portus to Naples and beyond, the Goths overland probably by way of Benevento and by sea certainly to Sicily and perhaps also to Naples.

We should note here the great diversity of Naples' population from the earliest Middle Ages: Greeks from its original population and then from the vast array of peoples in the Byzantine Empire, Romans and neighboring Samnites from Campania, merchants, traders and missionaries from the Middle East, including its first Christians (according to tradition, St. Paul landed in Italy first at Pozzuoli, St. Peter at Naples), Jews, Goths and — as revealed in the mosaic portraits of the catacomb of S. Gennaro[15] — North Africans. This is only natural, given Naples' position as one of the major ports of the Mediterranean and as the major Byzantine launching point for campaigns in southern Italy and the Roman Campania.

Then, as even today, the city shared the same cosmopolitan culture and connections as other major centers of the inland sea: Barcelona, Marseilles, Palermo, Tunis, Venice, Alexandria, Constantinople and the ports of the Levant. Our selection is taken from Procopius, *History of the Wars*, 239–41, 397–99.

V.25. When the Goths had been repulsed in the fight at the wall [of Rome], each army bivouacked that night in the manner already described. But on the following day Belisarius

---

15. See Bruzelius & Tronzo, 12–24; and Italica Press web gallery: http://www.flickr.com/photos/80499896@N05/sets/72157630152526498.

commanded all the Romans to remove their women and children to Naples, and also such of their domestics as they thought would not be needed by them for the guarding of the wall, his purpose being, naturally, to forestall a scarcity of provisions. And he issued orders to the soldiers to do the same thing, in case anyone had a male or female attendant. For, he went on to say, he was no longer able while besieged to provide them with food to the customary amount, but they would have to accept one half their daily ration in actual supplies, taking the remainder in silver. So they proceeded to carry out his instructions. And immediately a great throng set out for Campania. Now some, who had the good fortune to secure such boats as were lying at anchor in the harbor of Rome [at Portus, near Ostia], secured passage, but the rest went on foot by the road that is called the Appian Way. And no danger or fear, as far as the besiegers were concerned, arose to disturb either those who travelled this way on foot or those who set out from the harbor. For, on the one hand, the enemy were unable to surround the whole of Rome with their camps on account of the great size of the city, and on the other, they did not dare to be found far from the camps in small companies, fearing the sallies of their opponents. And on this account abundant opportunity was afforded for some time to the besieged both to move out of the city and to bring provisions into it from outside.... Consequently, the great majority were able to withdraw from Rome, and some went to Campania, some to Sicily and others wherever they thought it was easier or better to go.

VI.13. And Belisarius at about the time of the summer solstice marched against Vitiges and the Gothic army, leaving a few men to act as a garrison in Rome, but taking all the others with him. And he sent some men to Tudera [Todi] and Clusium [Chiusi] with orders to make fortified camps there, and he was intending to follow them and assist in besieging the barbarians at those places. But when the barbarians learned that the army was approaching, they did not wait to face the danger, but sent envoys to Belisarius, promising to surrender both themselves and the two cities, with the condition that they should remain free from harm. And when he came there, they fulfilled their promise. And Belisarius removed all the Goths from these towns and sent them to Sicily and Naples, and after establishing a garrison in Clusium and in Tudera, he led his army forward.

10. MOUNT VESUVIUS, 537

Fig. 7. Bacchus standing before Vesuvius, from the House of the Centenary's Lararium, Pompeii, Naples, Museo Archeologico.

While Procopius reports only a rumble of the volcano, his description offers what appears to be a first-hand account of the ascent of the mountain and of the crater and its activity. Procopius also relates one of the chief attractions of Naples and its region: the great fertility and abundance caused by the repeated deposits of volcanic ash from the mountain. His description fits into a millennia-old tradition of travel writing on Naples and its vicinity. Our selection is taken from Procopius, *History of the Wars*, 325–27.

VI.4. At that time, the mountain of Vesuvius rumbled, and though it did not break forth in eruption, still because of the rumbling it led people to expect with great certainty that there would be an eruption. And for this reason it came to pass that the inhabitants fell into great terror. Now this mountain is seventy stades distant from Naples and lies to the north [actually southeast] of it — an exceedingly steep mountain, whose lower parts spread out wide on all sides, while its upper portion is precipitous and exceedingly difficult of ascent. But on the summit of Vesuvius and at about the center of it appears a cavern of such depth that one would judge that it extends all the way to the bottom of the mountain. And it is possible to see fire there, if one should dare to peer over the edge, and although the flames as a rule merely twist and turn upon one another, occasioning no trouble to the inhabitants of that region, yet, when the mountain gives forth a rumbling sound that resembles bellowing, it generally sends up not long afterward a great quantity of ashes. And if anyone travelling on the road is caught by this terrible shower, he cannot possibly survive, and if it falls upon houses, they too fall under the weight of the great quantity of ashes. But whenever it so happens that a strong wind comes on, the ashes rise to a great height, so that they are no longer visible to the eye and are borne wherever the wind that drives them goes, falling on lands exceedingly far away. And once, they say, they fell in Byzantium [in 472 CE] and so terrified the people there that from that time up to the present the whole city has seen fit to propitiate God with prayers every year; and at another time they fell on Tripolis in Libya.

Formerly this rumbling took place, they say, once in a hundred years or even more, but in later times it has happened much more frequently. This, however, they declare emphatically, that whenever Vesuvius belches forth these ashes, the country round about is bound to flourish with an abundance of all crops. Furthermore, the air on this mountain is very light and by its nature the most favorable to health in the world. And indeed those who are attacked by consumption have been sent to this place by physicians from remote times. So much, then, may be said regarding Vesuvius.

■

CHAPTER 2: DUCAL NAPLES

INTRODUCTION

Surviving records for the ducal period[1] include the inventories and *vitae* in the *Liber Pontificalis* and the administrative details found in the letters of Pope Gregory I. Narrative sources include Paul the Deacon's *History of the Lombards*. New digital resources, such as the ALIM Project,[2] are now also making available online large runs of previously edited Neapolitan archives from this period.

11. GREGORY THE GREAT, LETTERS, 590–604

Fig. 8. Gregory the Great in his study. Book cover, c.980. Kunsthistorisches Museum, Vienna.

Gregory[3] was one of the most important figures in the history of the West. He was a monastic leader and writer, reformer and creator of liturgies, pope, missionary strategist and brilliant administrator, politician and diplomat who steered the Roman church skillfully toward independence from both the Byzantine Empire and the Lombard dominion of Italy and reached out to the new peoples of Europe. He was born into a highly placed, possibly patrician,

---

1. For a survey of this period, see Introduction, pp. xxv–xxxiv.

2. At http://www.uan.it/alim.

3. For background see Carole Ellen Straw, *Gregory the Great* (Berkeley: University of California Press, 1988); R.A. Markus, *Gregory the Great and His World* (Cambridge: Cambridge University Press, 1997); and John Moorhead, *Gregory the Great* (London: Routledge, 2005).

family in Rome in 540 and was a child of 7 when Totila destroyed Rome and massacred most of its population in 547. His family returned from their Sicilian estates in 549 and settled at their villa on the Caelian Hill amid the ruins of Rome's ancient monuments. Among Gregory's family were a former pope (Felix III) and numerous clerics and monks, both male and female. On his father's death Gregory converted the family villa into a monastery, now S. Gregorio Magno in Celio. Pope Pelagius II ordained Gregory a deacon of Rome and in 579 appointed him ambassador of Rome to the imperial court in Constantinople. Gregory remained in the Greek capital, pleading unsuccessfully for military aid against the Lombards, until 585, when he returned to Rome. On Pelagius's death in 590 during an outbreak of the plague, Gregory was elected pope by acclamation of the Romans.

As pope, Gregory turned his considerable diplomatic skills both to missionary work in the North, especially to England, and to relations with the new kingdoms of the Franks and Lombards. At the same time, he reformed and strengthened Roman liturgy, administrative practice and claims, both religious and secular, devoting considerable energies to securing food supplies and political security for Rome and extending the reach of the Roman bishopric through Italy and in the new kingdoms of the West.

Gregory played a key role in the creation of the independent duchy of Naples.[4] The relative frequency of Gregory's relations with the Neapolitans points both to Rome's strong role in the city's affairs and to Naples' own importance to the political and material fate of Rome itself during the early duchy.

Gregory was a prolific writer, and many of his works survived and had a profound influence on the thought and practice of the Middle Ages and subsequent western Christianity. His works include his *Sermons* (forty on the Gospels are recognized as authentic, twenty-two on Ezekiel, two on the

---

4.   See Jean-Marie Martin, "Grégoire le Grand et l'Italie," in *Histoire et culture dans l'Italie byzantine: Acquis et nouvelles recherches,* A. Jacob, J.-M. Martin and G. Noyé, eds., Collection de l'École Française de Rome 363 (Rome: l'École Française de Rome, 2006), 239–78 at 273–75.

Song of Songs); his *Dialogues*, a collection of miracles, signs, wonders and healings including the popular *Life of Saint Benedict*; his *Commentary on Job (Magna Moralia)*; and his *Rule for Pastors.* Copies of 854 letters have survived, out of an unknown number recorded in Gregory's time. This register is known to have existed in Rome, its last known location, in the ninth century. It consisted of fourteen papyrus rolls, now missing. Copies of letters had begun to be made, the largest batch of 686 by order of Pope Adrian I (772–95). The majority of the copies, dating from the tenth to the fifteenth century, are now in the Vatican Library.

The letters have been edited in the original Latin, translated into English and are now available online in both forms. We have excerpted from a good number of Gregory's letters to highlight many aspects of the religious, political, social and material life of Naples and its close relationship to Rome. These selections are taken from the *Nicene and Post-Nicene Fathers.*[5]

Book II, letter 46. To John, bishop of Ravenna, c.592

Gregory refers to immediate political circumstances: an alliance of Lombard princes aimed against the still-independent city-state of Naples. Arechis I, the second Lombard duke of Benevento (591–641), had allied with Ariulf, second Lombard duke of Spoleto (592–602), and was about to lay siege (unsuccessfully it turned out) to Naples. The city retained its place under the Byzantine exarchy but is here already recognized as a "republic." Note Gregory's testimony to the evolving role of the "duke" from Byzantine military *dux* to a political leader. Here also is clear evidence of the continued existence of ancient slavery and the changing nature of the rural population

---

5. *Nicene and Post-Nicene Fathers,* 2nd ser. 12-13. Philip Schaff and Henry Wace, eds., James Barmby trans. (Buffalo, NY: Christian Literature Publishing, 1895), with selections on the website of Greek Orthodox Christian Church of Greater Omaha Nebraska at http://www.synaxis.org/cf/volume35; and http://www.synaxis.org/cf/volume36. Accessed 10/30/12. The letters have recently been edited and translated in John R.C. Martyn. *The Letters of Gregory the Great* (Toronto: Pontifical Institute of Mediaeval Studies, 2004).

in Italy as freemen fall into slavery both as a result of war and, most likely, the economic and agrarian collapse produced as a by-product of decades of invasion, upward economic consolidation and devastation.

Gregory to John, bishop of Ravenna

...With regard to the city of Naples, in view of the urgent insistence of the most excellent exarch, we give you to understand that Arigis [Arechis I], as we have ascertained, has associated himself with Ariulf, and is breaking his faith to the republic, and plotting much against this same city; to which unless a duke be speedily sent, it may already be reckoned among the lost.

As to what you say to the effect that alms should be sent to the city of the schismatic Severus, which has been burnt, your fraternity is of this opinion as being ignorant of the bribes that he sends to the court in opposition to us. And, even though these were not sent, we should have to consider that compassion is to be shown first to the faithful, and afterwards to the enemies of the Church. For indeed there is near at hand the city Fanum [Fano], in which many have been taken captive, and to which I have already in the past year desired to send alms, but did not venture to do so through the midst of the enemy. It therefore seems to me that you should send Abbot Claudius thither with a certain amount of money, in order to redeem the freemen whom he may find there detained in slavery for ransom, or any who are still in captivity. But, as to the sum of money to be thus sent, be assured that whatever you determine will please me. If, moreover, you are treating with the most excellent Romanus Patricius for allowing us to make peace with Ariulph, I am prepared to send another person to you, with whom questions of ransom may be better arranged....

BOOK III, LETTER 1. TO PETER, SUBDEACON OF CAMPANIA, C.592

The letter's reference to Scholasticus, the "judge of Campania" and then its addressee, Peter, subdeacon of Campania, appears to provide evidence of the city as the center of a parallel administrative organization: one a secular inheritance of the Romano-Byzantine system, which at least held legal claim over the region, and one ecclesiastical, directed from Rome.

Here also is evidence for the transition of the Villa Lucullana into the *castrum Lucullanum* (now Castel dell'Ovo) and to the monastery of S. Severino, apparently one of several then within the bounds of the *castrum*.[6] The letter offers clear-cut evidence of the existence — and acceptance— of slavery and of women owning property. Gregory's letter refers to some unknown crime committed in the *castrum*, presumably by the servants of Clementina, against an unnamed cleric. The perpetrators had taken refuge in the monastery of S. Severinus inside the *castrum Lucullanum* and had apparently attempted to stir up some form of revolt.

Gregory to Peter, subdeacon of Campania.

What a crime has been committed in the Lucullan fort against our brother and fellow-bishop Paul, the account of which has been sent to us has made manifest. And, inasmuch as the magnificent Scholasticus, judge of Campania, happens at the present time to be with us here, we have especially enjoined on him the duty of visiting the madness of so great perversity with strict correction. But, since the bearer of the aforesaid account has requested us to send someone to represent ourselves, we therefore send the subdeacon Epiphanius, who, together with the aforesaid judge, may be able to investigate and ascertain by whom the sedition was raised or instigated, and to visit it with suitable punishment. Let your experience then make haste to give aid in this case with all your power, to the end both that the truth may be ascertained, and that vengeance may proceed against the guilty parties. Wherefore, since the slaves of the glorious Clementina are said to have had to do with this same crime and to have used language calculated to stir up the sedition, do you subject them strictly to immediate punishment, nor let your severity be relaxed in consideration of her person, since they ought to be smitten all the more as they have transgressed out of mere pride as being the servants of a noble lady. But you ought also to make thorough enquiry whether the said lady was privy to so atrocious a crime, and whether it was perpetrated with her knowledge, that from our visitation of it all may learn how dangerous it is not only to lay hands on a priest,

---

6. See discussion above, pp. xxxviii–xxxix.

but even to transgress in words against one. For, if anything should be done remissly or omitted in this case, know that you especially will have to bear the blame and the risk; nor will you find any plea for excuse with us. For in proportion as this business will commend you to us if it be most strictly investigated and corrected, know that our indignation will become sharp against you, if it be smoothed over.

Moreover, for the rest, if any slaves from the city should have taken refuge in the monastery of S. Severino, or in any other church of this same fort, as soon as this has come to your knowledge, by no means allow them to remain there, but let them be brought to the church within the city; and, if they should have just cause of complaint against their masters, they must needs leave the church with suitable arrangements made for them. But, if they have committed any venial fault, let them be restored without delay to their masters, the latter having taken oath to pardon them.

BOOK III, LETTER 35. TO PETER, SUBDEACON OF CAMPANIA, c.592

The letter offers evidence of Rome's dominant role in Naples' ecclesiastical affairs and of the existence already of a clear-cut class of Neapolitan "nobles," who shared in the election of the city's bishops. At the same time, Gregory's letter offers evidence of a transition from popular election of bishops to their papal appointment.

Gregory to Peter, subdeacon of Campania.

Our brother and fellow-bishop Paul has often requested us to allow him to return to his own church. And, having perceived this to be reasonable, we have thought it needful to accede to his petition. Consequently let your experience convene the clergy of the Neapolitan church, to the end that they may choose two or three of their number, and not omit to send them hither for the election of a bishop. But let them also intimate, in their communication to us, that those whom they send represent them all in this election, so that their church may have its own bishop validly ordained. For we cannot allow it to be any longer without a ruler of its own. Should they perchance try in any way to set aside your admonition, bring to bear on them the vigor of ecclesiastical discipline. For he will be giving proof of his own perverseness, whosoever does not of his own accord assent to this proceeding. Moreover, cause to be given to the aforesaid Paul, our brother and fellow-bishop, one hundred *solidi*,[7] and one little orphan boy, to be selected by himself, for his labor in behalf of the same church. Further, admonish those who are to come hither as representing all for the election of a bishop, to remember that they must bring with them all the episcopal vestments and also as much money as they may foresee to be necessary for him who may be elected bishop to have for his own use. But lose no time in dispatching those of the clergy who are selected as we have said, that, seeing that there are present here divers nobles of the city of Naples, we may treat with them concerning the election of a bishop, and take counsel together with the help of the Lord.

BOOK VI, LETTER 32. TO FORTUNATUS, BISHOP OF NAPLES, 593–600

This letter offers important evidence of Naples' Jewish population, of the persistence of ancient slavery into the Christian era, of the continued mix of Jewish, pagan and Christian slaves in the city, and of clear-cut legal divisions and separate status between the Jewish and Christian communities there.

Gregory to Fortunatus [II], bishop of Neapolis.

We have written before now to your fraternity that, if any [slaves] by the inspiration of God, desire to come from Jewish superstition to the Christian faith, their masters have no liberty to sell them, but that from the time of their declaring their wish they have a full claim to freedom. But since, so far as we have learnt, they [i.e., Jewish masters], weighing with nice discrimination neither our wish nor the ordinances of the law, think that they are not bound by this condition in the case of pagan slaves, your fraternity ought to attend to such cases, and, if any one of their slaves, whether he be a Jew or a

---

7.   See below, Reading 41, pp, 141–43 and nn. 22 and 23.

pagan, should wish to become a Christian, after his wish has been openly declared, let not any one of the Jews, under cover of any device or argument whatever, have power to sell him; but let him who desires to be converted to the Christian faith be in all ways supported by you in his claim to freedom. Lest, however, those who have to lose slaves of this kind should consider that their interests are unreasonably prejudiced, it is fitting that with careful consideration you should observe this rule: that if pagans when they have been brought out of foreign parts for the sake of traffic should chance to flee to the Church, and say that they wish to become Christians, or even outside the Church should announce this wish, then, till the end of three months during which a buyer to sell them to may be sought for, they [the Jewish owners] may receive their price; that is to say, from a Christian buyer. But if after the aforesaid three months any one of such slaves should declare his wish and desire to become a Christian, let not either any one afterwards dare to buy him, or his master, under color of any occasion whatever, dare to sell him; but let him unreservedly attain to the benefit of freedom; since he [i.e., the master] is in such case understood to have acquired him not for sale but for his own service. Let, then, your fraternity so vigilantly observe all these things that neither the supplication of any nor respect of persons may avail to inveigh you.

BOOK IX, LETTER 36. TO FORTUNATUS, BISHOP OF NAPLES

Gregory is well known for his supposed pun on seeing Anglo-Saxon slave boys brought to him in Rome as "not Angles but Angels!" and his decision then and there to send a mission to convert the English. England was apparently not the only source for fair-haired slaves in Italy. Here we have evidence for slaves captured in an already Christian Gaul. Again Gregory, and early medieval society, accepted slavery. Here the pope seeks only to adjudicate the market and by inference the larger issue of relations between the Jewish and Christian populations of Naples. Note that the Jewish slave trader Basilius bears not a Hebrew but a Greek name, indicative of the Neapolitans' continued ties of the

Byzantine East. Just as important, such evidence of Gallic slaves — and older Gothic inhabitants — tends to discredit the racialist myth for the origins of Naples' non-Mediterranean types in the Norman barons of the eleventh century.

Gregory to Fortunatus, &c.

Having learnt what zeal inflames your fraternity on behalf of Christian slaves whom Jews buy from the territories of Gaul, we apprize you that your solicitude has so pleased us that it is also our own deliberate judgment that they should be inhibited from traffic of this kind. But we find from Basilius, the Hebrew, who has come here with other Jews, that such purchase is enjoined on them by divers judges of the republic and that Christians along with pagans come to be thus procured. Hence it has been necessary for the business to be adjusted with such cautious arrangement that neither they who give such orders should be thwarted, nor those who say they obey them against their will should bear any expense unjustly. Accordingly, let your fraternity with watchful care provide for this being observed and kept to: that, when they [i.e., the Jewish dealers] return from the aforesaid province, Christian slaves who may happen to be brought by them be either handed over to those who gave the order, or at all events sold to Christian purchasers within forty days. And after the completion of this number of days let none of them in any way whatever remain in the hands of the Jews. But, should any of these slaves perchance fall into such sickness that they cannot be sold within the appointed days, care is to be taken that, when they are restored to their former health, they be by all means disposed of as aforesaid. For it is not fit that any should incur loss for a transaction that is free from blame. But since, as often as anything new is ordained, it is usual so to lay down the rule for the future as not to condemn the past in large costs, if any slaves have remained in their hands from the purchase of the previous year, or have been recently taken away from them by you, let them have liberty to dispose of them while they are with you. So may there be no possibility of their incurring loss for what they did in ignorance before the prohibition, such as it is right they should sustain after being forbidden.

Further, it has been reported to us that the above-named Basilius wishes to concede to his sons, who by the mercy of God are Christians, certain slaves, under the title of a gift, with the view that, under cover of the opportunity thus afforded, they may serve him as their master all but in name; and that, if after this any should perchance have believed that they might fly to the Church for refuge in order to become Christians, they may not be reclaimed to freedom, but to the dominion of those to whom they had before been given. In this matter it befits your fraternity to keep suitable watch. And, if he should wish to give any slaves to his sons, that all occasion of fraud may be removed, let them by all means become Christians, and let them not remain in his house; but, when circumstances may require that he should have their services, let them be commanded to render him what, even in any case, from his sons, and for God's sake, it is fitting should be supplied to him.

BOOK X, LETTER 24. TO FORTUNATUS, BISHOP OF NAPLES

This letter provides evidence that monastic life was already well established in Naples. Gregory's warning against accepting former soldiers into religious life was a standard element of church policy and developing canon law during the period and was a clear legacy of the early Church's discomfort with military service. At the same time, it is also probably evidence of the clear necessity of guaranteeing a source of military service in a violent world that could not be escaped by fleeing to a monastery.

Gregory to Fortunatus, &c.

When your fraternity pays too little attention to the monasteries that are under you, you both lay yourself open to reproof and make us sorry for your laxity. Now it has come to our ears that one Mauricius, who lately became a monk in the monastery of Barbacianus, has fled from the same monastery, taking other monks with him. In this case the hastiness of the aforesaid Barbacianus inculpates him exceedingly in our sight, in that he rashly tonsured a secular person without even previous probation. Did we not write to you that you should prove him first, and then, if he were fit, should make him abbot? Even now, then, look well after him whom you chose. For you are delinquent in his delinquency, if he has begun so to demean himself as to show himself unfit to have the government of brethren.

Further, let your fraternity more strictly interdict all monasteries from venturing by any means to tonsure those whom they may have received for monastic profession before they have completed two years in monastic life. But in this space of time let their life and manners be carefully proved, lest any one of them should either not be content with what he had desired or not keep firm to what he had chosen. For, it being a serious matter that untried men should be associated under obedience to any master, how much more serious is it that any who have not been proved should be attached to the service of God?

Further, if a soldier should wish to become a monk, let no one for any cause whatever presume to receive him without our consent or before it has been reported to us. If this rule is not diligently observed, know that all the guilt of those that are under you redounds on yourself, seeing that you prove yourself by the very facts of the case to be too little anxious about them.

BOOK X, LETTER 62. TO THE NEAPOLITANS

This letter, concerning the election of the city's bishop, probably dates from after 600, the year of Bishop Fortunatus' death. Gregory's letter demonstrates that Naples was already a "republic," appointing its own officers and higher clergy. Neapolitan politics probably reflect what was happening throughout the surviving Roman *civitates* of the old empire: parties were forming around the election of rival candidates for the bishop's seat, which — as Gregory clearly states — had become the highest political office in the city. John the Deacon, the opposition's choice in the election, was apparently disqualified, probably for fathering a child. The ultimate victor was Paschasius, bishop from 600 to 615, to whom Gregory addresses letter XIII.12.

Gregory to the clergy and noble citizens of Naples.

It is not a new thing, nor is it reprehensible, that in the election of a bishop the votes of the people should be divided between two parties, but it is a serious matter when in cases of this kind the election goes not by judgment, but by favor only. For before your letter reached us we had learnt from the report of certain persons that the deacon John, who has been elected by the other party, has a little daughter. Hence, if they had had a mind to attend to reason, neither would others have elected him nor would he have consented. For what presumption must his be who dares to approach the episcopate while convicted by the evidence of the little girl, of not having had long control over his own body! Moreover, Peter the Deacon, who you say has been elected by you, is, according to what is said, quite without astuteness. And you know, at the present time the person to be constituted in the highest place of government should be one who knows how to be careful, not only for the salvation of souls, but also with regard to the external advantage and safeguard of his subjects. But know further that it has come to our ears concerning him, that he has given money on usury; which you ought to enquire into thoroughly, and, if it is so, elect another, and without delay hold yourselves aloof from a person of this kind. For we will on no account lay hands on lovers of usury. If, however, after accurate enquiry made, this should prove to be false (since his person is unknown to us, and we know not whether what has been reported to us of his simplicity be true), he must needs come to us with your decree in his favor that, having made careful enquiry into his life and manners, we may at the same time become acquainted with his intelligence; and thus, in case of his satisfying this enquiry, we may in him, with the Lord's help, fulfill your desires. Further, let it be your care to look out also for another person who may be suitable, so that, if this one should by any chance appear unfit for appointment to this order, there may be someone else to whom you may transfer your choice. For it will be a serious disgrace to your clergy, in case of this man by any chance not being approved, if they should say that they have no one else fit to be elected.

BOOK XIII, LETTER 12. TO PASCHASIUS,
BISHOP OF NAPLES, 600–615

Paschasius was the victor in the election of 600, into which Gregory had intervened against deacons John and Peter.

This letter provides further evidence of a strong Jewish community with open religious practice, protected by the papacy, and of the tension between the Christian and Jewish communities implicit in several of the letters above. Gregory deplores the anti-Semitic actions of certain Neapolitans and urges the ending of policies seeking to curtail Jewish religious practice, if only to make the process of conversion to Christianity all the easier.

Gregory to Paschasius, &c.

Those who with pure intent desire to bring to the true faith aliens from the Christian religion should study kindness and not asperity; lest such as reason rendered with smoothness might have appealed to, should be driven far off by opposition. For whosoever act otherwise, and under cover of such intention would suspend people from their accustomed observance of their own rites, are proved to be intent on their own cause rather than on God's. To wit, the Jews dwelling in Naples have complained to us, asserting that certain persons are endeavoring unreasonably to drive them from certain solemnities of their holidays, so that it may not be lawful for them to observe the solemnities of their festivals, as up to this time since long ago it has been lawful for them and their forefathers to keep and observe them. Now, if this is true, these people appear to be taking trouble to no purpose. For what is the use, when even such long unaccustomed prohibition is of no avail for their faith and conversion? Or why should we lay down rules for the Jews as to how they should observe their ceremonies, if we cannot thereby win them? We should therefore so act that, being rather appealed to by reason and kindness they may wish to follow us, and not to fly from us; and that proving to them from their own scriptures what we tell them, we may be able, with God's help, to convert them to the bosom of Mother Church.

Therefore let your fraternity, so far as may be possible, with the help of God, kindle them to conversion and not allow them any more to be disquieted with respect to their solemnities; but let them have free license to observe and celebrate all their festivals and holidays, even as hitherto both they and their forefathers for a long time back have kept and held them.

12. THE REVOLT OF JOHN OF COMPSA, 618/19

There is some evidence that amidst the chaos of the invasions, a local aristocracy was already maneuvering to assert it independence from the Byzantine Empire in the early seventh century.

This selection briefly touches on the little known episode of John of Compsa and is taken from Davis, *Book of Pontiffs*, 61.

70. 1. [Pope] Deusdedit (615–18) born in Rome, son of the subdeacon Stephen, held the see three years twenty-three days. He greatly loved the clergy; he restored the *sacerdotes* and clergy to their original places.

2. At that time the patrician and chamberlain Eleutherius came to Ravenna and killed all who had been implicated in the death of Exarch John and the judges of the state. He came to Rome and was excellently received by the holy pope Deusdedit. Leaving Rome he came to Naples, which was held by the rebel John of Compsa. Eleutherius fought his way against him into Naples and killed that upstart <and many others with him>. He returned to Ravenna, gave the soldiers their stipend, and <great> peace was achieved throughout Italy.

3. He established the second *missa* among the clergy. Then in August of the sixth indiction [618] there was a major earthquake. Afterwards ensued a disaster among the people, affliction with the scab, so no one could recognize his own deceased.[8]

4. On his death he was buried in St. Peter's; for his funeral he left an entire stipend to all the clergy. He performed three ordinations, fourteen priests, five deacons; for various places twenty-nine bishops. The bishopric was vacant one month, sixteen days. <Buried on the 8th day of November.>

---

8. Davis does not identify this disease, perhaps the plague, which certainly raged intermittently during the period and affected Naples. References to the plague are certainly found in Gregory's correspondence. See Lester K. Little, ed., *Plague and the End of Antiquity: The Pandemic of 541–750* (New York: Cambridge University Press, 2007), 14.

13. PAUL THE DEACON ON JOHN OF COMPSA, 619

Paul the Deacon offers another version of the same events in the *History of the Lombards*. See Foulke trans., 176–77.

Fig. 9. Paul the Deacon (Eutropius?). Eutropius, Historia Romana. Florence, Biblioteca Medicea-Laurenziana, MS Plut. 65.35, fol. 16v.

Book 4, chapter XXXIV.

At this time John of Consia [Compsa, Conza] took possession of Naples, but not many days afterwards Eleutherius, the patrician, drove him from that city and killed him. After these things that same patrician Eleutherius, a eunuch, assumed the rights of sovereignty. While he was proceeding from Ravenna to Rome he was killed in the fortress of Luceoli [Luciuolo, between Perugia and Urbino] by the soldiers and his head was brought to the emperor at Constantinople.

14. NAPLES AS A BYZANTINE MILITARY BASE, 663

Naples remained an outpost of Byzantine rule in Italy throughout the Gothic and Lombard wars, and it was often the jumping-off place for campaigns aimed at defending or regaining Rome. Here Paul the Deacon offers evidence of the city's usefulness as a Byzantine base for Emperor Constans II (641–68). Our source also reveals that Naples appears to be well situated as a naval base for communication with southern Italy, Sicily, Sardinia and North Africa.

Our selection is taken from Paul the Deacon, *History of the Lombards*, Foulke trans., 220, 223–25.

Book 5, chapter VII.

Meanwhile the army of the emperor was assaulting Beneventum vigorously with various machines of war and on the other hand Romuald [duke of Benevento, 662–77] with his Langobards was resisting bravely, and although he did not dare to engage hand to hand with so great a multitude on account of the smallness of his army, yet frequently dashing into the camp of the enemy with young men sent out for that purpose, he inflicted upon them great slaughter upon every side. And while Grimuald [king of the Lombards, 662–71] his father was now hastening on, he sent to his son to announce his approach, that same tutor of his of whom we have spoken. And when the latter had come near Beneventum he was captured by the Greeks and brought to the emperor, who asked of him whence he had come, and he said he had come from King Grimuald and he announced the speedy approach of that king. Straightway the emperor, greatly alarmed, took counsel with his followers in what way he could make a treaty with Romuald so as to return to Naples.

Fig. 10. *The Byzantine army, from the Battle of Gibeon. The Joshua Rolls. 10th c. Vatican City, BAV, MS Pal. Gr. 431.*

Book 5, chapter XI

Emperor Constans, when he found that he could accomplish nothing against the Langobards, directed all the threats of his cruelty against his own followers, that is, the Romans. He left Naples and proceeded to Rome. At the sixth milestone from the city, Pope Vitalian [657–72] came to meet him with his priests and the Roman people. And when the emperor had come to the threshold of St. Peter, he offered there a pallium woven with gold and, remaining at Rome twelve days, he pulled down everything that in ancient times had been made of metal for the ornament of the city, to such an extent that he even stripped off the roof of the church of the blessed Mary, which at one time was called the Pantheon, and had been founded in honor of all the gods and was now by the consent of the former rulers the place of all the martyrs; and he took away from there the bronze tiles and sent them with all the other ornaments to Constantinople.

Then the emperor returned to Naples and proceeded by the land route to the city of Rhegium (Reggio); and having entered Sicily during the seventh indiction [after September 663], he dwelt in Syracuse and put such afflictions upon the people — the inhabitants and land owners of Calabria, Sicily, Africa and Sardinia — as were never heard of before, so that even wives were separated from their husbands and children from their parents [sold into slavery to satisfy tax debts]. The people of these regions also endured many other and unheard of things so that the hope of life did not remain to any one. For even the sacred vessels and the treasures of the holy churches of God were carried away by the imperial command and by the avarice of the Greeks.

And the emperor remained in Sicily from the seventh to the twelfth [11th] indiction, but at last he suffered the punishment of such great iniquities and while he was in the bath he was put to death by his own servants [July 15, 668].

15. NAPLES RETAKES THE FORTRESS OF CUMAE, 716

From the mid-seventh century the "duke" and people of Naples seem to have exerted considerable independence from their nominal overlords in Constantinople, and the duchy of Naples was taking firm shape as it resisted the incursions of the Lombards from neighboring Benevento. But complete independence became a reality no sooner than the fall of Ravenna — the capital of the Byzantine exarchate — to the Lombard Aistulf in 751. The duchy of Naples was rather circumscribed, hugging the coast northward from the Sorrentine peninsula, going inland as far as Capua (soon lost) and Nola, north to include the area of the Campi Flegrei, Pozzuoli and Cumae (and Gaeta for a time) and, in the Bay itself, Capri and Ischia.

In such a small area, virtual independence of any of these centers was a practical impossibility. By 840, Sergius I had moved from being count of Cumae to duke of Naples. Most modern visitors know Cumae only from its classical association, as the site of the famous ancient Sibyl and from its mysterious cave-like shrine. But all around the site atop its seaside promontory lie the remains of a substantial late ancient and early medieval city-state, rivaling neighboring Puteoli (Pozzuoli) for regional supremacy and finally surpassing it. Cumae's importance to Naples was paramount.[9] With the fall of Capua to the Lombards and the closing of the via Appia,

Fig. 11. The ruins of medieval and ancient Cumae. Photo: Campania Tourist Board.

the only land route connecting Naples and Rome was the via Domitiana, which was dominated by the fortress of Cumae. When the Lombard Romuald II took the fortress in 715, with no help coming from Constantinople, then under siege by the Arabs, the Neapolitans were forced to rely on their own devices. As duke of Naples, Giovanni I was the only local military and political commander on whom the pope could appeal.

Our selection is taken from Davis, *The Lives of the Eighth-Century Popes*, 7.

---

9.   See Jean-Pierre Brun and Priscilla Munzi, "La città di Cuma tra Tardoantichità e Altomedioevo: Le ricerche del Centre Jean Bérard," in Amedeo Feniello, ed. *Napoli nel Medioevo 2: Territorio e isole* (Galatina: Congedo, 2009) 1-34.

7. At that time too the Lombards, though pretending peace, seized the *castrum* of Cumae; at this news all were utterly dismayed at the loss of the *castrum*. The holy pontiff urged and advised the Lombards to return it — he declared in his writings that if they would not do so their treachery would incur God's wrath; he was even willing to give them many gifts to get them to restore it. But in their haughtiness they would endure neither to hear his advice nor to return it. This made the holy pontiff smart greatly; he entrusted himself to his hope in God and supplied leadership by devoting himself to advising the duke and people of Naples, writing to them every day how they were to act. Obeying his instruction they adopted a plan and entered the walls of that *castrum* by force in the quiet of the night — that is to say, the duke Giovanni [I], with Theodimus the subdeacon and rector [of Naples, for the papacy], and the army. They killed about 300 Lombards including their gastald [local Lombard official], and they captured more than 500 and took them to Naples. In this way they managed to get the *castrum* back; even so the holy pope paid [to Giovanni] the 70 lb of gold he had promised for its ransom.

16. DUKE STEPHEN (II) SEEKS A HOME, 763

While the grand narratives relate high politics and destruction, not all our sources for early medieval Naples speak of war. Archival materials have long been of great value to historians both because they provide so many priceless details of everyday life — economy, housing, property, marriage, births, deaths and inheritances — and because they speak with a less clearly defined narrative voice and are thus considered impartial, more "true" evidence. Both types of sources — as well as visual and archaeological evidence — are essential to any complete history. The transition from Byzantine outpost to autonomous duchy was apparently not continuous or smooth, even in the minds of the Neapolitans.

A parallel administrative structure seems to have been overlapping between imperial and Lombard dukes in the minds of the Neapolitans. Here, in an instrument recording a real-estate transaction, Stephen is referred to as "consul" not "duke." We can also see that, as in medieval Rome, large tracts of land within the walls had been converted into *hortus* or small agricultural holdings, in this case in the southeast of the city close to the site of the late ancient and early medieval mint, "ad monetam," probably in the area between Portanova and S. Agostino alla Zecca. In addition, the text indicates that Naples' housing type — the *domus* with interior courtyard or *curtis* — had probably not yet changed much from the basic forms used in antiquity.[10]

The following text is excerpted from Matteo Camera, *Annali delle Due Sicilie dall'origine e fondazione della monarchia fino a tutto il regno dell'augusto sovrano Carlo III Borbone*, 2 vols. (Naples: Fibreno 1841–60), 1:xlvi. Translation by R.G. Musto.

March 1, indiction 1, year 763, Naples. Lord Stephen, most eminent consul, requests a house, with a courtyard and garden, located in this city of Naples in the region of the Nola Gate [Porta Nolana] called "ad monetam" [at the mint]. It is located next to the garden of Lord Gregory [I, last Byzantine duke, 740–55], the most eminent consul, imperial expatarius and duke.

17. PAUL THE DEACON AND HAGIOGRAPHY, c.750

Paul the Deacon (c.720–13 April, probably 799) translated Sophronius' *Metrical Life of St. Mary of Egypt*. His translation is most likely the source of the abbreviated version of her life found in both the *Legenda Aurea* of Jacobus of Voraigne and Vincent of Beauvais' *Speculum Historiale* (15:65–73). As a saint's life, this work typifies the medieval interest in stories of morals and marvels from exotic places. It also reinforces the cultural ties between Naples and the eastern Mediterranean.

On the other hand, although we classify such tales as "hagiography," in an era before the celibate reforms of the eleventh century, and in a region rich in the visual remains of pagan antiquity and its celebration of the flesh, how piously did Neapolitan clerics and literate laity read these stories? Here on the Bay of Naples hagiography looks back to such narratives as the *Satyricon* and forward to Boccaccio and then

---

10.   See Arthur, *Naples*, 46–56.

to the erotic "autobiography" of Cleland's *Fanny Hill* and its successors.

Mary tells the story of her free-wheeling early life and conversion to Abba Zosimas, who encounters her wandering in the desert east of the Jordan River and appears to maintain his control in the face of her obsessive narrative. St. Mary of Egypt was later honored in Naples with a church, Sta. Maria Egiziaca, an ascetic religious foundation of Augustinian nuns, founded in the Forcella area by Queen Sancia in 1342.

Our text is taken from PL 73:671–90. The following English translation is found at http://www.fordham.edu/halsall/basis/maryegypt.html. Accessed 11/30/2012.

The elder [Zosimas] wept and the woman began her story. "My native land, holy father, was Egypt. Already during the lifetime of my parents, when I was twelve years old, I renounced their love and went to Alexandria. I am ashamed to recall how there I at first ruined my maidenhood and then unrestrainedly and insatiably gave myself up to sensuality. It is more becoming to speak of this briefly, so that you may just know my passion and my lechery. For about seventeen years — forgive me — I lived like that. I was like a fire of public debauch. And it was not for the sake of gain — here I speak the pure truth. Often when they wished to pay me, I refused the money. I acted in this way so as to make as many men as possible to try to obtain me, doing free of charge what gave me pleasure. Do not think that I was rich and that was the reason why I did not take money. I lived by begging, often by spinning flax, but I had an insatiable desire and an irrepressible passion for lying in filth. This was life to me. Every kind of abuse of nature I regarded as life.

"That is how I lived. Then one summer I saw a large crowd of Lybians and Egyptians running towards the sea. I asked one of them, 'Where are these men hurrying to?' He replied, 'They are all going to Jerusalem for the exaltation of the precious and life-giving Cross, which takes place in a few days.' I said to him, 'Will they take me with them if I wish to go?' 'No one will hinder you if you have money to pay for the journey and for food.' And I said to him, 'To tell you truth, I have no money, neither have I food. But I shall go with them and shall go aboard. And they shall feed me, whether they want to or not. I have a body — they shall take it instead of pay for the journey.' I was suddenly filled with a desire to go, Abba, to have more lovers who could satisfy my passion. I told you, Abba Zosimas, not to force me to tell you of my disgrace. God is my witness, I am afraid of defiling you and the very air with my words."

Zosimas, weeping, replied to her: "Speak on for God's sake, mother, speak and do not break the thread of such an edifying tale."

And, resuming her story, she went on: "That youth, on hearing my shameless words, laughed and went off. While I, throwing away my spinning wheel, ran off towards the sea in the direction that everyone seemed to take. And, seeing some young men standing on the shore, about ten or more of them, full of vigor and alert in their movements, I decided that they would do for my purpose (it seemed that some of them were waiting for more travelers whilst others had gone ashore). Shamelessly, as usual, I mixed with the crowd, saying, 'Take me with you to the place you are going to; you will not find me superfluous.' I also added a few more words calling forth general laughter. Seeing my readiness to be shameless, they readily took me aboard the boat. Those who were expected came also, and we set sail at once.

"How shall I relate to you what happened after this? Whose tongue can tell, whose ears can take in all that took place on the boat during that voyage! And to all this I frequently forced those miserable youths even against their own will. There is no mentionable or unmentionable depravity of which I was not their teacher. I am amazed, Abba, how the sea stood our licentiousness, how the earth did not open its jaws, and how it was that hell did not swallow me alive, when I had entangled in my net so many souls. But I think God was seeking my repentance. For He does not desire the death of a sinner but magnanimously awaits his return to Him. At last we arrived in Jerusalem. I spent the days before the festival in the town, living the same kind of life, perhaps even worse. I was not content with the youths I had seduced at sea and who had helped me to get to Jerusalem; many others — citizens of the town and foreigners — I also seduced.

"The holy day of the Exaltation of the Cross dawned while I was still flying about — hunting for youths. At daybreak I saw that everyone was hurrying to the church, so I ran with the rest. When the hour for the holy elevation approached, I was trying to make my way in with the crowd, which was struggling to get through the church doors. I did at last squeeze through with great difficulty almost to the entrance of the temple, from which the life-giving Tree of the Cross was being shown to the people. But when I trod on the doorstep, which everyone passed, I was stopped by some force that prevented my entering. Meanwhile I was brushed aside by the crowd and found myself standing alone in the porch. Thinking that this had happened because of my woman's weakness, I again began to work my way into the crowd, trying to elbow myself forward. But in vain I struggled. Again my feet trod on the doorstep over which others were entering the church without encountering any obstacle. I alone seemed to remain unaccepted by the church. It was as if there was a detachment of soldiers standing there to oppose my entrance. Once again I was excluded by the same mighty force and again I stood in the porch.

"Having repeated my attempt three or four times, at last I felt exhausted, and had no more strength to push and to be pushed, so I went aside and stood in a corner of the porch. And only then with great difficulty it began to dawn on me, and I began to understand the reason why I was prevented from being admitted to see the life-giving Cross. The word of salvation gently touched the eyes of my heart and revealed to me that it was my unclean life that barred the entrance to me. I began to weep and lament and beat my breast and to sigh from the depths of my heart. And so I stood weeping when I saw above me the icon of the most holy Mother of God. And turning to her my bodily and spiritual eyes I said: 'O Lady, Mother of God, who gave birth in the flesh to God the Word, I know, O how well I know, that it is no honor or praise to thee when one so impure and depraved as I look up to thy icon, O ever-virgin, who didst keep thy body and soul in purity. rightly do I inspire hatred and disgust before thy virginal purity. But I have heard that God who was born of thee became man on purpose to call sinners to repentance. Then help me, for I have no other help. Order the entrance of the church to be opened to me. Allow me to see the venerable Tree on which He who was born of thee suffered in the flesh and on which He shed His holy blood for the redemption of sinners and for me, unworthy as I am. Be my faithful witness before thy son that I will never again defile my body by the impurity of fornication, but as soon as I have seen the Tree of the Cross I will renounce the world and its temptations and will go wherever you wilt lead me.'

"Thus I spoke and as if acquiring some hope in firm faith and feeling some confidence in the mercy of the Mother of God, I left the place where I stood praying. And I went again and mingled with the crowd that was pushing its way into the temple. And no one seemed to thwart me, no one hindered my entering the church. I was possessed with trembling, and was almost in delirium. Having got as far as the doors that I could not reach before — as if the same force, which had hindered me, cleared the way for me — I now entered without difficulty and found myself within the holy place. And so it was I saw the life-giving Cross. I saw too the mysteries of God and how the Lord accepts repentance. Throwing myself on the ground, I worshipped that holy earth and kissed it with trembling. Then I came out of the church and went to her who had promised to be my security, to the place where I had sealed my vow. And bending my knees before the Virgin Mother of God, I addressed to her such words as these: 'O loving Lady, you hast shown me thy great love for all men. Glory to God who receives the repentance of sinners through thee. What more can I recollect or say, I who am so sinful? It is time for me, O lady to fulfill my vow, according to thy witness. Now lead me by the hand along the path of repentance!' And at these words I heard a voice from on high: 'If you cross the Jordan you will find glorious rest.'

"Hearing this voice and having faith that it was for me, I cried to the Mother of God: 'O lady, lady, do not forsake me!'

"With these words I left the porch of the church and set off on my journey. As I was leaving the church a stranger glanced at me and gave me three coins, saying: 'Sister, take these.' And, taking the money, I bought three loaves and took them with me on my journey, as a blessed gift. I asked the person who sold the bread: 'Which is the way to the Jordan?' I was directed to the city gate that led that way. Running on I passed the gates and still weeping went on my journey. From those I met I asked the way, and after walking for the rest of that day (I think it was nine o'clock when I saw the Cross), I at length reached at sunset the church of St. John the Baptist, which stood on the banks of the Jordan. After praying in the temple, I went down to the Jordan and rinsed my face and hands in its holy waters. I partook of the holy and life-giving mysteries in the church of the Forerunner and ate half of one of my loaves. Then, after drinking some water from Jordan, I lay down and passed the night on the ground. In the morning I found a small boat and crossed to the opposite bank. I again prayed to Our Lady to lead me whither she wished. Then I found myself in this desert and since then up to this very day I am estranged from all, keeping away from people and running away from everyone. And I live here clinging to my God who saves all who turn to Him from faintheartedness and storms."

Zosimas asked her: "How many years have gone by since you began to live in this desert?"

She replied: "Forty-seven years have already gone by, I think, since I left the holy city."

Zosimas asked: "But what food do you find?"

The woman said: "I had two and a half loaves when I crossed the Jordan. Soon they dried up and became hard as rock. Eating a little I gradually finished them after a few years."

Zosimas asked: "Can it be that without getting ill you have lived so many years thus, without suffering in any way from such a complete change?"

The woman answered: "You remind me, Zosimas, of what I dare not speak. For when I recall all the dangers which I overcame, and all the violent thoughts which confused me, I am again afraid that they will take possession of me."

Zosimas said: "Do not hide from me anything; speak to me without concealing anything."

And she said to him: "Believe me, Abba, seventeen years I passed in this desert fighting wild beasts — mad desires and passions. When I was about to partake of food, I used to begin to regret the meat and fish, of which I had so much in Egypt. I regretted also not having wine, which I loved so much. For I drank a lot of wine when I lived in the world, while here I had not even water. I used to burn and succumb with thirst. The mad desire for profligate songs also entered me and confused me greatly, edging me on to sing satanic songs that I had learned once. But when such desires entered me, I struck myself on the breast and reminded myself of the vow that I had made, when going into the desert. In my thoughts I returned to the ikon of the Mother of God, which had received me and to her I cried in prayer. I implored her to chase away the thoughts to which my miserable soul was succumbing. And after weeping for long and beating my breast I used to see light at last, which seemed to shine on me from everywhere. And after the violent storm, lasting calm descended.

"And how can I tell you about the thoughts that urged me on to fornication, how can I express them to you, Abba? A fire was kindled in my miserable heart, which seemed to burn me up completely and to awake in me a thirst for embraces. As soon as this craving came to me, I flung myself on the earth and watered it with my tears, as if I saw before me my witness, who had appeared to me in my disobedience and who seemed to threaten punishment for the crime. And I did not rise from the ground (sometimes I lay thus prostrate for a day and a night) until a calm and sweet light descended and enlightened me and chased away the thoughts that possessed me. But always I turned the eyes of my mind to my protectress, asking her to extend help to one who was sinking fast in the waves of the desert. And I always had her as my helper and the accepter of my repentance. And thus I lived for seventeen years amid constant dangers. And since then even till now the Mother of God helps me in everything and leads me as it were by the hand."

Zosimas asked: "Can it be that you did not need food and clothing?"

She answered: "After finishing the loaves I had, of which I spoke, for seventeen years I have fed on herbs and all that can be found in the desert. The clothes I had when I crossed the Jordan became torn and worn out. I suffered greatly from the cold and greatly from the extreme heat. At times the sun burned me up and at other times I shivered from the frost, and frequently falling to the ground I lay without breath and without motion. I struggled with many afflictions and with terrible temptations. But from that time till now the power of God in numerous ways has guarded my sinful soul and my humble body. When I only reflect on the evils from which Our Lord has delivered me I have imperishable food for hope of salvation. I am fed and clothed by the all-powerful word of God, the Lord of all. For it is not by bread alone that man lives. And those who have stripped off the rags of sin have no refuge, hiding themselves in the clefts of the rocks [Job 24; Heb. 11:38]."

Hearing that she cited words of scripture from Moses and Job, Zosimas asked her: "And so you have read the psalms and other books?"

She smiled at this and said to the elder: "Believe be, I have not seen a human face ever since I crossed the Jordan, except yours today. I have not seen a beast or a living being ever since I came into the desert. I never learned from books. I have never even heard anyone who sang and read from them. But the word of God, which is alive and active, by itself teaches a man knowledge. And so this is the end of my tale. But, as I asked you in the beginning, so even now I implore you for the sake of the incarnate Word of God, to pray to the Lord for me who am such a sinner."

Thus concluding her tale she bowed down before him.

Fig. 12. Solidus of Sicard. Wikimedia. The Marc Poncin Collection.

18. THE *PACTUM SICARDI*, JULY 4, 836

One of the best-known documents in the history of early medieval Naples is the *Pactum Sicardi*, or peace treaty between Duke Sicard of Benevento (832–39) and Duke Andrea II of Naples (834–40), Sorrento, Amalfi and Capua. The treaty recognizes important elements of the situation on the ground in the mid-ninth century, after the withdrawal of effective Carolingian and Byzantine power from the South.

The duchy of Naples by that date had expanded to include the coastal arc of territory between Capua and the Volturno River on the north, along the circle of the Bay of Naples, including Sorrento and the Sorrentine peninsula, and extending south to include the territory of Amalfi itself. This meant that Naples, while officially still a Byzantine outpost, had created an independent bulwark against Lombard encroachment from Capua all the way to Salerno. It controlled much of the most fertile lands of Campania and several of its most important seaports. The *Pactum* also indicates that Lombard Benevento laid claim to almost all of southern Italy, as far south as Lucania, without any reference to Byzantine or far-off Carolingian imperial prerogatives.

The pact, however, also reveals a good deal about the effective power balance in the region. Sicard and Lombard Benevento appear officially to have the upper hand in dictating, for example, terms of trade, including the prohibition of slave trading by the Neapolitans (of Christian Lombards to Arab slavers). However, the overall mutuality of the pact indicates that Naples was willing to acknowledge some larger supremacy in Benevento, but that it clearly expressed both its independence from any external authority and its effective equality in power relationships.

In the previous year, 835, Andrea of Naples had hired mercenaries to help fend off Lombard pressures on the duchy. These mercenaries were unusual, however, since they were Arabs from Aghlabid North Africa then in the process of conquering Byzantine Sicily. It was to be the beginning of the Arab presence in Campania that would last, intermittently, for nearly a century. As Lopez and Raymond noted, the abolition of the *lex naufragii*, the law of shipwreck (in clause 13), "was a step far in advance of the times," far ahead of northern Europe; but other clauses, such as 15, reflect the suspicion of merchants and other travelers crossing boundaries found "in Frankish and Anglo-Saxon laws, which also express suspicion of the merchant unless he is well known."[11]

Though the term of the treaty was stated clearly as five years, within two years the parties had broken most of its clauses.[12] It seems that few promises or allegiances lasted long in the southern Italy of the time. Then again, the same uncertainties haunted Anglo-Saxon England or Carolingian Francia in the face of the Vikings.

This text has been excerpted from Lopez and Raymond, *Medieval Trade*, 33-35, translated by them from the edition in Guido Padelletti, *Fontes iuris italici medii aevi* (Turin: E. Loescher, 1877), 318–24, et passim.

July 4, 836. In the name of the Lord God and of our Savior, Jesus Christ, and of the blessed and glorious Mary, Mother of God and ever Virgin. As long as the parties obey the commandments of God, then His orders are fulfilled and are shown to have led to concord of peace for the salvation of Christian souls. Wherefore we, the lord, the most glorious man, Sicardo, prince of the Lombard people, promise to you, Giovanni [IV, "the Scribe," bishop c.842–49], elect of the holy Neapolitan church, and to Andrea, *magister militum* [II, duke 834–40], and to your subject people of the Neapolitan duchy, Sorrento, Amalfi and the other fortified places or localities that are under your rule, that we shall give you our true peace and grace by land and sea from this fourth day of July, fourteenth indiction, that is, for five full years....

3. It is agreed that you shall not by any means buy Lombard [subjects] nor shall you sell them overseas. And if this is done, the person himself who bought, together with the one who bought [from him], shall be delivered to us, so that both — the one who bought and the one who sold — shall at the same time be delivered to us. And if not, and if there is a delay, [the guilty party] shall pay 100 *solidi* and the above-said persons shall be delivered; and if the sale has been made overseas, the one who committed this evil deed shall pay 200 *solidi*....

---

11.   Lopez and Raymond, 35 n. 82.

12.   See Kreutz, *Before the Normans*, 20–23.

5. In regard to the merchants of both parties, then, it is agreed that they are to be allowed to conduct their business within the borders of our Beneventan principality, and no matter by what way they may have entered the territory they are not to be injured or arrested or made to put up pledges, but shall return to their own country uninjured and without any loss. But if for any reason they are made to put up a pledge, that pledge is to be returned to them in its entirety; and whoever presumes to act contrary shall pay 24 *solidi* to the one he injured....

13. Also, it is agreed in regard to the rivers that are on the Capuan borders, that is, the Patria, the Volturno and the Minturno, that permission to cross their fords[13] be given to merchants as well as to *responsales* [legates or ambassadors] or *milites* or to other persons of your Neapolitan duchy; our customs being preserved, they are to cross uninjured. The boats, indeed, which have remained there [moored] by cable or have taken refuge from a storm, or have landed anywhere on that entire coast, or have come anywhere within the borders of our principality, are to be secure and uninjured, as is stated above. If however, they also want to do business there, they shall pay according to the old customs. This much [will be granted], that if a ship is wrecked because of the fault [of the men aboard] the goods found in it are to be returned to the one to whom they belonged and still belong; the men, however, are to return to their own country sound and uninjured. And it is agreed that from this time forward your ships are not to be detained for any reason in the territory of Lucania or anywhere else within our borders....

15. Also, it is agreed that no one from the territories outside a city is to have permission to buy a horse or an ox except within the city or in the market in the presence of the judges, and the seller himself should be known to them; and if the seller is not known to the judges, he is by no means to have permission to buy. If, however, he bought outside the city, or in the market or in the city and also in the presence of the judges, as is stated above, but the seller not being known, the buyer himself is to be regarded as a thief....

---

13.   One therefore presumes that any Roman bridges across these rivers had long been broken and not yet restored.

19. THE BATTLE OF OSTIA, 849 *Naples defends Rome against Arabs*

This incident is evidence less of the defeat of the Saracens than of Naples' active military engagement in the region and its relationship to Rome during the decline of Carolingian power in the mid-ninth century. We have already noted above Naples' close alliance with Arab forces when the need arose; and Rome itself had been devastated in a Saracen sack in 846 that saw many of its citizens massacred and its treasures in relics and precious church goods stolen. The event shocked all of Western Christendom and prompted the Carolingians to send military and reconstruction aid to the city. The famed Leonine Walls around the Vatican are a result of this rebuilding under Pope Leo IV.

The engagement here is a naval one, only several years later, and the text indicates that the Neapolitan fleet under Caesar, the son of Duke Sergius I, was a match for the Saracens. This "Battle of Ostia" was later to be commemorated in Raphael's frescos in the Vatican Stanze. There already existed a loosely shifting alliance among Naples, Amalfi and Gaeta, but only later — after 902 and Arab conquest was imminent — was this to become a major factor in the ongoing campaign against the Muslims in Campania. Note that the pope was by no means certain that the arriving Neapolitans had peaceable intentions toward Rome.

Our selection is taken from the life of Leo IV (pope 847–55) in *The Lives of the Ninth-Century Popes (Liber Pontificalis)*, Raymond Davis, trans. and ed. (Liverpool: Liverpool University Press, 1995), 132–34.

48. But so that those faithful to the Lord might rightly be yet more faithful and not doubt that his signs and wonders from of old freshly spring forth, there must now be an abridgment from the beginning of what God's mercy venerably achieved for them at that time, and in what great wretchedness and disasters that plague-bearing race [Muslims] were justly crushed and dissolved. So, remembering their former profit and the plunder they had had, they cruelly decided to come again to storm the city of Rome during the 12th indiction with a teeming band of

perverse men and with many ships. For many days they lingered at a place called Totarum close to the island of Sardinia. Leaving thence, they essayed to depart to the port of Rome, with no help from God.

49. Their hostile and wicked arrival frightened the Romans in no small way. But because almighty God has always kept his church inviolate and afterwards does not stop doing so, he then stirred up the hearts of all the men of Naples, Amalfi and Gaeta amongst others, that they too, along with the Romans, had to rise up and contend mightily against them: then they left their own localities, came with their ships ahead of the unwanted Saracens, suddenly informed the blessed pontiff Leo IV of their arrival and professed that they had come for no other reason than to win a victory with the Lord's help over the pagans.

50. Then the venerable pontiff bade some of them come on ahead to him in Rome, as he particularly wanted to know from them whether their arrival was peaceful or not; and so it happened. Among them then was one who had been appointed over the army, Caesarius by name, the son of Sergius I [duke of Naples] master of the soldiers. Giving them a kind reception at the Lateran Palace, he inquired the motive for their arrival. They swore they had come for no other purpose than that which can be read set down above. The godly *apostolicus* believed their account, then made his way to the city of Ostia with a great retinue of armed men and welcomed all the Neapolitans with grand and notable devotion.

51. When they saw the supreme pontiff, they prostrated themselves on the ground at his feet, kissed them reverently and gave thanks to the Almighty throned on high, who had decided to send such a bishop to strengthen them. That they might better be the victors over the sons of Belial, they begged him earnestly that they might deserve to receive the Lord's body from his sacred hands. With his own lips he chanted mass for them in St. Aurea's Church [in Ostia], and from his hands, as has been said, they all took communion. Before this happened, with Christ's help he made his way to that church with the Neapolitans, accompanied by hymns, litanies and distinguished chants. In it he knelt and besought the Highest that by his prayers he might see fit to hand over the enemies of Christians into the hands of the defenders.

His prayer was: "O God, whose right hand raised up St. Peter the apostle lest he sink when walking on the water [Mt. 14:29], and delivered from the depths of the sea his fellow-apostle Paul when three times shipwrecked [Acts 27–28], graciously hear us and grant that, by the merits of them both, the limbs of these thy faithful, contending against the enemies of thy holy church, may be fortified by thy almighty right hand and gain strength; that by their gaining triumph thy holy name may be seen glorious among all races; through [our Lord Jesus Christ]."

52. Next day, after the venerable prelate had returned from that city, those allies of and consorters with evil men appeared with many ships close to the seashore of Ostia. The Neapolitans launched an attack on them, meaning to contend mightily, and even wounded some of them — and they would have been triumphant, had it not been for one hindrance that speedily occurred. This was, that while they were contending earnestly with each other a very mighty and overpowering wind was suddenly stirred up, such as no one in these times can remember, and it immediately scattered both fleets, but that of the Saracens more so. So they came to the seashore; then, with the wind blowing and the sea billowing in the storms, they were scattered, and after a time they retreated with their strength broken. Almighty God, as we truly believe, had "brought forth this wind from his storehouse" [Ps. 135:7], and it would not let them sally forth to cause harm.

20. THE LIFE OF BISHOP ATHANASIUS I BY JOHN THE DEACON, 872

Athanasius I was the bishop of Naples from 850 to his death in 872. He was the second son of Sergius I of Naples and became bishop at the same time his brother, Gregory, became co-duke. Athanasius was an intimate of both the court of the Western emperor and that of the pope. He was a member of the royal household of emperors Lothair I and Louis II and was appointed a papal legate.

His *Vita* was commissioned by his nephew Athanasius II, bishop (876–98) and duke (878–98), and composed by John the Deacon of Naples, who lived from the end of the ninth to the beginning of the tenth century and who brought up to date the *vitae* of Naples' bishops, the equivalent of Rome's *Liber Pontificalis*. John also translated into Latin the Greek *Vita* of St. Nicholas, the patron saint of Myra in Asia Minor until "holy thieves" brought his relics west to Bari.

⟨The following sections from the *Vita* record Athanasius' building programs, his institutional foundations and his promotion of the arts and letters.⟩They also offer valuable information on the development of Naples' ecclesiastical architecture during the ducal period and provide tantalizing details for several sites, including the cathedral complex — the basilica of Sta. Restituta, the Stefania or episcopal church and the episcopal palace[14] — and the Baptistery of S. Giovanni in Fonte.[15] The narrative extends out to the areas beyond the walls: to the Campus Neapolis, the monastery of S. Salvatore on the island of Megaris, Sta. Lucia in Pizzofalcone, and to the basilica of S. Gennaro extra Moenia.[16]

The reign of Athanasius seems to have been a prosperous one for Naples, judging from the generous endowments he provided to a variety of churches and monasteries and by the rich liturgical gifts he made to several churches.

The following is excerpted from the Latin text of the *Vita S. Athanasii in the Chronicon episcoporum S. Neapolitanae ecclesiae*,[17] Bartolomeo Capasso, ed., *Monumenta ad Neapolitani ducatus historiam pertinentia* 1 (Naples: Francesco Giannini, 1881; repr., Salerno: Carlone, 2008), 213–20, and translated by R.G. Musto.

…As soon as he had taken the episcopal throne, therefore, he began to bestow generously the abundant milk of learning that he had suckled as a youth. He arranged for schools of lectors and

14. See Bruzelius & Tronzo, 24–32; and Italica Press web gallery: http://www.flickr.com/photos/80499896@N05/sets/72157630149817080.

15. See Bruzelius & Tronzo, 32–41; and Italica Press web gallery: http://www.flickr.com/photos/80499896@N05/sets/72157630149953976.

16. See Bruzelius & Tronzo, 16–23.

17. A modern critical edition is available in Antonio Vuolo, ed., *"Vita" et "Translatio" S. Athanasii Neapolitani episcopi: BHL 735 e 737, Sec. IX* (Rome: Istituto Storico Italiano per il Medio Evo, 2001).

cantors, he arranged for not a few to learn the grammatical arts, and he brought together others for the office of scribe. In this way the wise shepherd strengthened the fold for his flock....

Fig. 13. Mosaic, Sant'Apollinare, Ravenna. Wikimedia, The Yorck Project.

In addition to this he restored the chapel of San Gennaro at the cathedral and had the effigies of noble doctors painted in it. He also had built there a marble altar, set off with silver doors. He covered this with a screen on which he had embroidered the martyrdom of S. Gennaro and his companions. Of the same embroidered work he had thirteen tapestry screens set up in the church of the Stefania, on them depicting gospel histories, and he ordered that these be hung as ornaments between the capitals of the columns there.[18] For the altar of the same church he donated four screens of the same embroidered work, decorated with much gold and many gems.

He took care to have manufactured many tapestry screens, which he preferred to offer as church ornaments. For the same church [of the Stefania] he had quite a few vessels made of silver. And he spent forty-eight pounds [*libras*] of silver for the fabrication of large and small crowns and other sacred vessels. Also of silver he had made a large paten, with the faces of the Savior and of angels engraved on it in gold incision. He also provided the church with two silver basins, each weighing twenty pounds, on which one had incised the name of Sergius [I, duke 840–64]. He also built the assembly hall [*comitidos*, sic]

---

18. E.g., see Fig. 13 above or Fig. 8 above.

that the cantors use on festivals. He also donated nearly one hundred pounds of silver spoons and bowls to the same episcopal complex [*episcopio*] for its daily ministries.

In addition, he ordered that a public mass be celebrated with the [ecclesiastical] diptychs every day in the church of the Savior [Stefania].[19] He offered that church lands, from which its collegiate clergy would be supported. In the atrium of the said church he then set up a *xenodochium* intended for the lodging of the needy and of foreigners. This lodging was supported by [the income of] many properties.

Then, in the church of S. Gennaro situated outside the walls [*extra Moenia*], he set up a college of monks under the rule of an abbot, offering them a garden field located in the Campus Neapolis.[20] In this way he took care to support many churches, whose priests labored in poverty, with donations from his own generosity and with other items on his own initiative. If we were to recite all of these, we would take a long time to go through each of them, and our readers would grow quite weary.

At the same time the church of Misenum was destroyed by the pagans [Saracens] in punishment for its sins. Almost everything came to a standstill there, and so at the plea of the bishop, his father Duke Sergius [I] granted it to the diocese of Naples. On the altar of the church of the Stefania he adorned a tapestry with gold and gems and bands of cloth that contained Sergius' and his wife Drusa's names. He also donated to the library of the episcopal palace three codices of Flavius Josephus....

A variant contains the following details (pp. 216–17 nn. 8–9):

Trusting in divine zeal, he set up priests for daily services in the church [cathedral] of the Lord Savior, which is called the Stefania, who were to celebrate public masses continuously all week, as is the custom of the Roman church. He also distributed the necessary resources toward their expenses. He also delegated a custodian for the churches of S. Andrea the Apostle [ad Erculem?] and of S. Stefano the Protomartyr,[21]

---

19. See Bruzelius & Tronzo, 31.

20. Outside the walls, NE of the present Porta Capuana.

21. Mentioned in the *Chronicon Episcoporum XVIII* as founded by Victor, 486/89–98, otherwise unknown.

where he donated resources for the lighting arrangements and for the expenses of their custodians.

He joined to the church of Sta. Restituta — which as we have said was founded by Constantine, the first Christian emperor — to that of John the Baptist and the precursor of the Lord and the evangelist[22] and established a custodian and clerical officials for it, and he arranged for their support. He also built a *xenodochium* for the reception of pilgrims on the entry steps of the atrium, on which he conferred not a few landed estates, and to which many of the faithful made similar grants at his urging.

On the island known by the name of the Savior [Megaris, the Villa Lucullana], which is barely twelve stadia [1 stadion = 600 ft.] from the city of Naples, for many years already monks had established themselves, each living in a cell, according to his own will [i.e., eremitic monks, according to the Greek Basilian style]. Hastening there frequently he advised them with repeated admonitions, and he appointed one abbot as a pastor over those who then lived [communally] there as cenobites, and he encouraged them to live under the strictness of a rule. He granted to them for their expenses in perpetual holding the church of Sta. Lucia the Martyr [ad Mare, on Pizzofalcone] with all its belongings.

In addition, in the church [basilica] of the most holy and blessed S. Gennaro the Martyr, which is called S. Gennaro Maggiore [extra Moenia] by the citizens, and which was founded close by the walls of the said city, where previously only one priest used to observe the rites, he established a monastery under the protection of a single abbot, and for its religious life he set up one man as its father....

21. GIOVANNI III AND THEODORA BUILD THEIR LIBRARY, 947

Duke Giovanni III (928–69)[23] is well known to historians of medieval Naples for his fluid allegiances and open-ended policies toward his fellow Campanians, southern Lombards, Muslims, Byzantines and the German emperors,

---

22. The Baptistery of S. Giovanni in Fonte. See Bruzelius & Tronzo, 31–41.

22. See above, p. xxxv and n. 54.

Fig. 14. Duke Giovanni III. Cava de' Tirreni, Abbazia della Ss. Trinità, MS 4, fol. 196v.

all aimed at maintaining the independence of Naples and the power of his Sergian dynasty. Giovanni forged a marriage alliance with Rome under Alberic II (932–54) and in 949 with the Lombards of Benevento and Capua against Constantinople and Salerno. He launched an attack on Greek Siponto in Apulia also in 949, succumbed to a Byzantine naval blockade in 956 and, with the promised help of an imperial Greek fleet equipped with "Greek fire," he bought off a Saracen naval attack and siege of the city in 958, using the cathedral treasury (later recovered) to finance the deal. He managed to maintain the duchy's independence throughout his reign.

Giovanni's contributions to the cultural and literary life of the city and of western Europe were of great importance. His library was among the wonders of the early medieval world. As part of what must have been the official embassy to Constantinople to confirm the nomination of their son Marino II as co-duke in 944, Giovanni and his wife Theodora commissioned the archpriest Leo to inquire there and to bring together rare and important Latin and Greek texts. According to his own preface to the translation of the *Historia Alexandri Magni (History of Alexander the Great)*,[24] Leo returned to Naples with this *History*, the *Chronographia* of Theophanes, the *Antiquities of the Jews* by Flavius Josephus, the *Decades* or *Histories* by Livy and the *De coelesti hierarchia* of Pseudo-Dionysius the Areopagite. Giovanni and Theodora also paid for translations from these Greek manuscripts into Latin, including the *History of Alexander the Great*, which owes its subsequent European fame to their patronage.

Theodora was the Roman senatrix and daughter of Theodora and Theophylact I, count of Tusculum, and thus the niece of the infamous Marozia.[25] As the text below makes clear — whatever the truth of the Roman

---

24. See Reading 22.

25. See Ferdinand Gregorovius, *History of the City of Rome in the Middle Ages,* Annie Hamilton, trans., 8 vols. in 13 (London: George Bell & Sons, 1909–12; new edition, with intro. by David S. Chambers, New York: Italica Press, 2000–2004), 3 (800–1002 A.D.): 254–58, 278–79 et passim.

"prostitute narrative" around Marozia and the elder Theodora — the Neapolitan Theodora was a cultured and devout Christian, performing the works of mercy and collaborating with Giovanni on the assemblage of these learned and sacred texts. According to the archpriest Leo, she was also highly skilled in Latin and Greek. Theodora's power in Naples is also evidence of the continued affinities of Rome and Naples throughout the Middle Ages and of these cities' shared Roman heritage, their intertwined family, political and religious history, and their porous geographical boundaries — much of this independent of papal history — into the early-modern period.

Our text is taken from the *Notitia quaedam de Johanne et Marino ducibus, et de Theodora Iohannis ipsius uxore* (Ex Perzii Archiv, etc. t. IX, p. 692) in Capasso, *Monumenta*, app. I:339–40. Translation by R.G. Musto.

During the reign of Constantine [VII, Porphyrogenitus, 908–59] and Romanus [I, Lekapenos, 920–44], the magnificent emperors of the Christians, and during the rule of the excellent dukes and consuls Giovanni [III, 928–69] and Marino [II, co-duke 944–69, duke 969–92] over the duchy of Campania, it became necessary for them to send a representative to the aforesaid emperors at Constantinople [probably in 947].

Therefore they sent the archpriest Leo, a most faithful man, who travelled to that city of Constantinople and began to seek out books that should be read. Among these he discovered a history containing the battles and victories of Alexander the king of Macedonia.[26] Being a man neither neglectful nor lazy, without delay he copied it out [*scripsit*] and brought it back with him to Naples to his most excellent lords, and to his [Giovanni's] most devout wife, Theodora, senatrix of Rome, who used to meditate on the sacred scriptures both day and night. From her youth to the end of her life she remained the tireless protector of widows and orphans and of all those seeking her out, and in her thirty-eighth year she passed on to the Lord.

After her death the aforementioned Giovanni, a most excellent consul and duke, her husband and God's friend, took it into

---

26. Calisthenes, *History of the Deeds of Alexander the Great*. See Reading 22.

his mind to look into the proper order of the scriptures and to arrange them very clearly. But first he took the books that he already found in his collection and he restored and corrected them. Then, like a philosopher, he undertook painstaking research into who might have heard about or owned others. He thus acquired many different books, either discreetly inquiring after, or publicly requesting, them. He also commissioned the diligent copying of others. He therefore especially restored or had copies made of ecclesiastical books, namely of the Old and New Testament.

Among these ecclesiastical books that he arranged for were a *Historiography* and the *Chronographia* [perhaps of Theophanes], [*The Antiquities of the Jews* of Flavius] Josephus, [the *Decades* or *Ab urbe condita* of] Titus Livy, and [the *De coelesti hierarchia* of Pseudo-] Dionysius [the Areopagite], the excellent preacher of the celestial virtues, as well as the works of very many other famous and diverse doctors, which would be too many for us to enumerate here.

Now, at that time that most learned man, the aforesaid duke and consul, remembered that the archpriest Leo possessed that book mentioned above containing the *History of King Alexander*. He therefore summoned him and commissioned him to translate it from Greek into Latin. This Leo did, and the results are well known.

Giovanni rewarded the worthy labors of everyone engaged in this project, both the scholars and the scribes. He did this as much for the salvation of his soul as for the memory of his good name.

22. *THE ROMANCE OF ALEXANDER* BY PSEUDO-CALLISTHENES, c.950

The romance tradition flourished in Naples with translations from afar and creations by local literati. As noted in the selection above, the *Romanzo di Alessandro* of Pseudo-Callisthenes was translated from the Greek by the archpriest Leo at the request of Giovanni III after Theodora's death.

In our text Alexander recounts his adventure in the land of darkness. It is excerpted from *The Greek Romance*

Translation of Greek Play requested
By Giovanni III from Pope leo

of Alexander, trans. **Richard Stoneman (London: Penguin, 1991), 119–21.**

Book 2, c.39. After we had advanced for another two days, we came to a place where the sun does not shine. This is, in fact, the famous Land of the Blessed. I wanted to see and explore this region; I intended to go with just my personal servants to accompany me. My friend Callisthenes, however, advised me to take 40 friends, 100 slaves and 1,200 soldiers, but only the most reliable ones. So I left behind the infantry with the old men and the women, and I took only hand-picked young soldiers, giving orders that no old men should accompany us.

But there was one inquisitive old man who had two young sons, real soldiers, and he said to them, "Sons, heed the voice of your father and take me with you; you will not find me a useless burden on the journey. In his moment of danger King Alexander will have need of an old man. If he finds that you have me with you, you will receive a great reward."

"We are afraid of the king's threats," they replied. "If we are found disobeying his orders, we may be deprived not only of our part in the expedition, but of our lives."

"Get up and shave my beard," the old man replied. "Change my appearance. Then I will march with you in the midst of the army, and in a moment of crisis I shall be of great use to you." So they did as their father ordered.

After we had marched for three days we came to a place filled with fog. Being unable to go further, because the land was without roads or paths, we pitched our tents there. The next day I took 1,000 armed men with me and set off to see whether this was in fact the end of the world. We went towards the left, because it was lighter in that direction, and marched for half a day through rocky country full of ravines. I counted the passing of time not by the sun, but by measuring out the leagues we covered and thus calculating both the time and the distance. But eventually we turned back in fear because the way became impassable. So we decided to go instead to the right. The going was much smoother, but the darkness was impenetrable. I was at a loss, for my young companions all advised me not to go further into that region, for fear the horses should be scattered in the darkness over the long distance, and we should be unable to return. Then I said to them, "You who are so brave in war, now you may see that there is no true bravery without intelligence and understanding. If there were an old man with us, he would be able to advise us how to set about advancing in this dark place. Who among you is brave enough to go back to the camp and bring me an old man? He shall be given 10 pounds of gold."

Then the sons of the old man said to me, "Lord, if you will hear us without anger, we have something to say to you."

"Speak as you wish," I replied. "I swear by Providence above that I will do you no harm." Then they told me all about their father, and how they had brought him along with them, and they ran and fetched the old man himself. I greeted him warmly and asked him for his advice.

"Alexander," the old man said, "it must be clear to you that you will never see the light of day again if you advance without horses. Select, then, mares with foals. Leave the foals here, and advance with the mares; they will without fail bring you back to their foals."

I sought through the whole army and found only 100 mares with foals. I took these, and 100 selected horses besides, as well as further horses to carry our provisions. Then, following the old man's advice, we advanced, leaving the foals behind.

'The old man had advised his sons to pick up anything they found lying on the ground after we had entered the Land of Darkness, and to put it in their knapsacks. There were 360 soldiers: I had the 160 unmounted ones go on ahead. So we went on for about fifteen leagues. We came to a place where there was a clear spring, whose water flashed like lightning, and some other streams besides. The air in this place was very fragrant and less dark than before. I was hungry and wanted some bread, so I called the cook Andreas by name and said, "Prepare some food for us." He took a dried fish and waded into the clear water of the spring to wash it. As soon as it was dipped in the water, it came to life and leapt out of the cook's hands. He was frightened, and did not tell me what had happened; instead, he drank some of the water himself, and scooped some up in a silver vessel and kept it. The whole place was abounding in water, and we drank of its various streams. Alas for my misfortune, that it was not fated for me to drink of the spring of immortality, which gives life to what is dead, as my cook was fortunate enough to do.

23. DUKE GIOVANNI III GRANTS AN ESTATE, 951

In Reading 21, we met Giovanni and Theodora as patrons of learning. Here our text focuses on the source of their wealth and patronage. While this document is dated following Byzantine protocols, it reflects the realities of Neapolitan power, based on the lands of the *publicum* controled by the Sergian dynasty.

The text includes several unidentifiable places and names, but it offers a clear delineation of property boundaries. Since the property exchanged by Cesario Ferrario included his pledge to protect it against either Lombard or Neapolitan encroachment, we might assume that it lies somewhere on the duchy's boundaries with Lombard holdings to the east and north.

Though the language appears to follow the forms of a simple property exchange with Cesario, the actual grant reflects some form of clientage, if not an actual feudal relationship. This is underscored by Giovanni's pledge to allow Cesario Ferrario unimpeded use of the holding and to uphold and defend the granted land. It thus may indicate the use of the Neapolitan *publicum*, or ducal holdings, to provide for the city's administration and defense. In this sense it is both a private and a public transfer, one with an obligation on Cesario's part to protect his lands granted in exchange. The form of this charter is also noteworthy as it seems to require the consent of Theodora and the assent of their son, Marinus.

Also note the use of surnames so early in Naples: fully three to four centuries ahead of rest of Italy and at least five to six ahead of northern Europe. At the same time, note the ethnic mix reflected in this document. The agreement provides for the protection of the transferred land from either Lombards (of the duchy of Benevento) or Neapolitans and includes both Latin and several Greek signatories. It is uncertain at this point in relations with

Constantinople whether these are actually Greek-speaking residents or citizens of Naples or whether they were merely transliterating their Latin names into Greek characters as a sign of elite status. The document is reproduced below in Fig. 61.

Our selection is taken from Capasso, *Monumenta*, 2.2:13–14, edited from Naples, Archivio Reale, RNAM 2:21, and translated by R.G. Musto.

In the name of the Lord God our Savior Jesus Christ, in the forty-fourth year of the reign of our great Emperor Constantine [VII Porphyrogennetos, 908–59], and in the seventh [sic] year of his son the great emperor Romanus [II, 959–63], in the third day of the month of November, in the tenth indiction, at Naples.

It is certain that we, Giovanni, by the grace of God, consul and duke, and with our son the venerable lord Duke Marinus [II, co-duke 944–69, duke 969–92] with the attendance, consent and the will of the glorious Duchess Theodora my wife, have commuted and handed over to you, Cesario Ferrario, son of Giovanni Ferrario and [nephew of] the monk Maiorarius, on this day with the most active will the following:

That is, my entire half of the land that is called Ad Mulianum Pictulum, located in Calbetiani, along with its trees and along with its reclaimed land [*introitus*] and all its other holdings. There are two rows of trees and it abuts on one side the land of Leone Demaria in the place called Calbetiani. On the other side and at the top is our land, which we reserve under our control [*potestatem*], which belongs to us as part of the farm [*fundum*] that is called De Fracta located in that place. On the other [bottom] side is also our land, which we retain under our control, which belongs to us from our other farm, which place is called De Romano.

From this point on nothing further remains or has been reserved by us, nor have we commissioned it to another person, nor do we commit it to such control. And from the present day forward the aforesaid named and recorded half of our named land, which is named Ad Mulianum Pictulum, located in the named place, which is called Calbetiani and on which are two rows of trees with their reclaimed lands and all its other holdings, to the extent that I have included him [Cesario] among the named co-heirs as is read above, may it be commuted and given to you by us in your name, Cesario Ferrario, and in that of your heirs, and may it be under your control to do with as you wish.

And neither by us, the aforesaid Giovanni, by the grace of the Lord, consul and duke, along with the consent and will of the aforenamed Theodora the glorious duchess my wife, nor by our heirs nor by our subjects at any time nor in any name might you, the aforenamed Cesario Ferrario, or your heirs, be subject to any requisition or molestation [over the aforesaid transfer] from this point forever.

As above and by anyone, anywhere, at any time, we have granted to you and to your heirs our aforenamed two rows of trees from the aforenamed land that we have granted to you, which is called Ad Mulianum Pictulum and which in all cases we are bound to uphold and defend.

On account of which, in place of any commutation or compensation, we accept from you the following: an entire land holding from your estate [*campese*] which is called Ad Arbustum in the fields before S. Iacobo, along with its reclaimed lands and all its other holdings. These are two *tertiaria* ["thirds," probably a measure of land], and it has as its boundary on one side the land of the monastery of S. Gregorio and on the other side the hereditary land of Stefano Maiorarius, your uncle [*thii*]. At the top end of the holding is the land of Landemar the Lombard, and at the other end is the land of the heirs of Marino Tata, plus some others along the boundary. Nothing further of this remains with you, nor do you reserve anything. Furthermore, for all time it is incumbent upon you and your heirs to defend these from all men and persons whether Lombard or Neapolitan, just as it is incumbent upon us.

If, however, we or our heirs or our subjects presume to go against this charter of commutation as written above, in whatever manner, then we will bind ourselves and our heirs to pay to you or your heirs ten gold Byzantine *solidi*.

This charter of commutation, as written above, has been signed by the hand of Gregorius the court official and notary [*scrinarius*], who has been asked to write this, and by the witness of the undersigned, in the tenth indiction.

By this sign † and the hand of the aforenamed glorious Duchess Theodora I have written those named below on their behalf:

IOANNEC KONCOYΛ EΘ ΔΟΥΞ COYB, i.e., I, Giovanni, consul and duke, have signed.

ΕΓΟ IOANNEC ΦΙΔΙΟΥC ΔN EYCTPATI POΓATOYC A CCTOC IOYΓAΛEC TECTI COYB † i.e., I, Giovanni, son of Lord Eustrazio, surrogate for the above-written parties, have signed as witness.

ΕΓΟ ΓΡΕΓΟΡΙΟΥC ΦΙΔΙΟΥC ΔN KECAPII POΓATOYC A CCTOC IOYTAΛEC TECTI COYB. † i.e., I, Gregorius, son of Caesarius, surrogate for the above-written parties have signed below as witness.

† I, Gregorius, son of Lord Sergius, surrogate for the above-written parties, have signed as witness below.†

† I, Gregorius, court official and notary, here below the signatures of the witnesses, have completed and discharged this on behalf of the above-named. Tenth indiction.†[27]

24. VESUVIUS ERUPTS ON THE DEATH OF GIOVANNI III, 969

Duke Giovanni III also had a reputation as a reprobate. Perhaps this was due to his history of flexible alliances among Latins, Greeks and Muslims, and perhaps to his reputation for secular and classical learning — as well as for a layman's command of the scriptures and mystical texts. In the monastic literature of later generations he was portrayed as an unreliable ally of the Ottonian imperial cause in southern Italy, an unspiritual man more concerned with accumulating wealth and the fruits of pagan culture, including its philosophers. As such he was condemned by the cardinal and reformer Peter Damian (c.1007–72). The following description of Vesuvius need not be first-hand but could have derived from literary tradition.

Our text is taken from *De Iohanne III Neapoli duce et Pandulpho principe in infernum damnatis, ex S. Petri Damiani*

---

27. See Fig. 61.

Opusculis, XIX, c. 9 et 10, in Capasso, *Monumenta,* app. I:346–47. Translated by R.G. Musto.

As soon as Duke Giovanni III had died, Mount Vesuvius — from which Gehenna itself belches up — burst into flames. Thus clearly it is proven that the debt that was being held by the demons was nothing other than the fire of savage flame that is owed by depraved and reprobate men. For in these parts, whenever a rich reprobate dies, fire appears to erupt from that mountain; and such huge, heaping sulfurous globs flow continuously from Vesuvius that they create a fiery torrent that races down into the sea. Here, in fact, one can see embodied what John says of the damned in the Apocalypse [21:8]: "they shall have their portion in the pool burning with fire and brimstone, which is the second death."

Fig. 15. Sta. Maria ad Plateam.
Photo: Italica Press.

25. SERGIUS VI MAKES GRANTS TO S. GREGORIO ARMENO, 1084

Into the end of the eleventh century, at the beginning of the Crusades era, Naples continued to give lip service to its official status as part of the Byzantine Empire, as in this document dated by the regnal year of Alexius Comnenus. Several sections of the city are involved in this transaction: the first to the north, in the area around the church and catacombs of S. Gennaro, called Capo di Fuga; the second the Greek monastery of S. Gregorio Maggiore, or Armeno, in the heart of the city; and the third toward the southeast of the city, on the present via Forcella.[28]

The following text is excerpted from Camera, *Annali,* 1:xlvi. Translated by R.G. Musto.

28.   See Musto, Interactive Map: http://www.italicapress.com/index287.html.

Twentieth day of April, indiction VII [1084]. Naples. In the third year of the reign of Emperor Alexius [I, Comnenus, 1081–1118] Sergius [VI] Morsapane promises to the monastery of S. Gregorio Maggiore [Armeno] two parcels of land located outside this city not far from the church of S. Gennaro [*fuori le Mura* or *extra Moenia*], which is called Capo di Fuga. These parcels cohere with the properties of the church of Sta. Maria ad Plateam,[29] in the rione Forcellaria.

26. THE *PACTUM* OF SERGIUS VII, 1130

The *Pactum* or *Promissio* was probably written up in 1130. It reflects the effects of the new communal movement through-out Italy, most clearly emergent in the North, and it appears to be the first documentation of the commune or *societas* in the South. Read closely, however, it reflects less a defeat for the duke than a recognition of existing power relationships.

Duke Sergius retains his ancient Byzantine (and Roman) titles of "consul," "duke" and "master of soldiers"; but he acknowledges that he rules with the consensus of the ma-jor stakeholders in the city: the *nobiles* and the "middling" people, the merchants and artisans. The pact covers many areas of urban life: jurisdiction over justice, trade, contrac-tual arrangements, war and peace.

The pact reveals many long-standing or emerging social arrangements: the continued existence of what seems to be slavery or at least a strong clientage system, the ame-lioration of corporal punishment just beginning to ef-fect the Italian communes, recognition of the individual rights of both female and male in marriage arrangements, the rights of free movement of people and goods in this port city, and of non-Neapolitans to take up residence.[30] Among the recognized checks on the power of the duke are strong limitations on his rights to seize persons and property, to destroy homes in punishment, and the re-quirement to seek the consensus of the *nobiles* in major decisions.

---

29.   Sta. Maria in Piazza. See Fig. 15.

30.   For trade and commerce conditions, see Readings 18, 41, 61.

Like the Magna Carta in England nearly a century later, the *Pactum* is evidence not of a sharp break with the past but a recognition of the emerging power of a hereditary class of *nobiles* to curb the excesses of rulers and to insert themselves into the decision-making process. With the surrender of Sergius VII to the Norman king Roger II in 1137, it was this class of *nobiles* who assumed effective rule over the city until its final surrender to the Normans in 1140. During this three-year interim, the grouping of noble families within the city's *regiones* began to take formal shape. These would evolve into the *seggi* of the later Middle Ages.

The Latin text is available in Capasso, *Monumenta*, 2.2: 157–58. The text has been discussed and translated by Giovanni Italo Cassandro, SN 2.1:331–37; and edited by him in "La «promissio» del duca Sergio e la «societas napoletana»," *Archivio Storico Italiano* 1.3–4 (1942): 135 ff. It has been recently discussed by Amedeo Feniello, *Napoli*, 247–52. English translation by R.G. Musto.

Sergius, by the grace of God, consul, duke and master of the soldiers [*magister militum*].

I promise and swear to you all Neapolitan nobles, and to all the middling people [*medianis*], and to all inhabitants and residents of Naples, in the name of the Father, the Son and through the life-giving wood of the Holy Cross on which hung our Lord, and by these sacrosanct mysteries.

That henceforth I will not consider, nor will I allow, that either you or someone [belonging to] you lose your hand or any member of your persons, in any way.

Nor shall you be seized or exiled or put into prison or held as a hostage in any way to your harm or to the harm of anyone among your people, so long as you or someone [belonging to you] do no such harm to me.

If such harm is done, you, or anyone among your people, shall make indemnification [and vice-versa] by the just judgment delivered by the Neapolitan nobles of my court, within fifteen days following the notification delivered to you or to anyone of your people [after which no one shall be able to do so].

I will not take, nor will I remove, your property from you or from any of your people with violence.

Nor will I demolish, nor I will I cause someone to demolish, your houses.

Nor will I introduce nor cause to be introduced into this city of Naples or its possessions any new custom without the advice of as many Neapolitan nobles as possible.

Nor will I force a woman to marry a man, or a man a woman without their free will, or permit others to do so, and if someone ventures to do this, I will help you if it is requested by you or one of your people.

I do not intend nor will I consent that this *societas* that you have created among you or that you shall create in the future, be disbanded or weakened [*corrumpere*]; and if someone tries to do so, I will aid you in good faith so that it remains firm.

And I will not make war or peace or a truce or a treaty without the advice of the greatest possible number of Neapolitan nobles.

I shall not disturb men who arrive by land or by sea at Naples — with or without merchandise — and there take up abode, nor will I cause them to be disturbed. Nor will I seize their goods by force or cause them to be seized.

I will observe for you and for your people all the things written above with right faith and pure intention as long as I live, and I shall never knowingly violate them.

■

Fig. 16. Christ crowning Roger II king of Sicily, 1143–48. Mosaic from the church of La Martorana, Palermo.

CHAPTER 3: THE NORMANS

INTRODUCTION

Documents presented for this period include narrative sources, mirabilian and other travel accounts, *chansons* and poetry, religious, liturgical and legal records.

When the Norman prince Robert Guiscard died in 1085, he was succeeded by his younger brother, Roger of Calabria. Once he had consolidated Calabria, Roger crossed to Messina in 1061 and by 1091 had conquered all of Sicily from the Muslims. By 1130, Roger's son, Roger II (1130–54) had taken his cousins' inheritances in Apulia and Calabria and had formed the kingdom of Sicily on both sides of the Straits of Messina. In Palermo, on Christmas Day 1130, he was crowned "king" of Sicily by Antipope Anacletus II.

The document authorizing this, now somewhat mutilated and preserved in the Vatican,[1] is of fundamental importance for the history of Naples, for — even though Anacletus was an antipope — it established the papal right to crown (and thus to depose) the kings of Sicily, a right that would establish the theoretical vassalage of the king of Sicily to the papacy and reverberate through Neapolitan history for centuries. Note that Anacletus also concedes to Roger the rule of Naples, even though Roger did not manage to finally take the city until 1140.

The text has been edited and translated by G.A. Loud in his *Roger II and the Creation of the Kingdom of Sicily*, 304–6.

27. ANACLETUS II'S PRIVILEGE TO ROGER II, AUTHORIZING THE CREATION OF THE KINGDOM OF SICILY, SEPTEMBER 27, 1130

[Your father, Roger I] zealously served the Church in many ways in the time of our predecessors the Roman pontiffs of

---

1. Cod. Vat. Ottobon. Lat. 2940, fols. 18–19.

distinguished memory Urban and Paschal. And your mother of happy memory, following nobly in the footsteps of her husband, and in return for the advantages given her by the Lord, took pains to honor most ceremonially this same Church of God and to sustain it with a generous hand. You yourself, to whom divine providence has granted greater wisdom and power than the rest of the Italian princes, have tried splendidly to honor our predecessors and to serve them generously. It is proper [then] to raise up your person and those of your heirs and to adorn them with permanent titles of grace and honor.

Fig. 17. Anacletus II crowning Roger II king of Sicily. Peter of Eboli, Liber ad honorem Augusti, 1196. Bern, Burgerbibliothek, MS 120 II.

Therefore we concede, grant and authorize to you, your son Roger and your other sons following you in the kingdom as you shall decree, and to your heirs, the crown of the kingdom of Sicily, and Calabria, Apulia and all those lands which we and our predecessors have granted and conceded to your predecessors the dukes of Apulia, namely Robert Guiscard and his son Roger [Borsa], to hold and rule this kingdom in perpetuity, and to have by hereditary right [iure perpetuo] royal dignities and regalian rights.

We decree that Sicily shall be the capital of the kingdom [capud regni]. Furthermore we authorize and concede that you and your heirs shall be anointed as kings and at the appointed times crowned by the hands of those archbishops of your land whom you wish [to do this], assisted if you wish by other bishops of your choice. Also, we grant, concede and consent that you, your sons and heirs shall have and possess in perpetuity all the concessions, grants and rights that our predecessors have conceded and granted, and to which they have given their consent, to your predecessors as dukes of Apulia, Robert Guiscard, his son Roger [Borsa] and the latter's son William and to you. We also grant to you and your heirs and authorize [to rule] the principality of Capua with all its appurtenances, as the princes of the Capuans have held it in the past and [as they do] at the moment.

We grant and confirm the honor of Naples and its possessions and the aid of the men of Benevento against your enemies.

Kindly assenting to your repeated requests, we concede to the archbishop of Palermo and to his successors and the Palermitan church the consecrations of three of the bishops of Sicily, namely those of Syracuse, Agrigento and Mazzara or Catania, on condition that they shall suffer no damage to their dioceses or possessions from the archbishop of Palermo or the Palermitan church. We reserve our full rights over the other two bishops.

We concede, grant and authorize these our concessions, as laid out above, to you, your sons and heirs, to hold and possess in perpetual right, provided that you shall have sworn, or they shall have sworn, homage and fealty to us and our successors, which you shall do, or they shall do, at the time sought by us and at a place safe for you, unless it shall be remitted by us or our successors, [in which case] they [i.e., your successors] shall not on this account suffer loss of honor, dignity or their land. You and your heirs will however pay the census, namely the 600 *scifati*,[2] which you ought to pay every year to the Roman church, if you are requested to do this. If you are not so requested, you shall pay what is requested, but no case shall be made about the rest left unpaid. If indeed in the future any ecclesiastical or secular person tries to breach this our concession, then unless he makes suitable satisfaction, he shall be struck by the sword of anathema. Let the peace of our Lord Jesus Christ be on all those observing these our conditions, amen.

I Anacletus, bishop of the Catholic Church
I Matthew Eudoxie priest
John, son of Peter Leone, consul of the Romans

2. Loud, citing Grierson, notes that this was the south Italian name for Byzantine gold *nomisma*. derived from the borders (*scifae*) along the edges of these coins.

Roger his brother
Peter son of Uguccio
Cencius ...
... son of Guido
Peter Leone of Fondi
Abucio
Giovanni Habdiricio
Milo....

Dated at Benevento by the hand of Saxo, cardinal priest and chancellor of the Holy Roman Church, 27th September, ninth [year] in the indiction, in the year from the Lord's incarnation 1130, [first] year of the pontificate of our lord Pope Anacletus II.

28. ROGER II ATTACKS NAPLES, 1130

In 1030, the Normans seized the castle at Aversa and began their drive to conquer the duchy of Naples and principality of Capua. In 1059, the Norman Richard Quarrel, count of Aversa, was named prince of Capua, who then turned his eyes on the duchy of Naples. The city resisted Richard's blockade in 1077, but in 1078 accepted a nominal Norman protectorate.

Only a few territories remained outside Roger's kingdom, including the principalities of Salerno and of Capua and the duchy of Naples. Despite a series of revolts against his rule, by 1127 Roger had made an accord with Salerno, and by 1135 Capua had capitulated to him. That left Naples as the only independent state in the South. It became a haven for Roger's enemies, including Prince Robert of Capua, Count Rainulf II of Alife and almost one thousand exiles from Benevento. Roger's reconquest was destructive and bloody, and so in 1131 Duke Sergius of Naples offered his submission to the Norman king at Salerno. But Naples' leading citizens had already extracted their *Promissio* from Sergius, and the city was by no means ready to submit to the Normans. Throughout the following narrative the mentions of Pisan naval aid to Naples call to mind Pisa's imperial alliance and the imminent arrival of Roger II's greatest enemy: the German Emperor Lothair II.[3]

---

3. For a narrative of these events, see above, xli–xlvi.

The following passages recounting Roger's campaigns against Naples from 1130 to 1136 are taken from Alexander of Telese's *The Deeds Done by King Roger of Sicily*. Not much is known about Alexander other than that he was the abbot of S. Salvatore, near Telese, 30 km. west of Benevento, from before 1127 to before November 1143. The work was probably written in 1136 and shows no evidence of the subsequent resistance and final conquest of Naples.[4]

The following passages have been translated from the Latin by Loud and excerpted from his free online edition, since published in print in his *Roger II*, 77–122.

Book II [1130–34]

(1) With so many successes achieved, all the lands of Bohemond and the whole duchy seemingly in his power, the prince [Robert] of the Capuans, the *magister militum* of Naples [Sergius VII] and all the land up to the borders of the city of Ancona subject to him, and his opponents in war subdued, those close to Duke Roger, and particularly his uncle Count Henry by whom he was loved more than anyone, began very frequently to suggest to him the plan that he, who with the help of God ruled so many provinces, Sicily, Calabria, Apulia and other regions stretching almost to Rome, ought not to have just the ducal title but ought to be distinguished by the honor of kingship....

(2) After turning over in his own mind their well-intentioned and praiseworthy suggestion, he wanted to have sure and certain counsel. He journeyed back to Salerno, and just outside it, he convoked some learned churchmen and most competent persons, as well as certain princes, counts, barons and others whom he thought trustworthy to examine this secret and unlooked for matter....

(12) While he was staying there [in 1131] the *magister militum* of the city of Naples, by name Sergius [VII], realizing that

---

4. For links to Loud's translation, see Wikipedia article on Alexander of Telese, http://en.wikipedia.org/wiki/Alexander_of_Telese, accessed October 30, 2012. For background, see Oldfield, *City and Community*, 1–81; for detailed political and military history see John J. Norwich, *The Kingdom in the Sun, 1130–1194* (New York: Harper & Row, 1970), 1–72, esp. 38–41; and Loud, *Roger II*, 1–50.

in Roger there was such mighty strength and valor, went to him, constrained not by warlike means but by fear alone, and surrendered to him lordship over this city which, amazing to say, after the Roman Empire has never been subjected by the sword. Now he surrendered it to Roger, constrained by word alone....

(50) Count Rainulf [of Alife, in 1132 now in open revolt], hearing of the king's approach so near to him, and suspecting that he would indeed be moving against him, devoted himself even more energetically to his defences. On this account he went to Naples where he harangued the *magister militum* [Duke Sergius VII] and citizens, begging them all to help him; then he went on to Aversa where he encouraged all those who were capable of bearing arms to join him against the enemy. After that he returned to the Caudine Valley where he had left his army, waiting there for the *magister militum* and all those as yet absent....

(67) When the city [of Capua] had submitted to him [in July 1134] and the king was about to enter, he was honourably received, as was proper, by a procession organized in advance of the clerics and all the townspeople and was led to the archiepiscopal church with hymns and *laudes*. Then immediately afterwards he marched out with his army and commanded Sergius [VII of Naples], the *magister militum*, to come and surrender to him immediately, otherwise he should know that his city would undoubtedly be placed under siege. And indeed he was afraid that if he declined to do this the king would march upon him and attack his city. Thus he decided to yield, came to the king and on bended knee placed his hands between his, rendered homage to him and swore fealty [in July 1134]. This was indeed an amazing thing, for as we have already said in Book Two [Book I, c. 12], Naples had after the time of the Roman Empire never been subjected by the sword, and now it seemed to be constrained by word alone.

Book III [1134–35]

(1) It happened in the same year not long after King Roger returned to Sicily [in July 1134] that he was afflicted with a serious illness. But while with God's aid he rapidly recovered, his wife Queen Alberia [Elvira] soon became very ill indeed

and died [in February 1135]. This woman was during her lifetime distinguished by the grace of religion and by the generosity of her almsgiving. On her death the king was afflicted by such bitter grief that for many days he shut himself away in his chamber and was only seen by a few of his personal attendants. Hence little by little the rumor spread, not just to those who were far away but even to those who were close by, that he himself had died. As a consequence of this rumor Prince Robert [of Capua, who had fled to Pisa] travelled by sea with a very large force of Pisan troops and was welcomed in Naples with the agreement of Sergius, the *magister militum* of the city, who had already been conspiring with him against the king — for these two had been sending messengers to each other.

(2) [1135] Count Rainulf was deceived by this rumor and believed that the king had really died. When he found out that the prince had returned with a huge armed force he took heart and rejoiced greatly....

(5) Prince Robert [of Capua] was still uncertain about the king's death, but he did not desist from formulating plans through which he could recover his lost principality. Thus he sent to Count Rainulf [asking] that he hurry to him since he would be quite unable to do what had to be done without his strength [*strenuitas*]. The latter indeed, as has already been said, had never had any doubts about the king's death, and with those forces he had collected hastened enthusiastically to him in Naples. With his arrival the prince and Sergius the *magister militum* regained greater boldness and were imbued with greater vigor, thinking that through him, because he was a man of the most warlike mettle, they would achieve a happy result in what they desired. Their mutual conspiracy was therefore confirmed, and thus it was at length decided that the prince and count should restore to themselves all their lost possessions and the *magister militum* should retain Naples and all his other property[5] which legally belonged to him in security. The king was still, as before, believed to be dead, and many even of his faithful supporters despaired of his life, especially since he delayed his arrival more than usual in the face of declared enemies....

---

5.   The Byzantine *publicum* of the Neapolitan dukes. See above, xxvii, 76.

(11) When therefore the prince [Robert of Capua] decided to disdain the message sent to him, the king mustered in one place the huge force of knights and footmen whom he had recruited. He decided as a matter of first priority to attack Aversa, which Count Rainulf had remained behind to defend. He devoted his whole attention to this, and the Aversans, fearing the fierceness of his attack, all began as best they could to seek flight and to hasten to Naples to save themselves. The count realized that he was being abandoned by everyone in this timorous flight, that the king would undoubtedly immediately commence operations against him, and at length he too fled with scarcely a handful of men. He retired in confusion to the walls of Naples, where the prince and the *magister militum* had joined forces, and once shut up there he did not dare to stir forth, and in the depths of his mind was cruelly tortured with regret by the thought that he had been ill-advised to have begun the war and never to have given credence to those who had advised him towards peace....

(13) [June 1135] When Aversa had thus been destroyed, the king afterwards ordered its suburban area to be burned. Then approaching Naples between the town called Cuculo[6] and the Lago di Patria,[7] he pitched camp and remained here for some time, from whence he had all this part of the suburban area of Naples consumed by fire, and all the fields were laid bare by his army's foragers. Prince Robert, Count Rainulf and the *magister militum* Sergius were kept by their fear of him inside the city and did not dare to make a sortie outside the gate. And when all had been consumed, the king once again had Aversa laid waste, and he ordered that matters be conducted so diligently that if there was anything between Aversa and Naples that might be burned which had [so far] remained unburned then it was to be consumed. After thus staying for a long time, until the crops which had been abundant had been totally destroyed, the whole region was left a desert.

---

6. There is a Cercola about 17 miles due east of Naples, in a direct line between Somma and Acerra, both mentioned below; but Cuculo itself is over 100 miles to the east, too far for besieging Naples. It is unclear what town is meant here.

7. Patria is on the coast northwest of Naples, north of Cumae, and south of the River Volturno.

(19) Following this he rejoined his army which he had left at the River Volturno, and set off to besiege Naples where those enemies who had rebelled against him had taken refuge. It was a most ancient city, which Aeneas was said to have founded when he had landed there on his voyage: it was of great size and was defended on its southern flank not only by the height

of its walls but by the Tyrrhenian Sea. On its other sides it was protected by very high walls. Because of this it was considered to be unstormable, and indeed impregnable except for the danger of famine. Once upon a time the ruler of the city, by the order of Octavianus Augustus, had been Virgil, the greatest of poets, and in it he had composed a huge volume of verses in hexameters.

Fig. 18. Duke Roger II of Sicily. Peter of Eboli, Liber ad honorem Augusti, 1196.

(20) Thus when King Roger besieged this city from the eastern side [the Campus Neapolis], he foresaw that its capture would be very time-consuming. He decided to recruit a vast number of workmen and to build a large [siege] castle, protected by surrounding ramparts, next to it, by means of which, provided that it was sufficiently garrisoned, Naples could (even in his absence) be closely blockaded. Thus when Naples was put under siege, the ground was dug to raise the rampart for the siege castle; but due to the crumbling of the parched earth the rampart started to collapse. Because of this the work seemed to be in vain, and it was impossible to finish the castle, which had been begun while the rampart kept on collapsing. On seeing this the magnates quickly came to the king and began muted complaints. "This work to build the castle is," they said, "in vain, since every day the ground is dug to throw up the rampart, but the castle comes no nearer completion. The earth dug is unsuitable for building the rampart, and it is so unstable that it keeps on collapsing. Let's therefore abandon this operation and

find another plan, which will give us a better chance to abase the pride of this rebel city."

(21) "And [they said] there is also another thing that we must greatly lament, since many among the army find the heat of the summer here too much for them and begin to sicken, while others cannot endure the ghastly smell of the corpses of the horses that have died because there is such a lack of water. Furthermore the land on which we are situated, because it is so dry, gives forth an impure heat. On this account we greatly fear the harmful consequences, and indeed that the whole army might fall sick and at the worst be entirely wiped out. Hence, if it is not displeasing to your piety, we ought immediately to move, for by not remaining here and thus recovering our health we could not only blockade Naples in the summer but if it was necessary in the winter as well." On hearing this the king was moved by compassion for them and ordered the siege to be raised. He decided on another way to put pressure on his enemies without endangering his own men, for dispersing the greater part of his army among the various towns closest to Naples, he ordered it to blockade the city closely even in his absence, and if the rebels should ever happen to make a sortie, they could be driven back by those nearest to them.

(22) After making these dispositions, he went to Cuculo which had, while he had delayed his return from Sicily, been in part destroyed by the Pisans, whom the prince had brought with him to so little effect. [They had done this] because his order [to do so] had been opposed by the Neapolitans. Since this town was so very close to Naples, he ordered that work be started to rebuild it as fast as possible and stronger than it had been before as part of his blockade. Then, seeing that the rebuilding of Aversa could restrain the pride of rebel Naples, he went there and ordered that it be rebuilt on the same site as before and permitted all those who had lived there before to return and settle there once again.

(23) Meanwhile, with this city being energetically rebuilt in the presence of the king and his army, the prince, count and the *magister militum* Sergius, trapped within the walls of Naples, had no idea what to do, realizing that they were very close to disaster unless help was to be very quickly forthcoming from

somewhere or other. For they were all the time menaced by their shortage of supplies, since nothing could be brought in from outside by land to sustain them and their men. Of their knights, who had apparently enlisted for wages, some very much feared capture by the king, and fled from the city whenever they had the opportunity, others were unwilling to lose their property and were prepared to change sides if they were able to gain the king's sanction for its recovery.

(24) Finding themselves blockaded in the city, the princes finally decided, after exhaustive discussion, immediately to send messengers to Pisa to deafen the ears of the citizens with their prayers and beg their compassion upon them that they might send a mighty army by sea by which speedy help might be brought to those who were at their last gasp. When the immense force which they had sent had crossed the sea and arrived with its ships at Naples, the decision was taken to make a sudden dawn attack on the city of Amalfi, with the intention either of plundering it or of seizing it from the king, assuming that ill-fortune did not prevent this.

(27) These pirates returned to Naples with the Pisans whom the prince had brought with him. Then, leaving some of their number there as a garrison, they went back to Pisa with the prince himself, [intending] to return to aid the Neapolitans in the spring. Sergius the *magister militum* and Count Rainulf with his son Robert remained in the city to defend it. Robert had been made a knight [*miles constitutus*] in his earliest adolescence, at a time when despite his youth he was already beginning to attract praise for his great courage and daring.

(28) Then the king, re-uniting his forces in one huge army, returned to cut down all the vines belonging to the Neapolitans that he could get his hands on. Having accomplished this destruction far and wide he returned to Aversa to finish the rebuilding which, as we have said, had for a time been left incomplete....

Book IV [1136]

(1) After the king's departure for Sicily, according to the periods of office that he had arranged (as was discussed above), Count Adam entered Aversa to take command of its knights

and, conducting himself bravely and well, gathered a great reputation by his vigorous military activity. For he launched continuous sorties all round the outskirts of the city [of Naples] and was not afraid to penetrate right up to the city gate. The city was already vexed with such a shortage of bread that a penny of Rouen would scarcely buy two little loaves of millet. The knights whom Adam commanded numbered about a thousand; some of these blockaded Naples, others were placed in the town of Somma and at Acerra, some in the fortress of Cuculo, but the majority were ordered to garrison Aversa.

(2) After a large number of knights had deserted from Naples, either from fear of the king or from shortage of food, barely three hundred remained who were unable because of their lack of numbers to wage open resistance, although sorty-ing in the silence of the night without the besiegers knowing they managed to burn and rob....

(5) ...When the aforementioned Count Robert took com-mand of the royal troops at Aversa in succession to Adam, he instantly blockaded the borders of Naples with such military prowess and energy that its defenders never dared to sortie to inflict injury on their enemies, except occasionally at night when they could not be seen. After the king had left for Sicily the *magister militum* Sergius had sailed to Pisa in an attempt to gain assistance for himself and his accomplices for the mo-ment when the king himself returned to besiege Naples....

29. VIRGIL'S BONES PROTECT NAPLES, c. 1136

Naples retained its independence through several pro-tracted sieges, starvation and disease, united under Duke Sergius VII. It withstood both Roger's land attacks and his naval blockade of 1136. In order to save the city further hardship, however, Sergius finally submitted to Roger in 1137 but was killed shortly thereafter while participating in the Normans' siege of Capua. Naples' nobles had already formed a *societas*, or commune, under an agreement with Sergius c. 1130 (*Pactum* or *Promissio Sergii*[8]), and they con-tinued to resist Roger's renewed siege until 1139, when they

---

8.   See Reading 26.

formally submitted to the king at Benevento. In September 1140, Roger finally entered the city.

According to Alexander of Neckham (8 September 1157 –1217), Naples was able to resist Roger's overwhelming force through the magical powers bequeathed to it by Virgil: the magic egg and walls, and the "magic fly" (perhaps the malaria mosquito) through which the people sent pestilence against his soldiers. On another occasion, according to Alexander, his fleet of sixty ships was scattered by a magical tempest.

Our text is taken from the *Anecdota de Vergilio (The Secret History of Virgil)* attributed to Alexander Neckham. Alexander was born at St. Albans and was educated at the St. Albans abbey school and began to teach as schoolmaster at Dunstable. He later spent several years at the school of Petit Pons in Paris (c.1175–82). By 1180 he had become a distinguished lecturer on the arts at the University of Paris. By 1186 he was again in England as a schoolmaster, first at Dunstable and then as master of St. Albans School itself until c.1195. An Augustinian canon, he was appointed abbot of Cirencester Abbey in 1213. He died at Kempsey in Worcestershire and was buried at Worcester.[9]

This selection was edited and translated by "Joannes Opsopoeus Brettanus."[10]

Because of his defeats, King Roger [II] realized that Naples had supernatural protection, and that its source was the hidden bones of Vergilius [Virgil], the city's patron. For in his opulent coronation ceremony in Panormus [Palermo], he had learned that that city was protected by a hero. For Panormus possessed the bones of Aristoteles [Aristotle], which were held in a vessel hung in mid-air in a sanctuary that had originally been a pagan temple, but was later a Christian church and then a mosque. The people prayed to these relics for many reasons, but chiefly for protection.

---

9.   See Joannes Opsopoeus Brettanus, "Praefatio ad Lectorem (Preface to the Reader)" at http://web.eecs.utk.edu/~mclennan/BA/AV/praefatio.html; and Richard William Hunt and Margaret T. Gibson, *The Schools and the Cloister: The Life and Writings of Alexander Nequam (1157–1217)* (Oxford: Clarendon Press, 1984).

10.   At http://web.eecs.utk.edu/~mclennan/BA/AV, accessed 10/30/12.

For Aristoteles was the hero who protected Panormus, just as
Orestes' bones gave victory to the Spartans, and Alcmene's bones
guarded Thebes; so also other cities are protected by the bones
of Orpheus, Pelops, Antaeus, Hector, Hesiod, Plato and others.

Now King Roger supported learning of all kinds, but especially
of the Saracens, including their secret lore; and he was acquainted
with many scholars and professors. Therefore he sent Ludowicus,
an English scholar of the Stoic school, who had exiled himself
to Apulia [the Norman kingdom of Sicily], to obtain Vergilius'
bones through trickery. For this philosopher had told him that
after many vigils and fasts he could locate Vergilius' bones, which
he wanted to take to France. Therefore King Roger gave him a
letter granting permission to seek the bones.

Indeed, through his secret arts Ludowicus quickly found the
bones in a grave mound in the midst of a mountain near the
city.[11] Beneath Vergilius' skull he found a book, the master's *Ars
notaria*, as well as other secrets [*alia arcana*]. When Ludowicus
had taken these things from the tomb, the Neapolitan people
became frightened that the city would suffer some disaster, so
Sergius, the *magister militum* [Duke Sergius VII], gathered a great
number of people and, in spite of Roger's plotting, they took
the bones from the Englishmen.

Then the people put the bones in a leather bag [*culleus*]
and took it to the Castrum Ovi [the Castel dell'Ovo or Castle
of the Egg] and placed them for protection in a wooden ark
[*arcus ligneus*] in the Shrine of the Egg [*Sacellum Ovi*].

30. THE EXULTET IN NAPLES, c.1150

**The Exultet rolls were lavishly illustrated parchment scrolls,
datable from the tenth into the fourteenth centuries, used for
the Holy Saturday candle-lighting liturgy and derived from
both Beneventan and Gallo-Roman traditions. Naples took
its place among many other important centers in the South,
including Benevento, Gaeta, Montecassino, Capua, Salerno
and elsewhere in Campania in their production and use.
While the only attributable Neapolitan example dates from
1334–42, the following, contemporary text describing the**

---

11.   Probably at Virgil's tomb at Piedigrotta.

Fig. 19. *Exultet roll. Naples, Biblioteca Nazionale, 11th c.*

liturgy in Naples, notes that the ceremony dates "from ancient times" there. The Exultet rolls are witness to elaborate liturgies generally presided over by a bishop in a cathedral. Thomas Forrest Kelly dates the Neapolitan Exultet roll, possibly described in the text below, to the twelfth century.[12]

According to Kelly, "in 1337, Archbishop Giovanni Orsini drew up constitutions for the church of Naples, including customs 'which from ancient times have been, and ought to be, observed.' The description of the Holy Saturday rite places the Exultet in the Beneventan position." Kelly's translation (*Exultet*, 140–41) was transcribed from the now-lost original in the seventeenth century by Camillo Tutini (Naples, BN, Bibl. Brancacciana I.F.2).

On Holy Saturday the lord archbishop was accustomed to vest in the chapel of his palace, to which the deacons and cardinal priests should come to put on their copes. The count also, dressed in a cope, and four deacon acolytes in tunics, with the cross, candles, candelabra, thurible and everything else necessary, should assemble in the same chapel.

The said archbishop with all these mentioned goes in procession to the church, using the manner and order as at Christmas, with the addition that at the beginning of the office the lord

---

12. See above, Introduction, pp. xxxv–xxxvi and n. 56.

archbishop, dressed in a purple cope, proceeds to the blessing of new fire by the cimilarch in front of the basilica, and he lights the candle and carries it in his hand to the altar, which he then used to give to the sacristan of the church of Naples; and thus vested, the lord archbishop was accustomed to sit in the seat near the altar, and while he is seated there, twelve lections are to be read; when they are finished, immediately the deacon who reads the Gospel comes and blesses the candle, dressed in a white alb.

The said lord archbishop used to give to the deacon who blesses the candle the rest of the chrism, which he reserved in a vessel on Maundy Thursday. When the candle has been blessed, the said lord archbishop with the whole chapter goes in procession to bless the font, and going and returning the master of the scholars of the choir of Primicerii sings the litany with one colleague, and he used to receive from the lord archbishop one *tarenus* from Amalfi.

31. *FLORIO E BIANCOFIORE*, c.1150

Eastern roots, broad propagation and a popular audience[13] throughout Europe mark the legend of *Florio and Biancofiore*. Born on the same day in the same place to a Christian and a Muslim mother, two young lovers endure a series of tricks, trials, separations and journeys before they are united.

The story itself has certain associations with Naples, but there is also a Neapolitan literary tradition, which may date from as early as the twelfth century. A printed edition of 1481 from Naples provides concrete evidence for such a version, which probably existed in manuscript in the fourteenth century. An oral tradition is thought to be the groundwork for the lost manuscript heritage. Although the Neapolitan printed text is similar to other, particularly Italian, versions, there are nine unique stanzas (out of 38) in the version from Naples. Those stanzas include Biancofiore's complaint to God, Mary and Mary Magdalene

---

13. On *Florio e Biancofiore* and general reading taste, see Maria Bendinelli Predelli, "The Textualization of Early Italian *cantari*, in William Randolph Robins, ed., *Textual Cultures of Medieval Italy* (Toronto: University of Toronto Press, 2011), 145-66, at 147.

when she is about to be executed for serving a poisoned bird to King Felix, Florio's father. The literary tradition of the falsely accused royal woman had a broad European life and may have reappeared as background to the real trials of Queen Giovanna I. See below, Readings 77 and n. 123.

Our text is taken from Antonio Altamura, "Un' ignota redazione del cantaro di *Florio e Biancofiore* (contribuito all storia del *Filocolo*)," *Biblion* 1 (1946–47): 92–133 and translated by Eileen Gardiner.

If Florio knew of my death
neither irons nor chains would hold him,
since my love binds him so forcefully
he'd quickly come to take care of this struggle.
O almighty God, who restrains death,
have mercy on my wretched soul.
I believe Florio must be ill,
since from me he has been called away.

O almighty God, who raised Lazarus
through the mercy of your death-memory,
and Mary Magdalene, comfort
from such great torment,
shake the heart of Florio so that he does not tarry,
that he comes without delay.
If I cannot see him, just a little,
I think I will end up in heaven.

Heavenly queen crowned,
who helps the sinners,
have mercy on this disconsolate one.
Pray for me who is beaten down by difficulty and sorrow:
the seneschal, that false traitor, has denounced me
to the king for a great wrong
and says that I sent that chicken.
Protect me, Virgin Mary. (35.2–4)

The stanzas unique to Naples also elaborate on Florio's combat with the seneschal, who had conspired with the king to slander Biancofiore:

Then the seneschal was thrown
to the ground from his horse
and humbly he began to speak:
"Please, I pray you, O knight,
one last wish: let me live.
Grant that I may be your prisoner
in Greece where you want to send me."
Floria answered: "Fallen knight, be courageous
for I will knock you down."

The seneschal remounted his horse
and started from the field with all his will
like a lion when he is very hungry.
He struck Florio with such force
(he lowered his spear and gave him a blow)
that he knocked him from his good steed.
Florio got to his feet and said meanwhile:
"The gift that I gave you, I demand back from you."

The seneschal, infidel dog,
put his hand on the fervent sword
and said: "No. Why would I not act?
I'll have to take your life."
And so Florio, made wise and understanding,
gave him a good blow in the lists,
cutting his horse's feet out from under him
and the seneschal ended up on his own two feet. [49.2–4]

32. ABÛ 'ABDALLÂH AL-IDRÎSÎ IN CAMPANIA, c.1150

Despite the crusading spirit often cited as driving such works as *Florio e Biancofiore*, travel, trade and the exchange of culture and ideas across the Mediterranean was never interrupted for long throughout the Middle Ages, but became even more easily facilitated with the Norman control of Sicily and southern Italy.[14] Such exchanges continued even in the era of the Crusades, as the selection below attests.

---

14. See above, Introduction, xli–xlvi.

Abû 'Abdallâh al-Idrîsî was an Arab prince, descended from Muhammad and related to the noble families of North Africa. He traveled to Sicily in 1139 and took up a position at the Norman court. He completed his geographical treatise, *The Book of Roger*,[15] some time before the king's death in 1154. In it al-Idrîsî combined earlier geographical treatises with his own travel observations.

In the selection below he describes Naples, the Sorrentine peninsula and the Amalfi coast at the height of their maritime ascendency. Note the author's comments on Naples as a thriving commercial center, on the Bay of Naples as an easily travelled unit, on Vesuvius and on the prosperity of the towns on the Amalfi coast.

These selections are taken from G.A. Loud, *Roger II*, 362–63.

Naples is a beautiful town, ancient, prosperous and filled with busy markets where one may carry out transactions because merchandise, and commodities in general, are abundant. From there to the port of Stabia, which has excellent mooring, deep water and is in a bay, at the mouth of a river that runs year round and whose water is sweet,[16] is thirty [16] miles

Those who wish to travel directly by land to Amalfi must continue for fifteen miles. Between Naples and Stabia one notices the "mountain of fire" [Vesuvius], a mountain that one does not climb because it continually vomits forth fire and stones. Someone who wishes to follow the coast must go from Stabia to Sorrento, which is thirty miles.

Sorrento is built on a cape that juts out into the sea. It is a prosperous town where the houses are good and resources are abundant. It is surrounded by trees. It has a narrow harbor, in which boats cannot winter if they are not beached. Ships are built there. From there to Cape *Râs M.n.tîra* [Punta Campanella] is twelve miles; then to the little port of Positano fifteen, and [thereafter] to the port town of Amalfi eighteen.

Amalfi is a prosperous town and has a harbor. It is fortified on the landward side but is easy to access from the sea. If one

---

15. See Henri Bresc and Annliese Nef, trans. and eds., *Idrîsî: La première géographie de l'Occident* (Paris: Flammarion, 1999).

16. Probably the Sebeto.

attacks it, one will take it. It is ancient and has fine surroundings. Its people are numerous and rich. From there to the river mouth of Vietri, a beautiful place where ships can find anchorage, is ten miles. This river takes its name from a place situated on its upper reaches, which is fortified and only accessible at two points, and where one can find water and wood.

From this river to Salerno, a remarkable town, with well-stocked markets and all sorts of goods, in particular wheat and other cereals, is two miles.

33. BENJAMIN OF TUDELA IN CAMPANIA, c. 1165

The kingdom of Sicily was a natural crossroads in the Mediterranean, attracting exchange not only between North and South, but between East and West. Benjamin was a native of Tudela, in Navarre, perhaps a rabbi, and began his travels 1165 in what may have started as a pilgrimage to the Holy Land. A full century before Marco Polo, Benjamin's itinerary brought him through much of the world then known to Europeans, and to its Jewish communities. From Saragossa he proceeded to France, and then set sail from the port of Marseilles. After visiting Genoa, Pisa and Rome, he travelled south to Naples and the Amalfi coast and then went overland to Apulia. From there he visited Greece and Constantinople, Syria, Lebanon, the Holy Land and northern Mesopotamia (which he called Shinar) before reaching Baghdad. He went next to Persia, then cut back across the Arabian peninsula to Egypt and North Africa, returning to the Iberian peninsula in 1173. In all he visited over 300 cities, including many of importance in Jewish history, such as Susa, Sura and Pumbedita in southern Persia. In addition, he gathered information on many more areas that he heard about on his travels, including China and Tibet.[17]

---

17. There has not been much research on Benjamin of late; but see Joseph Shatzmiller, "Jews, Pilgrimage, and the Christian Cult of Saints: Benjamin of Tudela and His Contemporaries," in Walter A. Goffart and Alexander C. Murray, eds., *After Rome's Fall: Narrators and Sources of Early Medieval History* (Toronto: University of Toronto Press, 1998), 337–47.

While Benjamin concentrates on the Jewish communities he encounters, he does offer very useful observations of Campania, including Capua, Pozzuoli with its famous baths and bradyseismic activity, Naples and further south to the Amalfi coast with its steep and fertile terracing. In stark contrast to al-Idrîsî, Benjamin notes the impregnability of Amalfi. Some of his geographical notes for the region appear muddled, and some of his information seems derived from ancient foundation myths or hearsay, perhaps recorded on the spot from local guides. He miscalculates the length of the ancient tunnels between Pozzuoli and Naples at fifteen miles, for example; whereas the Grotta di Cocceio between Cumae and Pozzuoli measures one kilometer, while the Crypta Napoletana from Fuorigrotta to Mergellina is 700 meters. This may indicate that his itinerary from the Pozzuoli area took him to Naples via the bay and not by land, or perhaps point to a transcription error in his text. Upon his arrival by sea at Naples, he would have disembarked at one of the largest Jewish communities in the region: that around Portanova and the harbor.

Benjamin is clear, however, that Jews served on the faculty of the medical school of Salerno, and he names several physicians by name. One of these, Abraham Narboni, may indeed have come from Narbonne in Languedoc, evidence both of the continued toponym usage for surnames still in effect in the twelfth century and of the easy access of travel and communication along the western Mediterranean littoral during this period. In any case, his testimony of Jewish communities in Campania is invaluable historical evidence.

Our selection is taken from *The Itinerary of Benjamin of Tudela: Critical Text, Translation and Commentary*, Marcus Nathan Adler, ed. (New York: Philipp Feldheim, 1907; rev. ed., Michael A. Signer, Malibu, CA: Joseph Simon Publishers, 1983), 64–66.

From Rome it is four days to Capua, the large town that King Capys built. It is a fine city, but its water is bad, and the country is fever-stricken. About 300 Jews live there, among them great scholars and esteemed persons, at their heads being

Rabbi Conso, his brother Rabbi Israel, Rabbi Zaken and the chief rabbi Rabbi David, since deceased. They call this district the Principality [of Capua].

From there one goes to Pozzuoli, which is called Sorrento the Great, built by Zur, son of Hadadezer, when he fled in fear of David the king. The sea has risen and covered the city from its two sides, and at the present day one can still see the markets and towers that stood in the midst of the city.

A spring issues forth from beneath the ground containing the oil, which is called petroleum. People collect it from the surface of the water and use it medicinally. There are also hotwater springs to the number of about twenty, which issue from the ground and are situated near the sea, and every man who has any disease can go and bathe in them and get cured. All the afflicted of Lombardy [i.e., the interior of the old Lombard duchies] visit it in the summertime for that purpose.[18]

From this place a man can travel fifteen miles along a road under the mountains [probably the Grotta di Cocceio and Crypta Napoletana], a work executed by King Romulus who built the city of Rome. He was prompted to this by fear of King David and Joab his general. He built fortifications both upon the mountains and below the mountains reaching as far as the city of Naples.

Naples is a very strong city, lying upon the sea-board, and was founded by the Greeks. About 500 Jews live here, amongst them Rabbi Hezekiah, Rabbi Shallum, Rabbi Elijah Hacohen and Rabbi Isaac of Har Napus, the chief rabbi of blessed memory.

Thence one proceeds by sea to the city of Salerno, where the Christians have a school of medicine. About 600 Jews dwell there. Among the scholars are Rabbi Judah, son of Rabbi Isaac, the son of Melchizedek, the great rabbi, who came from the city of Siponto; also Rabbi Solomon [the Cohen], Rabbi Elijah the Greek, Rabbi Abraham Narboni and Rabbi Hamon. It is a city with walls upon the land side, the other side bordering on the sea, and there is a very strong castle on the summit of the hill.

Thence it is half a day's journey to Amalfi, where there are about twenty Jews, amongst them Rabbi Hananel, the physician, Rabbi Elisha and Abu-al-gir, the prince. The inhabitants

---

18.   For context, see Martin, "Les bains."

of the place are merchants engaged in trade, who do not sow or reap, because they dwell upon high hills and lofty crags, but buy everything for money. Nevertheless, they have an abundance of fruit, for it is a land of vineyards and olives, of gardens and plantations, and no one can go to war with them.

34. *THE SONG OF ASPREMONT*, c.1190

The Norman expedition from Messina to join the Third Crusade in the spring of 1191 is the probable cause for the composition of the *Song of Aspremont (Chanson d'Aspremont)*. Manuscripts of this work, composed originally in Old French, survive in English, Italian and Old Norse. Probably written in Sicily or Calabria, the action is set on the mountain of Aspromonte in Calabria and exploits the memory of the Muslim invasions of Italy in 813, 846 and 870.[19]

The work belongs to an epic cycle — the *chanson de roi* — that included Charlemagne as a central figure among a multinational cast, transplanting his deeds to a region that he probably never saw. His presence, however, bolsters aspirations for the descendants of the Carolingians in their claims to the South. In the following selection the fictitious Pope Milon himself travels down to Calabria to baptize the captured Saracen queen and her suite of princesses.

Though set in the distant Carolingian past of the *chansons*, the poem appears to reflect the political situation of Sicily and Calabria during the early Norman period, when the Hauteville dukes and their vassals were carving out their new realm from the Muslims. While the mixture of cultures reflected the characters and situations is certainly reflective of the Norman Regno, the courting of the Muslim princess by the Christian knight is typical of the genre.[20]

Our selection is taken from Michael A. Newth, trans. and ed., *The Song of Aspremont: Chanson d'Aspremont* (New York: Garland Publishing, 1989), ll. 10890–11003, pp. 258–60.

---

19. See above, pp. xxx–xxxiii, and Reading 19.

20. See, for example, *Fierabras and Floripas: A French Epic Allegory*, ed. and trans. Michael A.H. Newth (New York: Italica Press, 2010), 214–15.

Before the duke the queen now stands and waits,
While Girart much upon her face does gaze;
He sees how wan her visage is and pale,
Whence with her fast the color has all drained:
"My lord, if you would hear me now," she says,
"Then I shall tell a short and sorry tale;
We are twelve ladies from foreign parts and strange,
Wherein we all have worn a crown of state,
And twenty maidens, the eldest still a babe,
Who crossed the sea and came here for my sake;
When I the wife of Agolant was made,
I was much honored according to our ways;
Yet now I see my pride has proven vain;
Take pity, lord, upon us wretched waifs,
Till we have had the little food we crave,
And at the font have been baptized and raised;
Give me not over to your varlets or knaves."

The duke hears this, then shakes his head and says:
"By this my beard that turns to white with age,
On this account you need not be afraid;
For there is none, so high he sets his blade,
Who should he jostle or push one of these maids
Or even open his mouth to say 'good day,'
Who would not stand more chance of tempting fate
If he had pulled the beard upon my face;
I wish these maids to be such honor paid
As if my father had fathered them the same."

This said, all Girart's men without delay
Vacate the room where the queen is to stay;
Each of those maids goes with her and remains;
They ask for water without one moment's waste;
See now, my lords, so many towels ornate,
So many basins each with its water-chain!
The queen, when she is treated in this way
And has with food her strength somewhat regained,
So that the blood comes to her cheeks again,

To look upon is colored now as gay
As is the rose upon a morn in May,
Whose dewy head is struck by the sun's rays.

When now the queen sits down to eat and dine,
To serve her plate no prompting they require;
Girart acts now like a fine courtly knight,
Who was ere this so fierce, so proud and wild;
Lords, see him now! He stands to his full height,
An olive branch within his hand entwined!
He calls Gamier, his seneschal, aside:
"See that the queen has all that she desires!"
Then he instructs his chief butler alike:
"Make ready for me now my choicest wines,
The best of them that you can fetch and find;
See that the queen is sumptuously supplied!"
"Well granted this, my lord," the man replies,
And does the same, wasting no further time:
"My lady queen, you should regain your pride
And love Lord God and cherish Him likewise,
If by Baptism you may His love acquire."
She says: "I owe great thanks for this much, sire,
And if my prayers proved worthy in His sight
I would not cling to one more day of life."

The pope decides to visit there meanwhile;
He sends a message by means of a young squire
And asks to lodge in Reggio town that night;
The duke strides down before the pope arrives,
And when he does, runs up and clasps him tight;
Of his great tower two thirds he gives Pope Milon;
He says: "Good Pope, I will not try to hide
That I've rushed here to tell you of my prize;
I have here both the emir and his wife!
Within the hall of this great palace high
I've had his corpse placed in a coffin wide;
The severed head I sent to Charles betimes;
He has the head in its steel helmet bright;
I've thirteen queens whom you must now baptize,

And twenty maids whom you with cross must sign!"
"Well granted this, my lord," the pope replies,
"But let it be tomorrow at first light;
I scarcely can stand up, I am so tired."

At break of day, when dawn's first light appears,
The pope makes haste the Holy Mass to hear,
Which is intoned by Archbishop Guimer;
Duke Girart summons the queen of the emir
And asks those girls and maidens all to meet;
He sets large tubs next to the font and near,
Then has fresh water brought to fill them deep;
They ask for oil, for holy salts and cream
And then remove the clothes from all those queens;
Their mantles swapped for simple shirts and sheets,
Downcast and dumb, not one word dare they speak;
In their great fear they scarcely move their feet
To where they see so many folk convened;
They are quite sure that their fate has been sealed;
Yet each can see that there is no retreat;
Will they or not all of those maids proceed;
As they come up the pope surveys them each
And shows Girart what he himself perceives:
"These creatures, sire, whom I see standing here,
Were made by God to serve a lord and keep."
"Indeed," says Girart, "I cannot but agree;
For in no land so far across the sea
Could girls be found as beautiful as these;
If Charlemayn my counsel were to heed,
He'd marry them to men of high degree."

Milon the pope would now proceed at once;
Among the clergy are seven archbishops,
Who will this day the baptism conduct;
With sign of cross they firstly bless each one
And then of each the mantle is undone;
In simple shirts and nothing else dressed up,
That day they plunge and bathe them in those tubs
And raise their souls to Christian favor thus;

This done they change the fair queen's name at once:
She's called Clarence — what honor hence she won;
In her own time no better wife there was —
In clothes and shoes they dress them afterwards.

■

Fig. 20. Emperor Henry VI. Universitätsbibliothek Heidelberg, Cod. Pal. Germ. 848, Große Heidelberger Liederhandschrift (Codex Manesse), fol. 6r. Zürich, c.1300–c.1340.

CHAPTER 4: THE HOHENSTAUFEN

HENRY VI

The Hauteville dynasty ruled the kingdom of Sicily for the next two generations. By the end of the twelfth century and the reign of William II (the Good, 1166–89) the Normans had ties to the most illustrious royal families of Europe, and they took advantage of the system of marriage alliances to insure their status and position in Europe and the Mediterranean. William was making plans to lead the Third Crusade when he died suddenly, and childless, in Palermo on November 18, 1189. His claims to the throne were immediately assumed by Emperor Henry VI Hohenstaufen, the husband of William's aunt Constance, his declared heir.

While William had made the Norman barons swear their fealty to Constance, the Neapolitans joined many other southerners in siding with William's nephew, Tancred of Lecce, against the Hohenstaufen claim. Tancred had offered Naples substantial concessions, recognized what appear to have been already existing rights to a consular government, its own mint, courts, trade and financial controls. In April 1191, Naples fought off a three-month siege by Henry VI; but with Tancred's death, the city finally surrendered to the emperor on August 23, 1194. In revenge for Naples' resistance, imperial troops under Chancellor Conrad of Querfurt entirely destroyed the walls of the city.

35. HENRY VI INVADES THE REGNO, 1191

Sources for the period include narrative accounts, mirabilian literature and poetry, legal texts and commercial contracts. Our selection here is taken from the translation by G.A. Loud, *The Chronicle of Richard of S. Germano, 1189–1207*. According to Loud, "This chronicle, which in its final form covers the years from the death of King William II of Sicily in 1189 until 1243, is the most important narrative

source for the history of southern Italy under the rule of the Staufen emperors. Its author, Richard, was active as a notary at S. Germano (renamed Cassino in 1863), the town at the foot of Montecassino subject to the abbey of that name, from February 1186 until March 1232."[1] Our text has been translated from the standard edition, *Ryccardi di Sancto Germano Notarii Chronicon*, C.A. Garufi, ed., 2nd. ed. (Bologna: RIS, 1938), 3-25.

Fig. 21. *The Coronation of Henry VI. From Peter of Eboli, Liber ad honorem Augusti.*

(1191) ...King Henry [VI] came to Rome with his wife Constance, to whom the kingdom of Sicily belonged by hereditary right. Pope Celestine [III, 1191–98] crowned him as emperor and his wife as empress at St. Peter's. Tusculum was given by the emperor to the Romans, who raised it to the ground.

Then in the month of May, the emperor entered the Regno, despite the pope's prohibition, and came through Campania to Rocca d'Arce, which Matthew Borrellus held for the king; his soldiers attacked and stormed it. Because of this the men of S. Germano took refuge in [Monte] Cassino with their goods and sent envoys through whom they swore fealty to the emperor. At that time Abbot Roffred of Cassino lay seriously ill at the

Fig. 22. *Henry VI arrives in the Regno. From Peter of Eboli, Liber ad honorem Augusti.*

---

1.   Leeds Medieval History Texts in Translation Website (Leeds: University of Leeds, 2002) at http://www.leeds.ac.uk/arts/downloads/file/1123/the_chronicle_ of_richard_of_s_germano_1189-99, p. 1.

monastery. On the urging of the men of S. Germano, he went to the emperor to swear [fealty]. Sora, Atina and Castrocielo surrendered in fear to the emperor, and in them he placed castellans. Then the counts of Fondi and Molise did fealty to him, and marching into the Terra di Lavoro, Teano, Aversa and Capua surrendered to him.

He welcomed Count William of Caserta, and after Aversa he went to Naples, to which he laid siege, joined by the said counts and barons of the principality, as well as the abbot of Montecassino with his troops. To oppose him the count of Acerra took refuge within the city and energetically defended it for the king [Tancred]. Next

Fig. 23. Henry VI besieges Naples. From Peter of Eboli, Liber ad honorem Augusti.

the city of Salerno surrendered to the emperor, and he sent his wife the empress [Constance] to stay there while he repeatedly attacked and harried the city of Naples. But when, with neither his men nor their efforts making any headway, he was stricken by illness, he retired from there, albeit unwillingly. He left the empress, his wife, at Salerno and stationed Muscancervello [Conrad of Lutzelnhard] in the citadel of Capua. He came to S. Germano with his army much weakened, and the whole convent of Montecassino swore fealty to him. He then took the abbot away with him to Germany. For greater security he left the latter's brother Gregory as a hostage with the duke of Spoleto and seized some of the leading men from the land of S. Germano as hostages, whom he left with a German called Diepold in Rocca d'Arce. He left the latter and Conrad of Marlenheim at Sora as castellans and then retired from the Regno through the land of Count Peter of Celano, who was loyal to him, and returned to Germany in September.

Then the count of Acerra, whom I have mentioned, sortied from Naples with the Neapolitans and other troops, recruited from many other places, and came to Capua and besieged the citadel, which Muscancervello held for the emperor. Since the latter was not sufficiently supplied with food, he came to an agreement with the count, surrendered himself and the castle, and departed with a safe conduct for wherever he wished to go. The count then recovered Aversa, Teano and S. Germano for the king's [Tancred's] authority, and coming to Cassino entered the monastery's walls without opposition. He had a friendly enough discussion with Atenulf of Caserta, dean of Montecassino, to persuade him to join in fealty to the king. But when he was unable to obtain this from him, either through entreaties or promises, he descended from that place and departed. Then he was joined by the count of Molise and placed as large a garrison as he could in S. Germano and Sant'Angelo in Theodice, and set off [once again] in the service of the king, his brother-in-law.

Count Richard of Fondi was afraid because he had bought Suessa and Teano from the emperor. He abandoned his county and retreated into the Campania, and the county of Fondi was granted by the king to a certain brother of Aligern Cotrone of Naples. Atenulf of Caserta, the dean of Montecassino, was excommunicated by Pope Celestine [III] for not joining the king's party, and the monastery placed under an interdict.

Fig. 24. Empress Constance besieged. From Peter of Eboli, Liber ad honorem Augusti.

The Salernitans detained the empress [Constance] and sent her to the king in Sicily so that they might secure King Tancred's favour. The king received her honourably, loaded her with presents and sent her back to the emperor in Germany. In that year Paganus, lord of Casalvieri, treacherously killed the Germans who had been left by the emperor in Atina, and a certain Roger de Foresta was sent by the king to Atina.

(1194) After preparing his fleet and land army, Emperor Henry entered the kingdom. Abbot Roffred of Montecassino gave him a magnificent reception. The count of Fondi and all the other Germans and Italians were waiting

for his arrival; with them he invaded the Terra di Lavoro, took Naples, captured Salerno, which resisted him, by storm and gave it to his men to plunder and sack.…

(1196) …At that time Count Richard of Acerra wanted to flee from the emperor and leave the kingdom in secret. He abandoned Campania and Burgentia, the fortresses which he was [still] holding, but was betrayed by a certain white monk in whom he trusted, captured by Diepold and thrown into prison to await the emperor. The latter sent the bishop of Worms[2] from Germany to be his representative in the kingdom, who,

Fig. 25. Henry VI prepares his fleet. From Peter of Eboli, Liber ad honorem Augusti.

coming to Naples with the abbot of Cassino and other Italians and Germans and fulfilling imperial orders, had the walls of Naples and Capua razed to the ground.…

36. PETER OF EBOLI, *THE BATHS OF POZZUOLI*, c.1195–1220

Peter of Eboli (Pietro da Eboli), historian, biographer and naturalist, was born after 1150 in Campania and was probably a monk at Montecassino, although he apparently spent a considerable part of his life in Sicily. Peter wrote a verse chronicle for Emperor Henry VI, the *Liber ad honorem Augusti* or *De rebus Siculis carmen*, c.1195–97.[3] Peter is best known for his *De balneis Puteolanis*,[4] an illustrated Latin poem on the

---

2.   Conrad of Querfurt, then bishop of Hildesheim and imperial chancellor. See Reading 37 below.

3.   It survives in a unique manuscript: Bern, Burgerbibliothek, Cod. 120.

4.   For a good introduction see Claus Michael Kauffmann, *The Baths of Pozzuoli: A Study of the Medieval Illuminations of Peter of Eboli's Poem* (Oxford: B. Cassirer,

medicinal benefits of springs, formed from local reports and probably first-hand experience of the curing quality of each bath at Pozzuoli. The work was presented to Frederick II, who had made nearby Naples one of his capitals and presumably enjoyed the waters at Pozzuoli and at Baiae, as had the ancient Roman and more recent Carolingian emperors. Peter died c.1220.

The work survives in several manuscripts, including two from the mid-fourteenth century Angevin court at Naples.[5] Our selection is taken from Erasmo Pèrcopo, *I bagni di Pozzuoli* (Naples: F. Furchheim, 1887) and is translated by Eileen Gardiner.

Fig. 26 (L) 27 (R) La Solfatara, Peter of Eboli, De balneis puteolanis. *L: Rome, MS Angelica 1474, fol. 4r. R: Cologny, Foundation Martin Bodmer, Cod. Bodmer 135, fol. 3r.*

1959). See also Giuseppe Zampino, Filomena Sardella, et al., *Le terme Puteolane e Salerno nei codici miniati di Petro da Eboli* (Naples: Casa Editrice Fausto Fiorentino, 1995), which analyzes Rome, Biblioteca Angelica MS 1474. E-Codices also hosts an online version of a MS probably produced in Naples c.1350–70. See Cologny, Fondation Martin Bodmer, Cod. Bodmer 135 at http://www.e-codices.unifr.ch/en/list/one/cb/0135.

5.   The Cologny MS cited in Fig. 26 and n. 2; and Paris, Bibliothèque nationale de France, MS Latin 816.

There is a bath named Solfatara. This bath calms the nerves, cleanses the kidneys and soothes debilitated members, and it is very useful for helping sterile women become pregnant. It relieves every weakness brought about by a headache, controls the tears and expels vomit and makes the eyes stronger. It dissolves phlegm and relieves fever, which comes from the cold, and especially if the person is first purged before the bath. This bath has a horrid odor, not on account of the water, but you will love the effects of its character.

Peter ends his book on the baths by mentioning his other works, the second of which is now lost:

Sun of the World, pick up this little book I offer you:
This is the third of the three to reach my Lord.
The first contains our national victories in civil war;
The second contains the remarkable deeds of Frederick;
This third sets in order the waters of the Euboean colony,[6]
Their locations, their powers and their almost buried names.

37. CONRAD OF QUERFURT DESCRIBES NAPLES, C.1196

Conrad of Querfurt was born c.1160, the son of Burchard II, burggraf of Magdeburg. He was educated at the cathedral school of Hildesheim and then studied in Paris under Lothair of Segni, later Pope Innocent III. He was appointed to the cathedral of Magdeburg in 1182. In 1188 Conrad became a member of the royal chapel and pastor at the imperial palace at Goslar. In 1190 he became provost at Magdeburg and in 1194 at Aachen.

Conrad served as bishop of Hildesheim (1194–99) and bishop of Würzburg (1198–1202). He accompanied Emperor Henry VI on his Italian campaign of 1191 and then served as imperial chancellor from 1194 to 1200. Conrad was a man of deep learning, with a wide circle of European colleagues. At his instigation Peter of Eboli composed his *Liber ad honorem Augusti sive de rebus Siculis*. Conrad's inquiring mind and classical training made him

---

6.   Puteoli (Pozzuoli) was first settled by Greeks, not from Euboea but from Samos, in 530 BCE.

eager to learn the ancient (or more recently invented) stories of Virgil and of Naples' past. He died in 1202.

The source of the following reading is Conrad's letter to Hartbert, prior of Hildesheim, written shortly after Conrad's arrival in Naples. Conrad's letter takes its place in a long tradition of literary descriptions of Naples and of the miraculous work of Virgil there. Among his antecedents are John of Salisbury and Alexander of Neckham,[7] and after him Gervaise of Tilbury, Vincent of Beauvais, the *Cronaca di Partenope*, Petrarch and Boccaccio, among many others. Conrad was also writing in the new twelfth-century genre of mirabilian literature, describing the wonders and deep cultural memories held by the citizens of various ancient cities. Perhaps the most famous example of this literature is the *Mirabilia urbis Romae, the Marvels of Rome*.[8]

Conrad was also a powerful and apparently hard-headed official of the German emperor and had been entrusted by Henry VI to destroy Naples' famed walls. Historians have therefore wondered why he appears so gullible in accepting many of the legends recorded here. On the one hand, one ought not to approach such texts from a modern "scientific" perspective: Conrad was a man of his times and was open to all the information that could be provided from his classical sources, from the cultural memory passed down for centuries around the Bay of Naples and from his own personal observations and the reports from his entourage. In his story of the snakes (perhaps borrowed from the medieval legend of Pope Sylvester and the buried dragon of Rome), Conrad does make note of the many underground cisterns and water tunnels that honeycomb Naples' tufa platform to this day and, in his story of Monte Barbaro, of the ancient underground works by Lucius Cocceius Auctus in the Campi Flegrei.

On the other hand, the archbishop appears to be writing with a bit of tongue-in-cheek: his very light irony about the

---

7. See Reading 29.

8. The two best-known versions are Benedict of St. Peter's *The Marvels of Rome (Mirabilia Urbis Romae)*, Francis Morgan Nichols, ed.; rev. ed., Eileen Gardiner (New York: Italica Press, 1986); and Magister Gregorius, *The Marvels of Rome*, John Osborne, ed. and trans. (Toronto: Pontifical Institute of Mediaeval Studies, 1987).

crack in Naples' palladium or his dry retelling of the story of the bronze archer are only two examples of a letter-writing art that leaves much to his correspondent's sense of humor, intelligence and high culture. He would not be the last visitor to record the tales of his Neapolitan guides with a straight face. Conrad was also, no doubt, highly aware of the cultural sensibilities of a proud city that had only just recently been conquered after nearly a millennium of virtual autonomy. He himself had been ordered to destroy its walls, and he reports the fact without any pride and with a very full sense of the city's long cultural and political history.[9]

The letter was included in the *Chronica Slavorum* of Arnold of Lübeck (d. c.1214). The Latin text was edited by I.M. Lappenberg in *Scriptores Rerum Germanicarum 14*, Georg Heinrich Pertz, ed. (Hannover: Hahn, 1868), book V.19, pp. 174–83. Translation by R.G. Musto.

We also saw the industrious work of Virgil at Naples, of which the judgments of the three Fates were miraculously dispensed upon us, so that the walls of this city, that so great a philosopher had founded and raised up, we were ordered to destroy at the emperor's command. It did not benefit the citizens of that city that its image [the palladium] was encased with magical arts by that same Virgil in a crystal ampulla with the most artful gold work. The Neapolitans held the greatest faith in its integrity, believing that as long as that ampulla remained whole, the city could not suffer any harm. But we now hold that city and that same ampulla in our power, and we also destroyed its walls. Yet the ampulla remains undamaged. But perhaps the city has suffered harm because the ampulla might be slightly cracked.

In the same city there is a horse constructed by the magic incantations of Virgil in such a manner that, as long as it remains whole, no horse can develop swayback. Perhaps this

---

9.   For analyses of the legends around Virgil and Naples, see Jan M. Ziolkowski and Michael C.J. Putnam, eds., *The Virgilian Tradition: The First Fifteen Hundred Years* (New Haven: Yale University Press, 2008); Domenico Comparetti, E.F.M. Benecke, and Jan M. Ziolkowski, *Vergil in the Middle Ages* (Princeton: Princeton University Press, 1997); and John W. Spargo, *Virgil the Necromancer: Studies in Virgilian Legends* (Cambridge: Harvard University Press, 1934).

happens from some natural defect native to that land, so that before the construction of that horse and until the corruption of that horse, however minor, no one was able to sit on a horse's back without fracturing it.

Also there is a most powerful gate built in the image of a castle. It has bronze doors, which the imperial guard now holds and onto which Virgil built a bronze fly. As long as that fly remained intact, not a single real fly could enter the city.

The bones of Virgil are also there in a castle, at the rim of the city with the sea all around [the Castel dell'Ovo]. If these bones are left exposed to the open air, the sky grows dark, and without warning the sea rises up from its depths, boils up and swells, surging with the crashing of the tempest. We ourselves saw and experienced this.

Nearby is Baiae, which many authors have commemorated. It includes the baths of Virgil, useful against the various passions of the body. Among these baths is the largest and principal one, in which there are images,[10] today eaten away by long age, demonstrating the various passions of the body appropriate to each body part. There are other images in each bath illustrating the results of each of the passions. Also there is the palace of Sybilla [the queen of William II or a confusion with Cumae?], built with painstaking construction, in which are the baths that nowadays are called the Baths of Sybilla....

We also recall that at Naples there is a gate, called the Iron Gate, behind which Virgil closed up all the serpents of the region. Because of the numerous subterranean buildings and crypts, they multiplied. This gate we fear exceptionally among the many other gates, lest the serpents closed up there escape their prison and molest the land and its inhabitants.

Also in the same city there is a market, likewise constructed by Virgil, so that animals slaughtered in it remain fresh and unspoiled for six weeks, but if the meat is exported from there it becomes fetid and looks putrefied.

Outside this city is Mount Veseus [Vesuvius], from which fire, hurling out many stinking ashes, usually erupts once every ten years. [As protection] against this mountain, Virgil set up a man of bronze holding a drawn bow with an arrow set in the string.

---

10.   It is unclear whether the author is referring to sculpture, mosaics, frescos or all of these forms. Ancient Baiae was known as a center of sculptural production.

Now a certain rustic wondered why the man of bronze always threatened to shoot, but never released, the arrow. And so he pulled the string. The arrow went hurling forward and struck the crater of the volcano. Flames shot out without stop, so that to this day certain areas around the mountain are uninhabitable.

Off the same city of Naples is an island, which is called Iscla [Ischia] in the local language, on which fire and sulfurous fumes vomited out continuously so that little by little they ate up a castle that was nearby, as well as its rocks and its cliffs, with the result that all traces of the castle have disappeared.

There also people firmly assert is a mouth of hell, and there they say are the places of punishment. [Lago d'Averno in the Campi Flegrei.] There also legend says Aeneas descended into hell. Around the same spot on any Saturday, around the ninth hour, appear winged creatures in a certain valley made foul by black and sulfurous fumes. There these creatures rest all day Sunday, but at vespers they return back down amid great wailing and sorrow. And they never return until the next Saturday, and then they descend into the burning lake. Some people say that these are afflicted souls or demons.

There is also Monte Barbaro [above Pozzuoli], which we approached along a subterranean road right through the middle of the highest mountain, in the midst of infernal shadows, as if we were about to descend into hell. On this mountain, in the heart of other mountains, there are many palaces and estates, as in a very great city, and there are underground rivers and boiling underground waters, which some of our entourage saw, and these flow underground for the length of almost two miles. There too some say lie buried the treasures of the seven kings [of Apoc. 17:9–10], whom demons keep shut up inside bronze effigies, which hold out various terrifying images, some with bows taut, some with swords, some with other threatening weapons. We saw these and many other things, of which we cannot now recollect the details.

Fig. 28. Emperor Frederick II. From De arte venandi cum avibus. *13th c. Vatican City, BAV, MS Pal. Lat. 1071, fol. 1v.*

FREDERICK II

Frederick II (1194–1250)[11] was the son of Emperor Henry VI (d.1197) of Germany and of Constance, the daughter of Roger II and the heiress of the Norman kingdom of Sicily. Frederick thus inherited not only the imperial lands of Germany, imperial Burgundy and northern Italy but the entire south of Italy from Sicily to the borders of the papal states. In addition Frederick inherited the title of "king of Jerusalem" through his marriage in 1225 with Yolande of Jerusalem, the heiress of the Latin crusader king John of Brienne. The title would become a prestigious inheritance of the rulers of Naples from then on.

When Constance died in 1198, Frederick was left an orphan and was entrusted to the care of his feudal suzerain for the kingdom of Sicily, the pope himself. Raised in Sicily, he received an excellent education both in the classical tradition and in the arts of statecraft.

Crowned king of Germany in 1215 and emperor in 1220 through the influence of the pope, he soon established his independence, much to the chagrin of the papacy, which now found itself caught between the twin pincers of a revived imperial power to its north and south. Frederick was a German emperor in name, but he preferred his Italian holdings and centered his court at his mother's ancestral capital of Palermo. There he established a brilliant court that combined the cultures and learning of its Latin, Byzantine, Islamic and Jewish traditions. His prodigious learning and his early record of political achievements soon earned him the title of *stupor mundi*, "the wonder of the world." He was literate in six languages: Latin, Sicilian, German, French, Greek and Arabic; and his command of both contemporary literature and science

---

11. For good introductions see Abulafia, *Frederick II*; idem, "The Kingdom of Sicily under Hohenstaufen and Angevin Rule," *New Cambridge Medieval History*. Vol. 5, *c.1198–c.1300*, ed. David Abulafia (Cambridge: Cambridge University Press, 1999), 497–524; William Tronzo, ed., *Intellectual Life at the Court of Frederick II Hohenstaufen* (Washington, DC: National Gallery of Art, 1994); and Giovanni Vitolo, "L'età svevo-angioina," in Carratelli, 87–144.

were legendary. He was the author of the *De arte venandi cum avibus (The Art of Falconry)*.

His importance for the history of Naples was on several fronts: he established a unified and forward-looking state based on Roman law that attempted to normalize all the diverse territorial and feudal customs of his realms in southern Italy. These were enshrined in his Constitutions of Melfi *(Liber Augustalis)* in 1231. He also decided that his rivalry with the growing power of the papacy required his presence closer to the papal states on the Italian mainland. He therefore established Naples as an alternate capital, refortified it and helped establish it as a cultural and an economic center.

38. THE LIFE OF FREDERICK II, FROM GIOVANNI VILLANI, 1220

Giovanni Villani (c.1280–1348) was born into a prosperous Florentine merchant family.[12] He was inspired to write his *Cronica* after visiting Rome for the Jubilee of 1300 and taking in the city's ancient remains. His work was composed in Italian

and derives from a long tradition of medieval writing, recording a ongoing narrative from antiquity to the author's own time on a year-by-year basis, becoming more detailed and less derivative of other sources and full of local memory and legend as events approached Villani's own period.

Fig. 29. Empress Constance gives birth to Frederick II. Giovanni Villani, Cronica. Vatican City, BAV, MS Chigi L. VIII.296 (cat. XI.8).

---

12. For a recent introduction to the Villani and their work, see Paula Clarke, "The Villani Chronicles," in *Chronicling History: Chroniclers and Historians in Medieval and Renaissance Italy,* Sharon Dale, Alison Williams Lewin and Duane J. Osheim, eds. (University Park: Pennsylvania State University Press, 2007), 113–43.

Villani supplemented his annals with many rich details of politics, religion and natural phenomenon. He died during the first outbreak of the Black Death in Florence in 1348. His work was continued by his brother Matteo (d.1363) and Matteo's son Filippo, who brought the work up to 1364. Together they form one of the most important and reliable narrative sources that we possess for late medieval Italy.

In the following passages Villani reflects the ambiguous attitudes of late medieval Italians toward Frederick II and his legacy. Villani loathed the emperor's reputed impieties and persecutions of the Church and its Guelf[13] allies in Italy (including Florence) but also admired his learning, his cosmopolitanism and his commanding political and military genius.

The following readings are taken from *Selections from the First Nine Books of the* Croniche Fiorentine, trans. Rose E. Selfe, Philip H. Wicksteed, ed. (London: Archibald Constable, 1906). We have modernized some usage and spellings from Selfe's deliberately archaizing style.

BOOK VI

1. In the year of Christ 1220, on the day of St. Cecilia in November [22], there was crowned and consecrated emperor at Rome Frederick II, king of Sicily, son of Emperor Henry of Swabia, and of Empress Constance, by Pope Honorius III, with great honor. In the beginning he was a friend of the Church, and well might he be, so many benefits and favors had he received from the Church, for through the Church his father Henry had for wife Constance, queen of Sicily, and for dowry the said realm, and the kingdom of Apulia [later of Naples]; and when his father was dead, he being left a little child, was cared for and guarded by the Church as by a mother, and also his kingdom was defended, and he was elected king of the Romans against Emperor Otto IV, and he was afterwards crowned emperor, as aforesaid. But he, son of ingratitude that he was, not acknowledging Holy Church as

---

13. From *Guelfo*, an Italian form of Welf, the family of the dukes of Bavaria and German rivals to the Hohenstaufen, who used the name Waiblingen (Italianized as *Ghibellino*, our Ghibelline), the name of one of their castles, as their battle cry.

a mother, but as a hostile stepmother, in all things was her enemy and persecutor, he and his sons, almost more than his forefathers, as hereafter we shall make mention.

This Frederick reigned thirty years as emperor and was a man of great capacity and of great valor, wise in books, and of natural intelligence, universal in all things; was acquainted with the Latin tongue and with our vernacular, with German and French, Greek and Arabic, of abounding talents, liberal and courteous in giving, courageous and prudent in arms, and was much feared. And he was dissolute and licentious after divers fashions and had many concubines and catamites, after the manner of the Saracens, and he sought indulgence in all bodily pleasures and led an epicurean life, not taking account that there were ever another life; and this was one chief cause why he became the enemy of the clergy and of Holy Church. And the other was his greed in taking and occupying the lands of Holy Church, to squander them evilly. And many monasteries and churches he destroyed in his kingdom of Sicily and Apulia, and throughout all Italy, and this, either through his own vices and defects, or by reason of the rulers of Holy Church who could not or would not deal with him, nor be content that he should have the imperial rights, wherefore he subdued and smote Holy Church; or because that God permitted it as a divine judgment, because the rulers of the Church had been the means through whom he became the child of the holy nun, Constance, they not remembering the persecutions which Henry, his father, and Frederick, his grandfather, had caused Holy Church to endure.

This Frederick did many noteworthy things in his time, and raised in all the chief cities of Sicily and of Apulia, strong and rich fortresses, which are still standing, and built the fortress of [Castel] Capuano in Naples[14] and the towers and gate upon the bridge over the river of Volturno at Capua, which are very marvelous; and he made the park for sport on the marsh of Foggia in Apulia, and made the hunting park near Gravina and Amalfi in the mountains. In winter he abode at Foggia, and in summer in the mountains for the delights of the chase. And many other noteworthy things he caused to be made, as the castle of Prato and the fortress of S. Miniato, and many

---

14. Actually begun under the Normans. See above, p. xlvii.

other things, as we shall make mention hereafter. And by his first wife he had two sons, Henry and Conrad, whom he caused each one during his lifetime to be elected king of the Romans; and by the daughter of King John of Jerusalem he had King Giordano, and by others he had King Frederick (from whom are descended the lineage of those who are called of Antioch), King Enzo and King Manfred, who were great enemies to Holy Church; and during his life he and his sons lived and ruled with much earthly splendor; but in the end he and his sons because of their sins came to an ill end, and their line was extinguished, as we shall make mention hereafter.

14. HOW EMPEROR FREDERICK CAME TO ENMITY WITH THE CHURCH

After that Frederick II was crowned by Pope Honorius, as we have aforesaid, in the beginning he was the friend of the Church, but a little time after, through his pride and avarice, he began to usurp the rights of the Church throughout all his empire, and in the realm of Sicily and Apulia, appointing bishops and archbishops and other prelates, and driving away those sent by the pope, and raising imposts and taxes from the clergy, doing shame to Holy Church; for which thing by the said Pope Honorius, who had crowned him, he was cited and admonished that he should leave to Holy Church her rights and render the dues. But the emperor perceived himself to be great in power and estate, alike through the force of the Germans and through that of the realm of Sicily, and that he was lord over sea and land and was feared by all the rulers of Christendom and also by the Saracens and was buttressed around by the sons whom he had of his first wife, daughter of the landgrave of Germany, to wit Henry and Conrad, whom Henry he had caused to be crowned in Germany king of the Romans, and Conrad was duke of Swabia, and Frederick of Antioch, his first natural son, he made king, and Enzo, his natural son, was king of Sardinia, and Manfred prince of Taranto; wherefore he would not yield obedience to the Church, but rather was he obstinate, living after the fashion of the world, in all bodily delights.

For which thing by the said Pope Honorius he was excommunicated the year of Christ 1220 and did not for that reason cease from persecuting the Church, but so much the more usurped its rights, and so remained the enemy of the Church and of Pope Honorius as long as he lived. This pope passed from this life the year of Christ 1226, and after him was made Pope Gregory IX, born at Alagna [Anagni] in the Campania, who reigned as pope fourteen years and who had a great war with Emperor Frederick, because the emperor would in no wise relinquish the rights and jurisdiction of Holy Church, but rather the more usurped them; and many churches of the kingdom he caused to be pulled down and deserted, laying heavy imposts upon the clergy and the churches; and whereas there were certain Saracens in the mountains of Trapali in Sicily, the emperor — that he might be the more secure in the island and might keep them at a distance from the Saracens of Barbary, and also to the end that by them he might keep in fear his subjects in Apulia — by wit and promises drew them from those mountains and put them in Apulia in an ancient deserted city, which of old was in league with the Romans, and was destroyed by the Samnites, to wit by those of Benevento, which city was then called Lucera[15] and now is called Nocera, and they were more than 20,000 men-at-arms; and that city they rebuilt very strong; and they often overran the places of Apulia to lay them waste. And when the said Emperor Frederick was at war with the Church, he caused them to come into the duchy of Spoleto and besieged at that time the city of Assisi and did great harm to Holy Church; for which the said Pope Gregory confirmed against him the sentence given by Pope Honorius his predecessor, and again gave sentence of excommunication against him, the year of 1230.

22. How the emperor laid hold of King Henry, his son

In these same times (albeit it had begun before) Henry Sciancato [the Lame], the first-born of the said Emperor Frederick, who had had him chosen king of the Romans by the electors of Germany as aforesaid, perceiving that

---

15. For the colony's history, see Julie Taylor, *Muslims in Medieval Italy: The Colony at Lucera* (Lanham, MD: Lexington Books, 2005); and her "Muslim–Christian Relations in Medieval Southern Italy," *The Muslim World* 97.2 (2007): 190–99.

the emperor his father was doing all he might against Holy Church and feeling the same heavy upon his conscience, time and again reproved his father, for that he was doing ill; whereat the emperor set himself against him, and neither loving him nor dealing with him as with a son, raised up false accusers who testified that the said Henry had it in his mind to rebel against him as concerning his empire, at the request of the Church. On which plea (were it true or false), he seized his said son, King Henry, and two sons of his, little lads, and sent them into Apulia, into prison severally; and there he put him to death by starvation in great torment, and afterward Manfred put his sons to death. The emperor sent to Germany, and again had Conrad, his second son, elected king of the Romans in succession to himself; and this was the year of Christ 1236. Then after a certain time the emperor put out the eyes of that wise man Master Pietro della Vigna, the famous poet,[16] accusing him of treason, but this came about through envy of his great estate. And thereon the said M. Piero soon suffered himself to die of grief in prison, and there were those who said that he himself took away his own life.

23. How the war began between Pope Innocent IV and Emperor Frederick

1241. It came to pass afterwards, as it pleased God, that there was elected pope Messer Ottobuono dal Fiesco, of the counts of Lavagna of Genoa, who was cardinal and was made pope as being the greatest friend and confidant whom Emperor Frederick had in Holy Church, to the end there might be peace between the Church and him; and he was called Pope Innocent IV, and this was the year of Christ 1241, and he reigned as pope eleven years, and added to the Church many cardinals from divers countries of Christendom. And when he was elected pope, the tidings were brought to Emperor Frederick with great rejoicing, knowing that he was his great friend and protector. But the emperor, when he heard it, was greatly disturbed, whence his barons marveled much, and he said: "Marvel not, for this election will be of much hurt to us, for he was our friend when cardinal,

---

16. See below, Reading 40.

and now he will be our enemy as pope." So it came to pass, for when the said pope was consecrated, he demanded back from the emperor the lands and jurisdictions that he held of the Church, as to which request the emperor held him some time in treaty as to an agreement, but all was vanity and deception. In the end, the said pope seeing himself to have been led about by deceitful words, to the hurt and shame of himself and of Holy Church, became more an enemy of Emperor Frederick than his predecessors had been; and seeing that the power of the emperor was so great that he ruled tyrannously over almost the whole of Italy and that the roads were all taken and guarded by his guards so that none could come to the court of Rome without his will and license, the said pope seeing himself in the said manner thus besieged, sent secret orders to his kinsfolk at Genoa and caused twenty galleys to be armed and straightway caused them to come to Rome and thereupon embarked with all his cardinals and with all his court and immediately caused himself to be conveyed to his city of Genoa without any opposition. Having tarried some time in Genoa, he came to Lyons on the Rhône, by way of Provence; and this was the year of Christ 1241.

24. OF THE SENTENCE THAT POPE INNOCENT PRONOUNCED AT THE COUNCIL OF LYONS-ON-RHÔNE UPON EMPEROR FREDERICK, 1245

When Pope Innocent was at Lyons, he called a general council in the said place and invited from throughout the whole world bishops and archbishops and other prelates, who all came thither; and there came to see him as far as the monastery of Cluny in Burgundy the good King Louis of France, and afterwards he came as far as to the council at Lyons, where he offered himself and his realm to the service of the said pope and of Holy Church against Emperor Frederick and against all the enemies of Holy Church; and then he took the cross to go over seas. And when King Louis was gone, the pope enacted sundry things in the said council to the good of Christendom and canonized sundry saints, as the *Martinian Chronicle*[17]

---

17. According to Pierre Bayle, *A General Dictionary, Historical and Critical*, John Peter Bernard et al., trans. (London: James Bettenham, 1739), 8:459, this refers to the chronicle of Martinus Carsulanis, a contemporary of Pope John XXII.

makes mention where it treats of him. And this done, the pope summoned the said Frederick to the said council, as to a neutral place, to excuse himself of thirteen articles proved against him of things done against the faith of Christ, and against Holy Church. The emperor would not appear there but sent his ambassadors and representatives — the bishop of Freiburg in Germany and Brother Hugh, master of the mansion of S. Mary of the Germans, and the wise clerk and Messer Pietro della Vigna of the kingdom, who, making excuses for the emperor that he was not able to come by reason of sickness and suffering in his person, prayed the said pope and his brethren to pardon him and averred that he would cry the pope mercy and would restore that which he had seized of the Church; and they offered, if the pope would pardon him, that he would bind himself so to frame it that within one year the soldan of the Saracens should render up to his command the Holy Land over seas. And the said pope, hearing the endless excuses and vain offers of the emperor, demanded of the said ambassadors if they had an authentic mandate for this, whereon they produced a full authorization, under the golden seal of the said emperor, to promise and undertake it all. And when the pope had it in his hand, in full council, the said ambassadors being present, he denounced Frederick on all the said thirteen criminal articles, and to confirm it said: "Judge, faithful Christians, whether Frederick betrays Holy Church and all Christendom or no: for according to his mandate he offers within one year to make the soldan restore the Holy Land, very clearly showing that the soldan holds it for him, to the shame of all Christians." And this said and declared, he caused the process against the said emperor to be published and condemned him and excommunicated him as a heretic and persecutor of Holy Church, laying to his charge many foul crimes proved against him; and he deprived him of the lordship of the empire and of the realm of Sicily and of that of Jerusalem, absolving from all fealty and oaths all his barons and subjects, excommunicating whoever should obey him or should give him aid or favor, or further should call him emperor or king. And the said sentence was passed at the said council at Lyons on the Rhône, the year of Christ 1245, the 17th of July....

25. HOW THE POPE AND THE CHURCH CAUSED A NEW EMPEROR TO BE
ELECTED IN PLACE OF FREDERICK, THE DEPOSED EMPEROR

The said Frederick being deposed and condemned, as has
been aforesaid, the pope sent word to the electors of Germany
who elect the king of the Romans, that they should without
delay make a new choice for the empire; and this was done, for
they elected William, count of Holland and landgrave, a valiant
lord, to whom the Church gave her support, causing a great
part of Germany to rebel, and gave indulgence and pardon
as if they were going over seas, to whoever should be against
the said Frederick; whence in Germany there was great war
between the said elected King William of Holland and King
Conrad, son of the said Frederick; but the war endured but a
short time, for the said King William died, the year of Christ
... and the said Conrad reigned in Germany, whom his father
Frederick the emperor had caused to be elected king, as we shall
make mention. From this sentence Frederick appealed to the
successor of Pope Innocent [IV] and sent his letters and messengers throughout all Christendom, complaining of the said
sentence and setting forth how iniquitous it was, as appears by
his epistle written by the said Messer Pietro della Vigna, which
begins, after the salutation: "Although we believe, that words
of the already current tidings, etc." But considering the real
facts as to the process, and as to the deeds of Frederick against
the Church, and as to his dissolute and uncatholic life, he was
guilty and deserving of the deposition, for the reasons set forth
in the said process; and afterwards for the deeds done by the
said Frederick after his deposition; for if before he was and had
been cruel and persecuting to Holy Church and to the believers
in Tuscany and in Lombardy, afterwards he was much more so,
as long as he lived, as hereafter we shall make mention....

41. HOW EMPEROR FREDERICK DIED AT FIRENZUOLA IN APULIA

In the said year 1250, Emperor Frederick being in Apulia, in
the city of Firenzuola, at the entrance to the Abruzzi, fell griev-
ously sick, and for all his augury he knew not how to take heed;
for he had learned that he must die in Firenze [Florence], wherefore, as aforesaid, never would he set foot in Firenze, neither in
Faenza; yet ill did he interpret the lying word of the demon, for

he was bidden beware lest he should die in Firenze, and he took no heed of Firenzuola. It came to pass that, his malady increasing upon him, there being with him one of his bastard sons, named Manfred, who was desirous of having the treasure of Frederick, his father, and the lordship of the kingdom of Sicily, and fearing that Frederick might recover from that sickness, or leave a testament, the said Manfred made a league with his private chamberlain, and promising him many gifts and great lordship, covered the mouth of Frederick with a bolster and so stifled him, and after the said manner the said Frederick died, deposed from the empire and excommunicated by Holy Church, without repentance or sacrament of Holy Church. And by this may we note the word that Christ said in the Gospel: "You shall die in your sins," for so it came to pass with Frederick, who was such an enemy to Holy Church, who brought his wife and King Henry, his son, to death, and saw himself discomfited, and his son Enzo taken, and himself, by his son Manfred, vilely slain, and without repentance; and this was the day of Sta. Lucia in December, the said year 1250. And him dead, the said Manfred became guardian of the realm and of all the treasure and caused the body of Frederick to be brought and buried with honor in the church of Monreale above the city of Palermo in Sicily, and at his burying he desired to write many words of his greatness and power and the mighty deeds done by him. But one Trottano, a clerk, made these brief verses, which were very pleasing to Manfred and to the other barons, and he caused them to be engraved on the said sepulcher, which said:

Si PROBITAS, SENSUS, VIRTUTUM GRATIA, CENSUS NOBILITAS ORTI, POSSENT RESISTERE MORTI, NON FORET EXTINCTUS FEDERICUS, QUI JACET INTUS.

In sense or frankness bold, if virtues' grace or gold. If birth from noble source, could stay death in his course, Frederick who here doth lie, would ne'er have come to die.

39. FREDERICK II FOUNDS THE UNIVERSITY OF NAPLES, JUNE 5, 1224

Frederick clearly intended his new *studium generale* to rival that of Bologna and to counter its influence in canon and secular law as part of his ongoing efforts to establish a strong unified state and to counter the influence of the papacy over the Regno.[18] In so doing he established the first state-sponsored university in Europe. The emperor took seriously his role as heir of the ancient Roman Empire, and he attempted to apply Justinian's *Corpus Juris Civilis* over the Regno as the law of the land. The university at Naples was to become the chief center of the teaching of this revived Roman law and of the creation of a new secular civil service for his Italian holdings. Frederick was also a student of ancient and Muslim science and medicine, and over the years Naples also became renowned for the study of medicine, first established at the medical school in neighboring Salerno. The university also soon became a center of the study of rhetoric, long established in neighboring Capua. This was key to the work of a civil bureaucracy, of diplomacy and court life and helped produce a circle of propagandists and apologists for Frederick's imperial policies and for his struggle with the papacy.

In the time-honored fashion of college admissions, Frederick lured students with promises of an easy life, low costs, affordable textbooks, comfortable accommodations, charming surroundings and friendly neighbors. Once they arrived at the university they would have the best curriculum, the most renowned faculty and generous prizes and financial aid. In what reads like a surprisingly modern note, parents are reassured that they will not lose contact with their children. In the year 1224, Frederick also makes a clear-cut connection between a university degree and professional advancement, higher income and upward social mobility.

The following is from Frederick's *Licterae generales*. It has been translated by Mario Spagnuolo and is taken from the online *Medieval Sourcebook* hosted at Fordham University.[19]

---

18. See Martin Kintzinger, "Macht des Wissens: Die Universitäten Bologna und Neapel," in *Die Staufer und Italien: Drei Innovationsregionen im mittelalterlichen Europa*, Alfried Wieczorek, Bernd Schneidmüller and Stefan Weinfurter, eds., 2 vols. (Stuttgart: Konrad Theiss Verlag, 2010), 395-40; and Paul Oldfield, "The Kingdom of Sicily and the Early University Movement," *Viator* 40.2 (2009): 135–50.

19. http://www.fordham.edu/halsall/source/1224fred2-lictgen.asp.

Frederick etc., to all the archbishops, bishops, priests, counts, barons, judges, executors of justice, bailiffs and all authorities of the kingdom: With the favor of God, thanks to whom we live and reign, and to whom we attribute all good deeds done by us, we wish that in all parts of the kingdom many will become wise and knowledgeable, by having access to a fountain of knowledge and a seminary of doctrine, so that they, made proficient by study and observation, will serve divine justice and will become useful to us for the administration of justice and of the laws, which we urge everyone to obey. We have therefore decided that in the most pleasant city of Naples there should be teaching of the arts and of all disciplines, so that those who are starved for knowledge will find it in our own kingdom and will not be forced, in their search for knowledge, to become pilgrims and to beg in foreign lands. We intend to provide for the good of our subjects who, after having become learned, will hope to acquire wealth, since the acquisition of what is good cannot be sterile, and will be followed by nobility, the halls of the tribunals, wealth and the grace and favors of friendship. Therefore we will invite those scholars who are not without merit, and without doubt we will entrust them with the administration of justice once they have become able to do so. Therefore be happy and ready for the teachings that scholars desire.

We will allow you to live in a place where everything is in abundance, where the homes are sufficiently spacious, where the customs of everyone are affable, and where one can easily transport by sea or land what is necessary to human life. To them we offer all useful things, good conditions, for them we will look for teachers, promise goods and offer prizes to those who are worthy of it. We will keep them under the gaze of their parents, we will free them from many labors and from the necessity of long trips, almost pilgrimages. We will protect them from the dangers of brigands who would deprive them of their goods on the long roads. Among the teachers that we have assigned to the school we have Roffredo of Benevento, a faithful judge, professor of civil rights, a man of great science and proven loyalty.

We order therefore to all of you who govern provinces and preside over administrations, to let all these things be known to all and everywhere, and to command, under danger of persons and goods, that no student will dare leave the kingdom for reasons of study and that no one dare to teach in other places of the kingdom. And that, through their parents, you order to those students who are outside the kingdom, to return here by the feast of St. Michael [September 29, "Michaelmas"].

These are the conditions that we offer to the students. First, that there will be doctors and teachers in every faculty. We assure the students, wherever they come from, that they will be able to come, stay and return without any risk to their persons or goods. The best houses will be given to them, and their rent will be at most two ounces of gold. All the houses will be rented for a sum up to that amount, based on an estimate by two citizens and two students. There will be loans given to students, based on their needs, by those who are designated to do so, with the pawning of the books, which will be temporarily returned after receiving the guarantee from other students. The student will not leave the city until he has paid back his debt or has given back the pawns given to him temporarily. Such pawns will not be requested by the creditor as long as the students remains in school. In civil trials all will have to appear before their teachers. As for grain, meat, fish, wine and other things that students need, we will not make any rule since the province has all these things in abundance and all will be sold to students as it is to citizens. We invite the students to such a laudable and great task, we promise to respect these conditions, to honor your persons and to order universally that you should be honored by all.

Syracuse, 5 June 1224.

40. Neapolitans in the Sicilian School of poetry, 1230–66

Poetry from the Sicilian court of Frederick II is an important strand in the literary history of medieval Europe. A few of the known poets from that court were from the region around Naples or lived at some point in that city.

Pietro della Vigna (c. 1190–1249), already discussed by Villani,[20] was a native of Capua. He studied law at Bologna and went on to serve as secretary to Frederick, ambassador to the papal court and governor of Apulia.

---

20.   See above, Reading 38, at pp. 131, 133, 134.

The following selections, from Pietro's *Canzone Amore, in cui disio ed ho speranza*, are taken from *Lyrics of the Middle Ages: An Anthology*, James J. Wilhelm, ed. (New York: Garland Publishing, 1990), 130.

Go, little song, and carry these laments
To her who holds my heart within her power.
Go, count for her the pains that I have felt
And tell her how I'm dying with desire,
And let her send a message back to tell
How I can console this love I bear for her;
And if I ever did a thing debased,
Let her give me penance as she wills.

Rinaldo d'Aquino (fl.1235–79), was from the town of Montella in Campania and was possibly the brother of, or at least from the same family as, Thomas Aquinas.[21] According to his reputation, he was the imperial falconer of Frederick II. He is well known for his *Complaint against the Crusade* (1227–28), written as a woman lamenting the departure of her lover. The work is excerpted from *The Crusades: A Reader*, S.J. Allen and Emilie Amt, eds. (Peterborough: Broadview Press, 2003), 215. It is still performed as an anti-war song. It opens:

Never again that comfort,
Never again that joyous heart.
The ships down in the harbor
Are straining to depart.
Away runs the noblest one
To the land across the sea
But me — poor weeping thing —
What shall become of me?

Giacomo da Lentini, who worked for Frederick II as an imperial *notarius* and *scriba* in 1233 and 1240, may have studied at Naples in the 1220s. He is considered the father of the sonnet. Although Dante did not think very highly of his work, Dante Gabriel Rossetti found it to contain both beauty and feeling and chose the following sonnets for his own anthology of Italian poetry.

---

21.   See below, Reading 44.

These selections are taken from Dante Gabriel Rossetti, *The Early Italian Poets: From Ciullo D'Alcamo to Dante Alighieri* (London: Smith, Elder and Co., 1861), 41, 45, available online at http://www.rossettiarchive.org/docs/1-1861.yale.rad.html. Accessed 12/8/2012.

Of His Lady in Heaven
I have it in my heart to serve God so
That into paradise I shall repair,—
The holy place through the which everywhere
I have heard say that joy and solace flow.
Without my lady I were loth to go,—
She who has the bright face and the bright hair;
Because if she were absent, I being there,
My pleasure would be less than nought, I know.
Look you, I say not this to such intent
As that I there would deal in any sin:
I only would behold her gracious mien,
And beautiful soft eyes, and lovely face,
That so it should be my complete content
To see my lady joyful in her place.

No Jewel Is Worth His Lady
Sapphire, nor diamond, nor emerald,
Nor other precious stones past reckoning,
Topaz, nor pearl, nor ruby like a king,
Nor that most virtuous jewel, jasper call'd,
Nor amethyst, nor onyx, nor basalt,
Each counted for a very marvellous thing,
Is half so excellently gladdening
As is my lady's head uncoronall'd.
All beauty by her beauty is made dim;
Like to the stars she is for loftiness;
And with her voice she taketh away grief.
She is fairer than a bud, or than a leaf.
Christ have her well in keeping, of His grace,
And make her holy and beloved, like Him!

Prinzivalle Doria died in Naples in 1276. In his earlier years he wrote in Italian, although later he produced both poetry and prose treatises in Provençal. From his poetry at

least one Italian canzone, *Of his Love, with the Figure of a Sudden Storm*, survives.

This closing section of the poem is taken from Rossetti, *Early Italian Poets*, 139–40, http://www.rossettiarchive.org/docs/1-1861.yale.rad.html. Accessed 12/8/2012.

The sea is much more beautiful at rest
Than when the tempest tramples over it.
Wherefore, to see the smile which has so bless'd
This heart of mine, deem'st thou these eyes unfit?
There is no maid so lovely, it is writ,
That by such stern unwomanly regard
Her face may not be marr'd.
I therefore pray of thee, my own soul's wife,
That thou remember me who am forgot.
How shall I stand without thee? Art thou not
The pillar of the building of my life?

41. Two commercial insurance contracts, 1261

Naples had remained an important trading port for the entire Mediterranean since the decline of the Roman Empire, coming into its own as the major southern Italian port with the Hohenstaufen decision to make the city their capital.

The following two texts are insurance agreements drawn up to cover shipment of goods. They reflect common practice of developing international maritime and admiralty law on the verge of the Angevin conquest. Note the use of set terms, of specific ships and merchandise covered, guarantees, penalties and indemnities, and of witnesses, including a woman. Also worth noting is the existence of an established system of customs and duties on merchandise, of a "Pisan Port" or trading station, similar to the *fondaci* established by the Latins throughout the eastern Mediterranean. These served many purposes: as warehouses, consulates, safe compounds and as social gathering places for foreign colonies within the city.

These selections have been translated from the Latin in Lopez and Raymond, *Medieval Trade*, 257–58.

1. In the name of the Lord, amen. I, Uggeri Mascolino of Florence, acknowledge to you, Gogo, [son] of the late Giacomo de Marino, that I am under obligation to give to you 4 ounces gold *tarini*[22] according to the ounce of the kingdom [in consideration] and by reason of the freight charge of goods and merchandise that I possess and that I have loaded in your vessel named *Saint Nicholas*. This I promise to give and to pay, personally or through my messenger, to you or to your accredited messenger, within two days after you arrive with your aforesaid vessel at... <illegible in MS> in the said place, net and clear from all duties [*dacitis* or *dazio*] and customs [*avariis*]. Otherwise, the penalty of the double, etc.; for the penalty and for so observing I pledge to you as security all [my goods], etc. Witnesses: Lapo, Florentine, nicknamed Alnardino; Matteo Aurigemma; Vernaccio de Curia; Pietro of Porta Nuova. Done in Naples, in the Pisan port, 1261, third indiction, on March 12.

2. In the name of the Lord, amen. I, Uggeri Mascolino of Florence, acknowledge that I have had and have received from you, Gogo, [son] of the late Giacomo de Marino... <?> 14 ounces good gold *tarini* of legal weight according to the correct weight of Naples, and in regard to them I call myself well satisfied and paid, waiving, etc. In consideration of these I promise and agree to give and to pay to you in Rome, viz. at...<?> £39 s.18 Roman, viz. 57 *soldi [solidi]* in every ounce — and this in silver groats[23] Roman worth 12 Pisanos [?] each, net and clear

---

22. Up until 935, the Byzantine *solidus* was the official coinage of the city and duchy. By 987 the Muslim *tarì* or *tareni* of Sicily replaced the *solidus*, which then became only a unit of exchange (4 *tarì* = 1 *solidus*). In 1060, the Amalfitan *tarì* became the official currency. See Arthur, *Naples*, 133–43; and Feniello, *Napoli*, 202–4, citing J.-M. Martin, "Economia naturale ed economia monetaria nell'Italia meridionale longobarda e bizantina (secoli VI–XI)," in *Storia d'Italia. Annali 6: Economia naturale, economia monetaria*, Ruggiero Romano and Ugo Tucci, eds. (Turin: G. Einaudi, 1983), 181–219. See also below, Reading 64.

23. According to Allan Evans, ed., Francesco Balducci Pegolotti, *La Pratica della Mercatura* (Cambridge: The Medieval Academy of America, 1936), 239 n. 1, describing the exchange rates in Bruges in the 1330s, "1 soldo equals a sterling, and 3 sterlings or in other words 3 soldi of parisis equal a groat tournois." These are *"muneta di pagamento"* whose relative value could vary widely over time. See also below, Reading 61.

from all tolls and customs — and this within two days after the said vessel arrives there.

And in consideration of these I assign to you as security and in the name of security 3 *centenaria*[24] of wine and one fourth of a *centenarium* of filberts, which I have and I declare to have, as we acknowledge, in your vessel, and all and anything I have in the same vessel; [I do so] in such wise that if I do not make the aforesaid payment as [mentioned] above, you are to have full permission and power to sell the aforesaid goods and to receive and to retain the payment for yourself, by your authority, out of their price; and if you lack anything to complete [the payment of] said debt, I promise to make that good to you. Otherwise, the penalty of the double, etc.; and in consideration of the penalty and for so observing all this [my goods], etc.

Witnesses: Lapo Alnardino of Florence, Matteo Aurigemma, Vernaccio de Curia, Pietro of Porta Nuova, and Costanza Canevarius. Done in Naples, in the locality named Pisan Port, 1261, third indiction, on March 12.

■

---

24. A hundred weight by volume, also a 100 count of coinage.

Fig. 30. The Angevin Genaeology. c.1340. From the Anjou Bible, *Leuven, Maurits Sabbe Library, MS 1, fol. 4r.*

CHAPTER 5: THE ANGEVINS

CHARLES I

Despite the destruction of the Angevin archives in 1943,[1] sources for the period remain rich and plentiful. They include narrative, literary and epistolary, trade and economic, religious, legal and other documents. The best — and most engaging — narrative source for the early years of the Angevin conquest remains the *Nuova cronica* of Giovanni Villani (c.1280–1348).[2] His work combines traditional chronicle writing with narrative techniques found in the *chansons de geste* to create a vivid picture of events and personalities.

In 1263 Charles, count of Provence, the brother of King Louis IX (Saint Louis) of France, at the urging of Pope Urban IV, set out to conquer the kingdom of Sicily from the heirs of the excommunicated Emperor Frederick II Hohenstaufen. Financed by the papacy and from his and his wife Beatrice's holdings in France and Provence, Charles led a papally sanctioned crusade against Frederick's heir, Manfred. The Villani were great admirers of the Neapolitan Angevins, especially of their contemporary Robert of Anjou, and their writing reflects these prejudices.

The following selections describe Charles' character and narrate his coronation in Rome, his march south, the Battle of Benevento and Charles' victory. The next selection then traces the rise of Conradin, his defeat at Tagliacozzo and his execution in Naples. Villani's portrait of Charles I as the taciturn warrior of pithy reply has long been canonical but has recently been contested.[3]

The following readings are taken from Selfe and Wicksteed, 192–95, 199–217. We have modernized some usage and spellings from Selfe's deliberately archaizing style.

---

1. See above, xviii and n. 3.

2. See above, 126–27; and Clarke, "The Villani Chronicles."

3. See above, lvi–lvii.

42. CHARLES OF ANJOU CONQUERS NAPLES, 1263–65

BOOK VI. 88. HOW THE CHURCH OF ROME ELECTED CHARLES OF
FRANCE TO BE KING OF SICILY AND OF APULIA

Fig. 31. Charles I. From his golden carlino.

[1263] The said Pope Urban and the Church being thus brought down by the power of Manfred, and the two emperors-elect (to wit, the Spaniard and the Englishman) not being in concord nor having power to come into Italy, and Conradin, son of King Conrad, to whom pertained by inheritance the kingdom of Sicily and of Apulia, being so young a boy that he could not as yet come against Manfred, the said pope, by reason of the importunity of many faithful followers of the Church, who by Manfred's violence had been driven from their lands, and especially by reason of the Guelf exiles from Florence and from Tuscany who were continually pursuing the court, complaining of their woes at the feet of the pope, the said Pope Urban called a great council of his cardinals and of many prelates and made this proposal: seeing the Church was subjugated by Manfred, and since those of his house and lineage had always been enemies and persecutors of Holy Church, not being grateful for many benefits received, if it seemed well to them, he had thought to release Holy Church from bondage and restore her to her state and liberty, and this might be done by summoning Charles, count of Anjou and of Provence, son of the king of France, and brother of the good King Louis [IX], who was the most capable prince in prowess of arms and in every virtue that there was in his time, and of so powerful a house as that of France, and who might be the champion of Holy Church and king of Sicily and of Apulia, regaining it by force from King Manfred, who was holding it unjustly by force and was excommunicated and condemned and was against the will of Holy Church, and as it were a rebel against her; and he trusted so much in the prowess of the said Charles and of the barons of France, who would follow him, that he did not doubt that he would oppose Manfred and take from him the lands and all the kingdom in short time, and would put the Church in great state. To this counsel all the cardinals and prelates agreed, and they elected the said Charles to be king of Sicily and of Apulia, him and his descendants down to the fourth generation after him, and the election being confirmed, they sent forth the decree; and this was the year of Christ 1263.

89. HOW CHARLES, COUNT OF ANJOU AND OF PROVENCE, ACCEPTED THE ELECTION OFFERED HIM BY THE CHURCH OF ROME TO SICILY AND TO APULIA

When the said invitation was carried to France by the Cardinal Simon of Tours to the said Charles, he took counsel thereupon with King Louis of France and with the count of Artois, and with the count of Alençon, his brother, and with the other great barons of France, and by all he was counseled that in the name of God he should undertake the said enterprise in the service of Holy Church, and to bear the dignity of crown and kingdom. And King Louis of France, his elder brother, offered him aid in men and in money, and likewise offers were made to him by all the barons of France. And his lady, who was the youngest daughter to the good Count Raymond Berenger of Provence, through whom he had the inheritance of the county of Provence, when she heard of the election of Count Charles, her husband, to the intent that she might become queen, pledged all her jewels and invited all the bachelors-at-arms of France and of Provence to rally around her standard and to make her queen. And this was largely by reason of the contempt and disdain that a little while before had been shown to her by her three elder sisters, who were all queens, making her sit a degree lower than they, for which cause, with great grief, she had made complaint thereof to Charles, her husband, who answered her: "Be at peace, for I will shortly make you a greater queen than them"; for which cause she sought after and obtained the best barons of France for her service, and those who did most in the enterprise. And thus Charles wrought in his preparations with all solicitude and power, and made answer to the pope and to the cardinals, by the said cardinal legate, how he had accepted their election, and how, without loss of time, he would come into Italy with a strong arm and great force to defend Holy Church, and against Manfred, to drive him from the lands of Sicily and of Apulia; by which news the Church and all her followers, and whosoever was on the side of the Guelfs, were much comforted and took great courage.

When Manfred heard the news, he furnished himself for defense with men and money and with the force of the Ghibelline party in Lombardy and in Tuscany, who were of his league and alliance. He enlisted and equipped many more folk than he had before, and caused them to come from Germany for his defense, to the intent that Charles and his French following might not be able to enter Italy or to proceed to Rome; and with money and with promises he gathered a great part of the lords and of the cities of Italy under his lordship, and in Lombardy he made vicar Marquis Pallavicino of Piedmont, his kinsman, who much resembled him in person and in habits. And likewise he caused great defenses to be prepared at sea of armed galleys of his Sicilians and Apulians, and of the Pisans who were in league with him, and they feared little the coming of Charles, whom they called, in contempt, "Little Charles." And since Manfred thought himself, and was, lord over sea and land, and his Ghibelline party was uppermost and ruled over Tuscany and Lombardy, he held his coming for nought.

BOOK VII. HERE BEGINS THE SEVENTH BOOK, WHICH TREATS OF THE COMING OF KING CHARLES AND OF MANY CHANGES AND EVENTS THAT FOLLOWED

[1264] 1. Charles was the second son of Louis [VIII], king of France, and grandson of the good King Philip, the blear-eyed, his grandfather,... and brother of the good King Louis [IX] of France, and of Robert, count of Artois, and of Alfonso, count of Poitou; all these four brothers were the children of Queen Bianca [Blanche], daughter of King Alfonso of Spain [Castile]. Charles [was] count of Anjou, by inheritance from his father, and count of Provence, this side the Rhône, by inheritance through his wife, the daughter of good Count Raymond

Berenger. As soon as he was elected king of Sicily and of Apulia by the pope and by the Church, [he] made preparation of knights and barons to furnish means for his enterprise and expedition into Italy, as we before narrated. But in order that those who come after may have fuller knowledge how this Charles was the first of the kings of Sicily and of Apulia descended from the house of France, we will tell somewhat of his virtues and conditions; and it is very fitting that we should preserve a record of so great a lord and so great a friend and protector and defender of Holy Church and of our city of Florence, as we shall make mention hereafter.

This Charles was wise, prudent in counsel and valiant in arms, and harsh, and much feared and redoubted by all the kings of the earth, greathearted and of high purposes, steadfast in carrying out every great undertaking, firm in every adversity, faithful to every promise, speaking little and acting much, scarcely smiling, chaste as a monk, catholic, harsh in judgment, and of a fierce countenance, tall and stalwart in person, olive-complexioned, large-nosed, and in kingly majesty he exceeded any other lord, and slept little and woke long, and used to say that all the time of sleep was so much lost; liberal was he to knights in arms, but greedy in acquiring land and lordship and money, from wherever it came, to furnish means for his enterprises and wars. In jongleurs, minstrels or jesters he never took delight; his arms were those of France, that is an azure field charged with the golden lily, barred with vermilion above; so far they were diverse from the arms of France.

[1265] This Charles, when he passed into Italy, was forty-six years of age, and he reigned nineteen years in Sicily and Apulia, as we shall make mention hereafter. He had by his wife two sons and several daughters; the first was named Charles II and was somewhat crippled and was prince of Capua; and after the first Charles, his father, he became king of Sicily and of Apulia, as we shall make mention hereafter. The second was Philip, who was prince of the Morea in his wife's right; but he died young and without issue, for he ruptured himself in straining a cross-bow. We will now leave for a while to speak of the progeny of the good King Charles, and will continue our story of his passing into Italy, and of other things that followed.

3. How Count Charles departed from France and passed by sea from Provence to Rome

In the year of Christ 1265, Charles, count of Anjou and of Provence, having collected his barons and knights of France, and money to furnish means for his expedition, and having mustered his troops, left Count Guy of Montfort, captain and leader of 1,500 French horsemen, who were to journey to Rome by way of Lombardy; and having kept the feast of Easter, of the Resurrection of Christ, with King Louis of France and with his other brothers and friends, he straightway departed from Paris with a small company. Without delay he came to Marseilles in Provence, where he had had prepared thirty armed galleys, upon which he embarked with certain barons whom he had brought with him from France, and with certain of his Provençal barons and knights, and put out to sea on his way to Rome in great peril, inasmuch as King Manfred with his forces had armed in Genoa, and in Pisa, and in the kingdom, more than eighty galleys, which were at sea on guard, to the intent that the said Charles might not be able to pass. But the said Charles, like a bold and courageous lord, prepared to pass without any regard to the lying-in-wait of his enemies, repeating a proverb, or perhaps the saying of a philosopher, that runs: "Good care frustrates ill fortune." And this happened to the said Charles at his need; for being with his galleys on the Pisan seas, by tempest of the sea they were dispersed, and Charles with three of his galleys, utterly forespent, arrived at the Pisan port.

Hearing this, Count Guido Novello, then vicar in Pisa for King Manfred, armed himself with his German troops to ride to the port and take Count Charles; the Pisans seized their moment, closed the doors of the city, ran to arms and raised a dispute with the vicar, demanding back the fortress of Mutrone, which he was holding for the Lucchese, which was very dear and necessary to them; and this had to be granted before he was able to depart. And on account of the said interval and delay, when Count Guido had departed from Pisa and reached the port, Count Charles, the storm being somewhat abated, had with great care refitted his galleys and put out to sea, having departed but a little time before from the port, the great peril and misfortune being past; and thus, as it pleased God, passing afterwards hard by the fleet of King Manfred, sailing over the high seas, he arrived with his armada safe and sound at the mouth of the Roman Tiber, in the month of May of the said year. His coming was held to be very marvelous and sudden, and by King Manfred and his people could scarce be believed.

Having arrived in Rome, Charles was received by the Romans with great honor, inasmuch as they loved not the lordship of Manfred; and immediately he was made senator of Rome by the will of the pope and the people of Rome. Albeit Pope Clement [IV] was in Viterbo, yet he gave him all aid and countenance against Manfred, both spiritual and temporal; but by reason of his mounted troops, which were coming from France by land, and which through the many hindrances prepared by the followers of Manfred in Lombardy, had much difficulty in reaching Rome, as we shall make mention, it behooved Count Charles to abide in Rome, and in Campania, and in Viterbo throughout that summer, during which sojourn he took counsel and ordered how he might enter the kingdom with his host.

5. How King Charles was crowned in Rome king of Sicily, and how
he straightway departed with his host to go against King Manfred

Fig. 32. The coronation of Charles
I. From Grandes Chroniques de
France, (1375–1400). Paris, BNF,
MS Français 2813, fol. 342r.

When the mounted troops of Count Charles had reached Rome, he purposed to assume his crown; and on the day of the Epiphany in the said year 1265, by two cardinal legates dispatched by the pope to Rome, he was consecrated and crowned over the realm of Sicily and Apulia, he and his lady with great honor; and as soon as the festival of his coronation was ended, without any delay he set out with his host by way of the Campania, towards the kingdom of Apulia and Campania; and very soon he had a large part thereof at his command without dispute. King Manfred hearing of their coming, first of Charles and then of his people, and how through failure of his great host, which was in Lombardy, they had passed onward, was much angered. Immediately he gave all his care to defend the passes of the kingdom, and at the pass at the bridge at Ceprano, he placed the Count Giordano and the count of Caserta, who were of the house of da Quona, with many followers, both foot and horse; and in S. Germano [below Montecassino] he placed a great part of his German and Apulian barons and all the Saracens of Nocera with bows and crossbows and great store of arrows, trusting more in this defense than in any other, by reason of the strong place and the position, which has on the one side high mountains and on the other marshes and stagnant waters, and was furnished with victuals and with all things necessary for more than two years.

King Manfred having fortified the passes, as we have said, sent his ambassadors to King Charles to treat with him concerning a truce or peace. Their embassage being delivered, it was King Charles's will to make answer with his own mouth, and he said in his language, in French: *"Allez, et ditez pour moi au sultan de Nocere, aujourdhui je mettrai lui en enfer, ou il mettra moi en paradis"*; which was as much as to say: I will have nothing but battle, and in that battle, either he shall slay me, or I him. Once this was done, he set out on his road without delay. It chanced that King Charles having arrived with his host at Fresolone in Campania, as he was descending towards Ceprano, Count Giordano, who was defending that pass, seeing the king's followers coming to pass through, desired to defend the pass. The count of Caserta said that it was better to let some of them pass first so that they might seize them on the other side of the pass without stroke of sword. Count Giordano, when he saw the people increase, again desired to assail them in battle, then the count of Caserta, who was in the plot, said that the battle would be a great risk, seeing that too many of them had passed. Then Count Giordano, seeing the king's followers to be so powerful, abandoned the place and bridge, some say from fear, but more say on account of the pact made by the king with the count of Caserta, inasmuch as he loved not Manfred, who, of his inordinate lust, had forcibly ravished the count of Caserta's wife. Therefore he held himself to be greatly shamed by him and sought to avenge himself by this treachery. And to this we give faith, because he and his were among the first who gave themselves up to King Charles; and having left Ceprano, they did not return to the host of King Manfred at S. Germano, but abode in their castles.

6. HOW, AFTER KING CHARLES HAD TAKEN THE PASS OF CEPRANO, HE STORMED THE CITY OF S. GERMANO

When King Charles and his host had taken the pass of Ceprano, they took Aquino without opposition, and they stormed the stronghold of Arci, which is among the strongest in that country. This done, they encamped the host before S. Germano. The inhabitants of the city, by reason of the strength of the place, and because it was well furnished with men and with all things, held the followers of King Charles for nought, and in contempt they insulted the servants who were leading the horses to water, saying vile and shameful things, calling out: "Where is your little Charles?" For which reason the servants of the French began to skirmish and to fight with those of the city, whereat all the host of the French rose in uproar, and fearing that the camp would be attacked, the French were all suddenly in arms, running towards the city. Those within, not being on their guard, were not all so quickly in arms. The French with great fury assailed the city, fighting against it in many places; and those who could find no better protection, dismounting from their horses, took off their saddles, and with them on their heads went along under the walls and towers of the town. The count of Vendôme, with M. John, his brother, and with their standard, who were among the first to arm themselves, followed the grooms of the besieged who had sallied forth to skirmish, and pursuing them, entered the town together with them by a postern that was open to receive them; and this was not without great peril, since the gate was well guarded by many armed folk, and of those who followed the count of Vendôme and his brother, some were there slain and wounded, but they by their great courage and strength nevertheless were victorious in the combat around the gate by force of arms, and entered in, and straightaway set their standard upon the walls. And among the first who followed them were the Guelf refugees from Florence, of whom Count Guido Guerra was captain, and the ensign was borne by Messer Stoldo Giacoppi de' Rossi. At the taking of S. Germano, these Guelfs bore themselves marvelously and like good men, for which the besiegers took heart and courage, and each one entered the city as he best could.

The besieged, when they saw the standards of their enemies upon the walls and, the gate taken, fled in great numbers, and few of them remained to defend the town; wherefore King Charles's followers took the town of S. Germano by assault on the 10th day of February 1265, and it was held to be a very great marvel, by reason of the strength of the town, and rather the work of God than of human strength, forasmuch as there were more than 1,000 horsemen within and more than 5,000 footmen, among whom there were many Saracen archers from Nocera; but by reason of a scuffle which arose the night before, as it pleased God, between the Christians and the Saracens, in which the Saracens were vanquished, the next day they were not faithful in the defense of the city, and this among others was truly one of the causes why they lost the town of S. Germano. Of Manfred's troops many were slain and taken, and the city was all overrun and robbed by the French; and there the king and his host abode some time to take repose and to learn the movements of Manfred.

7. How King Manfred went to Benevento, and how he arrayed his troops to fight against King Charles[4]

King Manfred, having heard the news of the loss of S. Germano, and his discomfited troops having returned thence, was much dismayed and took counsel what he should do, and he was counseled by Count Calvagno, by Count Giordano, by Count Bartolommeo, by the count chamberlain and by his other barons to withdraw with all his forces to the city of Benevento, as a stronghold, in order that he might give battle on his own ground, and to the end he might withdraw towards Apulia if need were, and also to oppose the passage of King Charles, forasmuch as by no other way could he enter

---

4.   Dante also relates these events in Inferno XXVIII:1–21.

Fig. 33. The Battle of Benevento. From Grandes Chroniques de France, (1375–1400). Paris, BNF, MS Français 2813, fol. 343r.

into the principality[5] and into Naples, or pass into Apulia except by way of Benevento; and thus it was done. King Charles, hearing of Manfred's departure for Benevento, immediately departed from S. Germano to pursue him with his host. He did not take the direct way of Capua, and by Terra di Lavoro, since they could not have passed the bridge of Capua by reason of the strength of the towers of the bridge over the river, and the width of the river. But he determined to cross the Volturno River near Tuliverno, where it may be forded, whence he held on by the country of Alifi, and by the rough mountain paths of Beneventana, and without halting, and in great straits for money and victual, he arrived at the hour of noon at the foot of Benevento in the valley over against the city, distant by the space of two miles from the bank of the Calore River, which flows at the foot of Benevento.

King Manfred seeing the host of King Charles appear, having taken counsel, determined to fight and to sally forth to the field with his mounted troops to attack the army of King Charles before they were rested, but in this he did ill, for had he tarried one or two days, King Charles and his host would have perished or been captive without stroke of sword, through lack of provisions for them and for their horses, because the day before they arrived at the foot of Benevento, through want of victual, many of the troops had to feed on cabbages, and their horses on the stalks, without any other bread, or grain for the horses; and they had no more money to spend. Also the people and forces of King Manfred were

---

5. A century later Naples and its immediate vicinity were still called "Napoli di principato." See the *Pratica della mercatura*, Reading 61, at p. 219.

much dispersed, for M. Conrad of Antioch was in Abruzzi with a following, Count Frederick was in Calabria, the count of Ventimiglia was in Sicily; so that, if he had tarried a while, his forces would have increased; but to whom God intends ill, him He deprives of wisdom. Manfred having sallied forth from Benevento with his followers, passed over the bridge which crosses the said river of Calore into the plain which is called Sta. Maria della Grandella, to a place called the Pietra a Roseto. Here he formed three lines of battle or troops: the first was of Germans, in whom he had much confidence, who numbered fully 1,200 horse, of whom Count Calvagno was the captain; the second was of Tuscans and Lombards, and also of Germans, to the number of 1,000 horse, which was led by Count Giordano; the third, which Manfred led, was of Apulians with the Saracens of Nocera, which was of 1,400 horse, without the foot soldiers, and the Saracen bowmen who were in great numbers.

8. How King Charles arrayed his troops to fight against King Manfred

King Charles, seeing Manfred and his troops in the open field and arranged for combat, took counsel whether he should offer battle on that day or should delay it. Most of his barons counseled him to abide till the coming morning, to rest the horses from the fatigue of the hard travel, and M. Giles le Brun, constable of France, said the contrary, and that by reason of delay the enemy would pluck up heart and courage, and that the means of living might fail them utterly, and that if others of the host did not desire to give battle, he alone, with his lord Robert of Flanders and with his followers, would adventure the chances of the combat, having confidence in God that they should win the victory against the enemies of Holy Church. Seeing this, King Charles gave heed to and accepted his counsel, and through the great desire which he had for combat, he said with a loud voice to his knights, "*Venu est le jour que nous avons tant desiré,*" and he caused the trumpets to be sounded and commanded that every man should arm and prepare himself to go forth to battle; and thus in a little time it was done.

And he ordered, after the fashion of his enemies, over against them, three principal bands: the first band was of Frenchmen to the number of 1,000 horse, whereof were captains Philip of Montfort and the marshal of Mirapoix; of the second King Charles with Count Guy of Montfort, and with many of his barons and of the queen's knights, and with barons and knights of Provence, and Romans, and of the Campania, which were about 900 horse; and the royal banners were borne by William, the standard-bearer, a man of great valor. The third was led by Robert, count of Flanders, with his prefect of the camp, Marshal Giles of France, with Flemings, men of Brabant and of Aisne and Picards to the number of 700 horse. And besides these troops were the Guelf refugees from Florence, with all the Italians, and they were more than 400 horse, whereof many of the greater houses in Florence received knighthood from the hand of King Charles upon the commencement of the battle; and of these Guelfs of Florence and of Tuscany, Guido Guerra was captain, and their banner was borne in that battle by Conrad of Montemagno of Pistoia. And King Manfred seeing the bands formed, asked what folk were in the fourth band, which made a goodly show in arms and in horses and in ornaments and accoutrements: answer was made to him that they were the Guelf refugees from Florence and from the other cities of Tuscany. Then did Manfred grieve, saying: "Where is the help that I should receive from the Ghibelline party whom I have served so well and on whom I have expended so much treasure?" And he said: "Those people (that is, the band of Guelfs) cannot lose today"; and that was as much as to say that if he gained the victory he would be the friend of the Florentine Guelfs, seeing them to be so faithful to their leader and to their party, and the foe of the Ghibellines.

9. The battle between King Charles and King Manfred, and how King Manfred was discomfited and slain

[1265] The troops of the two kings being set in order on the plain of Grandella, after the aforesaid fashion, each one of the leaders admonished his people to do well. King Charles having given to his followers the cry, "Ho Knights, *Monjoie!*" and

King Manfred to his, "Ho, Knights, for Swabia!" the bishop of Alzurro as papal legate absolved and blessed all the host of King Charles, remitting sin and penalty, forasmuch as they were fighting in the service of Holy Church. And this done, there began the fierce battle between the two first troops of the Germans and of the French, and the assault of the Germans was so strong that they evilly treated the French troop and forced them to give much ground and they themselves took ground. The good King Charles seeing his followers so ill-bestead, did not keep to the order of the battle to defend himself with the second troop, considering that if the first troop of the French, in which he had full confidence, were routed, little hope of safety was there from the others; but immediately with his troop he went to succor the French troop, against that of the Germans, and when the Florentine refugees and their troop beheld King Charles strike into the battle, they followed boldly and performed marvelous feats of arms that day, always following the person of King Charles; and the same did the good Giles le Brun, constable of France, with Robert of Flanders and his troop; and on the other side Count Giordano fought with his troop, wherefore the battle was fierce and hard and endured for a long time, no one knowing who was getting the advantage, because the Germans by their valor and strength, smiting with their swords, did much hurt to the French.

But suddenly there arose a great cry among the French troops, whosoever it was who began it, saying: "To your daggers! To your daggers! Strike at the horses!" And this was done, by which thing in a short time the Germans were evilly treated and much beaten down and well-nigh turned to flight. King Manfred, who with his troop of Apulians remained ready to succor the host, beholding his followers not able to abide the conflict, exhorted the people of his troop that they should follow him into the battle, but they gave little heed to his word, for the greater part of the barons of Apulia and of the kingdom, among others the count chamberlain, and him of Acerra and him of Caserta, and others, either through cowardice of heart, or seeing that they were coming by the worse, and there are those who say through treachery, as faithless folk, and desirous of a new lord, failed Manfred, abandoning him and fleeing, some towards Abruzzi and some towards the city of Benevento. Manfred, being left with few followers, acted like a valiant lord, who would rather die in battle as king than flee with shame; and while he was putting on his helmet, a silver eagle, which he wore as crest, fell down before him on his saddle bow; and seeing this, he was much dismayed and said to the barons who were beside him, in Latin: *"Hoc est signum Dei*, for I fastened this crest with my own hand after such a fashion that it should not have been possible for it to fall"; yet for all this he did not give up, but as a valiant lord he took heart and immediately entered into the battle, without the royal insignia, so as not to be recognized as king, but like any other noble, striking bravely into the thickest of the fight. Nevertheless, his followers endured but a little while, for they were already turning; and straightway they were routed, and King Manfred slain in the midst of his enemies, it was said by a French esquire, but it was not known for certain. In that battle there was great mortality both on the one side and on the other, but much more among the followers of Manfred; and while they were fleeing from the field towards Benevento, they were pursued by the army of King Charles, which followed them as far as the city (for night was already falling) and took the city of Benevento and those who were fleeing.

Many chief barons of King Manfred were taken; among the others were taken Count Giordano and Messer Piero Asino degli Uberti, whom King Charles sent captive to Provence, and there he caused them to die a cruel death in prison. The other Apulian and German barons he kept in prison in divers places in the kingdom; and a few days after, the wife of the said Manfred and his children and his sister, who were in Nocera of the Saracens in Apulia, were delivered as prisoners to King Charles, and they afterwards died in his prison. And without doubt there came upon Manfred and his heirs the malediction of God, and right clearly was shown the judgment of God upon him because he was excommunicated as the enemy and persecutor of Holy Church. At his end, search was made for Manfred for more than three days, and he could not be found, and it was not known if he was slain, taken or escaped, because he had not borne royal insignia in the battle. At last he was recognized by one of his own camp-followers by sundry marks on his person, in the midst of the battlefield; and his body being found by the said camp-follower, he threw it across an ass he had and went his way crying, "Who buys Manfred? Who buys Manfred?" And one of the king's barons chastised this fellow and brought the body of Manfred before the king, who caused all the barons who had been taken prisoners to come together, and having asked each one if it was Manfred, they all timidly said "Yes." When Count Giordano came, he smote his hands against his face, weeping and crying: "Alas, alas, my lord," wherefore he was commended by the French; and some of the barons prayed the king that he would give Manfred the honor of burial; but the king made answer: "*Je le fairois volontiers, s'il ne fût excommunié*"; but forasmuch as he was excommunicated, King Charles would not have him laid in a holy place; but at the foot of the bridge of Benevento he was buried, and upon his grave each one of the host threw a stone; whence there arose a great heap of stones. But by some it was said that afterwards, by command of the pope, the bishop of Cosenza had him taken from that sepulcher, and sent him forth from the kingdom, which was Church land, and he was buried beside the river of Verde [Garigliano], on the borders of the kingdom and Campania; this, however, we do not affirm. This battle and defeat was on a Friday, the last day of February in the year of Christ 1265.

43. CONRADIN'S INVASION OF THE REGNO AND HIS DEATH IN NAPLES, 1268

The following selections continue the narrative taken from Villani, *Croniche*, book VII, Selfe, 228–42.

23. HOW THE YOUNG CONRADIN, SON OF KING CONRAD, CAME FROM GERMANY INTO ITALY AGAINST KING CHARLES

King Charles being in Tuscany, the Ghibelline refugees from Florence formed themselves into a league and company with the Pisans and Sienese, and came to an agreement with Don Henry of Spain [Castile], who was Roman senator and already at enmity with King Charles, his cousin.

Therefore, with certain barons of Apulia and Sicily, he made oath and conspiracy to make certain towns in Sicily and in Apulia rebel, and to send into Germany to stir up Conradin, who was the son of Conrad, the son of Emperor Frederick, to cross into Italy to take away Sicily and the kingdom from King Charles. And so it was done; for immediately in Apulia there rose in rebellion Nocera of the Saracens, Aversa in Terra di Lavoro, many places in Calabria and almost all in Abruzzi, if we except Aquila, and in Sicily almost all, or a great part of the island of Sicily, if we except Messina and Palermo; and Don Henry caused Rome to rebel, and all Campania and the country around; and the Pisans and the Sienese and the other Ghibelline cities sent of their money 100,000 golden florins to stir up the said Conradin, who being very young, sixteen years old, set forth from Germany, against his mother's will, who was daughter of the duke of Austria, and who was not willing for him to depart because of his youth.

And he came to Verona in the month of February, in the year of Christ 1267, with many barons and good men-at-arms from Germany in his train; and it is said that there followed him as far as Verona almost 10,000 men on horses or ponies, but through lack of means a great part returned to Germany, yet there remained of the best 3,500 German cavalry. And from Verona he passed through Lombardy, and by the way of Pavia he came to the coast of Genoa and arrived beyond Saona at the shores of Varagine, and there put out to sea, and by means of the forces of the Genoese, with their fleet of twenty-five galleys, came by sea to Pisa and arrived there in May in 1268, and by the Pisans and by all the Ghibellines of Italy was received with great honor, almost as if he had been emperor. His cavalry came by land, crossing the mountains of Pontremoli, and arrived at Serrazzano, which was held by the Pisans, and then took the way of the seacoast with an escort as far as Pisa.

King Charles, hearing how Conradin had come into Italy, and hearing of the rebellion of his cities in Sicily and Apulia, caused by the treacherous barons of the kingdom (most of whom he had released from prison), and by Don Henry of Spain, immediately departed from Tuscany, and by hasty marches came

into Apulia, and left in Tuscany M. William di Belselve, his marshal, and with him M. William, the standard-bearer, with 800
French and Provençal horsemen to keep the cities of Tuscany for
his party and to oppose Conradin so that he should not be able
to pass. Pope Clement [IV], hearing of the coming of Conradin,
sent to him his messengers and legates, commanding him, under pain of excommunication, not to go forward, nor to oppose
King Charles, the champion and vicar of Holy Church.

But Conradin did not by reason of this abandon his enterprise, nor would he obey the commands of the pope, forasmuch
as he believed that his cause was just and that the kingdom and
Sicily were his and of his patrimony, and therefore he fell under
sentence of excommunication from the Church, which he de-
spised and cared little for. But being in Pisa, he collected money
and people, and all the Ghibellines and whosoever belonged
to the imperial party, gathered themselves to him, whence his
force grew greatly. And being in Pisa, his host marched against
the city of Lucca, which was held for the party of Holy Church,
and within it were the marshal of King Charles with his people,
and the legate of the pope and of the Church, with the forces
of the Florentines and of the other Guelfs of Tuscany, and with
many who had taken the Cross, and through proclamations
and indulgences and pardons given by the pope and by his legates, had come against Conradin; and he remained over against
Lucca ten days with his host; and the two hosts met together to
fight at Ponterotto, two miles distant from Lucca, but they did
not fight, but each one shunned the battle, and they remained
one on each side of the Guiscianella; so they returned, the one
part to Pisa, and the other to Lucca.

24. How the marshal of King Charles was defeated at Ponte a
Valle by Conradin's army

Then Conradin departed with his followers from Pisa and
came to Poggibonizzi, and when the inhabitants thereof
heard how Conradin was come to Pisa, they rebelled against
King Charles and against the commonwealth of Florence and
sent the keys to Pisa to Conradin. And then from Poggibonizzi
he went to Siena, and by the Sienese was received with great
honor; and whilst he sojourned in Siena, the marshal of

King Charles, who was called, as we have said, M. William di Belselve, with his people, departed from Florence on St. John's Day in June [24] to go to Arezzo to hinder the movements of Conradin; and by the Florentines they were escorted and accompanied as far as Montevarchi; and they desired to accompany him till he should be nigh unto Arezzo, hearing that the journey was like to be disputed, and fearing an ambush in the region round about Arezzo. The said marshal, being beyond measure confident in his people, would have the Florentines accompany him no further, and in front of the cavalcade he set M. William, the standard-bearer, with 300 horsemen well armed and in readiness, and he passed on safe and sound.

The marshal, with 500 of his horsemen, not on their guard nor keeping their ranks, and for the most part unarmed, prepared to advance, and when they came to the bridge at Valle, which crosses the Arno close to Laterino, there sallied forth upon their rear an ambush of the followers of Conradin, which, hearing of the march of the said marshal, had departed from Siena under conduct of the Ubertini and other Ghibelline refugees from Florence. Coming to the bridge, the French, not being prepared, and without much defense, were defeated and slain, and the greater part were taken, and those who fled towards Valdarno to the region round about Florence were taken and spoiled as if they had been enemies; and the said M. William, the marshal, and M. Amelio di Corbano, and many other barons and knights were taken and brought to Siena to Conradin, and this was the day after the Feast of S. John, the 25th day of the month of June, in the year of Christ 1268. At which defeat and capture the followers of King Charles and all those of the Guelf party were much dismayed, and Conradin and his people increased thereupon in great pride and courage and held the French almost for naught. And this being heard in the kingdom, many cities rebelled against King Charles. And at this time King Charles was at the siege of the city of Nocera of the Saracens in Apulia, which had rebelled, to the end that the others on the coast of Apulia, which were all subject to him, might not rebel against him.

25. How Conradin entered Rome and afterwards with his host passed into the Kingdom of Apulia

Conradin, having sojourned somewhat in Siena, departed to Rome, and by the Romans and by Don Henry, the senator, was received with great honor, as if he had been emperor, and in Rome he gathered together people and money, and despoiled the treasures of St. Peter and the other churches of Rome to raise monies. He had in Rome more than 5,000 horsemen, what with Germans and Italians, together with those of the senator, Don Henry, brother of the king of Spain [Castile], who had with him full 800 good Spanish horsemen. And Conradin, hearing that King Charles was with his host in Apulia at the city of Nocera, and that many of the cities and barons of the kingdom had rebelled, and that others were suspected, it seemed to him a convenient time to enter into the kingdom, and he departed from Rome on the 10th day of August, in the year of Christ 1268, with the said Don Henry, and with his company and his barons and with many Romans; and he did not take the way of Campania, for he knew that the pass of Ceprano was furnished and guarded; wherefore he did not desire to contest it, but took the way of the mountains between the Abruzzi and Campania by Valle di Celle, where there was no guard nor garrison. Without any hindrance he passed on and came into the plain of S. Valentino in the country of Tagliacozzo.

26. How the host of Conradin and that of King Charles met in battle at Tagliacozzo

King Charles, hearing how Conradin had departed from Rome with his followers to enter into the kingdom, broke up his camp at Nocera, and with all his people came against Conradin by hasty marches, and at the city of Aquila in Abruzzi awaited his followers. And being at Aquila, he took counsel with the men of the city, exhorting them to be real and true, and to make provision for the host; whereupon a wise and ancient inhabitant rose and said: "King Charles, take no further counsel, and do not avoid a little toil, to the end you may have continual repose. Delay no longer, but go against the enemy, and let him not gain ground, and we will be real and true to you." The king, hearing such sage counsel, without any delay or further parley,

Fig. 34. *The Battle of Tagliacozzo*. From Grandes Chroniques de France, (1375–1400). Paris, BNF, MS Français 2813, fol. 345r.

departed by the road crossing the mountains and came close to the host of Conradin in the place and plain of S. Valentino, and there was nothing between them except the river of ...

King Charles had among his people between the French, Provençals and Italians, less than 3,000 cavaliers, and seeing that Conradin had many more people, he took the counsel of the good M. Alardo di Valleri, a French knight of great wisdom and prowess, who at that time had arrived in Apulia overseas from the Holy Land,[6] who said to King Charles, if he desired to be victorious it behooved him to use stratagems of war rather than force. King Charles, trusting much in the wisdom of the said M. Alardo, committed to him the entire direction of the host and of the battle, who drew up the king's followers in three troops, and of one he made captain M. Henry of Cosance, tall in person and a good knight at arms. He was armed with royal insignia, in place of the king's person, and led Provençals, Tuscans, Lombards and men of Campania. The second troop was of Frenchmen, whereof were captains M. Jean de Cléry, and M. William, the standard-bearer; and he put the Provençals to guard the bridge over the said river, to the end the host of Conradin might not pass without the disadvantage of combat. King Charles, with the flower of his chivalry and barons, to the number of 800 cavaliers, he placed in ambush behind a little hill in a valley, and with King Charles there remained the said M. Alardo di Valleri, with M. William de Ville and Arduino, prince of the Morea, a right valiant knight.

---

6.   Dunbabin, *French in the Kingdom of Naples*, 171–74 et passim, emphasizes the importance of such military experience.

Conradin, on the other side, formed his followers in three troops, one of Germans, whereof he was captain with the duke of Austria, and with many counts and barons; the second of Italians, whereof he made captain Count Calvagno, with certain Germans; the third was of Spaniards, whereof was captain Don Henry of Spain [Castile], their lord. In this array, one host over against the other, the rebel barons of the kingdom guilefully, in order to cause dismay to King Charles and his followers, caused false ambassadors to come into the camp of Conradin, in full pomp, with keys in their hands and with large presents, saying that they were sent from the commonwealth of Aquila to give him the keys and the lordship of the city, as his men and faithful subjects, to the end he might deliver them from the tyranny of King Charles. For which cause the host of Conradin and he himself, deeming it to be true, rejoiced greatly; and this being heard in the host of King Charles caused great dismay, since they feared to lose the victual which came to them from that side and also the aid of the men of Aquila. The king himself, hearing this, was seized with so great pangs that in the night he set forth with a few of the host in his company and came to Aquila that same night, and causing the guards at the gates to be asked for whom they held the city, they answered, "For King Charles!" He, having entered without dismounting from his horse, having exhorted them to good watch, immediately returned to the host, and was there early in the morning; and because of the weariness of going and returning by night from Aquila, King Charles laid down and slept.

27. How Conradin and his people were defeated by King Charles

[1268] Now Conradin and his host were puffed up with the vain hope that Aquila had rebelled against King Charles, and therefore, all drawn up in battle array, they raised their battle cry and made a vigorous rush to force the passages of the river and engage with King Charles. King Charles, albeit he was reposing, as we have said, hearing the din of the enemy, and how they were in arms and ready for battle, immediately caused his followers to arm and array themselves after the order and fashion whereof we before made mention. And the troop of the Provençals, which was led by M. Henry of Cosance, being at guard on the bridge to hinder the passing of Don Henry of Spain [Castile] and his people, the Spaniards set themselves to ford the river, which was not very great, and began to enclose the troop of Provençals who were defending the bridge. Conradin and the rest of his host, seeing the Spaniards had crossed, began to pass the river, and with great fury assailed the followers of King Charles, and in a short time had routed and defeated the Provençal troop and M. Henry of Cosance; and the standard of King Charles was beaten down, and M. Henry himself was slain. Don Henry and the Germans, believing they had got King Charles in person, inasmuch as he wore the royal insignia, all fell upon him at once. The Provençal troop being routed, they dealt in like fashion with the French and the Italian troop, which was led by M. Jean de Cléry and M. William, the standard-bearer, because the followers of Conradin were two to one against those of King Charles, and very fierce and violent in battle; and the followers of King Charles, seeing themselves so hard pressed, took to flight and abandoned the field. The Germans believed themselves victorious, not knowing of King Charles' ambush, and began to scatter themselves over the field, giving their minds to plunder and booty.

King Charles was upon the little hill above the valley, where was his troop, with M. Alardo di Valleri and with Count Guy of Montfort, beholding the battle. When he saw his people thus routed, first one troop and then the other thus put to flight, he was deadly grieved and longed even to put in motion his own troop to go to the succor of the others. M. Alardo, who was commander of the host, and wise in war, with great temperance and with wise words much restrained the king, saying that for God's sake he should suffer it a while, if he desired the honor of the victory, because he knew the cupidity of the Germans, and how greedy they were for booty; and he must let them break up more from their troops; and when he saw them well scattered, he said to the king: "Let the banners set forth, for now it is time"; and so it was done.

When the said troop sallied forth from the valley, neither Conradin nor his followers believed that they were enemies, but that they were of their own party; and they were not upon their guard; and the king, coming with his followers in close ranks, came straight to where was the troop of Conradin, with the chief among his barons, and there began fierce and violent combat, albeit it endured not long, seeing that the followers of Conradin were faint and weary with fighting and had not near so many horsemen in battle array as those of the king, forasmuch as the greater part were wandering out of the ranks, some pursuing the enemy and some scattered over the field in search of booty and prisoners; and the troop of Conradin, by reason of the unexpected assault of the enemy, was continually diminishing, and that of King Charles continually increasing, because his first troops, who had been put to flight through the first defeat, recognizing the royal standard, joined his company, so that in a little while Conradin and his followers were discomfited.

And when Conradin perceived that the fortunes of war were against him, by the counsel of his greater barons he took to flight, together with the duke of Austria, Count Calvagno, Count Gualferano, Count Gherardo da Pisa and many more. M. Alardo di Valleri, seeing the enemy put to flight, cried aloud, praying and entreating the king and the captains of the troop not to set forth either in pursuit of the enemy or other prey, fearing lest the followers of Conradin should gather together, or should sally forth from some ambush, but to abide firm and in order on the field; and so was it done. And this was very fortunate, for Don Henry, with his Spaniards, and other Germans, which had pursued into a valley the Provençals and Italians whom they had first discomfited, and which had not seen King Charles offer battle nor the discomfiture of Conradin, had now gathered his men together and was returning to the field. Seeing King Charles' troop, he believed them to be Conradin and his following, so that he came down from the hill where he had assembled his men, to come to his allies; and when he drew nigh unto them, he recognized the standards of the enemy, and how much deceived he had been; and he was sore dismayed; but, like the valiant lord he was, he rallied and closed up his troop after such a fashion that King Charles and his followers, which were spent by the toils of the combat, did not venture to strike into Don

Henry's troop, and to the end they might not risk the game already won, they abode in array over against one another a good space.

The good M. Alardo, seeing this, said to the king that they must needs make the enemy break their ranks in order to rout them; whereon the king bade him act after his mind. Then he took of the best barons of the king's troop from twenty to thirty, and they set forth from the troop, as though they fled for fear, as he had instructed them. The Spaniards, seeing how the standard-bearers of sundry of these lords were wheeling round as though in act to flee, with vain hope began to cry: "They are put to flight," and began to leave their own ranks, desiring to pursue them. King Charles, seeing gaps and openings in the troop of Spaniards and others on the German side, began boldly to strike among them, and M. Alardo with his men wisely gathered themselves together and returned to the troop. Then was the battle fierce and hard, but the Spaniards were well armed and by stroke of sword might not be struck to the ground and continually after their fashion they drew close together. Then began the French to cry out wrathfully and to take hold of them by the arms and drag them from their horses after the manner of tournaments; and this was done to such good purpose that in a short time they were routed, defeated and put to flight, and many of them lay dead on the field.

Don Henry, with many of his followers, fled to Montecassino, and said that King Charles was defeated. The abbot, who was lord of those lands, knew Don Henry, and judging by divers signs that they were fugitives, caused him and a great part of his people to be seized. King Charles, with all his followers, remained upon the field, armed and on horseback, until night, to the end that he might gather together his men, and to be sure of full victory over the enemy. This defeat was on the vigil of S. Bartholomew, on the 23rd day of August, in the year of Christ 1268. And in that place King Charles afterwards caused a rich abbey to be built for the souls of his men who had been slain; which is called Sta. Maria della Vittoria,[7] in the plain of Tagliacozzo.

---

7.   For the abbey, see Bruzelius, *Stones*, 27–36.

29. How Conradin and certain of his barons were taken by King Charles, and how he caused their heads to be cut off [1268]

Fig. 35. *The execution of Conradin and his barons. From Giovanni Villani,* Nuova cronica.

Conradin, with the duke of Austria and with many others, who had fled from the field with him, arrived at the beach near Rome on the sea-shore close by a place that is called Asturi and belonged to the Frangipani, noblemen of Rome; and when they had come there, they had a pinnace furnished to pass into Sicily, hoping to escape from King Charles; and in Sicily, which had almost all rebelled against the king, to recover state and lordship. They having already embarked unrecognized on the said vessel, one of the said Frangipani who was in Asturi, seeing that they were in great part Germans and fine men and of noble aspect, and knowing of the defeat, was minded to gain riches for himself, and therefore he took the said lords prisoners. Having learnt of their conditions, and how Conradin was among them, he led them captive to King Charles, for which cause the king gave him land and lordship at Pilosa, between Naples and Benevento.

And when the king had Conradin and those lords in his hands, he took counsel what he should do. At last he was minded to put them to death, and he caused by way of process an inquisition to be made against them, as against traitors to the Crown and enemies of Holy Church, and this was carried out; for on the <...> day were beheaded Conradin, the duke of Austria, Count Calvagno, Count Gualferano, Count Bartolommeo and two of his sons, and Count Gherardo of the counts of Doneratico of Pisa, in the market place at Naples, beside the stream of water that runs over against the

church of the Carmelite friars[8]; and the king would not suffer them to be buried in a sacred place, but under the sand
of the market place, since they were excommunicated. Thus
with Conradin ended the line of the house of Swabia, which
was so powerful both in emperors and in kings, as before we
have made mention. But certainly we may see, both by reason
and by experience, that whosoever rises against Holy Church
and is excommunicated, his end must needs be evil for soul
and for body; and therefore the sentence of excommunication of Holy Church, just or unjust, is always to be feared,
for very open miracles have come to pass confirming this, as
whoever wants may read in ancient chronicles; as also by this
present chronicle it may be seen with regard to the emperors
and lords of past times, who were rebels and persecutors of
Holy Church.

Yet because of the said judgment King Charles was much
blamed by the pope and by his cardinals, and by all wise men,
forasmuch as he had taken Conradin and his followers by chance
of battle, and not by treachery, and it would have been better to
keep him prisoner than to put him to death. And some said that
the pope assented thereto; but we do not give faith to this, forasmuch as he was held to be a holy man. And it seems that by
reason of Conradin's innocence, which was of such tender age to
be adjudged to death, God showed forth a miracle against King
Charles, for not many years after God sent him great adversities
when he thought himself to be in highest state, as hereafter in his
history we shall make mention. To the judge who condemned
Conradin, Robert, son of the count of Flanders, the king's son-in-
law, when he had read the condemnation, gave a sword-thrust,
saying that it was not lawful for him to sentence to death so great
and noble a man, from which blow the judge died; and it was
in the king's presence, and there was never a word said thereof,
forasmuch as Robert was very high in the favor of the king, and
it seemed to the king and to all the barons that he had acted
like a worthy lord. Now Don Henry of Spain [Castile] was likewise in the king's prison, but since he was his cousin by blood,

---

8.   That is, in the present Piazza del Mercato, next to Sta. Maria del Carmine.
See Musto, Interactive Map: http://www.italicapress.com/index287.html.

and because the abbot of Montecassino, who had brought him prisoner to the king, to the end he might not break his rule, had made a compact with him that he should not be put to death, the king would not condemn him to death, but to perpetual imprisonment, and sent him prisoner to the fortress in the hill Sanctae Mariae in Apulia; and many other barons of Apulia and of Abruzzi, who had opposed King Charles and been rebellious against him, he put to death with divers torments.

44. THOMAS AQUINAS, *TREATISE ON LAW*, C.1270

Fig. 36. *Thomas Aquinas. c.1300. Detail of Bernardo Daddi*, Madonna, St. Thomas Aquinas and St. Paul. *Tempera and gold leaf on panel. J. Paul Getty Museum.*

Thomas Aquinas[9] was born c.1225 in Roccasecca between Ceprano and Montecassino not far from Aquino, of a noble family of the kingdom of Naples and educated first at the monastic school of the neighboring Benedictine house of Montecassino and then at the *studium generale,* or University, of Naples, established by Frederick II. Against the wishes of his family, he entered the Dominican Order and in 1245 went north to pursue theological studies at the University of Paris. From there he began his teaching career at the University of Cologne and in 1256 returned to Paris as regent master in theology.

---

9.   On Aquinas' early career and his stay at Naples, see James A. Weisheipl, *Friar Thomas d'Aquino: His Life, Thought and Works* (Oxford: Blackwell, 1974,) 15–19. For the University of Naples in this context, see Dunbabin, *French in the Kingdom of Sicily,* 214–27. According to Jeremy Catto, one can understand Aquinas' political thought in the context of his experience in Naples. See "Ideas and Experience in the Political Thought of Aquinas," *Past & Present* 71 (1975): 3–21.

He returned to Naples between 1259 and 1261 to lecture at the Dominican school at the university, and after a second regency at Paris (1268–72), he returned to Naples in 1272 to head a revamped Dominican *studium generale* there. He began work on his *Summa theologiae* in 1265. While working on the third part of his *Summa* he suffered a collapse in December 1273 and died on 7 March 1274. His *Summa theologiae* follows the form of many medieval compendia of theology and philosophy, highly influenced by biblical, patristic, medieval and ancient philosophical thought, especially that of Aristotle and his later followers.

Since the University of Naples specialized in educating future legal experts and royal bureaucrats, we have selected a text from Aquinas that discusses the more theoretical aspects of the law in order to give some of the flavor of the intellectual atmosphere of late medieval Naples. This was influenced both by Roman law and by the legal theory and practice of the communes of northern Italy. Following Aristotle, Aquinas stresses the pubic, communal nature of human agency and law, culminating in the "common good."

The following sections are excerpted from his "Treatise on Law," *Summa*, part II, question 90, article four (II.90.4), translated by David Burr and used on *The Medieval Sourcebook*.[10]

TREATISE ON LAW

WHETHER LAW IS SOMETHING PERTAINING TO REASON

Law is a rule and measure of actions through which one is induced to act or restrained from acting. *Lex*, "law," is derived from *ligare*, "to bind," because it binds one to act. The rule and measure of human activity is reason, however, for it is the first principle of human acts. Indeed, it is the function of reason to order to an end, and that is the first principle of all activity according to Aristotle. That which is the first principle in any genus is the rule and measure of that genus, e.g., unity in the genus of number or first movement in the genus of movement. Thus it follows that law is something pertaining to reason.

---

10. At www.fordham.edu/halsall/source/aquinas2.asp. Accessed 11/5/12.

WHETHER LAW IS ALWAYS ORDERED TO THE COMMON GOOD

Law pertains to that which is the principle of human acts because it is a rule and measure. Just as reason is the principle of human acts, however, there is something in reason which is principle of all the rest. It is to this that law principally and mostly pertains. The first principle in activity, the sphere of practical reason, is the final end. The final end of human life is happiness or beatitude. Thus law necessarily concerns itself primarily with the order directing us toward beatitude.

Furthermore, since each part is ordered to the whole as imperfect to perfect, and since each single man is a part of the perfect community, law necessarily concerns itself particularly with communal happiness. Thus Aristotle, in defining legal matters, mentions both happiness and the political community, saying, "We term 'just' those legal acts that produce and preserve happiness and its components within the political community." For the state is a perfect community, as he says in his *Politics*.

In any genus, that which is called "most of all" is the principal of everything else in that genus, and everything else fits into the genus insofar as it is ordered to that thing. For example, fire, the hottest thing, is cause of heat in mixed bodies, which are said to be hot insofar as they share in fire. Thus, since law is called "most of all" in relation to the common good, no precept concerning action has the nature of law unless it is ordered to the common good.

WHETHER ANYONE CAN MAKE LAWS

Law principally and properly seeks the common good. Planning for the common good is the task of the whole people or of someone ruling in the person of the whole people. Thus lawmaking is the task of the whole charge of the whole people; for in all other matters direction toward an end is the function of him to whom the end belongs.

WHETHER PROMULGATION IS AN ESSENTIAL PART OF LAW

Law is imposed on others as a rule and measure. A rule and measure is imposed by being applied to those who are ruled and measured. Thus in order for a law to have binding power

— and this is an essential part of law — it must be applied to those who ought to be ruled by it. Such application comes about when the law is made known to those people through promulgation. Thus such promulgation is necessary if a law is to have binding force.

Thus from the four preceding articles we arrive at a definition of law: Law is nothing other than a certain ordinance of reason for the common good, promulgated by him who has care of the community.

WHETHER THERE IS AN ETERNAL LAW

A law is nothing more than a dictate of the practical reason emanating from a ruler who governs some perfect community. Assuming that the world is ruled by divine providence, however, it is clear that the whole community of the universe is governed by divine reason. Thus the very idea of the governance of all things by God, the ruler of the universe, conforms to the definition of a law. And since, as we read in Proverbs 8:23, the divine reason's conception of things is eternal and not subject to time, a law of this sort can be called eternal.

WHETHER THERE IS A NATURAL LAW IN US

Since law is a rule or measure, it can be in something in two ways: as that which regulates and measures, or as that which is regulated and measured, for insofar as something participates in a rule or measure it is itself regulated and measured. Since everything subjected to divine providence is regulated and measured by eternal law, it is clear that everything participates in the eternal law in some way. That is, everything inclines to its own proper acts and ends because such an inclination is impressed on it through eternal law.

The rational creature is subject to divine providence in a more excellent way than other beings, however, for he is a participant in providence, providing both for himself and for others. Thus he is a participant in that eternal reason through which he has a natural inclination to his proper act and end, and this participation of the rational creature in eternal law is called "natural law." Thus the psalmist says, "Offer a sacrifice of justice" (Ps. 4:6) and then, as if someone were asking him what the works of justice are, he adds, "Many say, 'Who shows us good things?'" He replies, "The light of your countenance is impressed upon us, Lord," thus implying that the light of natural reason, by which we discern what is good and bad (which is the function of natural law), is nothing else than an impression of the divine light upon us.

Thus it is clear that natural law is nothing other than the rational creature's participation in the eternal law.

WHETHER THERE IS A HUMAN LAW

Law is a certain dictate of practical reason. The process is the same in the case of practical and speculative reason. Each proceeds from certain premises to certain conclusions. Accordingly it must be said that, just as in speculative reason we draw from naturally known, in demonstrable principles the conclusions of various sciences, and these conclusions are not imparted to us by nature but discovered by the work of reason, so it is that human reason starts from the precepts of natural law as from certain common and in demonstrable premises, proceeding from them to more particular determinations of certain matters.

These particular determinations devised by human reason are called "human laws," provided that all the other conditions included in the definition of "law" are observed. Thus Tully [Cicero] says that "justice took its start from nature, then certain things became customary because of their usefulness. Later the things which started in nature and were approved by custom were sanctioned by fear and reverence for the law."

45. THE ANGEVINS IN MOREA, 1278

The Morea is the French name of the Peloponnese in Greece, conquered by Latins in the Fourth Crusade, which toppled the Byzantine Empire in 1204 and installed a series of Latin states in its place in what is now Greece and Albania. Charles I of Anjou inherited the Morea after his defeat of Manfred at Benevento, and Latin rulers there ceded titles to him in the Treaty of Viterbo in 1267. Historians often speak of an "Angevin Empire" in the Mediterranean. Yet, as the selection below indicates, Neapolitan rule over this area was less imperial than feudal. Difficulties of feudal rule, its mixed and conditional allegiances, the conservatism of colonial societies and the fragile — and very personal — nature of governance in the thirteenth and fourteenth centuries combined with the threat of rivals in the area, especially the growing power of the Turks, to make this empire as much a burden to the Angevins as an asset. Nevertheless, the allure of empire and its titles held strong influence over the Angevins of Naples, and they long held within the royal family the title of princes of the Morea and titular emperor of Constantinople.

The *Chronicle of the Morea* was composed in verse by an unknown French author, probably a court notary or clerk in Morea, in Greek for a bilingual French audience. It largely covers the period 1204–92. The Greek version, translated here into English, was probably based on a now lost French original, dating to about 1304–14. Another Greek version brought the narrative to 1388. These, and the Italian and Aragonese (to 1393) versions, all attest to the cosmopolitan nature of this region and its role as a cockpit of international colonial rivalry.

This selection was clearly composed after 1309, since it mentions Robert of Anjou as king of Naples. It is taken from Harold E. Lurier, ed. and trans., *Crusaders as Conquerors: The Chronicle of Morea* (New York: Columbia University Press, 1964), 191–94.

Now after Prince Guillaume [II de Villehardouin, died May 1, 1278], Sir Jean Chauderon, the grand constable (thus was he called throughout the principality, and he was left, indeed, as bailli in Morea), immediately wrote letters and sent messengers to Naples, where King Charles [I] was. In minute detail he announced to him and informed him of the death of the prince and his situation. And when the king heard this, he was sorely grieved; he ordered that the leaders of his council come to him. He asked counsel of them and that they counsel him about the land of Morea and how he should govern it. And his council told him to send a most wise man, an experienced soldier, to be bailli and governor throughout the principality and to have permission and power to govern everyone in accordance with the desires and well-being of the men of the land.

So, he thereupon appointed a certain knight: Rousseau was he named and de Sully was his surname. He was a noble man and an experienced soldier. And he [King Charles I] gave him fifty mercenaries on their steeds and 200 arbalesters, all excellent in the highest degree, whom the king ordered him to set to the protection on his behalf of the castles of Morea; he issued him orders, which he took with him. To the bishops, bannerets, knights, to the leading men who were then in Morea, to all of these he bore letters on the part of the king. He left Naples with these troops and arrived in Klarentsa in the beginning of May. Now, when he arrived, he sent missives to the bishops of the land, to all the bannerets and to the knights, including letters from the king, which he carried with him. At the same time, he wrote to them on his own behalf that they should gather in Klarentsa to see the commands which he had brought from the king. And they came in on receiving the letters; and as soon as they were gathered, small and great, they opened the orders and read them; the king ordered all men of Morea to accept Rousseau de Sully as bailli and all who were liege men and owed homages to perform them to Rousseau for their estates, altogether as if he were the king himself.

And as soon as they had read those commands, the bannerets, the bishops and the knights as well took counsel as to how they might release themselves. They chose the metropolitan of Patras, Sir Benoit by name, to speak for all. Thereupon, he undertook to tell the bailli that all the men of Morea, small and great, all respected the orders and commands which he had brought from the king and accepted him, to hold and respect him as though he were the king himself. But, the homage and act of allegiance that he ordered them to perform to the bailli de Sully, they would never do, for by so doing, they would, in fact, be straying from the customs, which are stipulated by the law of Morea and which they had from the time of the conquest and which were sworn to and written by those who conquered the principality of Morea and seized it by the sword.

For the law of Morea and the customs of the land stipulate that the prince, the lord, indeed, of the land, whoever he may be, when he comes to take up the suzerainty, must come in person into the principality to swear first of all to the troops who are in Morea, and he is to place his hand upon Christ's Gospel, that he will protect and justify them in the customs which they have and not disturb them in the franchise that they have. And when the prince has sworn in the way I have been telling you, then all the lieges of the principality begin to pay homage to the prince. For the liege act that takes place when they kiss upon the mouth is a mutual affair between the two of them; thus the prince owes good faith to the liege, just as the liege to him, and there is no difference, apart from the glory and honor which every lord receives. But should the prince happen to be in another land and should wish to appoint some other representative to receive the homage which the lieges owe, the liege men of Morea are not obliged to perform the act of homage and fealty to any other but to the prince, himself, and within the confines of the principality. "Therefore, the lieges of Morea ask you not to take this as a reflection upon you, for they would rather die and be disinherited than be removed from their customs. However, let the following take place for the glory of the king; and let him not in any way believe that they do this in defiance. Rather, since the sovereign authority of the prince has changed hands, we should come under the authority of our lord the king, if we had the power to do homage. We who are here in the presence of your highness do not have this power unless the others be here: the great lord, first of all, the duke of Athens; the three lords of Euripos and the duke of Naxos, and also the marquis of Boudonitza. However, to avoid a lengthy discussion, if it is your wish, whereas you are bailli today and have that power, and you are not rightful lord for them to do you homage, so that you may have confidence in the men of the land, and they, in turn, in you, that you will govern them with justice, let there be made a compromise in fear of God; you, first, to swear on the Gospels of Christ to rule and govern us according to the customs of the land, and then, after you, these to swear to you to be true to the king and to you as the king's official and his representative that you are."

When Rousseau de Sully heard that an oath was to take place, he immediately fell in with the suggestion and agreed to it.

Thereupon, he ordered that the Holy Gospel be brought, and the bailli swore first, and then the liege men, to be vassals and faithful, first to King Charles, and after him to his heirs, as is the custom. With this, Rousseau received the bailliage and he began to put his office into operation and to change the officials and put in others who were new. He changed the protovestiarios and also the treasurer, the purveyor of the castles and all the castellans; he distributed the arbalesters among the castles and then assigned the corvées [labor services] on of the land.

And so, after the dominion of the king was begun to spread in the name of the prince Sir Louis [Philip of Sicily],[11] who was the son of the king and husband of Isabeau [Isabelle de Villehardouin], the daughter of Prince Guillaume, there had hardly passed a short, brief time when, from the many sins that Morea has, and, thus, they do not have the luck to keep a good lord, Sir Louis [Philip], prince of Morea, died [1 January 1277]. Behold the evil that befell with this death, for he promised and he seemed to be a good lord. He was the younger brother of King Charles [II], the one who was lame, the father of King Robert. And after Sir Louis [Philip] died, the suzerainty of sinful Morea fell into the hands and power of King Charles [II, who then became the direct ruler].

46. THE SICILIAN VESPERS, 1282

The revolt of the Sicilian people on Easter Sunday, 30 March 1282, known as the Sicilian Vespers,[12] does not appear to have been a spontaneous uprising over one Sicilian's honor but most likely a carefully planned revolt against the Angevins by loyalists to the Hohenstaufen in alliance with Byzantine agents and the king of Aragon. Villani's narrative reflects these conflicting versions of events. Whatever the cause, the division of the kingdom and the loss of Sicily were ever after seen as a "mutilation," as is explicitly stated in King Robert's will in 1343.[13] The Angevins of Naples would make

---

11. The chronicle confuses Charles' eldest son, Louis, with his third son, Philip.

12. See above p. lxiii–lxv and n. 152.

13. See below, Reading 65, Item 14, p. 247.

the recapture of Sicily one of the cornerstones of their policy until the end of the dynasty. Nevertheless, the island of Sicily would be reunited to the Regno only with the Spanish conquest of 1504 and the creation of what would become known thereafter as the "Kingdom of the Two Sicilies."

The following selection is taken from book VII of Villani, *Croniche*, trans. Selfe, 267–68.

VII. 61. HOW AND AFTER WHAT MANNER THE ISLAND OF SICILY REBELLED AGAINST KING CHARLES

In the year of Christ 1282, on Easter Monday of the Resurrection, which was the 30th day of March, as had been purposed by Lord John of Procida, all the barons and chiefs who had a hand in the plot were in the city of Palermo for Easter, and the inhabitants of Palermo, men and women, going in a body, on horse and on foot, to the festival at Monreale, three miles outside the city (and as those of Palermo went, so also went the Frenchmen, and the captain of King Charles, for their disport), it came to pass, as was purposed by the enemy of God, that a Frenchman in his insolence laid hold of a woman of Palermo to do her villainy; she beginning to cry out, and the people being already sore and all moved with indignation against the French, the retainers of the barons of the island began to defend the woman, whence arose a great battle between the French and the Sicilians, and many were wounded and slain on either side; but those of Palermo came off worst. Straightway, all the people returned in flight to the city, and the men flew to arms, crying, "Death to the French!"

They gathered together in the market place, as had been ordained by the leaders of the plot; and the justiciary, which was for the king, fighting at the castle, was taken and slain, and as many Frenchmen as were in the city were slain in the houses and in the churches, without any mercy. And this done, the said barons departed from Palermo, and each one in his own city and country did the like, slaying all the Frenchmen who were on the island, except that in Messina they delayed some days before rebelling; but through tidings from those in Palermo giving account of their miseries in a fair epistle, and exhorting them to love liberty and freedom and fraternity with them, the men of Messina were so moved to rebellion that they afterwards did the same as what they of Palermo had done against the French, and even more. And there were slain in Sicily more than 4,000 French, and no one could save another though he were never so much his friend, no not if he would lay down his life for him; and if he had concealed him, he must needs yield him up or slay him. This plague spread through all the island, whence King Charles and his people received great hurt both in person and in goods. These adverse and evil tidings the archbishop of Monreale straightway made known to the pope and to King Charles by his messengers.

47. ADAM DE LA HALLE'S *JEU DE ROBIN ET MARION*, 1283

Fig. 37. *Adam de la Halle. La Vallière manuscript. Paris, BNF.*

Adam de la Halle (le Bossu or le Bossu d'Arras) was born c.1237 or 1245–50. He came to the Neapolitan court of Charles I of Anjou, possibly in 1282/83, as the guest of Charles' nephew, Robert II of Artois. Adam, the son on a burgher, was probably educated at the University of Paris. He is often called one of the last trouvères but was accomplished of many forms, including polyphony.[14]

At Naples he wrote *Jeu du Pélerin* and began his *Chanson du roi de Cécile*. He may have died in Naples in 1285–88 or perhaps even after 1306 in England. His *Jeu de Robin et Marion* was performed in Naples in the autumn of 1283 and had its first performance in the North at Arras in 1289.[15] Sung throughout with

---

14. See *Oeuvres complètes du trouvère Adam de la Halle (poésies et musique)*. Charles Edmond Henri de Coussemaker, ed. (Paris: Durand & Pédone-Lauriel, 1872).

15. See Jean Maillard, *Adam de La Halle: Perspective musicale* (Paris: H. Champion, 1982).

both songs and dialog, it has been seen as the first surviving comic opera and is indicative of the entertainments found in the Angevin court in Naples.

Our text[16] is taken from L.J.N. Monmerqué and Francisque Michel, *Théatre français au moyen age* (Paris: Firmin Didot Frères, 1842), 102–11, and is translated by Eileen Gardiner.

Marion: Robin loves me, Robin has me, if Robin asked me to, I would. Robin bought me a fine and beautiful scarlet blouse and belt to go with it! Robin loves me, Robin has me, if Robin asked me to, I would.

Knight: I returned from the tournament, and I found Marion, with her beautiful figure, all alone.

Marion: Oh, Robin, if you love me, for love take me.

Knight: Shepherdess, may God give you a fine day.

Marion: God bless you, sir.

Knight: For love, sweet girl, tell me now why you sing this song so willingly and so often. "Oh, Robin, if you love me, for love take me."

Marion: Good sir, there well enough: I love Robin and he loves me, and he even showed me that he cherished me: he gave me this box, this staff and this knife.

Knight: Tell me, have you seen any bird fly over this field?

Marion: Sir, I have seen, I don't know how many of them. There are even goldfinches in those bushes who sing so gaily.

Knight: So help me God, beautiful, sweet form, this is not what I asked at all, but did you see here, up near the river, any ducks?

Marian: There is a beast that sneers; yesterday I saw three on the road, all burdened, go to the mill. Is that what you wanted to know?

Knight: At this point I am well underway. Tell me, have you seen a heron?

Marion: A heron! Sir, by my faith, no I have not seen one since Lent, when I saw one eaten at the home of Lady Emma, my grandmother, who owns all these sheep.

---

16. A complete facsimile of the Mejanes manuscript of the work: Aix-en-Provence, Bibliothèque Méjanes, MS 166 (Rés. MS 14), is online at: http://toisondor.byu.edu/dscriptorium/aix166. Sample sound recordings are available online at http://www.youtube.com/watch?v=35f2Tg3Efoc.

Fig. 38. Marion and a knight. Aix-en-Provence, Bibliotèque Mejanes, MS 166, fol. 1v.

Knight: By my faith, I am dumbfounded, I have never been so mocked.

Marion: Sir, by the faith that you owe me, what kind of animal is that on your hand?

Knight: It is a falcon.

Marion: Does it eat bread?

Knight: No, only good food.

Marion: That animal?

Knight: Look! She has a leather head.

Marion: And where are you going?

Knight: To the river.

Marion: Robin is not that sort. There is much more gaiety in him. He enlivens our whole village when he plays the musette.

Knight: Now tell me, sweet shepherdess, would you love a knight?

Marion: Good sir, hold on. I don't know what knights are. Of all the men in the world, I would love only Robin. He comes to me here morning and evening, and all day long and always he brings here to me some of his cheese. I still have some of it in my blouse, and a large piece of bread that he brought me at dinner time.

Knight: Now tell me, sweet shepherdess, would you like to come with me to play on this beautiful palfrey, along the grove in the valley?

Marion: Oh, sir. Take away your horse. It would take very little for him to hurt me. Robin's does not rush at me when I go after his plow.

Knight: Shepherdess, be my friend and do what pleases me.

Marion: Sir, take yourself away from me. It's not right for you to be here. It would not take much for your horse to strike me. What is your name?

Knight: Aubert.

Marion: You waste your effort, Sir Aubert. I will never love anyone except Robin.

Knight: No one, shepherdess?

Marion: No one, by my faith.

Knight: Would you lie down with me? I am a knight and you are a shepherdess, who so far rejects my plea.

Marion: Never, because I don't love you. I am a shepherdess, but I have a good love, well bred and gay.

Knight: Shepherdess, may God give you joy. Since that is it, I'll be on my way. Today I'll say not another word.

Marion: *Trairi, deluriau, deluriau, deluriele, trairi, deluriau, delurau, delurot.*

Knight: This morning I rode near the edge of a forest. I found a gentle shepherdess, more beautiful than any king has seen. And *trairi, deluriau, deluriau, deluriele, trairi, deluriau, deluriau, delurot.*

Marion: Oh! Robin, *duere leire va,* come to me, *leure leure va.* We will play *du leure leure va, du leure leure va.*

Robin: Oh! Marion, *leure leure va,* here I come, *leure leure va.* We will play *du leure leure va, du leure leure va.*

Marion: Robin!

Robin: Marion!

Marion: Where are you coming from?

Robin: By what's holy. I took off my vest because it's cold, and I put on a homespun coat. I brought you some apples. Here.

Marion: Robin, I easily recognized your song when you came, and yet you did not recognize me?

Robin: Yes indeed, by your singing and by your sheep.

Marion: Robin, you didn't know, sweet friend — and I didn't want to hurt you — but here came a man on a horse, wearing a glove. He wore a mitten on his fist and instantly begged me to love him, but didn't succeed since I would not do any wrong.

Robin: Marion, you would have killed me, but if I had come here in time, me or Gautier the Stubborn or Baudon, my cousin, devils would get involved: it would not have ended without a fight.

Marion: Robin, sweet friend, don't be alarmed. Let's enjoy ourselves now.

Robin: May I sit, or must I kneel?

Marion: Come, sit down by my side. Let's eat.

Robin: I give in. I will sit here by your side. But I have not brought you anything. I've certainly made a big mistake.

Marion: Don't worry yourself, Robin. I still have some cheese in my blouse and a big piece of bread, and the apples that you brought me.

Robin: God, how big and fatty this cheese is. Sister, eat.

Marion: You too. When you want something to drink, tell me. Here is some drink in a pouch.

Robin: God. Whoever had some stuff from your grandmother's would not be angry.

Marion: Robin, we have none of it at all, since it is hung too high on the rafters. Let's make do with what we have. It's enough for the morning.

Robin: I'm tired of belly bile again.

Marion: Tell me, Robin, by the faith that you owe me, have you played ball? May God reward you.

Robin: You heard me right, dear, you heard me right.

Marion: Tell me, Robin, don't you want to eat anything more?

Robin: No, really.

Marion: Then put back the bread and the cheese in my blouse until we are hungry.

Robin: Put it all in the box.

Marion: And there it is. Robin, my dear. Pray and command and I will do it.

Robin: Marion, I feel that you are my true friend, since you have found me to be a friend. Shepherdess, sweet bachelorette, give me your little hat, give me your little hat.

Marion: Robin, would you like me to put it on your head, with love?

Robin: Yes, and you will be my little love. You have my belt, my purse and my clasp. Shepherdess, sweet bachelorette, give me your little hat.

Marion: Willingly, my sweet friend. Robin, let's have a little celebration.

Robin: Do you want my arms or my head? I tell you that I can do anything. You only have to say yes.

Marion: Robin, by the love of your father! Do you know how to turn on one foot?

Robin: Yes, by the love of my mother, see, my sweet, how it suits me in front and in back, in front and in back.

Marion: Robin, by the soul of your father, let's turn forward.

Robin:　Marion, by the soul of my mother, I will come very well in the end. Could there ever be so beautiful a figure, could there ever be so beautiful a figure?

Marion: Robin, by the soul of your father, let's turn arms.

Robin:　Marion, by the soul of my mother, just as you please. Is this the way, my sweet, is this the way?

Marion: Robin, by the soul of your father! Do you know how to dance in the evening?

Robin:　Yes, by the soul of my mother! But I have less hair in front than behind, my sweet, in front then behind.

Marion: Robin, do you know how to lead a braid?

Robin:　Yes, but the way is too cool, and my leggings are torn.

Marion: We are very well set, do not be afraid. Now do what I tell you, by your love for me.

Robin:　Wait, I will go and look for my tambour and musette of the bumblebee. I will bring here Baudon, if I can find him, and Gautier. I will very much need them if that knight returns.

Marion: Robin, return quickly. And if you find Péronnelle, my friend, call her. The more the merrier! She is behind those gardens, as one passes Roger's mill. And hurry.

Robin:　Let me roll up my pants, then I'll run.

Marion: Go now.

Robin:　Gautier, Baudon, are you there? Good cousins, open the door quickly for me

Gautier: You are welcome here, Robin. Why are you so out of breath?

Robin:　What, me? Alas! I am so tired that I cannot catch my breath.

Gautier: Tell me, has someone beaten you?

Robin:　Not at all. Truly.

Gautier: Tell me quickly if there's a problem.

Robin:　Lord, listen a bit. I have come here for you two since I know that fiddler on a horse asked for love from Marion just now. I fear that he will come back again.

Gautier: If he returns he will pay.

Baudon: Yes, truly, with his head!…

Fig. 39. Charles II. Detail of the Angevin Genaeology. Anjou Bible, *fol. 4r.*

CHARLES II

One of the more useful narrative sources for the history of the later Angevins is the *Cronaca di Partenope,* named after the ancient Greek name of the city. It had been thought by Bartolommeo Capasso, among others, that the text that we now possess is probably the work of several authors and was composed in Neapolitan some time between 1326 and 1380.[17] Samantha Kelly has now concluded that it was written by a single author: Bartolomeo Carracciolo-Carafa, who completed the text between the summer of 1348 and that of 1350.[18]

Like many medieval chronicles, the *Partenope* narrates its history from antiquity to the writer's time. Book I pays special attention to the history of Naples from its Greek foundations, the Roman period and to the city's early Christian history. Of special interest to students of Neapolitan sources are the *Cronaca's* early use of the Neapolitan dialect and its recounting of the many legends around Virgil and his mythic status as a magician.

The following selection was translated by R.G. Musto and is taken from Book II of the *Cronaca di Partenope,* Antonio Altamura, ed. (Naples: Società Editrice Napoletana, 1974), 129–31; now supplemented by Kelly's edition in *Cronaca,* 270–73.

---

17. Capasso, *Le fonti,* 131–37.

18. Samantha Kelly, *The Cronaca di Partenope: An Introduction to and Critical Edition of the First Vernacular History of Naples (c.1350)* (Leiden: Brill, 2011). Kelly summarizes and analyzes all previous scholarship on the chronicle in her introduction, 11–26, esp. 19–21. On Bartolomeo and his family, see pp. 21–26.

48. CHARLES II AND HIS REIGN, 1285

11. How Charles II succeeded King Charles I

To the aforesaid Charles I succeeded his son Charles II [in 1285]. Charles II ruled for twenty-four years and died in Naples in the year of the Lord 1309, on a Saturday, the fifth of May, in the seventh indiction. He was sixty [55] years of age [1254–1309]. He was buried in the church of S. Domenico Maggiore of the Dominican Order. Afterwards his body was transported to Aquis [Aix] in Provence and was buried in the convent of Notre-Dame-de-Nazareth of the Dominican sisters.

Samantha Kelly's new edition provides a parallel, more complete text of the first, version A (chapter 71) in her new version B, chapter 91. Translations by R.G. Musto.

To the aforesaid Charles I succeeded his first-born and only son Charles II. He was bent in body but sharp in mind, wise and full of infinite virtue. During the life of King Charles no one could be found more generous in giving gifts nor more munificent in providing private alms. He was glorious in peace and in war.

He had built in the city of Aix-en-Provence a monastery of friars and monks that is called Saint-Marie-de-Nazareth. In Naples he had built the monastery of S. Pietro a Castello of the same [Dominican] order, and at Aversa the monastery of S. Luigi of the [Dominican] order of Preachers, which he endowed and provided with great riches.

13. ON THE VIRTUE AND GOODNESS OF KING CHARLES II (KELLY A73, B93)

King Charles II was just and gracious, liberal and benign, and he was much loved by his vassals. He was in addition a most faithful Christian, and he promoted religious life, and in his lifetime built many churches and hospitals. He exalted the men of the Regno, giving them counties and baronies and honors.

He benefited the city of Naples both in general and in particulars, creating there cardinals, admirals, counts and high officials. He began the Molo there and he granted it a *gabella* of good currency and a series of great favors too long to record here....

49. Celestine V abdicates in Castel Nuovo, 1294

Pope Celestine V, the hermit Pietro da Morrone,[19] was a simple adherent of the radical branch of the Franciscan Order dedicated to absolute poverty and Joachite prophesy. His rapid rise and abdication of the papal throne in 1294 — an act almost without parallel — earned him Dante's condemnation for his *"gran rifiuto,"* the adjuration of his civic and religious duty. For this refusal Dante placed Celestine in hell (*Inf.* 3:58–60). Celestine's entire career took place within the kingdom of Naples. His abdication itself was performed in the Castel Nuovo, some say at the instigation of his successor Boniface VIII, and with the connivance of King Charles II. This selection is taken from Villani, *Croniche*, trans. Selfe, 304–6.

Fig. 40. Celestine V. Fresco. Castello di Casaluce, Campania. Wikimedia. Photo: Marie-Lan Nguyen.

Book VIII 5. How Celestine V was elected and made pope, and how he renounced the papacy

In the year of Christ 1294, in the month of July, the Church of Rome had been vacant after the death of Pope Nicholas [IV] d'Ascoli for more than two years, by reason of the discord of the cardinals, who were divided, each party desiring to make one of themselves pope. And the cardinals being in Perugia and straightly constrained by the Perugians to elect a pope, as it pleased God they were agreed not to name one of their own college, and they elected a holy man who was called Brother Peter of Morrone in Abruzzi.

This man was a hermit, and of austere life and penitence, and in order to abandon the vanity of the world, after he had

---

19. See Peter Herde and Stefano Tiraboschi, *Cölestin V. (1294): Peter vom Morrone, der Engelpapst. Mit einem Urkundenanhang und Edition zweier Viten* (Stuttgart: Hiersemann, 1981).

ordained many holy monasteries of his order, he departed as a penitent into the mountain of Morrone, which is above Sulmona. He, being elected and brought and crowned pope, made in the following September, for the reformation of the Church, twelve cardinals, for the most part from beyond the mountains,[20] by the petition and after the counsel of King Charles, king of Sicily and of Apulia.[21] And this done, he departed with the court to Naples, and by King Charles was graciously received and with great honor; but because he was simple and knew no letters, and did not occupy himself willingly with the pomps of the world, the cardinals held him in small esteem, and it seemed to them that they had made an ill choice for the well-being and estate of the Church.

The said holy father perceiving this, and not feeling himself sufficient for the government of the Church, as one who more loved the service of God and the weal of his soul than worldly honor, sought every way how he might renounce the papacy. Now, among the other cardinals of the court was one M. Benedetto Gaetani d'Alagna [Anagni],[22] very learned in books, and in the things of the world much practiced and sagacious, who had a great desire to attain to the papal dignity; and he had laid plans seeking and striving to obtain it by the aid of King Charles and the cardinals, and already had the promise from them, which afterwards was fulfilled to him.

He put it before the holy father, hearing that he was desirous to renounce the papacy, that he should make a new decretal, that for the good of his soul any pope might renounce the papacy, showing him the example of St. Clement, whom, when St. Peter came to die, he desired should be pope after him; but he, for the good of his soul, would not have it so, and in his place first St. Linus and then St. Cletus was pope. And even as the said cardinal gave counsel, Pope Celestine made the said decretal; and this done, the day of Sta. Lucia in the following December [13], in a consistory of all the cardinals, in their presence he took off the crown and papal mantle, and renounced

---

20.　That is, north of the Alps, or mostly French cardinals.

21.　That is, the kingdom of Sicily and Naples.

22.　Benedetto Gaetani, later Boniface VIII.

the papacy, and departed from the court, and returned to his hermit life, and to do his penance. And thus Pope Celestine reigned in the papacy five months and nine days.

But afterwards it is said, and was true, that his successor, M. Benedetto Gaetani aforesaid, caused him to be taken prisoner in the mountains of S. Angiolo in Apulia above Bastia, whither he had withdrawn to do penance; and some say that he would fain have gone into Slavonia, but the other secretly held him in the fortress of Fulmone in Campania in honorable confinement, to the intent that so long as he lived none should be set up as a rival to his own election, forasmuch as many Christians held Celestine to be the right and true pope, notwithstanding his renunciation, maintaining that such a dignity as was the papacy by no decretal could be renounced; and albeit St. Clement refused the papacy at first, the faithful nevertheless held him to be father, and it behooved him to be pope after St. Cletus.

But Celestine being held prisoner, as we have said, in Fulmone, lived but a short time in the said place; and dying there, he was buried poorly in a little church outside Fulmone belonging to the order of his brethren, and put underground more than ten cubits deep, to the end that his body might not be found. But during his life, and after his death, God wrought many miracles by him, whence many people held him in great reverence; and a certain time afterwards by the Church of Rome, and by Pope John XXII, he was canonized and called St. Peter of Morrone.

ROBERT OF ANJOU

Robert of Anjou, called "the Wise," was actually the third in line for the Neapolitan throne. When his eldest brother Charles Martel was named king of Hungary, however, the throne was to pass to Charles II's second-oldest son, Louis. With Louis' renunciation of the throne and his entering the Franciscan Order in 1295,[23] Robert became duke of

---

23. St. Louis of Toulouse. The best monographic study remains Margaret R.S. Toynbee, *Louis of Toulouse and the Process of Canonisation in the Fourteenth Century* (Manchester: University Press, 1929).

Calabria and official heir to the throne in 1296. He married Yolanda of Aragon in 1297 as part of a final peace treaty between Naples and Aragon to settle the war of the Sicilian Vespers. Yolanda died in 1302, after the couple had had two sons, Charles and Louis (d.1310). In 1304, Robert married Sancia of Majorca.[24] On the death of Charles II in 1309, he inherited the crown with the approval of the Pope Clement V.

Fig. 41. *Robert of Anjou. From the* Panegyric to Robert of Anjou *from* the Citizens of Prato. *c.1330. London, British Library, MS Royal 6 E IX, fol. 10v.*

Robert of Anjou was prudent in his diplomatic relations with his neighbors in Italy and his overlord the pope, a strong ruler who inherited and refined a late medieval bureaucratic state and used its apparatus to administer justice, encourage trade, keep a close eye on finances and avoid military conflict whenever possible. He was also a man of keen intellect who patronized or employed the most forward-looking artists and intellectuals of the age, including Petrarch, Boccaccio, François de Meyronnes, Paolino da Venezia, Giovanni Barrili, Barbato da Sulmona, Giotto, Simone Martini, Pietro Cavallini and Tino da Camaino. Robert was himself — with the aid of his many advisors and court intellectuals — the author of treatises on governance, personal and public ethics, church and state policy and theology.

These qualities gave him the title of "the Wise" even in his own lifetime. Recent students of the Angevins have

---

24. See Musto, "Queen Sancia of Naples"; and Gaglione, *Donne e potere*, 109–74.

demonstrated Robert's keen sense of statecraft and a public image-making that they see as epitomizing a Renaissance prince. Applying a theme ultimately from Jacob Burkhardt,[25] Pryds,[26] Kelly[27] and others have focused on Stephen Greenblatt's theory of Renaissance persona[28] as a key to Robert's rule.[29]

Yet Robert remains a paragon of medieval kingship and, with Queen Sancia of Majorca, of Franciscan Spiritual and Joachite religious belief.[30] In 1309, Robert traveled to Provence, where the papacy was about to take up its long residence in exile in Avignon, and was crowned king of Naples there.

This selection is taken from book VIII, 112 of Villani, *Chroniche*, trans. Selfe, 390–91.

---

25. Originally published in German in 1860, English trans. S.G.C. Middlemore; Benjamin Nelson and Charkles Trinkaus, eds., *The Civilization of the Renaissance in Italy*, 2 vols. (New York: Harper & Row, 1958), esp. 1:143–74.

26. In *The King Embodies the Word*.

27. In *The New Solomon*.

28. Best expressed in *Renaissance Self-Fashioning: From More to Shakespeare* (Chicago: University of Chicago Press, 1980). For some medievalist responses to this theory see, for example, Jeffrey F. Hamburger, "Medieval Self-Fashioning: Authorship, Authority, and Autobiography in Suso's Exemplar," in *The Visual and the Visionary: Art and Female Spirituality in Late Medieval Germany* (New York: Zone Books, 1998), 233–78. For a useful overview of the literature on self and self-fashioning in the Middle Ages, see Walter Pohl, "Introduction: Ego Trouble?" in *Ego Trouble: Authors and Their Identities in the Early Middle Ages*, Richard Corradini et al., eds. (Vienna: Verlag der Österreichischen Akademie der Wissenschaften, 2010), 9–21. For a recent critique of Greenblatt's methodology see Jim Hinch, "On *The Swerve*: Why Stephen Greenblat Is Wrong — and Why it Matters," *Los Angeles Review of Books* (Dec. 1, 2012), http://lareviewofbooks.org/article.php?type&id=1217& fulltext=1&media#article-text-cutpoint. Accessed 12/1/12.

29. Se also above lvii–lix.

30. See Musto, "Queen Sancia of Naples"; and "Franciscan Joachimism." For the most recent rejection of Joachite influence see Dunbabin, *French in the Kingdom of Naples*, 213, citing Kelly, *New Solomon*, 74–90.

50. How Robert was crowned king over the kingdom of Sicily and Apulia

In the month of June 1309, Duke Robert, now King Charles' [II's] eldest son, went by sea from Naples to Provence, to the court, with a great fleet of galleys and a great company, and was crowned king of Sicily and of Apulia by Pope Clement [V], on St. Mary's Day in September of the said year, and was entirely acquitted of the loan which the Church had made to his father and grandfather for the war in Sicily, which is said to have been more than 300,000 ounces[31] of gold. In the said year and month the Guelfs were driven out of Amelia by the forces of the Colonna.

51. King Robert expels prostitutes from central Naples, 1314

The port of Naples' position as an international entrepôt has long made it a center for prostitutes of all sorts. Angevin Naples was no exception. Here Robert attempts to clear the area between S. Biagio dei Librai and SS. Severino e Sossio, the heart of the old city.

Our selection is taken from Camera, *Annali*, 2:225–26. It is translated by R.G. Musto.

Robert, by the grace of God king of Sicily, etc., commands the Neapolitan noble Filippo de Pando to take action...against the intemperate women, prostitutes and scandalous women inhabitants of via S. Gennaro ad Iaconiam [S. Gennaro all'Olmo on S. Biagio dei Librai] near the monastery of S. Severino in the center of Naples.[32] He commands that all women whose lips are smeared by such filthy conduct, either living there now or who had previously been living there, be completely expelled according to the procedures in the new Constitutions of the Realm.

---

31. An *oncia* equalled 60 silver *carlini*, or *gigliati*, the standard coin of the Regno. See Reading 64 below.

32. SS. Severino e Sossio. See Musto, Interactive Map: http://www.italicapress.com/index287.html.

52. KING ROBERT ADDRESSES THE GENOESE, JULY 27, 1318

Robert's contemporary Dante first caricatured him as "the king who preaches sermons" (*Par.* VIII.145–48) for his many, and often long, sermons.[33] Of these 268 are now extant, most still unedited. And while many of these were not well received by his contemporaries, the practice of the *rex praedicans*, or preaching king, was not unheard of. The kings of Aragon, including Jaime II, and both Robert's near contemporaries Charles IV of Bohemia and Cola di Rienzo in Rome used public speaking to move forward public agendas that were simultaneously political and religious, in keeping with the world view of the time. In almost every sense they fulfilled a learned ruler's obligation to set an agenda and forge a consensus among important constituencies.

The extant collection of Robert's sermons, most recently analyzed by Darleen Pryds, included addresses to visiting ambassadors, speeches commemorating the signing of peace treaties, orations before other princes, sermons in honor of feast days, building dedications, academic ceremonies and the promotion or honoring of members of the court or barons of the realm. In short, it was a fairly typical collection that one would expect an articulate and well-read political leader to deliver over the course of a relatively long career. In addition to these, however, were many sermons delving into the spiritual mysteries of the Christian religion, heavily influenced by the Spiritual Franciscans whom both Robert and Sancia protected at court.

The following selection is a political speech delivered to the people of Genoa, Robert's close neighbors as count of Provence and sometime rivals for territories along the modern Italian Riviera. In the spring of 1318 the lord of Milan, Matteo Visconti, threatened the Genoese with war. They then invited Robert to accept the rule of the city for ten years to defend it against Visconti's encroachments. After delaying and being prodded by Pope John XXII, Robert accepted and entered

---

33. See Pryds, *King Embodies the Word.* On the specific political aspects of his address to the Genoese, see Jean-Paul Boyer, "La prédication de Robert de Sicile (1306–1343) et les communes d'Italie: Le cas de Gênes," in *Prêcher la paix et discipliner la société: Italie, France, Angleterre (XIIIe–XVe siècle),* Rosa Maria Dessi, ed. (Turnhout: Brepols, 2005), 383–411.

Genoa on July 21 in the company of Neapolitan troops, Queen Sancia and his brothers Prince Philip of Taranto and John of Gravina, duke of Durazzo.

This political address of July 27, 1318 offered Robert the opportunity to accept the seignory, to discourse at length on the political and moral virtues of a ruler and to set out a personal agenda for his rule. Chief among its themes are the two virtues that a ruler must possess: power and wisdom. From these come peace: both in the Roman imperial sense of order and tranquility and in the Christian sense of justice for, and among, the people. Robert uses the Bible[34] and Augustine as his main sources, and he speaks of peace in terms that would have been understood easily by his contemporary Italians, as in the frescos of *Good and Bad Government* by Ambrogio Lorenzetti from 1338–40 in the Palazzo Pubblico in Siena.[35]

The following sermon is number 142, from Rome, Bibl. Angelica, MS A 151, fol. 250r–v. It was edited in Darleen Pryds doctoral dissertation.[36] Another version of this book was later published as *The King Embodies the Word*, where the letter is given context, discussed and analyzed.[37] The Latin text appears in the dissertation[38] and has been translated by R.G. Musto. Biblical citations are from the Latin Vulgate Bible used by Robert and his contemporaries, and translations from the Douay-Rheims Bible.

---

34. For Robert's use of the Bible and Angevin commissioning of lavishly illustrated bibles under both Robert and Giovanna I, see Eva Irblich and Gabriel Bise, *The Illuminated Naples Bible: Old Testament, 14th-Century Manuscript*, trans. G. Ivans and D. MacRae (New York: Crescent Books, 1979); Andreas Bräm, *Neapolitanische Bilderbibeln des Trecento: Anjou-Buchmalerei von Robert dem Weisen bis zu Johanna I. 1: Bilderbibeln, Buchmaler und Auftraggeber; 2: Abbildungen* (Wiesbaden: Reichert, 2007); Watteeuw and Van der Stock, *The Anjou Bible*; and Fleck, *The Clement Bible.*

35. See, for example, Randolph Starn, *Ambrogio Lorenzetti: The Palazzo Pubblico, Siena* (New York: George Braziller, 1994); and Musto, *Apocalypse in Rome*, 130–34.

36. "The Politics of Preaching in Fourteenth-Century Naples: Robert d'Anjou (1309–1343) and His Sermons" (Ph.D. diss., University of Wisconsin-Madison, 1994).

37. On 56–59.

38. Appendix V, Sermon 142, pp. 322–26.

Address to the Genoese, July 27, 1318. "The Lord will give strength to his people: the Lord will bless his people with peace" Psalm 28 [10].

A king ought to possess Power: gaining victory over his enemies with strength. Wisdom: seeking concord on behalf of the gentle and meek with enlightenment.

The first attribute is understood in terms of the virtue that ought to be recognized as coming from God, according to Psalm [20:2]: "Yahweh, the king rejoices in your power." For blessed God himself will grant virtue and strength to his people. The second is understood as an expression the peace that he ought always to seek according to Psalm 33 [15]: "seek after peace and pursue it." Apropos of both these virtues together let us quote chapter 10 [6–7] of Jeremiah: "There is none like to thee, O Lord: thou art great and great is thy name in might. Who shall fear thee, O king of nations?"

Regarding the first virtue, "for thine is the glory: among all the wise men of the nations, and in all their kingdoms there is none like unto thee" [Jer. 10:7].

Regarding the second, we find this in two famous kings of the Old Testament. First, the holy King David, as much in the interpretation of the word as in the exercise of the deed. In the interpretation of the word, since "David" means "strong hand." In the execution of the deed as much as in the singular feat against Goliath as in the faithful multitude about whose conquest it is sung, "Saul slew his thousands, and David his ten thousands" [1 Kings 18:7]. Of this strength of virtue David himself says in Psalm [cf. 88:14]: "Thy arm is with might. Let thy hand be strengthened, and thy right hand exalted." And elsewhere [Ps. 17:40]: "And thou hast girded me with strength unto battle."

In his Sermon 4, concerning a barbarian age, Augustine writes, "When Samson had long been terrifying and exhausting the demonic tribes by the strength on his head, which he had accepted from God, whose strength grew greater along with the length of the hair on his head, grasping those two columns [Judges 16:23–30], one in each hand, he wanted to bring down ruin on himself along with the Philistines, rather than suffer listening freely to the praise of demons and insult

Fig. 42. Cristoforo Orimina, Samson Destoys the Palace of the Philistines, c.1330–43. From the Hamilton Bible, *Berlin, Staatliche Museen, Kupferstichkabinett, MS 78 E 3, fol. 83r.*

to his God. As Ecclessiaticus 46 [11] writes of Caleb, "And the Lord gave strength also to David, and his strength continued even to his old age."

Regarding the second virtue, that is Wisdom, which is understood as an expression of peace, we find it in King Solomon, since he was the wisest of kings either preceding or following him, and he made his kingdom universally tranquil in peace. For this he has also been called the peacemaker king. Concerning this 3 Kings 5 [12] writes precisely to the point: "And the Lord gave wisdom to Solomon, as he promised him: and there was peace between Hiram and Solomon, and they two made a league together." Concerning this the prophet Zachariah 8 [19] connects together the truth of wisdom and the unity of peace and concord when he says, "only love ye truth and peace!" Augustine in Sermon 74 [347, 2; PL 39:1525] on the fear of God, expounding on the text [Ps. 83:6–7] "in his heart he hath disposed to ascend by steps. In the vale of tears, in the place which be hath set": "What could this place be," he asks, "except one of quiet and peace?" For there in peace wisdom is clear and never withers.

These two virtues lived in Christ, the son of David, in fact, the second David, who according to the Apostle, is God.

Virtue overcoming the devil, wisdom reconciling the people. Peace follows from both, for peace rises out of victory, since according to Augustine [Letter 189] "war is sought so that peace can be found," and peace is born out of wisdom. Thus, once wisdom, that is Christ, is born in its time (as the saying goes), then a universal peace rises up and is announced through his angels to people of good will [cf. Luke 2:14].

53. THE VILLANI COLLECT PAPAL REVENUES, MAY 5, 1324

Ever since late antiquity, and increasingly from the reign of Pope Gregory the Great, the Roman papacy had based much of its charitable work, food distribution and activities on agricultural incomes derived from southern Italy, especially from Campania and from Sicily. These rights and revenues were developed into a full-scale theory and practice of feudal sovereignty over the Regno that overlapped with papal rights to raise revenues throughout Christendom. Especially important to these papal income streams in the later Middle Ages were the banks of Florence. Among these the Bardi, Peruzzi and Acciaiuoli were major financiers to the papacy, the kings of England and to King Robert of Anjou; while smaller companies like the Bonaccorsi and Villani also found lucrative incomes from acting as papal tax collectors.[39]

This selection has been translated from the Italian in Lopez and Raymond, *Medieval Trade*, 102–3.

In the name of the Lord, Amen. May 5, 1324.

We, Matteo Villani and companions, of the Bonaccorsi *compagnia* of Florence, resident in Naples, acknowledge and recognize by this present receipt [*poliga*] that we have received in Naples, May 5, 1324, from Messer Raymond of Toulouse, treasurer of Benevento, 408 ounces[40] of silver *carlini* marked with the lily, at [the rate of] 60 to the ounce, for which we promise to have paid in court to the chamberlain and treasurer of our lord the pope and his camera 400 ounces of the aforesaid *carlini* marked with the lily, at [the rate of] 60 to the ounce, in consideration of 2 percent [commission] for the transfer. And we promise that we shall hand over to him the receipt of the said chamberlain and treasurer as soon as we have received it, or sufficient guarantee of this payment.

---

39. For the currencies noted below and their equivalencies, see Reading 64.

40. According to Lopez and Raymond, 103 n. 59, "the ounce [*oncia*] was a money of account, whereas the *carlini* marked with the lily, or *gigliati*, were silver coins issued in the kingdom of Naples."

And for further confirmation of this matter and guarantee to the said Messer Raymond, I, the aforesaid Matteo Villani, have written this receipt and sealed it with the seal of the said *compagnia* by my own hand. And we are to deliver to him the said receipt or guarantee in Naples or in Benevento as he wishes.

54. ROBERT OF ANJOU ATTEMPTS TO REGAIN SICILY, 1325

Book III of the *Cronaca di Partenope* begins with Robert of Anjou's attempts to regain Sicily and concludes with the conquest of Naples by Charles III of Durazzo in 1380, just short of the death of Giovanna I in 1382. Our selections are from the *Cronaca di Partenope*, ed. Altamura, 134–36.[41] Translation by R.G. Musto.

III.1. Account of King Robert's attempt to retake Sicily

As already noted, the island of Sicily had rebelled against King Charles I and had come under the control of King Peter of Aragon, who held it in peace. Coming into the rule [*solio*] of the kingdom of Sicily, King Robert, son of King Charles II, who was prudent and rich, considered it an evil that the island of Sicily beyond the Faro [lighthouse at Reggio Calabria] should not be united with the kingdom of Sicily.

Wishing to regain it, he first sent ambassadors to the princes of that island to determine whether they wished to return to their fealty as was their duty, due to the fact that they had been his vassals and that he wished to forgive and forget all offenses committed in the past.

To this the Sicilians replied that they wished to maintain allegiance to the banners [*bandere*] of the most happy house of Aragon. Advised of that fact, King Robert proposed to take on the enterprise of Sicily.

2. How King Robert raised an armada against the Sicilians

Realizing the impertinence of the Sicilians, King Robert envisioned the enterprise of Sicily. He raised many knights, foot soldiers and horses; and he arranged a great fleet of ships, galleys

---

41. Kelly, *Cronaca*, ends her edition (pp. 280–81) with the murder of Andrew of Hungary and the invasion of the Regno by King Lewis, Andrew's brother.

and other vessels. He sent the said forces behind the fleet, and as captain general of the armada he commissioned his son Charles, duke of Calabria. Charles maintained the enterprise for three years with four thousand cavalry and ten thousand infantry. And among the great ships and galleys and other vessels he had one hundred and fifty ships.

To aid the enterprise he appointed Sir Bertram del Balzo, count of Montescaglioso and of Andria. In the company of Duke Charles there were eight counts, the best of the realm. The enterprise began in 1325 and continued into 1328....

3. How King Robert made the said Duke Charles his vicar general, and how he administered justice

Realizing the true virtue and integrity of his illustrious first-born son Duke Charles, and how he loved justice, King Robert appointed him vicar-general of the kingdom of Sicily. In this role he administered such infinite justice that his father took joy in it, and not only for his administration of humans, but also of beasts....

Charles died in 1328. He poor father cried out to the barons of the realm, "The crown has fallen from my head. Woe to you, woe to me!" And so poor old King Robert lost his first-born son and was left without a legitimate male heir. Charles left him a little daughter named Giovanna, and he was buried in the church of Sta. Chiara.

55. KING ROBERT'S CAVALCADES, JUNE 27, 1334

The following treasury record from the *Ratio thesauriarum*, fols. 70–72, notes Robert's donations to religious establishments as part of his regular rounds of cavalcades through the city. The royal family and other high nobility used the cavalcade to attend jousts, funerals, religious ceremonies and other public rituals as a display of both power and pomp for the urban population.

The document is interesting for several reasons. It provides an excellent record of the frequency and ubiquity of public jousts during Robert's reign and offers a checklist of the major churches of the city in the mid-fourteenth century.[42] On the coinage and their relative value, see below, Reading 64.

This reading is taken from Camera, *Annali*, 2:507 and translated by R.G. Musto.

Order to our treasury, that whenever we happen to ride to various places, 6 *tareni* should be given as alms to the poor.

In light of this order funds were consigned to Lord Pietro Baudet [Boudin],[43] our chaplain almoner and member of our household, when we rode to the church of Sta. Barbara, Sant'Andrea [Apostolo ad Diaconum], and Sta. Maria la Nova, Sta. Lucia and Sant'Agnello.

The same when we rode to S. Giovanni Maggiore,[44] the episcopal palace of Naples, Sant'Antonio a Carbonara [Abate?] in the city of Naples to view the jousts twice in the month of January.

The same on February 8, when the king rode to the jousts when the Astiludio games were held.

The same when the lord king rode to the funeral rites of the deceased Lord Giovanni de Haya[45] and when he rode to the church of S. Pietro a Castello [in Castel dell'Ovo].

The same on March 2, when he rode to the jousts organized by Lord Dragoneto, and on March 10, when he rode to the jousts, and again when he rode to the church of S. Domenico [Maggiore][46] of Naples for the feast of St. Thomas Aquinas.

The same when he rode to the church of S. Lorenzo [Maggiore][47] for the feast of the Forty Martyrs [of Sebaste, March 9] and again when he rode to the Tarsienatum [intarsia works?] newly constructed at Ponte Guizzardo [Maddalena].

---

42. See Musto, Interactive Map: http://www.italicapress.com/index287.html.

43. Also named as a witness to Robert's will. See below, Reading 65, at p. 240.

44. See Italica web gallery: http://www.flickr.com/photos/80499896@N05/sets/72157630159535292.

45. Regent of the Vicaria court. See Kelly, *New Solomon*, 66, 169.

46. See Italica web gallery: http://www.flickr.com/photos/80499896@N05/sets/72157630148664544.

47. See Italica web gallery: http://www.flickr.com/photos/80499896@N05/sets/72157630149709946.

Again when he rode to the church of Sta. Maria Annunziata on the feast of the Annunciation [March 25].

On April 29, when he rode to the church of S. Pietro Martire, on the saint's feast day.

On May 7, when he rode to the cathedral of Naples,[48] and on the sixth, when he rode to the church of S. Gennaro of Naples [extra Moenia].

On May 12, when he rode to the jousts.

On June 27, when he rode to the church of Sta. Chiara[49] for the feast of the Eucharist, and again when he rode to Castellamare [di Stabia] to go to the church of S. Bartolomeo di Stabia.

The lord king ordered payments to the monasteries listed below for the approaching feast of Christmas in the fifth indiction: for the Franciscans of S. Lorenzo, the Franciscans of Sta. Maria la Nova, the Friar Preachers of S. Domenico, the Friar Preachers of S. Pietro Martire, the Hieronimites of Sant'Agostino, the brothers of Sta. Maria del Carmine, for the poor of Sant'Eligio, for the sisters of Sta. Maria de Perceyo, for the sisters of Sta. Maria Donnaregina,[50] for the sisters of Sta. Chiara, for the nuns of S. Pietro a Castello, for the sisters of Sant'Agatha, for the sisters of S. Sepolcro, for the nuns of Sta. Maria Annunziata, and for the brothers of Sto. Spirito de Arminia. Distributed to the said religious were 12 *oncie*, 16 *tareni* and 10 *grani*.

56. Queen Sancia of Naples (1286–1345) writes to the chapter general of Assisi, July 25, 1334

This letter was written in 1334 to the chapter general of Assisi of that year and incorporated three earlier letters written by Sancia to the Franciscan Order between 1316 and 1331. The letter shows Sancia's deep loyalty to — and firm control over — the Franciscan Order and her adherence to the strict interpretation of the Franciscan Rule advocated by the Spiritual Franciscans.

---

48. See Italica web gallery: http://www.flickr.com/photos/80499896@N05/sets/72157630152316564.

49. See Italica web gallery: http://www.flickr.com/photos/80499896@N05/sets/72157630151262510.

50. See Elliott and Warr, *Church of Sta. Maria Donnaregina;* and Italica web gallery: http://www.flickr.com/photos/80499896@N05/sets/72157630164795244..

Fig. 43. Sancia of Majorca. From the Angevin Genaeology. Anjou Bible, fol. 4r.

Sancia, and through her Robert, protected such key Spirituals as her brother Philip of Majorca and Angelo Clareno. Her patronage and protection made Naples a center of religious dissent and of Joachite prophesy, confronting even Pope John XXII to do so. This Spiritual Franciscan influence extended perhaps even to her and Robert's design for the church of Sta. Chiara.[51] The letter is excerpted from Ronald G. Musto, "Queen Sancia of Naples (1286–1345) and the Spiritual Franciscans"[52] and was translated by R.G. Musto.

Letters of Lady Sancia, queen of Sicily and Jerusalem

To the venerable fathers and brothers and sons, the Friars Minor coming to the holy indulgence of Sta. Maria de Angelis, so called from antiquity but now named Sta. Maria de Portiuncula, where our common father, Francis, began the order and ended his life and blessed the brothers, present as well as future, and commended them to the glorious Virgin; Sancia, by the grace of God queen of Jerusalem and Sicily, the humble daughter and servant of blessed Francis, sends greetings in Jesus Christ crucified.

Know, fathers, that for this God caused me to be born into this world from such a lineage and family tree, just as was Lady Sclaramonda [de Foix] of holy memory, my lady mother, queen of Majorca and true daughter of blessed Francis. He also caused that my firstborn brother, namely Friar James of Majorca, my

---

51.   See Caroline Bruzelius, "Queen Sancia of Mallorca and the Convent Church of Sta. Chiara in Naples," *Memoirs of the American Academy in Rome* 40 (1995): 69–100; *Stones of Naples*, 132–53 et passim; Bruzelius & Tronzo, 98–106; and Musto, "Franciscan Joachimism."

52.   In Kirshner and Wemple, *Women of the Medieval World*, 207–14. It has recently been translated into Italian in Gaglione, *Donne e potere*, 168–74.

dearest brother, renounced royal power for the love of Jesus Christ and became a son of blessed Francis and entered his order. He also caused me to be a descendent of blessed Elizabeth [of Hungary], who was such a true and devoted daughter of blessed Francis and a mother of his order. She was the blood sister of the lady mother of my father, Lord James, well remembered king of Majorca. He also caused me to have as a husband the most illustrious lord, my lord Robert, king of Jerusalem and Sicily, who was the son of Lady Marie, the well-remembered queen of these realms and of Hungary. She was also the true daughter of blessed Francis and bore a son, blessed Louis [of Toulouse], who refused and renounced royal power for the love of Jesus Christ and became a Friar Minor.[53]

I also firmly believe that God and blessed Francis ordained that my lord, who was the third brother, would be king and would have all the virtues that were proper for him and more wisdom and knowledge than have been known of any prince of the world since the time of Solomon; and this knowledge he gathered from the friars of the order so that he — and I with him — might defend the order of blessed Francis.

I myself have recounted these things so that you may see how much I am held to be, and ought to be, a servant of so great a father and of his order. If I consider the example of those who preceded me in both my own and in my lord's family, I can accept that passage in John [15:13] when our Lord Jesus Christ said to his disciples: "For I call you not servants but sons." That passage I can also say myself to you and to the entire order as a mother, and a true mother, for three reasons.

I. First, since a mother is one with her dear son

And I am one in soul with any Friar Minor, as appears in the letter that I have from the chapter general of Naples [of May 1316] that was written by Lord Brother Cardinal Bertrand de Tour, then minister of the province of Aquitaine, in the holy convent of Assisi by order of Brother Michael [of Cesena],

---

53. Here Sancia lays out the *beata stirps* of the Angevin and Majorcan dynasties. See above, p. lvii. For recent work on Robert's sacred kingship see Mirko Vagnoni, "Una nota sulla regalità sacra di Roberto d'Angiò alla luce della ricerca iconografica," *Archivio Storico Italiano* 167.620 (2009): 253–67.

appointed minister general, and also in the letter that I myself sent to him, the tenor of which is such:

Reverend and venerable father in Christ, Brother Michael, minister general of the Order of Friars Minor, Sancia, by the grace of God queen of Jerusalem and Sicily, humble and devoted daughter of blessed Francis and of his order, sends herself with humble and devoted commendation.

Let it be known to you, dearest father, that the brothers of your order, who lately in the chapter general of Naples remarked our devotion and most sincere affection with which we embrace the order itself singularly among all the estates of the Church, by unanimous vote and in perfect concord favorably conceded and wished that certain things be confirmed through your office that we had humbly and devoutly sought from them for the salvation of our soul and the prosperity of our realms. For we had asked that the salvation of our soul and of our lord be firmly impressed upon the hearts of all the brothers and that our soul be one with the soul of each one of them in the unity of the spirit, and that through the bond of charity we might be partners fully in the benefits that are combined for you through individual brothers wherever on earth the clemency of the Savior deigns to work, so that any brother whatever might accept our soul as one with his own in the full participation of all merits. The brothers ought to do this since our soul is better in the order, which it loves most justly, than in our body, which it gives life and informs.

Furthermore, since that chapter general will have set aside for us — at our humble and affectionate petition — one mass for the living in every convent of the entire order for every day that we live and likewise, after our death, one mass for the dead forever wherever it is to be celebrated through the entire order, we devoutly and humbly beseech your reverend paternity that you deem to confirm all the above-said and that you embark to transmit under your seal those things confirmed for us through the minister of Terra di Lavoro to all the ministers so that they might be bound to announce in their provincial chapters and in each convent of their provinces those things conceded through you and through them to us and to bind each brother to all of the aforesaid.

We, for our part, beyond our person and our realm, offer as much as we can for the honor and utility and defense of your order. We also intend always to persevere in this course with the help of God. May the Almighty deign to keep your venerable person on behalf of this holy order for a long time to come. Dated in the castle [Castel Nuovo] at Naples, tenth day of June, fourteenth indiction [1316].

II. SECOND, A MOTHER LOVES HER SONS

And so I love my sons, the Friars Minor, as appears in the letter that I sent to the chapter general to be held in Paris [in 1329], whose tenor is noted below:

Venerable brothers and sons, the Friars Minor of the chapter general of Paris to be held soon; Sancia, by the grace of God queen of Jerusalem and Sicily, your humble and devoted daughter, sends greetings in the Lord Jesus Christ. You know how our common father, blessed Francis, founded your Rule upon the holy Gospel, and you know your wish, which is "namely to observe the holy Gospel of our Lord Jesus Christ by living in obedience without any property and in chastity" [RegB I.1]; and you know what are the commands and what are the admonitions of your Rule. I ask you [this] humbly, and I admonish you through our Lord Jesus Christ crucified, who by his precious stigmata deigned to mark his servant, our said common father, blessed Francis, about whom one reads in the Epistle to the Galatians [6:14]: "Brothers, God forbid that I should glory save in the Cross of our Lord Jesus Christ, through whom the world is crucified to me, and I to the world." Later he adds in the same epistle [6:16–17], "and whoever would follow this rule, peace and mercy upon them and upon the Israel of God. Henceforth let no man give me trouble," etc. because you follow the vestiges of our father.

Have no doubt that such a rule is founded upon such a foundation, namely the holy Gospel,[54] and is signed with such signs, namely the wounds of our Lord Jesus Christ, impressed upon the person of our said common father. No one could, nor can, nor will be able to break it. May our Lady — in whom our common father himself began and fulfilled your order in Sta. Maria

---

54. Sancia's assertion that the Franciscan Rule was based firmly and directly upon the Gospels was one of the chief tenents of the Franciscan Spirituals.

de Angelis, and in his death especially commended himself to her — defend and govern you, unless, God forbid, it be your fault by which you stray from the way of the father.

Also remember the word that the father himself spoke at his death [See I Celano II,7]: "Farewell, all my sons, in the fear of the Lord and remain in it always. And because the future tribulation approaches, happy are they who will persevere." Thus may no past or present or future tribulation terrify you, recalling the word of the Apostle in the Epistle to the Romans [8: 35–38]: "Who shall separate us from the love of Christ? Shall tribulation or distress or hunger or persecution or nakedness or danger or the sword? Even as it is written, 'For thy sake we are put to death all the day long. We are regarded as sheep for the slaughter.' For I am sure that neither death," etc.

I myself hope in the Lord Jesus Christ, who gave grace to his Apostle, that he will give to you and to me and to those who intend to follow the vestiges of our father that charity and happy fortitude of the above words, unless, God forbid, your or my fault impede it. As your devoted daughter, I offer to expose myself and my interests and my body to death, if necessary, for the defense of your Rule, which was sealed in the person of our common father by the stigmata of our Lord Jesus Christ.

Finally, in the election of the future minister general we warn and remind you to keep God before your eyes and not favor or reward. Let no individual allegiance seduce you in this election, but may you choose a person who will be prepared to follow the vestiges of our father and the words of the Apostle quoted above. I commend to you my lord husband, the king of Jerusalem and Sicily, father and brother, everyone in his household, my dearest son of good memory, the duke [Charles] of Calabria [d.1328], and all the deceased from the royal household and myself, your devoted daughter, and all those from our household of Majorca, living as well as dead, and all others both living and dead to whom I direct my thoughts.

Written in Naples by my own hand and dictated through us without any other assistance except divine on account of your merits, fifteenth day of March, twelfth indiction [1329].

III. THIRD, A MOTHER GIVES COUNSEL TO HER SONS AND ASSISTS THEM

So I have given counsel and aid to my sons the Friars Minor as is declared in the letter that I sent to the chapter general of Perpignan [May 1331], which begins thus:

To the venerable brother in Christ, Gerald [Odonis], minister general of the Order of Minors, and to the brothers assembled in the chapter general of Perpignan; Sancia, queen of Jerusalem and of Sicily, your humble and devoted, albeit unworthy, daughter of blessed Francis and of his entire order, sends greetings in the Lord Jesus Christ.

I ask and admonish your paternity that you do not stray from the vestiges of so great a father who is the standard-bearer of Christ, our common father, blessed Francis. I have heard that some of your brothers say that your Rule cannot be served, which Rule was revealed by God twice to our holy father Francis and ornamented with those five seals that are the precious wounds of Christ ensealed upon the body of the nourishing confessor. Let the brothers remember what the venerable father, Lord Giovanni of S. Paolo, bishop of Sabina,[55] and what the vicar of Christ, Lord Innocent III of holy memory, said when he confirmed the Rule: "For if anyone were to say that the intent and observation of evangelical perfection contained anything harmful or irrational or impossible to observe, he is guilty of blaspheming the author of the Gospel himself."[56] Do not believe them at all, since they are not sons of the father except in name only. If, God forbid, your father the general wishes to change anything one single iota, do not support it. Because if he were to tamper with it, he is not a pastor but a mercenary, and as such should you hold him.[57] Know for certain and do not doubt that God and the Blessed Virgin will govern and defend you who wish to be true sons of the father. Also remember the words that the Lord Jesus Christ said to the father: "I have called, I shall serve and I shall feed, and I shall choose others for those falling away, so that if they were not born, I shall cause them to be born. And by whatever shocks

---

55. Most likely not a Colonna, but a Bobone.

56. See Bonavenura, *Legenda maior* 3, 19.

57. On the Spiritual theory of legitimate resistance, see Musto, "Queen Sancia," 213 n. 265.

this poor little order may be battered, it shall always remain safe in my protection."[58]

I myself offer myself with all my ability to governing those who will wish to follow the vestiges of our own and your common father all the way to the death of the Cross. I also consider it the greatest grace if God causes me to die and to be a martyr for this cause. May that blessing descend upon you and me and all those who are or will be of this most holy will that the father gave in the chapter of Arles, when blessed Anthony [of Padua], brother and father, was preaching on the chapter of the Cross and on that grace that on Pentecost day came over the Apostles. May it not turn away because of our sins, as is written in the Gospel [Luke 9:62] and in your Rule [RegB 2:13]: "No one having put his hand to the plow and looking back is fit for the kingdom of God."

Since I am a sinner and insufficient and unlettered, and I speak literally, know nothing except from the grace and intimacy of God, and I trust nothing of my own, on Thursday, the eighteenth day of April, I entered the small chapel next to my chamber in the Castel Nuovo in Naples where well through three candles before daybreak, with the door closed, alone with the body of Christ, which was upon the altar, I commended myself to him and afterward began to write as the Lord directed me, without any counsel, human or earthly.

I commend to your prayers the lord king, my reverend husband and your father and special son, and all his household both living and dead, and especially the well-remembered duke of Calabria, that God may give his glory to him and to me and to all our people living as well as dead and to those to whom I direct my thoughts, and especially Lord Fernando, my dearest brother, who was the father of the king of Majorca who now reigns, my dearest nephew and my son.

Written by my own hand on the aforesaid day in the Castel Nuovo indiction..., in the year 1331.

Although I am not worthy on my own, nevertheless through the grace of God I can be called the true mother of the order of blessed Francis in several ways, not only in word or writing, but by works that I have performed continuously and that I intend

---

58. See *Prophetia* attributed to Francis, VI.

to do with his help all the days of my life. For, although I feel that I have nothing on my own except sin, nevertheless I can accept the word of the Apostle [I Cor. 15:10]: "What I am, I am by the grace of God." And later it continues [John 15:15]: "No longer do I call you servants, because the servant does not know what his master does,… but all things that I have heard from my father I have made known to you." And like a mother I can say to you and to the whole order: I do not call you servants, but intimate sons, as if you were born from my own body, and as much more as spiritual love is greater than physical love.

Dated in Quisisana near Castellamare di Stabia with my own secret ring on the twenty-fifth day of July, fourteenth indiction [1334].

57. KING ROBERT'S EDICT ON YOUTH FASHION, JANUARY 15, 1335

Fig. 44. A cavalcade of dandies. Detail from Buonamico Buffalmacco, Triumph of Death, c.1338. Fresco. Pisa, Camposanto.

Fourteenth-century sumptuary legislation[59] was as much an attempt to bind new generations and nobles to traditional modes of style and behavior as it was a reaction to rapid social and economic change and conspicuous consumption in a "thick" urban social context. Examples are numerous from Venice and Florence and reflect accurately the new changes in fashion and attitude among the nobility in the decades around the Black Death.

Here, however, Robert may be condemning the opposite trend: an ascetic poverty chic, probably influenced by the Spiritual Franciscans at Robert's and Sancia's court (who held strongest influence at precisely this time) and later

---

59.   For a general overview see Catherine K. Killerby, *Sumptuary Law in Italy, 1200–1500* (Oxford: Clarendon Press, 2002). For examples of sumptuary legislation and prohibitions of cross-dressing, see Dean, *Towns of Italy,* 199–207.

condemned by Petrarch in his letter on Roberto da Mileto, OFM, one of Robert's chief advisors.[60]

The document appears to indicate that such dress promotes illicit and secret sexual liaisons. Such a connection had a long tradition in Angevin Naples stretching as far as the first generation under Charles I.[61] Robert of Artois, vicar of the Regno, had first introduced harsh sumptuary legislation that included condemnations of sodomy — unusual among the Capetians at the time — in order to reinforce a presumed connection between norms of masculine dress and behavior and military preparedness, the same connections made by Robert in the selection below. The trial of Adenolfo IV, count of Acerra, for sodomy in 1293, and his harsh punishment, left a lasting impression on Neapolitan legislation.

Our selection is taken from Camara, *Annali* 2:411–12, and translated by R.G. Musto.

Robert by the grace of God king of Jerusalem and Sicily, etc.

To all and sundry readers of this edict, we who hold fast in imitating Christ the King of Kings through narrow frailty toward perfection with the little measure of human mediocrity or worse, and who seek the praiseworthy good for our subjects, and likewise condemn the detestable.

Apropos, among many of our young people an unusual fad has gained ground to such an extant that among them their style is uncertain, their behavior swinging, their worship divergent, their body language distorted and ridiculous. Their hats are elongated, hair unkempt, faces mostly covered by it, beards are long and more horrible than marvelous to behold. The higher and lower parts that God gives to man, these hypocrites destroy with we know not what false austerity.

Their clothes, which until recently they wore down to their knees, now end at their buttocks. Lookers-on no longer greet them with opprobrium as in days gone by; but the shortness of

---

60. The infamous *"horrendum tripes animal"* of Petrarch's *Familiares* V.3. See Vincenzo Forcellini, *"'L'horrendum tripes animal'* della lettera 3 del libro V delle *Familiari* di Petrarca,"* in *Studi di storia napoletana in onore di Michelangelo Schipa* (Naples: I.T.E.A., 1926)," 167–99; and Musto, "Queen Sancia," 198–99.

61. See Dunbabin, *French in the Kingdom of Sicily,* 241–49.

their clothes causes jealousy, and their style vanity, or more aptly fatuity. Some conceal their thin bodies amid the folds of their tunics, others deform and squeeze in their fat bulging bellies to such an extent that these appear consumptive, those dropsical.

They also perch crookedly upon their horses. They have to use both hands to hold the reins. Consequently they consider superfluous the military use of the shield, the shoulder plate and the lance. They carry short swords, their limbs exposed in war. Without armor plate their shoulder blades are exposed to wounds. They thrust out their chests uncovered and renounce manly customs, adopting womanly habits.

What's even more stupid, perhaps the most stupid of all, and contrary to the Arabum Anacoritarum [sic], they imitate the customs of philosophers with their hair and their beards. These signifiers usurp privileges and transgress professions. They also render testimony as to what secret hiding places there may be in which two of these people come together in the filthy associations to which they submit.

And what is even more demented, more perverse, than for the old — who ought to provide leadership and direction to youth with their advice — to chase after them even more in their mindless fads, wrapping on head bands to hold in their gray hair or to hide their bald spots? These habits take delight in contrary behaviors and despise the virtuous and honest customs with which their fathers and our predecessors advanced to our own days and by which the republic and other provinces subject to us have been exalted and promoted by steady progress.

They do not heed what the text of Maccabees 2 [15–17] says: "And setting nought by the honours of their fathers, they esteemed the Grecian glories for the best. For the sake of which they incurred a dangerous contention, and followed earnestly their ordinances, and in all things they coveted to be like them, who were their enemies and murderers. For acting wickedly against the laws of God doth not pass unpunished: but this the time following will declare." As Giosa [sic] comments in the beginning of Exodus [1:8], "'In the meantime there arose a new king over Egypt, that knew not Joseph.' The new king may be the ingrate who does not know the benefits Joseph has bestowed, or the new king may be the Devil, who rejoices in new fashions."

Therefore, lest our lordly warning fall on deaf ears, we order that all the aforesaid, under the grave penalty of our indignation, abstain from these habits and resume their original honest customs. We intend to enact this gradually lest their wealth be seriously impacted by a sudden change of clothing. Unless exemptions apply to them, we will add other penalties as we deem appropriate.

We therefore forbid long beards on poor men, and we order frequent shaving or at least the necessary and onerous imposition of the least costly head bands.

In witness of this we order that three copies of the present edict be posted, one each on the gates of Castel Nuovo, on the doors of the duomo, and on those of the Vicaria [Castel Capuano]. Let it not be hidden from a single person and let it be promulgated openly for the eyes of all.

Dated Naples, in the year of the Lord 1335, 15th day of January, third indiction, in the 26th year of our reign.

58. CONSTRUCTION AT STA. CHIARA AND BELFORTE, 1338

The following selection quickly notes some of the building projects begun under Robert of Anjou. Of note here is the author's remark that the campanile of Sta. Chiara had not yet been completed in 1328. The text follows entries for 1335 and 1337, and must have meant 1338, since the tower's four base inscriptions record dates of 1310, 1330 and 1340, the last the date of anticipated completion referred to below.

This selection is taken from the *Cronaca di Partenope*, book III, Altamura, p. 140. Translated by R.G. Musto.

In the year of our Lord 13[3]8, in the month of January, the first foundation was laid for the campanile of Sto. Corpo di Cristo. When the third story is completed, from what it appears, it will be the most beautiful tower in Italy. In the same year [1338], the lead roof was completed on the said church of Sto. Corpo di Cristo, called Sta. Chiara.

In the fortress of Belforte and the monastery of S. Martino, which rise above Naples on the summit called Sant'Erasmo, a great campanile was completed that same year. It is considered the greatest in all of Italy.

Kelly's edition of the *Cronaca* provides some additional details from version A75, p. 277, including the frescos in the Capella Palatina at Castel Nuovo. Translated by R.G. Musto.

He caused to be built during his reign many churches, among which were built the church of Sta. Chiara in Naples, and he had built the Castel Sant'Erasmo and the chapel that is inside Castel Nuovo, excellently painted, and the arsenal of Naples....

Kelly's edition, text B (p. 277) adds the following projects supported by Queen Sancia. Translated by R.G. Musto.

The renowned and Catholic lady Madam Sancia of Majorca, the queen and his wife, caused to be built the following monasteries: the noble monastery of Sto. Corpo di Christo of the order of Sta. Chiara.[62] The monastery of Sta. Maria Egiziaca, the monastery of Sta. Croce of Naples along with the convent of the Friars Minor and their religious nuns.... And she had built another monastery

of this order which is called Saint-Claire in the city of Aix-en-Provence. And she had another monastery built in Jerusalem called St. Mary of Mt. Sion.

59. THE CAMPANILE OF STA. CHIARA BEGUN, 1338

Written in Latin by an unknown author, the *Chronicon Siculum* covers the years 340 to 1396 and becomes useful with the reign of Robert of Anjou. Note that the *Chronicon* records Prince Andrew of Hungary's attendance, calls him "king," and omits reference to Robert's heir, the future Queen Giovanna I, who, the tower inscriptions attest, did attend.

Fig. 45. Sta. Chiara, campanile. Photo: Italica Press..

---

62. That is, the church of Sta. Chiara by its original foundation name. See Bruzelius, *Stones of Naples*, 137.

This selection is taken from Giuseppe de Blasiis, ed., *Chronicon Siculum incerti authoris de rebus siculis* (Naples: Giannini, 1887), 10. Translated by R.G. Musto.

In the year 1338 construction of the campanile of Sta. Chiara was begun. The cornerstone was laid by King Robert, Queen Sancia, King Andrew, the prince [Robert] of Taranto and his brothers, the duke [Charles] of Durazzo and his brothers. Many prelates attended the ceremony.

60. FAMINE IN NAPLES, 1338/39

Between 1315 and 1322 much of Europe north of the Alps was struck by what has come to be called the Great Famine.[63] Extended periods of severe weather, lowered grain production, harvest failures and massive die-offs of farm animals seem to have been the primary causes. But human intervention, first in the destruction to agricultural land, livestock production and distribution by war; then inefficient agricultural methods in farming very marginal lands in reaction to surging population; and then by hoarding, increased taxation and price increases may also have played a part.

In the South conditions were good enough that Italian merchants continued to supply the North with grain.[64] Yet by the 1330s conditions similar to those in the North began to affect the Mediterranean. The kingdom of Naples, which had become the major supplier of grain to the northern Italian communes,[65] was no exception. Prices of commodities are measured in *tarì* or *tareni*.[66]

This selection is taken from book III of the *Cronaca di Partenope*, Altamura, 141. Translation by R.G. Musto.

---

63. The best account remains Jordan, *The Great Famine*.

64. Jordan, *Great Famine*, 173–74. For Italy see Larner, *Italy in the Age of Dante and Petrarch*, 154–55, 256–57. Italians were well aware of conditions in the North: see Villani, *Croniche*, VIII.68 for 1303 and IX.80 for 1316 (Selfe, 355). For 1328, see Agnolo di Tura del Grasso, *Cronache senesi*, in Dean, *Towns of Italy*, 172–74.

65. Larner, *Italy in the Age of Dante and Petrarch*, 214–15.

66. See below, Reading 64.

14. The Famine

Between the years of the Lord 1338 and 1339, there was a very great food shortage, almost a famine, in the Regno. A *tumolo*[67] cost fourteen *tareni* [*tarì*], when provisions could be found for sale. One never knew such scarcity before, nor provisions valued at such a price. Then Death came to the Regno.

61. FRANCESCO BALDUCCI PEGOLOTTI, *LA PRATICA DELLA MERCATURA*. ON TRADE CONDITIONS IN NAPLES, C.1338–43

Pegolotti was the son of a prominent Florentine mercantile and banking family. Born before 1290, by the 1310s he had achieved high status at the Bardi bank, which employed 336 agents between 1310 and 1340 and had branches or connections in Antwerp, Bruges, Paris, London, Avignon, many Italian cities including Naples and Barletta, in Majorca, Rhodes, Cyprus and Constantinople. It enjoyed special privileges in the ports of Setalia in Asia Minor, Ayas in Armenia, Famagusta in Cyprus, and Seville in Spain. As one of their chief agents Pegolotti traveled widely through northern Europe, including London and the Low Countries. He served as a banker for the English court, and — like the Villani in Naples — as a collector of papal tithes. Between 1318 and 1321, he was in charge of transferring huge papal revenues to Avignon. It is highly likely that he served the Bardi bank in both Naples and Barletta, and his descriptions of Neapolitan tariffs and customs formalities are among the most detailed in his book.

Diplomatic work for the Florentine republic also took him to Cyprus for long periods and involved repeated travel between there and Avignon. In the later 1330s, Pegolotti also served on missions to Armenia. By 1331, he had been elected in Florence as a *Gonfaloniere di compagni*. By 1340, he was one of the college of Buonomini who advised the Florentine signoria, and by 1346, as *Gonfaloniere di justicia*, had risen to one of the highest elected offices in Florence. By 1347 he was representing the Bardi bank in the bankruptcy proceedings that followed upon the English crown's default of its huge loans from the Bardi.

---

67. About a half-bushel of grain. See Reading 61 below.

Pegolotti's *Pratica della mercatura* is a comprehensive guide for the merchant and banker to the ports, trade emporia, and local and emerging territorial states of the Mediterranean in the mid-fourteenth century. It is full of calendars, recipes for refining gold and silver, exchange rates, weights and measures, customs duties, tariffs and commodities traded, arranged geographically across the Mediterranean and northern Europe and including linkages to many of the exchange rates between each of these cities and its important trading partners. It is thus a database in manuscript and is a treasure trove for urban and economic historians.

Pegolotti seems to have compiled his *Pratica* over several decades but may have composed the complete book some time between 1330 and 1342. Its many borrowings from local merchant guides, customs handbooks and travel accounts may have been supplemented by reports from Bardi agents in many of the cities he covers. His information from Naples, including his advice on how to deal with Naples' customs officials, appears to be first-hand. Also worth noting is the wide variety of merchandise sold through Naples — everything from precious metals, dyes and industrial ingredients, to coral and pearls, silks, wools and pelts, to spices, nuts, fish, meat, oil and wines. One gets a vivid picture of a port participating in the vigorous commercial life of the wider Mediterranean.

The work survived in a single manuscript, Florence, Bibliotheca Riccardiana 2441, and was edited by Allan Evans in his Francesco Balducci Pegolotti, *La pratica della mercatura* (Cambridge: Mediaeval Academy of America, 1936). The sections below on Naples were translated by R.G. Musto from pp. 178–85.

Naples of the Principality Itself

In Naples one sells according to the weights used there, that is, by the thousand weight, the *kantar*, by the hundred, pound and ounce.

1 thousand weight equals four *kantar* [*cantara*]
1 *kantar* equals 100 *ruotoli*
1 *ruotolo* equals 2½ pounds gross
1 pound equals 12 gross ounces [*oncie*]

1 gross ounce equals 33¹/₃ *tarì*
1 pound fine [*sottile*] equals 12 ounces
1 ounce fine [*sottile*] equals 30 *tarì*....

SOLD BY THE HUNDRED WEIGHT IN NAPLES

Ginger, cinnamon, lacquer, zedoary, incense, galangal, long
pepper and all the said spices are subject to gabelle taxes.[68]

Sugar in cakes of any amount and barrels or shipping cases in
which it arrives remain with the buyer for nothing additional
to the total tariffed.

Granular sugar of any amount is tariffed in the cases in which
it arrives and then the case remains with the buyer at no cost.

Aloe, of any amount, and wax is tariffed with the sack and its
cordage and then the sack and cordage remain with the buyer at no additional cost.

Quick silver is measured in the bucket in which it is weighed,
and the bucket and all the cordage remain with the buyer at
no extra cost.

Vermilion and cinnabar are weighed along with their cases and
cordage, and then are tariffed along with the case and cordage, and after they are tariffed these [cases and cordage] remain with the buyer at no extra cost.

Uncleaned coral....

MERCHANDISE SOLD BY THE HUNDRED WEIGHT

Hazelnuts are sold in Naples by the hundred weight, and each
hundred weight is measured at 606 *tomboli*[69] iron-cut fine,
and the buyer pays for the measurement.

Walnuts and peeled chestnuts and chestnuts in their shells sell
in Naples in the same way as hazelnuts and at the same hundred weight.

---

68. These were generally indirect taxes across a range of items and financial
transactions, issued widely by the Italian communes. They included sales taxes,
customs duties and exchange taxes. Villani listed thirty *gabelle* in Florence in
1338. Venice imposed numerous *dazi*, and Rome under both barons and the
buon governo of Cola di Rienzo imposed a number of *gabelle* in the later 1340s.
See Waley and Dean, *Italian City-Republics*, 48–50; Musto, *Apocalypse*, 146–47,
336. Dean, *Towns of Italy*, records *gabelle* for Padua (p. 20), Florence (37), Ferrara
(175–76), and San Miniato (187–88).

69. In the sense of a pile, of volumetric measure, the *tumulo*. See Reading 60.

Oil is sold in Naples by the *staio* [from 20 to 70 liters], and 51 bushels [*staia*] make up a *mina* barrel of Naples, and the buyer pays for the barrel.

Greco and Latino wine are sold in Naples by the *mina* barrel of Naples....

Flax is sold in Naples by the hundred *dicine* at 10 pounds gross per *dicina*.

Almonds in the shell are sold in Naples by the *tombolo*, and so many *tomboli* per ounce.

Silk velveteen and silk drapery and cloth of gold, and camlets, buckram and sendal are all sold in Naples by the usual piece.

French wools are sold in Naples by the piece or by the *livrate*.[70]

[SOME OTHER MERCHANDISE ON THE MARKET]

Sicilian cow's leather...

Stag hide, deer hide...

Peltry, Sicilian shearling, rabbit fur, and all dressed hides sell in Naples by the hundred, at a rate of 104 pelts per hundred.

Barbary peltry...

Pelts tailored into robes sell in Naples by the robe.

Packed tuna sells wholesale in Naples in barrels by the hundredweight and is fragrant and free of any bad taste.

Sardines and anchovies sell in Naples by the barrel.

Salt from Sardinia sells in Naples by the hundred quarts

Wheat, barley and all grains sell in Naples by the *salma*[71]...

Pearls are sold in Naples by the fine ounce...

Silver in plates or in rods or bullion is sold in Naples by the pound, at 12 ounces per pound, and at 30 *tarì* per ounce.

THE MINT ALLOY OF THE *GIGLIATO*

Gigliati are of an alloy of 11 ounces and 3 sterling of fine silver, that is of 3 *tarì*. In Neapolitan pounds when they leave the mint they are 6 *soldi*, 8 *denarii* to the coined *gigliato* of account, to the equivalent of 4 *tarì* and 10 *grani* by weight to the *gigliato*. And so much should they weigh, and so they do weigh when they leave the king's mint.

---

70. Likely a reference to a scale, or by weight.

71. According to Evans, 188 n. 1, a *salma* is a volumetric measure equal to 11¼ *staia*, or bushels.

The small coins of Naples are called *gherardini*, because Gianni Gherardini of Florence had them struck, and the king, out of love for the said Gherardino, wanted them to bear the name Gherardino, and so they are called *gherardini*. They are an alloy of 18 fine silver *denarii* to the pound, and at a rate of 40 soldi to the pound. They were originally distributed through the Regno at a rate of 6 of the said small *gherardini* to one *grano*, and 10 *grani* to the *carlino*. And today one spends <…> per silver *gigliato*, and 1 *gigliato* is worth 10 *grani*, and 2 *gigliati* are worth 1 silver *tarì*.

The gold coinage of Naples is the gold *carlino*, and it is alloyed of fine gold of 24 carats of gold per ounce, and it is measured at an equivalent of 6 gold *carlini* to one ounce, and this comes to the equivalent in weight of one *carlino* to five *tarì*. To whomever deposits gold, the master of the mint of Naples gives per carat of fine gold 1 *tarì* and <...> *grossi*, or 17½ gold *grani*.

Gold in rods or in bullion, silver in plate or in bullion, pearls and precious stones pay no duty and are duty-free throughout the Regno. But insofar as they are not converted to gold or silver thread, because they have been worked into or beneath silkwork, one pays a duty of <…> *grani* per ounce. Truly neither gold nor silver in bullion nor in coined money can be used throughout the Regno except for the king's coin: gold *carlini* or silver *gigliati*; and if one wishes to use any but the king's coin, and if [such foreign coinage] is found among your fellow [travelers] while traveling, you would lose whatever might be found on you, and you will be at the lord's mercy, except if you are in agreement with your fellow travelers and they do you the favor of leaving [the Regno with such currency] and then you may go and come safely, but otherwise not, and not unless you agree to pay 3 *grani* per ounce.

From Naples one cannot export tallow [*grascia*] or lumber either milled or unmilled, neither by a citizen nor a foreigner if the customs court [*corta*] does not agree. And unless it has a bill of exchange for other merchandise, it is not worth anything. But with agreement of the court, a customs duty is imposed on the buyer at 2 *tarì* per ounce, and 21½ *grani* per *kantar* of weight, and 10 *grani* per ounce of good coin.

For all the merchandise that you bring into Naples by land or by sea you pay a customs of 18 *grani* per ounce at Neapolitan value, that is 3 percent; and you can then bring in any other merchandise at the value of what you can bring in within one year without paying customs. If you bring it in within that year, you would not pay 1 *tarì* and 5 *grani* per ounce, that is, the 15 *grani* for the fondaco fee and the 10 *grani* for the good coin of the realm. [184]

All the merchandise that enters the Regno by sea and goes on from there to Naples by land, and [all merchandise] from Naples you wish to carry and take outside the Regno without selling it, pays 15 *grani* per ounce, and 1 *tarì* and 6²/₃ *grani* for the sum that one calls *Refica*. The emperor Frederick II imposed this *Refica* and fondaco fee, and the current King Robert observes its articles.

Oil, meat, all fats, lumber and cheese pay duty in Naples at the royal customs at 3 *tarì* and 15 *grani* per ounce, that is, 3 for the customs and 15 *grani* for the fondaco. To tell the truth, unless you make an agreement with the customs officials of at least 2 *tarì* per ounce, as you can arrange with them, and unless you first make arrangements with the customs officials, you will pay the entire duty, that is, 3 *tarì* and 15 *grani* per ounce. In addition to the said duty, one pays another 10 *grani* per ounce in good coin, and the buyer pays this duty in good coin on all merchandise, and the seller pays nothing. And none of this duty in good coin [185] is ever refunded, so that in the end it happens that the buyer pays it for all the merchandise he buys.

Wines pay a duty of 2 *tarì* and 8½ *grani* per ounce, that is, 18 *grani* for the customs and 15 *grani* for the fondaco and 5½ *grani* for each cask and 10 *grani* in good coin. But on the wines that an individual wants for his own drink, either entering or leaving, he pays no duty on good wine.

Silk pays a duty called *Giusso*, which is 10 percent.

For the citizens of Naples and of the city's contado, Naples itself is free so that they pay no duty on any merchandise that they import or export from Naples, either by land or sea, and they can sell to whom they please without paying any duty. But if they wish to sell [at retail] out of their shops, they must pay for the buyer 1 *tarì* and 5 *grani* per ounce, that is 15 *grani* for the fondaco and 10 for the good coin.

Once again, the citizens of Naples and the inhabitants of its contado have the right that the fruits of their own possessions can be transported outside the Regno without paying any duty....

Fig. 46. Boccaccio. Fresco by Andrea del Castagno, 1449. Florence, Uffizi.

62. GIOVANNI BOCCACCIO'S NEAPOLITAN LETTER, 1339

The son of a Florentine banker, Boccaccio (1313–75)[72] went to Naples in 1327 to learn his father's trade. He went on to study at the University of Naples and was introduced by his father to the court of Robert of Anjou. There he soon became involved in the literary life of Robert's court through his relationship with Maria d'Aquino, Robert's natural daughter, which began in 1334. There he also befriended Niccolò Acciaiuoli, Barbato da Sulmona, Giovanni Barrili (named in the letter below) and other members of Robert's and then Queen Giovanna I's intellectual circle.

Boccaccio spent many years in Naples, including 1327–41, 1355, 1362–63 and 1370–71 in private and diplomatic capacities, moving freely through the city's merchant and noble circles, and having full opportunity to observe the Angevin court, its daily life and its public rituals. While Conrad of Querfurt[73] certainly approached Napes with some dry irony, Boccaccio might be seen as the literary source of Naples' "comic" tradition. The image of Naples that we derive from his *Decameron*, *Fiammetta*, *Amorosa Visione* and other works is of a city full of bustling commerce and urban life, of the *"lieta brigata"* of young noble men and women, of song and

---

72. See Francesco Torraca, "Giovanni Boccaccio a Napoli (1326–1339)," ASPN 39 (1914): 25–80, 229–67, 409–58, 605–96. For these early humanists at the Neapolitan court, see Kelley, *New Solomon*, 41–49 et passim.

73. See Reading 37 above.

dance and a playful lightness of being.[74] On the other hand, Petrarch[75] might be seen as the source of its "tragic" image: of grandeur fallen from grace, of nobility corrupted, of potential squandered. These "comic" and "tragic" images would characterize our views of Naples' up to the present.[76]

While in Naples, Boccaccio penned the following humorous letter in Neapolitan, signed by "Jannetto *Parisse*," on the birth of Machinta's and his son Antoniello. He wrote it to his friend, Francesco de' Bardi, of the banking family for which his father worked. It is taken from Antonio Altamura, ed., *Testi Napoletani dei secoli XIII e XIV* (Naples: Libreria Perrella, 1949), 143–45.[77] English translation by Eileen Gardiner.

This is to let you know, dear brother, that the first day of this month of December, Machinta gave birth to a beautiful son. May God protect him and give him a long life full of good years. And what did the midwife say, who brought him from the womb? That he looks just like his father! And for God's sake we ought to believe her. Even the priest, who knows, says that she is a good person. O true God, born of our Lady, what a celebration would we all have for the love of him! If only you had been here with us, you also would have had as much joy as we did! And I must tell you that as soon as Machinta had given birth, instantly friends sent us the best octopus that you ever saw and we ate everything. Forgive us, because, being so contemptible, there is not even a little left to send you.

The complete, original text is worth including here for its record of medieval Neapolitan. Boccaccio takes as much delight in the flavor of Neapolitan names as in that of the *pulpo*

---

74. See also below Readings 73, 78, 81.

75. See below Readings 63, 69–70.

76. See above, lvi–lxi and below, 256–58, on the "black legend of the Angevins"; or "The Tragic Centuries," introduction by John Santore to his *Modern Naples: A Documentary History, 1799–1999* (New York: Italica Press, 2001), xxxi–l.

77. See also Francesco Sabatini, "Prospettive sul parlato nella storia linguistica italiana (con una lettera dell' Epistola napoletana)," in Francesco Sabatini and Vittorio Coletti, eds., *Italia linguistica delle origini: Saggi editi dal 1956 al 1996* (Lecce: Argo, 1996), 2: 425–66.

Francesco has missed. The letter may be the first recorded literary document in Neapolitan, today recognized as a distinct language and a protected UNESCO world heritage:

Facimmote, adunqua, caro fratiello, assaperi ca, lo primo iuorno de sto mese di dicembro, Machinta figliao e appe uno b(i)ello figlio masculo, ca Dio ncie-llo garde e li dea bita a tiempu e a biegli anni. E, per chillo ca nde dice la mammana, ca lo levao nella ncuccia, tutto s'assomiglia allu pate. E, per Deo, credemolielo, ca nde dice lu patino, ca la canosce, cad'è bona perzona perzí. O beneditto Dio ca nde apesse aputo uno madama nuostra la reina! Acco festa ca nde facieramo tutti per l'amore suoio! Ammacaro Deo, stato nci fussi intanto, c'apissimo aputo chillo chiacere inchietta con vuoi medemi! Et sacci ca, quanno appe figliato Machinta, a cuorpo li compari lie mannâro lo chiú biello purpo ca bidíssivingi mai; e manducuosselo tutto, ca ncie-lle puozza, si buoi tu, benire scaia, ca schitto tantillo non cie nde mandao.

E dapuoi arquanti iuorni lo faciemo batteggiare, e portàolo la mammana incombugliato in-dello ciprese di Machinta, in chillo dello mbelloso inforrato di varo: non saccio se ti s'aricorda qualisso boglio dicere eo. Et Ian[nello] Squarcione purtao la tuorcia allummata, chiena chiena, de carlini... chianchi; e foronc'i compari Iannello Corsario, Cola Scrignario, Tuczillo Parcietano, Franzillo Shizzaprévete, e Sarrillo Sconzaioco, e Martusciello Burcàno perzí, e non saccio quanta delli megliu megliu de Napoli. E ghiéronci inchietta con ipsi Mariella Cacciapúllece, Catella Saccone, Zita Cubitusa e Rudetula de Puorta Nova, e tutte chelle zitelle de la chiazza nuostra. E puoseronli nome Antuoniello ad onore de Santo Antuono, ca nce lo garde. E s'apissivi beduto quanta belle de Nido e de Capovana perzí e delle [autre] chiazze bénneno a bisitare la feta, pu cierto t'àppera maravigliato biasí a tene quant'a mene. Chiú de ciento creo ca fossero, colle zeppe encannellate e colle macagnane chiene chiene de perne e d'auro mediemmo ca nde sia laudato chillo Deo ca lle creao! Acco stavano bielle! Uno paraviso pruoprio parze chillo iuorno la chiazza nuostra! Quant' a Machinta, bona sta e allèrase molto dello figliu: nompequanto anco iace a lo lietto, come feta cad' è.

Apímmote ancora a dicere arcuna cuosa, se chiace a tene.

Lloco sta abbate Ia(nne) Boccaccio, come sai tune: ni iuorno ni notte perzí fa schitto ca scribere. Aggiolielo ditto chiú fiate, e sonbende boluto incagnare co isso buono buono. Chillo se la ride, e diceme: "Figlio meo, ba', spícciate! ba' iòca alla scola co li zitielli, ch'io faccio chesso pe volere addiscere!" E chillo, me dice Io[anne] Barrile ca isso sape quant'à lu demmòne e chiú ca non sape Scaccinopole da Surriento. Non saccio pecchene isso fa chesso; ma, pe la Donna de Pederotta, pésamende. Non pozzo chiú, ma male me nde sape. Biasí na perzona pòtera dicere: "Tune che 'nci ha' che fare a chesso?" Dicotielo. Sai ca l'amo quant'a pate. Non bòlzera nde lli abenisse arcuna cosa ca schiacesse a isso ned a mene mediemmo. Se chiace a tene, scríbelielo. E raccomannace, se te chiace, a nostro compare Pietro dallo Caneiano, ca lo pozímo bedere alla buoglia suoia.

Bolimmonce scusare ca no ti potíemo chiú tosto scrivere, c'appimo a fare una picca de chillo fatto ca sai tune ben. Se te chiace cubielle, scribiencelo. E beammoti inzorato alla chiazza nostra. Lloco sta Zita Bernacchia, ca sta trista pe tene. E aguàrdate.

Bolimmo buffoneiare na picca con tia, se chiace a tia. Che biene àiati sta tia minchia, che ne trasío a Machinta, che n'abíemo sí biello zitiello.

In Napole, lo iuorno de sant' Aniello [1339].

A Franciesco de' Bardi.

delli toi JANNETTO PARISSE, dalla rotta.

Fig. 47. Petrarch. *Fresco by Altichiero da Zevio. Padua, Oratorio di S. Giorgio, c.1376. Source: Wikimedia Commons.*

63. Petrarch on Naples, c.1341

In late February 1341, in preparation for Petrarch's coronation as poet laureate on the Capitoline Hill in Rome that April, King Robert hosted Petrarch in Naples. There the poet also became close to several of the Regno's early humanists.[78] Petrarch reminisced about his trip in his travel account, The *Itinerarium ad sepulchrum domini nostri Yeshu Christi,*[79] dated from both internal evidence and external notices to the 1350s.

King Robert conducted several interviews with the poet, testing Petrarch's and demonstrating his own knowledge of

---

78. See above, p. 224 and n. 72.

79. Trans. by Theodore J. Cachey, Jr. as *Petrarch's Guide to the Holy Land* (Notre Dame: University of Notre Dame Press, 2002).

the classics and of Naples' antiquities. The two men discussed Virgil's legacy in and around Naples, including conversations during a visit to the ancient poet's tomb at Mergellina. Petrarch describes several of the chief monuments around the Bay of Naples, its topography and famous wines, and Vesuvius.

Within Naples he also notes such important monuments as the new harbor, Giotto's frescos in the Capella Palatina of Castel Nuovo, Queen Sancia's construction of Sta. Chiara,[80] and the Certosa of S. Martino. While Petrarch's first visit was in February 1341, he is clearly describing Naples in the early 1350s: the city's two chief *seggi*, S. Nilo and Capuana, still depopulated from the chaos surrounding the Hungarian invasion, the Black Death and Giovanna I's exile and return.

Our selection is excerpted from Cachey, *Petrarch's Guide*, pars. 10.0–10.4, translated by Theodore J. Cachey, Jr.

Opposite Misenum and Baiae, distant three or four miles, appears Pozzuoli. Caligula, the fourth Roman emperor but worst of the worst after Nero, inspired by inane and presumptuous arrogance, connected these shores across this stretch of sea by a land bridge, which he himself first crossed on horseback, in triumphal pomp, in the company of many important citizens and with a more than imperial accompaniment. Not far from Pozzuoli rises the hill of Falernus, worthy of note for its beautiful vineyard.[81]

Between Falernus and the sea there is a rocky mountain, excavated by men, a work the common people foolishly believe was performed by Virgil with magic spells. Thus the fame of illustrious men, for whom true praises are inadequate, often encourages the creation of legends. And when King Robert, famous for his kingdom, but still more illustrious for his intelligence and his literary culture, in the presence of many other people, asked me what I thought about it, trusting myself to his regal humanity, in which he surpasses not only other kings but all other men, I answered playfully that I had nowhere read that Virgil was a marble worker. To which he assented with a nod of his serene brow, and confirmed that those were vestiges of iron and not magic.[82]

---

80. See below, Readings 58–59.

81. Falerno is still a well-known Campanian wine. On Petrarch's identification of its source, see Cachey, *Petrarch's Guide*, 181 n. 93.

82. Petrarch refers to the well known Virgilian and mirabilian traditions of Naples. See above, Readings 29, 37.

The entrances to the little caves are very narrow, but the tunnels are very long and dark, within which it is always an impenetrable and fearful night; in the middle there is an extraordinary path open to all, that has a nearly sacred aspect, unviolated even in times of war, if it is true what the people say, and it appears immune to acts of brigandage. They call it the "Neapolitan crypt," and Seneca mentions it in the letters to Lucilius. Towards the end of the dark passage, when one begins to see the light of the sun, one can see on another prominent height the tomb of Virgil, surely very old, and from which probably derives the belief that he excavated the mountain. At the exit from the crypt, there is a small but very much venerated shrine, and thereafter, at the foot of the hill, on the shore, is a church dedicated to the Virgin, to which a great number of people always flock by land and sea.[83]

Naples itself is situated in the nearby valley, one of few coastal cities. The port here is also man-made and the royal castle overlooks it.[84] If you disembark, don't miss visiting the king's chapel, in which the greatest painter of our times, my countryman, has left great monuments of his skill and his genius.[85] I don't dare urge you to go to the Charterhouse that is on the nearby hill.[86] I know how sailing can be tiring and tedious. Nevertheless, even if it is slightly distant from the coast, you must see the famous abode of the virgin Saint Clare: it is a beautiful work of the elderly queen.[87] No hurry or weariness should keep you from visiting two of the city's neighborhoods, Nido and Capuana,[88] worthy of mention for their extraordinary edifices and, before the plague

---

83.   Virgil's Tomb and Sta. Maria di Piedigrotta, built in 1352, and hence dating this text to at least that date.

84.   Castel Nuovo, the portus de Arcina, and the Arsenal. See Musto, Interactive Map: http://www.italicapress.com/index287.html.

85.   Giotto's frescos in Castel Nuovo. See Bruzelius, *Stones*, 103–4; and Cordelia Warr and Janis Elliott, *Art and Architecture in Naples, 1266–1713* (Malden, MA: Wiley-Blackwell, 2010), 46–48.

86.   The Certosa di S. Martino. See Reading 58.

87.   Sta. Chiara, built by Queen Sancia. See above, lxvii–lxviii, and Readings 58–59. Petrarch seems to indicate that it is a long walk from the waterfront.

88.   Two of Naples' most important *seggi*, or regional divisions. See above lxxi.

emptied the entire globe,[89] for their incredible concentration of nobility and wealth. In your role as soldier I send you to that sea of soldiers, which is proper to you, and not, since you love truth, to fables: for this reason it will be sufficient for you to observe from a distance that which is called Castel dell'Ovo.[90]

This is the city where our Virgil dedicated himself to liberal studies, after studying during his youth in your city Milan. Here he wrote the *Georgics*, here he recalls, with great modesty, having flourished in inglorious ease. He calls it "sweet Parthenope," which is in fact the other name of the city that derives from the name of she who founded it. Finally, as he lay dying far away, he remembered Naples amid last sighs and hoped to be returned there so that the city he had loved while living should have him after his death.

Having left there, you will have nearby the double summits of Vesuvius (called "Summa" by the people), and it is usually erupting flames. Pliny the Elder, a master of many sciences and of florid eloquence, went to witness that spectacle desiring experience and knowledge, only to be crushed by wind-driven volcanic ash and flames: what a miserable departure for such a great man! Thus on one side Naples guards the bones of a Mantuan and on the other those of a Veronese citizen.[91] The mountain possesses also many other characteristics, but first of all it is marvelously abundant with wine, which is called "Greek,"[92] because this part of Italy was possessed by the Greeks and was once called Magna Graecia. From there, on the right hand side one leaves behind the island of Capri which is surrounded by very steep cliffs....

---

89. Of 1348. See above, lxviii.

90. See Readings 1, 2, 29, 37 above and 79 below, pp. xxxviii–xxxix; and Musto Interactive Map: http://www.italicapress.com/index287.html.

91. See Reading 10. On Pliny's burial place, see Cachey, *Petrarch's Guide,* 184 n. 108.

92. The Greco wines, such as Greco di Tufo, are still a standard in Naples. See Reading 61 at p. 221 for Pegolotti's mention.

64. Papal revenues raised from Naples, December 1341

The passages below deal with incomes derived in 1341 from the kingdom and city of Naples.[93] The Matteo Villani noted here was one of the family of chroniclers already cited.[94] As noted here, he was authorized to collect revenues from the church of S. Pietro ad Aram and, like the other papal bankers, worked on a commission of 3 percent on average for their service of transporting the revenues to papal Avignon.

The confusion of currencies then widely used in the Regno is documented here and relative values noted. The gold florin (Fig. 48A) was the official currency of Florence, first minted in 1252 and a standard throughout Europe by the fourteenth century, widely used by the papal court. By the mid-fourteenth century the Angevins had ceased to mint their own gold coins, and Florentine bankers controlled the royal mint or zecca in Naples, minting their own gold florins.

The ducat (Fig. 48B) was the silver coin first minted by Roger II of Sicily and then from 1284 minted and circulated widely as a gold coin by the Venetians. The ducat became a standard in international trade in the Mediterranean, rivaling the florin and widely used in the Regno as a coinage of account, The *carlino* (Fig. 48C), first minted by Charles II and equal to one-twelfth of a ducat, was issued in both gold and silver. The *gigliato* (Fig. 49A) was a silver coin bearing the Angevin *giglio*, or fleur-de-lis, first minted by Charles II and by Robert of Anjou. One *carlino* equalled 10 *gigliati*. *Tareni* (or *tarì*, Fig. 49B) were another silver coin, equal to 2 *carlini*. These Neapolitan currencies and their value in florins are noted here.[95]

The following extract is taken from William Edward Lunt, *Papal Revenues in the Middle Ages* (New York: Columbia University Press, 1934), 1:316–17, translating the original Latin in Göller, *Die Einnahmen der apostolischen Kammer unter Benedikt XII*, 179, 186.

---

93. See Reading 53 above.

94. See above, Readings 38, 42–43, 46, 49, 50, 53; and below, 77.

95. On Neapolitan coinage, see Grierson and Blackburn, *Medieval European Coinage*, 3:406–29.

Fig. 48. 14th-century gold coinage: A. Florentine florin, B. Venetian ducat, C. Neapolitan carlino.

The discreet man, Bettinus Bonacursi, fellow of the said company staying at the Roman court — having deducted for the less value of 193 ounces 10 *tareni* of less weight, 9 ounces 20

Fig. 49. Neapolitan silver coinage: A. Silver gigliato, B. tarì.

tareni; and for the less value of 2900 gold florins 375 gold ducats of less weight, 10 ounces 27 *tareni* and 10 grains; and for carriage of 11,955 gold florins, namely 3 florins for each hundred, 358½ gold florins; and for the carriage of 620 ducats of gold, 18 ducats 7 silver *julhati [gigliati]*; and for the carriage of 34 gold *carlini*, 1 gold *carlino* — assigned to the camera 826 ounces 2½ *tareni* of gold in silver *carlini* — 59 *carlini* having been computed for an ounce of gold and an ounce for 5 florins, being of the value of 4200 gold florins, 5 silver *carlini* — and the aforesaid florins as well, in 15,797 gold florins; 601 gold ducats; 33 gold *carlini*; 4 silver *julhati*.

24 December. Whereas the venerable man, Lord Arnulf Marcellini, vice-rector of Benevento, deposited for the said lord, our pope, with Matteo Villani, merchant of the company of Bonacursi of Florence, in the city of Naples, of the moneys received by him from the fruits and revenues of the monastery of S. Pietro ad Aram of Naples to be paid and

assigned to the camera of our lord pope 400 ounces of gold in florins, each ounce having been computed at 5 florins, the discreet man, Bettinus Bonacursi, fellow-merchant of the aforesaid company staying at Avignon, assigned and paid to the aforesaid camera, in the name of the said Matteo and the aforesaid society, the said 400 ounces of gold, having retained for the carriage of the said ounces 3 gold florins for each hundred, namely the sum of 60 gold florins, 1940 florins gold.

65. KING ROBERT'S LAST WILL AND TESTAMENT, JANUARY 16, 1343

Robert of Anjou's will[96] remains one of the most important, most misinterpreted and least known documents of the later Angevin period. Despite its concise and careful arrangements for the succession of the Regno, Provence, Forcalquier and Piedmont in an undivided inheritance to his granddaughter Giovanna I, later political and then historiographical misrepresentations of the rights to the throne of Prince Andrew of Hungary, her second cousin and young husband, and of the legitimacy of Giovanna and the later Neapolitan Angevins have often been called into question. Robert's will is an essential starting point for any examination of this contested issue.

The process started with the Angevins of Hungary following the murder of Andrew in 1345 and continued through such influential writers as Petrarch, the Villani and Domenico da Gravina, who took up the Hungarian propaganda line that Robert of Anjou had named Andrew himself his successor in place of Giovanna. According to this line, Robert's supposed guilt over disinheriting his older brother Charles Martel and "usurping" the throne of Naples from Charles' son, his nephew Carobert, led him on the deathbed to pass the kingdom on to Charles' heirs: Andrew and then Lewis of Hungary.

---

96. For brief treatments, see Baddeley, *Robert the Wise*, 281–87; De Frede, "Da Carlo I," 223–24. For a good recent introduction see Shona Kelly Wray and Roisin Cossar, "Wills as Primary Sources," in *Understanding Medieval Primary Sources*, Joel T. Rosenthal, ed. (New York: Routledge, 2012), 59–71, esp. 61–68 for the Roman law traditions of Italy and southern Europe.

"Usurpation" in the nineteenth-century literary fiction of Alexandre Dumas and others[97] has evolved into "illegitimacy" in the not-unrelated literary theory of Greenblatt[98] and his followers among certain historians of Naples. This deep sense of illegitimacy supposedly led to Robert's creation of fictive personae of the wise and just ruler in order to compensate for this guilt. Whatever the merits of this theory,[99] such documents as the following will and testament do not seem to bear out this gesture toward the Hungarians. Rather, they stress the strong links between Robert and his granddaughter and his strong awareness of the rivalries among the Angevins.

The will relies less on French law and Capetian custom, including the Salic Law (*lex Salica*),[100] than on the traditions

---

97. "But the throne is usurped!" Alexandre Dumas, *Joan of Naples. Celebrated Crimes*, first published 1843, English trans. 1910, Etext #2750, David Widger, ed. (Oxford, MS: Project Gutenberg, 2001), http://www.gutenberg.org/files/2760/2760-pdf.pdf at dccclxviii (accessed 11/8/12); Marjorie Bowen, *The Sword Decides: A Chronicle of a Queen in the Dark Ages, Founded on the Story of Giovanna of Naples* (New York: The McClure Co., 1908), 43. Gregorovius enshrined the theme in his *History of the City of Rome*, 6:535.

98. Kelly, *New Solomon*, 1–21, 276–83 et passim, stresses Robert's illegitimacy and her debt to Stephen Greenblatt's *Renaissance Self-Fashioning* and to Burckhardt before him. See above, pp. lviii–lix n. 139 and 194 n. 28.

99. See Ronald G. Musto, review, "*The New Solomon: Robert of Naples (1309–1343) and Fourteenth-Century Kingship*, by Samantha Kelly," *Renaissance Quarterly* 57.3 (Autumn 2004): 984–85; and idem, review, "*The Anjou Bible: A Royal Manuscript Revealed. Naples 1340*, ed. Lieve Watteeuw and Jan Van der Stock; *The Clement Bible at the Medieval Courts of Naples and Avignon: A Story of Papal Power, Royal Prestige, and Patronage*, by Cathleen A. Fleck." *Renaissance Quarterly* 64.2 (Summer 2011): 587–90.

100. French jurists had "rediscovered" this supposed early Frankish law in the early stages of the Hundred Years War to prevent the inheritance to the French throne by Edward III of England through the maternal line and to justify the inheritance of Philip VI in 1328 as the first Valois successor to the Capetian dynasty. However, it appears that Angevin precedent may have provided the French with a legal framework in this regard. According to Michael Jones, "François de Meyronnes had already written a treatise on the [ancient Roman] *lex voconia*, which excluded women from succession, enshrining the fundamental principles adopted later in the century to justify royal practice in France."

of Roman law used in Naples from the time of Frederick II and encouraged under Angevin rule and among Robert's advisors.[101] But here Robert appears to have disregarded the thinking of his own advisors and of the Italian legal tradition of *exclusio propter dotem*, which had developed to exclude women from Justinianic equal-inheritance practice.[102] Even should Giovanna die, her heir was not to be Andrew, who would then become prince of Salerno (Item 4), but her younger sister Maria (Items 2, 3).

Also worth noting (Item 13) is the repeated, indissoluble link between the Regno and the other Angevin holdings: Provence, Forcalquier and Piedmont. Robert foresaw the danger of such a dissolution and reaffirmed the dynastic links of the Regno and counties with the same firmness as for the long-standing Angevin claims to Sicily (Item 14). His policies informed much of Giovanna's later actions, including plans for the reconquest of Sicily and the earmarking of the royal treasury in the Torre Bruno of the Castel Nuovo toward this enterprise.

Central to the execution of the will are several personalities that reflect Robert and Sancia's support of the Franciscan Spirituals. These include Roberto da Mileto, OFM, a follower of Angelo Clareno OFM, and the target of one of Petrarch's most venomous letters,[103] and Pietro de Cadeneto, OFM. Their role on the regency council would become the target of both

---

See Jones, "The Last Capetians and Early Valois Kings, 1314–1364," *The New Cambridge Medieval History* 6, c.1300–c.1415 (Cambridge: Cambridge University Press, 2000), 388–421 at 394. Dean, *Towns of Italy,* 198, notes that King Robert had excluded women from law courts in 1332. On the Provençal François de Meyronnes (d. c.1328), and his role in the Neapolitan court and intellectual life, see Kelly, *New Solomon,* 34–36, 112–19 et passim. Such influence *from* Angevin Naples to Capetian France, as well as vice-versa, is a central theme of Dunbabin's *French in the Kingdom of Naples.* For general background see Andrew W. Lewis, *Royal Succession in Capetian France: Studies on Familial Order and the State* (Cambridge: Harvard University Press, 1981).

101. Dunbabin, *French in the Kingdom of Naples,* 235–49, esp. 237; Kelly, *New Solomon,* 168–69 et passim.

102. Wray and Cossar, "Wills," 66.

103. *Familiares* V.3. See above Reading 57 at pp. 212–13 and n. 60.

papal and princely attacks on the provisions of the will and the make-up of Giovanna's court.

Robert also guaranteed a strong place for both his widow Sancia and for the regency council (Items 6 and 22), made of up largely of his new nobility of the robe: men and women of the lower nobility or merchant classes, even in the case of the de' Cabannis, the descendents of a former African slave, who had risen up through the Neapolitan court because of their talents and strong loyalty.[104] Part of Robert's emphasis upon this civil bureaucracy was to insure continuity of policy (Item 8).

---

104. Raimondo de' Cabanni was a former slave, and a Moor. According to Boccaccio, who knew him, "people said that Raimondo was a black man, an Ethiopian, and his looks did not contradict them." King Charles II's household seneschal, Raimondo Cabanni, had purchased the African from corsairs, gave him his own name, set him free and appointed him his successor in the royal kitchens. Filippa, Giovanna I's governess, was reported to be a laundry woman. She had grown up in Catania, and hence was known as "La Catanese." According to Boccaccio's *The Fall of Famous Men*, some time during his campaigns (1298–1300) to reconquer Sicily for his father Charles II, Robert of Anjou, then prince and duke of Calabria, had encamped close to Trapani. There his wife Violante gave birth to a son — probably Charles of Calabria — and needed an attendant. Filippa soon came to the princess's attention for her beauty and imposing figure. She was already married to a local fisherman and had just given birth to a son of her own, and so was taken into Violante's service as a wet nurse. She accompanied the princely party when they returned north and became a trusted servant to Robert and Violante. After Violante's death, La Catanese, now a widow, became a favorite too of Queen Sancia, who arranged her marriage to Raimondo de' Cabanni. In 1332, after Giovanna and her sister were orphaned, their step-grandmother Queen Sancia named Filippa the girls' *magistressa* or governess. Filippa and Raimondo's diligence and talents gained them the trust and favor of both the crown and the nobility, and they began to accumulate wealth and property. He achieved knighthood and higher offices, ultimately rising to the office of seneschal of the court. The sons of the de' Cabanni — Carlo, Roberto and Perrotto — were made prominent feudatories by Robert and Sancia. Roberto, in fact, became count of Eboli and grand seneschal of the realm. Carlo's daughter was also named Sancia. The name is not Italian, or Neapolitan, and was most likely given her in honor of the Majorcan queen. Sancia de' Cabanni married Carlo di Gambatesa and in 1346 became countess of Morcone. She had become a playmate of the young princesses in her grandmother's care and was later described as "the queen's intimate friend." On their fates, see below, Readings 74–76.

Note that Robert's heirs' affirmation of their consent to his will carries a double guarantee (Item 24): the oath on the Gospel book in addition to the public witness of the notary and judge. Yet, despite Robert's attempts to have this family swear to adhere to its provisions, the will reflects the growing tension between the old nobility of the sword — including Robert's own siblings and their heirs — and the new nobility of the robe. This friction would erupt into bloodshed with Prince Andrew's murder and the attack on Giovanna's throne by her cousins, the Angevin princes.

While we possess only a copy from the Angevin and then royal archives in Marseilles, based on the public instrument derived from the original will, the authenticity of the document itself has never been doubted by the leading scholars of the Angevins, including Léonard and Baddeley.

The text is taken from Johann Christian Lünig, *Codex Italiae diplomaticus* (Frankfurt: Lanckisianorum, 1725–35), 2:LXXXII, cols. 1101–10.[105] Translated by R.G. Musto.

The Testament of Robert, king of Sicily, 16 January 1343

In the name of our Lord [col. 1101], Jesus Christ, Amen, in the year of His incarnation, one thousand, three hundred forty-three, 11th indiction, 27th day of January, in the first year of the pontificate of the most holy father and lord in Christ, Lord Clement VI, pope by divine providence. At Naples, in the Castel Nuovo.

Let all know both present and in future, who will inspect the tenor of the present instrument or of its public transcript, that in our presence by the notary and the undersigned witnesses, in the presence of our most serene Lady Sancia, by the grace of God queen of Jerusalem and Sicily, that the lady queen herself caused to be presented and exhibited and read a certain public instrument of the last will and testament of our most serene prince and lord Robert of shining memory, by the grace of God illustrious king of Jerusalem and of Sicily, her husband, with his and our golden seal [1102] of his royal majesty impressed

---

105. Lünig's note reads: "Extracted from the registers. Copies of the testaments of the kings of Sicily and counts of Provence, fol. 18, conserved in the archives of the king in Provence. Collated by me, his councillor to the said secretary and to the archbishop of the said county."

with silk threads affixed by the public notary Mapillo Ruffulo[106] of Naples and by Master Niccolò d'Alife,[107] appointed by royal authority chief judge for the entire kingdom of Sicily, and collaborated by the signatures of the undersigned witnesses. The tenor of this instrument, with nothing in it changed, deleted or added, is understood word for word to be the following:

In the name of our Lord, Jesus Christ, in the year of His nativity one thousand, three hundred forty-three, in the reign of our most serene prince and lord Robert, felicitously by the grace of God the renowned king of Jerusalem and Sicily, duke of Apulia and prince of Capua, count of Provence and Forcalquier and of Piedmont, in the thirty-fourth year of his reign, Amen.

On the sixteenth day of January, the eleventh indiction, at Castel Nuovo in Naples, in the chamber of the same lord king, [1103] we Niccolò d'Alife, by royal authority appointed chief judge for the entire kingdom of Sicily; and Mapillo Ruffulo of Naples, by royal authority public notary for the whole of the same kingdom of Sicily; and by the undersigned literate witnesses, summoned and sworn especially for this, namely:

Venerable father, Lord Brother Guglielmo, bishop of Salon [Scala], the confessor of the lady queen [Sancia]; the venerable and religious friar Giovanni de Bertolio of the Friars Minor, confessor of the illustrious lady the duchess of Calabria [Giovanna I]; Lord Giovanni Grillo, vice-protonotary of the

---

106. On the Ruffulo, see Kelly, *New Solomon*, 168. On the process of recording notarial wills in Italy, see Steven Epstein, *Wills and Wealth in Medieval Genoa, 1150–1250* (Cambridge: Harvard University Press, 1984), esp. 5, 17–18.

107. D'Alife was a member of Robert's household *familia* from at least 1331, was appointed *magister rationarum* in 1342 and in 1363 Giovanna I's grand seneschal. He died on Dec. 31, 1367. The famed Anjou Bible (Figs. 30, 39, 43, 50, 51) was probably intended as a wedding present from King Robert for Giovanna and Andrew of Hungary, but it was completed under d'Alife's patronage at Giovanna's request after Andrew's assassination in 1345. The painting-over of Andrew's coats of arms with d'Alife's provides poignant evidence of this transfer. D'Alife then bequeathed the bible to the Celestine house of the Ascension before his death. See Fleck, "Patronage, Art," esp. 47–49; Michelle Duran, "The Politics of Art: Imaging Sovereignty in the Anjou Bible," in Watteeuw and Van der Stock, *The Anjou Bible*, 73–93, esp. 74 and n. 6; Kelly, *New Solomon*, 32, 42, 44 n. 81.

kingdom of Sicily[108]; Brother Roberto da Mileto, OFM[109]; Lord Pietro Baudet,[110] master of the royal chapel and almoner; Lord Egidio de Bevania, master of the Ratio of the royal court[111]; Master Guy de Cavaillon; Lord Hugo de Figueria, knight; Master Giovanni de Arianco; Master Bartolomeo de Biscuto, physician; the royal secretaries Raimondo de Roca and his son Audibert de Roca, his chamberlains and *familiares.*

By the present public document we declare, make note and swear, that summoned to the presence of the lord king, residing in his chamber in the said Castel Nuovo, the said lord king, with attention for [making] salubrious provision, called to our attention that our first parents lost paradise because of a carnal sin. The punishment of death for their transgression was propagated upon all their future offspring; and, transfused in miserable fragility, this punishment has lain silent and without certitude, so that mortals in this vale of tears end their lives in angry dissolution amid the shadows of this world and can perceive nothing else. Thus the unspoken law of death itself is applied equally to each and every of their posterity so that death's gluttony does not distinguish among kings and princes. In the end he consumes all equally in common.[112]

Therefore after some pious consideration, the king grew doubtful about whether his earthy life would be prolonged for many more days. Completely uncertain of the end, and reasonably fearing a sudden calling, he considered how he might provide and arrange for the happy liberation of his soul from the

---

108. Originally from Salerno. He taught civil law at the University of Naples until 1306, worked in the royal treasury until 1317 and then served as vice-protonotary from 1324 to 1342. See Kelly, *New Solomon,* citing Minieri-Riccio, "Geneaologia," ASPN 7 (1882): 254.

109. See above, 212–13 and n. 60; 236–37; Forcellini, "'L'horrendum tripes *animal';* and Musto, "Queen Sancia of Naples," 197–99.

110. Also Benedeti or Bandetto. See Baddeley, 284 n. 3.

111. In 1345 named by Giovanna I the *giudice de mercanzia* for the commune of Florence. See Baddeley, 284 n. 4. He is also named above in Reading 55 at p. 203. The *ratio* was part of the treasury.

112. It seems that Robert had time and energy for yet another sermon, even on his deathbed.

weighty prison of the flesh and for confessing the name of the Lord. In anticipation, he arranged and considered his last day in the Lord and the hour of his passing, in the hope of divine clemency for his living in the heavenly mansions among the blessed.

The lord king, sound of body and of mind, and speaking clearly, and disposing of everything in order, both for the kingdom of Sicily all the way to the Faro,[113] and for the counties of Provence and Forcalquier and of Piedmont, and of all his other dominions and lands, jurisdictions, goods and other possessions moveable and immovable of whatever place and condition before us, the judge, notary and aforesaid witnesses,[114] disposed of all as described below and made his last testament.

[Item 1]. First, since any testament must begin with the head, he named as his universal heir Giovanna the princess of Calabria, the daughter of his first-born son, the illustrious lord Charles, duke of Calabria and his heir as lord king in the kingdom of Sicily as far as Faro as well as of the counties of Provence and Forcalquier and Piedmont and all other lands, places, lordships, jurisdictions, [1104] places and things moveable and immovable, wherever and in whatever way they might belong to him.

Item [2].[115] He established the distinguished Lady Maria, also his granddaughter, as the duchess of Calabria and [his] heir next in line, with the county of Alba and the justiciarship of Valle di Crati and Terra Giordana,[116] with all the lands, castles,

---

113. The lighthouse at Reggio Calabria. The mainland portion of the dismembered kingdom of Sicily was understood to encompass all territories from the borders of the papal states to the toe of Italy.

114. Roman law required at least seven witnesses to a "nuncupative" testament, that is, a will made aloud before witnesses and a notary, as this one was. See *The Institutes of Justinian*, trans. J.B. Moyle, 5th ed. (Oxford: Clarendon Press, 1913), 63. See also Epstein, *Wills and Wealth*, 11.

115. Gaglione, *Donne e potere*, 177, offers a translation of items 1 and 2. It is, however, his translation of a synopsis in Lorenz Enderlein's *Die Grablegen des Hauses Anjou in Unteritalien: Totenkult und Monumente, 1266–1343* (Worms: Wernersche Verlagsgesellschaft, 1977), 117 n. 1.

116. Since the Norman period, the duchy of Calabria had been divided into three administrative regions: "Calabria" proper; Valle di Crati (Valle Gratis), centered around Cosenza; and Terra Giordana, centered on Catanzaro. The latter two had comprised a single royal justiciarship since the Norman period, when

men, vassals, plains, mountains, groves, waters and waterways, fruits, rights and all their appurtenances whatever, along with 30,000 *uncie*[117] in coin as her dowry for maintaining the agreed terms. With these he wishes her to be content, so that she will not be able to request above or beyond that for her inheritance. Nor should she seek anything else at any time by any law, reason or cause, or in any other way whatsoever. The aforesaid Lady Maria ought to hold these counties and jurisdictions in direct fief from the same lady duchess [Giovanna I] and her heirs or from the royal council, under the terms of the services owed as well as under this condition: that the aforesaid lady duchess [Giovanna I] grants and assigns, or causes to be granted and assigned by others on her behalf, to the said Lady Maria her sister through agreed terms another 10,000 *uncie* of similar coin in compensation for the said justiciarship of Valle di Crati and Terra Giordana above the said 30,000 *uncie*. [In that case] the said county and justiciarship will remain with the lady duchess [Giovanna I] for herself and for her heirs and will revert into her hands and into those of her aforesaid heirs. But [if] the said county remains in the hands of the Lady Maria, along with the aforesaid 30,000 *uncie*, and in the aforesaid cases, with the consent each to one another, and with the agreement of the present lord king, [then] she has renounced voluntarily and expressly the aforesaid royal and whatever other inheritances, especially in the case of the exchange written below.

Item [3]. The lord king willed and commanded that — God forbid — it happen that the Lady Duchess Giovanna should die without legitimate issue born to her or should her legitimate descendants not survive, then her sister the aforesaid Lady Maria or her heirs or the heirs of her heirs [shall inherit] the kingdom of Sicily all the way to the Faro, as well as all the counties and all the other inheritances already described. Equally, should — God forbid — the Lady Maria predecease her without

---

they were the possession of the counts of Catanzaro. See Hiroshi Takayama, *The Administration of the Norman Kingdom of Sicily,* The Medieval Mediterranean 3 (Leiden: Brill, 1993), 107.

117. In Reading 64, at pp. 232–33 above, an *uncia* (ounce) was calculated by papal revenue collectors to be five golden florins. The justiciarship of Valle di Crati and Terra Giordana alone therefore was worth 150,000 florins annually.

physical heirs, then Lady Giovanna now duchess, the first-born sister, or her heirs, or her heirs' heirs, shall inherit each and every item already named. And in the aforesaid exchange, each for each, voluntarily and freely, with the agreement and assent and the intercession of the king himself, he has consented, and they wish expressly, that this agreement remain in inviolable efficacy and vigor. And for the greater confirmation and more complete warranty, he has exchanged the one for the other in the above-mentioned cases. And for this commission of good faith, he has asked them, and he has wished that the same exchanges retain validity in every way and manner in which they can and should maintain better worth *de jure*. In this way, however, under the present disposition and exchange, the aforesaid may sell no holding from her Trebellian, Falcidian or any other fourth,[118] howsoever allocated to her.

Item [4]. He commanded and willed that — God forbid — [1105] the situation arises that Lady Giovanna the duchess dies, and she leave no legitimate heirs born to her, then Lord Andrew, the duke of Calabria her husband, shall hold, and ought to hold, the principality of Salerno with the title of Prince and all its dues, fruits, revenues, jurisdictions and appurtenances whatsoever. He [Robert] also commanded that additional revenues be attached to this said principality in the amount of 2,000 gold *uncie*, as befits the tenancy of these privileges. Hence, as [has been] said of the tenancy held through him immediately and in chief from the lord king or the queen of Sicily, either he [Andrew] or she [Giovanna] shall be held to the customary duty and service, according to the use and custom of the said Regno.

---

118. Trebellian inheritance decree: Bas. 41, 3; D. 36.1 *Ad senatus consultum Trebellianum*. For the Falcidian portion, see Bas. 41.1.95; D 35.2; Inst. 2.22, *Ad legem Falcidiam*. Both laws, incorporated into Justinian's *Corpus Iuris Civilis*, guaranteed a fourth of any inheritance to "heirs" (more like modern executors), notwithstanding any specific legacies in a testament, and established that these "fourths" were the heir's by right. This reference is an important indication that Robert's testament owed as much to his court experts in Roman law as to any French legal principles, thus diminishing the importance of the Salian and other practices of the contemporary Capetian and Valois courts. See the articles on both as PDF downloads in Fred H. Blume, *Annotated Justinian Code*, Timothy Kearley, ed. http://uwacadweb.uwyo.edu/blume%26justinian (accessed 11/11/12).

Item [5]. The king willed and commanded that his body be buried in his royal monastic church of Corpus Christi in Naples,[119] where certain special alms shall be provided, such as the most serene lady Queen Sancia, his consort, and the other undersigned executors of his testament below specify.

Item [6]. He commands and orders that the aforesaid lady queen [Sancia] principally, as well as the venerable father Lord Philippe bishop of Cavaillon,[120] the vice-chancellor of the kingdom of Sicily; and his magnificence Lord Filippo de Sanguineto, count of Altomonte, the seneschal of Provence; Lord Goffredo de Marzano, count of Squillace and admiral of the Regno; and Carlo Artus[121] shall be and ought to be governors, stewards, rectors and administrators and whatever other office or title they shall better determine on behalf of the said illustrious lord king Andrew, duke of Calabria[122] and the

---

119. Corpo di Cristo or Sta. Chiara. See Bruzelius, *Stones of Naples*, 137; and Italica web gallery: http://www.flickr.com/photos/80499896@N05/sets/72157630151262510, and images 18–19, 34, 36 for Robert's tomb and sepulcher.

120. Philippe de Cabassoles (1305–72), bishop of Vaucluse in Provence, was a very close friend and correspondent of Petrarch, in both the *Familiares* and the *Liber sine nomine*. As vice-chancellor of the Regno, he was a major figure in the regency council at Naples. He served as a papal nuncio in the 1350s, was named titular patriarch of Jerusalem in 1361, rector of Comtat-Venaissin in 1362, administrator of Marseilles in 1366 and cardinal priest of SS. Marcellino e Pietro in 1368. A member of the papal curia from 1369, he was named governor of Avignon and created cardinal bishop of Sabina and papal legate in 1370. Petrarch dedicated his *De vita solitaria* to him. Philippe was removed from Giovanna I's regency council by Clement VI, first by summoning him to Avignon during the Angevin princes' attempt to topple her and then, despite her entreaties for his return, permanently, thus crippling her court. See Ernest Hatch Wilkins, *Life of Petrarch* (Chicago: University of Chicago Press, 1961), 17–118, 121–22, 137–38 et passim; and E. Cerasoli, "Clemente VI e Giovanna I di Napoli: Documenti inediti dell'Archivio Vaticano (1343–1352)." ASPN 21–22 (1896–97) 21:3–41; 227–64, 427–75 667–707; 22:3–46.

121. Robert's natural-born son, sometimes known as Charles of Artois.

122. …dicti illustris domini Andreae regis, ducis Calabriae…. The designation "regis" seems to contradict Item 1, p. 241 above, where Robert explicitly excludes Andrew from the line of royal inheritance. One must therefore interpret this phrase either as a later interpolation by someone sympathetic to the Hungarian

aforesaid ladies and sisters, the duchess [Giovanna] and Lady
Maria, and of the council of the realm and of all the others
mentioned until the aforesaid lords, the duke [Andrew] and
duchess [Giovanna] and Lady Maria reach their twenty-fifth
year. Further, that the aforesaid lords, the duke, duchess and
Lady Maria ought not — nor can — contract, grant or alienate
anything either judicially or extra-judicially in any form or in
any manner either expressly without the knowledge or consent principally of the lady queen [Sancia] or of the aforesaid
administrators, rectors, stewards and governors. Further, until
the completion of their twenty-fifth year, should they do any
such things — which the lord king himself neither believes
nor intends that they do — *ipso jure* these shall be null, void
and empty.

Item [7]. He willed and ordained that the aforesaid Lady Maria
be betrothed to marry the illustrious Prince Lewis, the king of
Hungary, excepting certain secret conditions that induced the
lord king [Robert] himself, as he has expressed. Namely, that if
the said marriage encounters any impediment because an oath
and an agreement between the lord king of Hungary himself
and the king of Bohemia,[123] then either his [grand]daughter
ought to be married to the first-born son of the excellent Lord
Jean, duke of Normandy,[124] the first-born son of the illustrious
King Philip [VI] of France[125] or, in case of his death, with the
second-born son of the said king of France.[126]

Item [8]. He established and commanded that each and every one of his officials and members of his royal household

party — for which we have no evidence — or as a simpler honorific, in fact,
meaning, "king consort."

123. A reference to Lewis of Hungary's betrothal to Margaret of Bohemia (24
May 1335–49, before October). Margaret was the second child of Emperor
Charles IV of Bohemia and was actually married to Lewis of Hungary in 1342.
This clause therefore may well be one of the older ones in Robert's will and
appears not to have been altered to reflect the new realities.

124. Born 16 April 1319, duke of Normandy from 1322, king of France 22
August 1350–8 April 1364.

125. Reigned 1 April 1328–22 August 1350.

126. This probably referred to the second surviving son, Philip of Valois, duke of
Orléans (1336–75).

of whatever condition and status ought to remain on and continue in their various grades in the service of the aforesaid lords, the lord duke and lady duchess and Lady Maria, in the same manner as they were in the [1106] service of the same lord king, and these aforesaid ought to be preferred to all and sundry. And he commanded expressly to the same lady queen [Sancia] principally, as well as to the aforesaid stewards, rectors and administrators, that they take care and cause these things to be effectually commanded, executed and tenaciously observed.

Item [9]. He willed and ordained that in each and every archdiocese and important diocese of the aforesaid Regno and in the counties of Provence and Forcalquier, one priest ought to be designated who will continuously celebrate masses for the soul of the said king and for his predecessors and successors. For these priests provision shall be made for food and other necessities according to the wishes of the said lady queen, principally, and then of the other aforesaid governors, stewards and administrators.

Item [10]. He willed and ordained that in each and every incorporated town [*universitas*] of the Regno and of Provence, on whatever day, commemoration should be made in masses and vespers for his soul and for that of his predecessors and successors, and for this purpose certain alms shall be established according to the will of the said last queen, principally, and also of the other governors already named.

Item [11]. He established and ordered that monies from the treasury, which is in the said Castel Nuovo, shall serve and ought to serve as has been and is its intended use: for the reconquest of Sicily and the defense of the Regno as occasion warrants.

Item [12]. He has entrusted, with every reverence, humility[127] and devotion to our most holy and clement lord the pope and to the reverend fathers the lord cardinals of the Sacred College, the aforesaid lady queen [Sancia] as well as the lords duke [Andrew] and duchess [Giovanna] and her aforesaid

---

127. Lünig's text reads "humanitate," perhaps a transcription error, as the context seems to call for "humilitate."

sister[128] [Maria], the Regno and the [aforesaid] counties and whatever other benefices, lands and places. The aforesaid lord king also hopes that the said lady queen, the lord duke, the duchess and her sister maintain, defend and hold from harm the Regno, the counties and the other aforesaid possessions with the favor and the assistance of the aforesaid lord our pope and the lord cardinals. [And he hopes that they will be] especially attentive to the filial reverence and devotion of the lord king himself and of his predecessors toward them [the pope and cardinals] and that this [reverence and devotion] will be handed on to his successors just as it has been handed down until now.

Item [13]. He willed and ordained that always and forever the aforesaid counties of Provence and Forcalquier be united inseparably with the Regno in one dominion and that a separation never can be, nor ought to be, made even if there should be more sons and daughters [born] or for whatever other reason and cause, since this union is especially important for the mutual defense and the prosperous state of the Regno and the aforesaid counties.

Item [14]. Concerning the island of Sicily, he established and commanded through his aforesaid heir [Giovanna] and other successors that — at no time whatever and in perpetuity — no pact, convention, transaction or whatever else be made that Sicily be separated and mutilated from the more notable remaining and larger part of the Regno. Rather, it shall be and ought to be expressly and thoroughly joined and united to the remaining part of the said Regno, like a part mutilated from the rest, so that there may be one shepherd and one flock,[129] for it is written, "any kingdom divided against itself is laid waste."[130]

Item [15]. With clear knowledge and expressly he confirms all the lands, locales and jurisdictions of the lady queen [Sancia] that she now holds and ought to hold [1107] by whatever reason or cause, and that whatever demesne lands that she holds in

---

128. Lünig reads "Sorores ejus praedictos," surely another error of transcription, since only one sister (Maria) is referred to four lines below.

129. John 10:16.

130. Mt. 12:25.

exchange at present in execution of any provision for her shall especially be preserved in each and every detail. It is reasonable and worthy that this be allowed by every intelligible means and by every sane and straightforward understanding and sense and any other interpretation by whatever laws and interpretations and new readings however torturous, notwithstanding whatever privileges conceded to the contrary, or to be conceded in the future, by using whatever sequence or expression of words. According to that certain knowledge, from this point on, by every means, these are to be considered empty and without basis.

Item [16]. He willed and ordered from this time on, and from his own sure knowledge he made immune, and he wished to keep immune, any administrative acts carried out by the lady queen [Sancia] either in the Regno or in the lands of the aforesaid ladies and sisters, the duchess [Giovanna] and Maria. And if perhaps at some time it is discovered or appears or happens to be discovered or made apparent that for any reason of the aforesaid administration she [Sancia becomes a] debtor and repays or delegates anything from what has been left to her, then the aforesaid sisters — the lady duchess [Giovanna] and Maria — shall consent freely and voluntarily to this immunity, remission and delegation [*legato*] in as far as they are affected or could be affected.

Item [17]. He decreed and willed that the Hospital of Sta. Elisabetta[131] be constructed, completed and endowed in the location that he the lord king had arranged and provided for it to be, so that there might be received forever one hundred of his and his family's court circle [*familiaribus*] and so that they might be comfortably maintained there. This is incumbent especially upon the lady queen and the other executors named below.

Item [18]. He willed, decreed and expressly commanded that whatever and of whatever type of detrimental laws, statutes and ordinances both especially within the Regno and within the said counties that were promulgated unnecessarily against justice be revoked and be understood to be revoked and nullified. It was never the intention of the lord king to enact or ordain anything that would be repugnant to justice, and the lord king from

---

131. Identity unknown, perhaps the hospital of Sta. Elisabetta just north of Sorrento toward the royal castle of Quisisana.

henceforth from his certain knowledge expressly revokes the detrimental laws, statutes and ordinances and cancels, abolishes and annuls them *ipso jure* and holds them to be cancelled, abolished and annulled. And he especially and expressly decreed and set forth in certain clauses, notwithstanding contrary and derogatory ordinances, which he revokes with the said full knowledge and wills to be empty and meaningless.

Item [19]. He willed and commanded that all the surplus from the general subventions, collections and gifts and the dispositions made from those surpluses, including those not yet expended, shall be cancelled and remitted to each and every land and place of the Regno for all past debts right up to the day of his death, and that at no time shall they ever be exacted.[132] Nor shall those lands and places, or their citizens or inhabitants, be asked for them [subventions, etc.] either from their person or in the form of a penalty. And because, inasmuch as one levy a year is otherwise imposed and raised, the aforesaid lord king nevertheless hopes that his faithful subjects will subvent his said heir and successors freely as the need arises.

Item [20]. He willed and commanded that all things improperly exacted shall and ought to be restored as well and salubriously as can be done for the salvation of his soul. This is incumbent principally upon the same lady queen [Sancia] and upon the other undersigned executors of this testament.

Item [21]. He ordered and ordained that on the day of his death all those imprisoned in punishment for their crimes ought to be freed, with the exception of brigands and others under [the ban of] public infamy and any individual enemies [of the king], and without prejudice to any law.

Item [22]. He decreed and ordered that the aforesaid lady the queen and the above-mentioned lords, Archbishop Philippe de Cavaillon, Filippo de Sanguineto, the admiral of the Regno [Goffredo de Marzano], and [Carlo] Artus shall be the executors of his last will in this form that he has wished to validate by the power of the testament. And if he does not

---

132. Such cancellations had recent precedent in Capetian royal practice, for example. See Elizabeth A.R. Brown, "Moral Imperatives and Conundrums of Conscience: Reflections on Philip the Fair of France," *Speculum* 87.1 (January 2012): 1–36, esp. 3–6 and nn.

or shall not validate it by right of the testament, he ought to validate it by right of the codicils and of the grants occasioned by his death, or whatever else of his last wishes, and by every other right and way by which he can and should better validate it.

Item [23]. He wished and ordered that from the aforesaid governors, rectors, stewards, administrators and executors, along with the aforesaid lady the queen, as long as she shall live and as long as she remains willing and able to participate, or [even] after her death, even if two other [testators] be dead or in some way unable to participate, then the aforesaid [officials] shall be required to exercise the government, rule, dispensation, administration and execution of all and each of the aforesaid items just as set forth above, according to the wish of the above-said testator.

The aforesaid lord king concedes to his said executors, or any two of them as said above, the taking of free faculty and complete power by their own authority, the disposition of all his moveable goods, wherever and in whatever form, as well as their proceeds, revenue and returns, by the laws of the Regno and the aforesaid counties, with the aforesaid express exceptions, and of their selling, withdrawing, alienating and contracting as they shall see best for the complete execution of the said testament.

Item [24]. The aforesaid lord duke [Andrew] and lady duchess [Giovanna] and her sister Maria, affirming themselves to be adults — and so it seems from their appearance — in the presence of the said lord king and of our judge, notary and the above written witnesses, have promised and sworn, grasping the sacred Gospels of God, to tenaciously and inviolably observe each and every article of the above, and at no time ever through themselves, or through any way by means of others, to cause or bring about the contrary, exchanging with one another the same aforesaid promise and sacred oath.

I as notary and as public witness also received the very same promise and sacred oath from the aforesaid lord duke and lady duchess and Maria her sister. By legal stipulations on the part of one and all who are concerned and who might be concerned in any way with each and every article of the aforesaid — notwithstanding for all of the above whatever laws, constitutions, oaths, customs, rites and whatever else, in whatever manner opposing or thwarting the aforesaid royal dispositions or this last will, with whatever series or expression of words, even if special or explicit mention ought to be made here by anyone or any of their [dependent] men or women in the presence of us, the judge and notary and witnesses above — the aforesaid lord king, unbound by the laws, by his own certain knowledge and in the plenitude of his royal power, has wished and resolved that each and every one of the above be null of strength, effect and vigor [1109] and be considered specified, assigned and expressed. He also made up for every omission in such a way so that for every eventuality of this type his disposition or last will, obtaining the position of law in the prescribed way, obtained its effect in reality and infallibly in each and every case. As testimony of this by the aforesaid lord duke and lady duchess, and her sister Lady Maria and of each and every one who have or will have an interest in this, there have been executed from the same testament four copies of the public instruments by the hand of me, the aforesaid notary, sealed by my usual seal, with my signature, and collaborated above by the judge and our witnesses signed below.

And I, Mapillo Ruffulo of Naples, public notary for the entire kingdom of Sicily by the same royal authority, have written the above. I, who was among the aforesaid witnesses, have signed below, and upon request I have written and signed with my usual notarial device. For the aforesaid lord king through this, his last will, from his certain knowledge, has expressly voided, invalidated, annulled and nullified in its force and efficacy any testament or testaments, codicil or codicils and any other last will or donation or donations put into effect by his death that he might have executed in singular or plural, and that might happen to be discovered in the future or appear in whatever manner. And he [the king] wishes, decrees and commands that his present testament or last will be the final one and that it obtain the firmness of strength in each and every way, as has been expressed above. Furthermore, for the greater certitude, strength and warranty of each and every one the aforesaid lord king's orders and wishes that the said four copies of the instrument be strengthened with his gold royal seal affixed with the communal stamp [*typario*].

I, as above, Nicolaus de Alisia,[133] appointed for the entire afore-said kingdom of Sicily, have signed below by royal authority.

I, as above, Brother Guillelmus, bishop of Scala, have signed below.

I, as above, Brother Joannes de Bertolio, have signed below.

I, as above, Joannes Gulli de Sallucio, have been among the aforesaid, and I have made my mark below.

I, as above, Brother Robertus de Mileto, have signed below.

I, Petrus Baudet, master of the royal chapel and of the almonry, have made my mark below.

I, as above, Egidio de Bujana, knight, master of the Ratio of the great royal curia, have signed below.

I, as above, Guigo Guigonis de Carelliome, have signed below.

The mark of the cross by his own hand of Hugo de Figueria, knight, who does not know how to write.

I, as above, Bartholomaeus de Biscuto, professor of medical sci-ence and salaried physician, have signed below.

I, as above, Joannes de Arriano [Arianco?], royal secretary, was witness among the aforesaid, and I have signed below.

I, as above, Raymundus de Roca have signed below.

Onto which instrument or last will of the aforesaid Lord King Robert of famous memory, strengthened with his afore-said gold and royal seal and with the subscriptions of the aforesaid judge and witnesses, diligently examined and read, not struck out, nor corrupted, nor annulled, nor torn out in any of its parts, to us the notary and witnesses, at the request of our aforesaid Lady Sancia, by the grace of God queen of Jerusalem and Sicily, confirming that this work has been [properly] copied, and that its making and the summation for sending the public instrument from the aforesaid [official] instrument from the said original of the royal testament, as is expedient, to other parts, we the notary and the witnesses

---

133. Perhaps a transcription or typographical error for Niccolò d'Alife. See above p. 239 n. 107.

authenticate it as a warranty for that original sealed document, to remain with the other in evidence of the aforesigned witnesses of all whom it concerns or will be able to concern, a more complete warranty and certification and tenor of the above-written instrument of the said royal testament.

I, the aforesaid notary, who have copied word for word everything from the original instrument and have brought the redaction to this public form, and for the greater warranty and corroboration of all the aforesaid by order of the aforesaid lady the queen, by the seals of the said lady the queen and of the regency council of the kingdom of Sicily the present public instrument *extitit communitum.*

Each and every one of these things has been done at Naples in the said Castel Nuovo, in the chamber of the aforesaid lady the queen, in the presence of the magnificent and noble men, the said lord admiral of the kingdom of Sicily Lord Pietro de Cadeneto,[134] and Lord Roberto de Ponziaco, professor of civil law, knight, and the regents of the said regency council, and Lord Joannes de Lando de Capua, professor of civil law, and of the aforesaid Lord Egidio de Bujana, knight, and of the magistrates of the *rationes* of the great royal curia, and the masters Bartolomeo de Bastivo [de Biscuto?] and Joannes de Arriano, and of many other aforesaid witnesses to the above. Year, indiction, the 27th of January, the pontificate written below.

I, Matteo di San Giorgio, of the diocese of Casmen,[135] the aforesaid notary public of the royal chamber by apostolic authority, with the exhibition, presentation and reading of the aforesaid signatories to the instrument of the testament of the aforesaid lord king, with his said golden seal and corroborated by the aforesaid signatories, and to each and all the aforesaid, prefaced and ratified, I was present along with the afore-named witnesses, as was the instrument or public transcript made from it by me at the request of the aforesaid royal excellence, just as proclaimed. I copied it word for word from

---

134. Another Franciscan Spiritual at the royal court. See Musto, "Queen Sancia," 194 and n. 137.

135. Perhaps a transcription or typographical error for Casiensis or Montecassino.

the original instrument itself, changing nothing in the process, just as proclaimed, nothing added or subtracted. I wrote
it with my own hand and I redacted it into this public form,
and with my own notarial mark along with the affixing of the
seals of the aforesaid, with my usual notarial mark.

In the above recorded year, indiction, day, month, place
and pontificate [in the year of His incarnation, one thousand,
three hundred forty-three, 11th indiction, 27th day of January,
in the first year of the pontificate of the most holy father and
lord in Christ, Lord Clement VI, pope by divine providence.
At Naples, in the Castel Nuovo, in the presence of all the
aforesaid. Etc.

66. ROBERT OF ANJOU'S DEATH AND LEGACY, JANUARY 20, 1343

The *Cronaca di Partenope* adds to the growing chorus of
fourteenth-century writers — including his wife Sancia
as early as 1334[136] — who hailed Robert as the "new
Solomon" and conferred on him the title of "the Wise,"
even in his own lifetime. This summary of his accomplishments succinctly surveys his foreign policy, his fis-
cal management and his patronage of religious life and
the arts, all key elements of medieval rulership and of his
subsequent historical reputation. The list of Robert's civil
servants and counts highlights his practice of elevating
the lower nobility (of the robe) to positions of high power and authority within the Regno as a counterpoise to the
hereditary great barons (of the sword), a practice of most
of the emerging monarchial states in the later fourteenth
century, most notably in England under Richard II.

The following selections are taken from the *Cronaca di
Partenope*, II.14–15, Altamura, 131–33; Kelly, *Cronaca*, A75,
p. 276. Translated by R.G. Musto.

14. King Robert succeeded Charles II

Robert lived as king for twenty-three [sic] years, eight months
and fifteen days. He died in Naples and was entombed in the
church of Sta. Chiara in Naples in the year of our Lord 1343,

---

136. See above, Reading, 56 at p. 206.

on a Sunday [January 20], in the eleventh indiction, in the sixty-eighth year of his life.

15. Of the virtues and achievements of King Robert and how he honored his ministers and his vassals

This King Robert was the wisest man on earth since Solomon, and he was most strenuous in arms from the time of his youth. He demonstrated this as much in the Regno as in Sicily, Tuscany and Genoa, as well as when the Regno was invaded by the forces of the emperor [Henry VII in 1313]; and Robert managed things in such a manner that he preserved the Regno without harm.

He created the following officials and counts: Tomaso di Marzano, count of Squillace[137]; the Catalan Diego de la Ratta, count of Caserta; Nicola de Iamvilla, count of Sant'Angelo; Giordano Ruffo, count of Mont'Alto; Gullielmo Ruffo, count of Sinopoli; Filippo di Sanginito [Sanguineto], count of Altomonte[138]; Ruggiero di S. Severino, count of Melito; Giovanni di Cirigliano; Nicola de Iamvilla, given the title count of Terranova through his wife; Nicola Pipino, count of Minervino[139]; Galasso [Gasso] di Nissiaco, count of Terlizzi[140]; Berardo d'Aquino, count of Loreto; Corrado d'Acquaviva, count of S. Valentino; Zuccardo de Brasson, count of Satriano; Roberto di Capua, count of Altavilla [Hauteville]; Roberto Visconte, count of Mirabella; Nicola d'Eboli, count of Trivento; Pietro Cossa, count of Bellante; Tomaso d'Aquino, count of Bellocastro.

Robert's successor as ruler was Lady Queen Giovanna I, his granddaughter. She was the daughter of Lord Charles, duke of Calabria, the first-born son of the said King Robert. Giovanna was the wife of our Lord King Louis [of Taranto]. The said duke

---

137. Goffredo Marzano, count of Squillace, was named as grand admiral in Robert's will. See Reading 65, at p. 244.

138. See above, Reading 65, at p. 244.

139. On the Pipini of Minervino, see Reading 72 below.

140. Gace de Denisy was marshal of the realm and later head of the inquest into Andrew of Hungary's murder and then himself implicated in the plot and executed. See below, Reading 74.

of Calabria died in Naples of natural causes and was buried in the aforesaid church of Sta. Chiara in the year 13[2]8, on the 11th of November, in the twelfth indiction. May God save his soul and let him reign in the glory of paradise, Amen. He was the most just prince who ever lived in the Regno. Deo gratias, Amen.

Fig. 50. *Giovanna I. From the* Anjou Bible, *fol. 309r.*

GIOVANNA I

Born in 1326, Giovanna was the elder daughter of Charles of Calabria, the heir of Robert of Anjou. On Charles' death in 1328, Giovanna became the heir to the throne of Naples, and Robert of Anjou held lengthy negotiations with his brothers' families in the houses of Taranto and Durazzo to guarantee his granddaughter's inheritance. He also made sure that the rival claims of the Angevin house of Hungary, descended from his elder brother Charles Martel, were also settled. This process involved the betrothal of Giovanna first to Robert's grandnephew Lewis, king of Hungary, and then when Lewis was engaged to Margaret of Luxemburg, to his younger brother Andrew.

Giovanna and Andrew were married in Naples on August 27, 1342. But with Andrew's brutal murder in the royal place of Aversa on September 18, 1345, Giovanna's rivals — both in Naples and in Hungary — attempted to place the blame for the murder on her and her closest courtiers, many of whom had been loyal officials of Robert of Anjou. Pope Clement VI, the feudal suzerain of Naples, attempted to hold off Lewis of Hungary's invasion of Naples, while he sided with Giovanna's cousins in Naples — Charles of Durazzo and Robert of Taranto — to capture, try and execute many of Giovanna's closest friends and advisors in 1346. In alliance with Louis of Taranto, Giovanna attempted to resist Lewis of Hungary's invasion in 1347/48, but in January 1348 was forced to flee to the papal court in Avignon both to vindicate herself of her husband's murder and to raise funds to return and retake the kingdom.

With Clement VI's eventual blessing, Giovanna married Louis of Taranto and returned to retake Naples from Hungarian forces in August 1348. Giovanna and Louis were officially crowned in Naples on Pentecost day, May 23, 1352. Giovanna's relations with Louis soon cooled as Louis attempted to seize control of the government from her, and she found herself defending her rule against Louis and her grand seneschal Niccolò Acciaiuoli. Louis died on June 5, 1362, and Giovanna then married Jaime IV, titular king of Majorca, on September 26, 1363. Jaime quickly proved to be an unreliable and personally unstable consort.

By the time of Jaime's death at Soria near Roussillon in 1375, Giovanna was also confronted by the political catastrophe of the Great Schism. She had allied with the Avignon line of popes and found herself defenseless against the Roman line. Declaring Giovanna deposed, Pope Urban VI sanctioned an invasion of the kingdom, led by the son of her former rival Charles of Durazzo. Charles III entered Naples in July 1381, despite the attempts of Giovanna's fourth husband, Otto of Brunswick, to save her and the Regno. With the approach of an army led by Giovanna's adopted heir, Louis of Anjou, Charles had Giovanna removed to a distant fortress in Basilicata and there ordered her strangled to death in the Spring of 1382.

Giovanna's reign and her subsequent reputation have been the object of centuries of legend, false accusation and fantasy on the part of historians and other writers. She is held responsible for the decline of Angevin Naples and for a life of dissolute immorality, for which comparisons to Marie

Antoinette's reputation are not inappropriate.[141] This "black legend" of Angevin greatness and decline is not a modern construction but had its origins first in Hungarian propaganda, but more importantly in the pen of Francesco Petrarch. It was the poet laureate who first constructed the "tragic" image of a radical shift in Neapolitan fortunes — and character — from the wise and prosperous rule of Robert of Anjou to the decadent, corrupt and irrational rule of his granddaughter Giovanna I.

Fig. 51. Giovanna I and Prince Andrew. From the Anjou Bible, *fol. 249r.*

67. GIOVANNA I IS ENGAGED TO ANDREW OF HUNGARY, 1333

Prince Andrew of Hungary was King Robert's second choice of husband for his granddaughter Giovanna; but after Lewis of Hungary was engaged to Margaret of Luxemburg, Robert's nephew, King Carobert (Charles Robert) of Hungary traveled to Naples to officially arrange the betrothal of his second son, Andrew, to Giovanna. The event recorded below was actually the formal betrothal ceremony, not the actual marriage, which took place in August 1342. While the Hungarians may have held high hopes for Andrew's becoming king — and the custom of the French royal house from which the Angevins of Hungary and Naples descended favored only male heirs — Robert's final will and testament was clear: Andrew was to be prince consort only.[142] Giovanna was to rule as queen without giving up or sharing power. On this point, however, many sources, including Villani and the *Cronaca di Partenope,* sided with the Hungarians' claims and referred to Andrew as "king."

---

141. See Chantal Thomas, *The Wicked Queen: The Origins of the Myth of Marie-Antoinette* (New York: Zone Books, 2001).

142. See above, Reading 65 and items 2–4, pp. 241–43.

The following selection is taken from the *Cronaca di Partenope*, book III, Altamura, 138. Translated by R.G. Musto.

6. How the marriage was contracted between King Andrew and Queen Giovanna, and how the king of Hungary then departed.

King Robert was left without a legitimate male heir, because Charles, duke of Calabria and vicar general, had died without a legitimate male heir. Only Giovanna was left, the daughter of Duke Charles, and the king wished to arrange things correctly for her. The king of Hungary came to Naples at the arranged time of the year 1333, and his son King Andrew was betrothed to the said Giovanna. There were plenty of triumphs and feasts in the city of Naples, both among the nobility and among all the common people of Naples in all the piazze. The feast lasted for one month. When these feasts and the marriage were completed, the king of Hungary, named Charles [Carobert], departed and returned to Hungary. He left King Andrew behind as the legitimate successor of King Robert for the said Regno.

68. GIOVANNA I GRANTS A MEDICAL LICENSE TO MARIA INCARNATA, MAY 7, 1343

While the medical school of Salerno was less a formal institution than a circle of medical masters, by the fourteenth century the Angevins were issuing licenses to both men and women to practice various forms of medicine, pending a board examination for skill and knowledge. While it was normal — for moral purposes — for women to treat other women, here the text seems to indicate more than sexual morality, stressing the appropriateness of female physicians due both to their character and to their special knowledge of female diseases. Maria Incarnata was a native of Naples, apparently independent enough to practice outside the city in Molise and the Terra di Lavoro. As the text below indicates, Queen Sancia approved the licence for Giovanna, and this was appropriate to her role as the head of the new regency council.[143] The license was issued by Adenulfo Cumano, a vice-protonotary of the Regno.

Our text is taken from Katherine L. Jansen, Joanna Drell and Frances Andrews, *Medieval Italy: Texts in Translation* (Philadelphia: University of Pennsylvania Press, 2009), 324–25, and was translated by Monica H. Green.

Giovanna, etc. To all those throughout the province of Terra di Lavoro and the county of Molise who will be reading these letters both now and in the future, her faithful servants, greetings, etc.

With respect to the public weal as it relates to the upstanding women of our [kingdom], we have been attentive and we are mindful in how much modesty recommends honesty of morals. Clearly, Maria Incarnata of Naples, our faithful servant, present in our court has proved that [she] is competent in the principal exercise of surgery, in the treatment of wounds and apostemes [tumors]. She conducts herself with circumspect judgment in such cases, because of which she has supplicated our highness most attentively that we might deign to concede to her a license to practice on diseases or conditions of this kind. Because, therefore, by trustworthy testimony presented to our court, it is clearly found that the above-said Maria is faithful and comes from a worthy family and, having been examined by our surgeons, she is found to be competent in treating the above-said illnesses.

Although it should be alien to female propriety to be interested in the affairs of men lest they rush into things abusive of matronly shame and for this reason they risk the sin of forbidden transgression, [nevertheless] because the office of medicine is expediently conceded to women by an unspoken rule of law, it being noted that females, by their honesty of character, are more suited than men to treat sick women, especially in their own diseases, we, having first received from this same Maria the customary oath of fidelity sworn on the Gospels and [the promise] that she will faithfully treat [patients] according to the traditions of this art, impart to her a license to treat and to practice on the mentioned afflictions throughout the whole of the abovesaid principality, by the

---

143. According to Robert of Anjou's will. See above, Reading 65, Item 6.

counsel and consent of the glorious lady, Lady Sancia, by the grace of God queen of Jerusalem and Sicily, reverend lady mother, administrator and our principal governor, and by the public authority of our other administrators.

Therefore by our faith from the counsel and assent of the above-mentioned, we command that it be ordered that in so far as this same Maria treats and practices on the above-said diseases through the whole of the above-said principality, to the honor of us and our heirs and the utility of our faithful servants of these same provinces, you should permit her freely [to do so], posing no impediment or obstruction to her.

Given at Naples by Adenulf Cumano of Naples, professor of civil law, vice-protonotary of the kingdom of Sicily, in the year of Our Lord 1343, the seventh day of May of the eleventh indiction, the first year of our reign.

69. Petrarch recounts his tour around the Bay of Baiae, October 1343

In October 1343, Francesco Petrarch arrived in Naples and in the company of noted court intellectuals took a tour around the upper Bay of Naples including Pozzuoli, the Campi Flegrei and Baiae. His description, like much of his image of Naples under Giovanna, is less bright than that of Cassiodorus c.534, at the end of the Gothic period. His account of Baiae closely resembles that of Conrad of Querfurt in Reading 37.

Petrarch describes the various scenes in his letter to Cardinal Giovanni Colonna, *Familiares* V.4.[144]

Fig. 52. The Baths of Baiae. Cologny, Fondation Martin Bodmer, Cod. Bodmer 135, fol. 2r.

144. Edited in Petrarch, *Letters on Familiar Matters*, 1:238–42.

I saw Baiae along with the very famous Giovanni Barrili and my Barbato [da Sulmona].[145] I do not recall a happier day in my life, not only because of my friends' company and the variety of notable sights but because of the recent experience of many sad days. I saw in the winter months that very attractive bay which, if I am not mistaken, the summer sun must overwhelm. This is nothing but an opinion, for I was never there during the summer. It is now three years since I was first brought here in the middle of the winter with the north winds raging [1340], a time when one is particularly subject to danger in a sea journey. Therefore, I was unable to view from up close the many things I wished to see. However, I have today finally satisfied the desire that has occupied my mind as a result of that brief taste of things and of wishes that have been with me since my youth. I saw the places described by Virgil; I saw the lakes Avernus and Lucrinus as well as the stagnant waters of Acheron; the laguna of Augusta rendered unhappy by the fierceness of her son; the once proud road of Gaius Caligula now buried under the waves; and the obstacle against the sea built by Julius Caesar. I saw the native land and the home of the Sibyl [at Cumae] and that dreadful cave from which fools do not return and which learned men do not enter. I saw Mt. Falernus distinguished for its famous vineyards [of Falerno wine] and the parched soil exhaling continuously the vapors that are good for diseases [La Solfatara]. There I also saw balls of ashes and boiling water as in a boiling copper vessel spilling over with a confused rumbling. I saw the wholesome fluid which the cliffs everywhere dripped and which as a gift of mother nature was once employed for all kinds of illnesses and later, as the story goes, were mixed with the regular baths [at Pozzuoli] because of the envy of the doctors.

Now many people of all ages and of both sexes throng from neighboring cities to the waters. I saw not only what is called the Neapolitan grotto, which Annaeus Seneca recalls in his letter to Lucilius, but everywhere mountains full of perforations and suspended on marble vaults gleaming with brilliant

---

145. The famous early humanists and correspondent of Petrarch. See above, p. 224 and n. 72; Musto, *Apocalypse*, 165.

whiteness, and sculpted figures indicating with pointing hands what water is most appropriate for each part of the body. The appearance of the place and the labor devoted to its development caused me to marvel.

Henceforth I shall be less astonished by the walls of Rome and her fortresses and her palaces, when such care was taken by Roman leaders so far from the homeland.... Their winter delights included Anzio, Terracina, Formia, Gaeta and Naples. However none was more pleasant nor more popular than Baiae. This is attested to by the authority of the writers of that period and by the huge remains of the walls, although I am not ignorant of the fact that this was a place of dwelling suited rather to human pleasures than to the gravity of the Romans....

70. Petrarch describes the tidal storm on the Bay of Naples, November 25, 1343

Francesco Petrarch arrived in Naples in 1341, probably shortly after Boccaccio departed, and developed a number of friendships with important and learned men of the kingdom, including Robert of Anjou, who sponsored Petrarch as the poet laureate. In 1343 he was again in the city serving on a diplomatic mission from the papal court in Avignon. In a famous letter dated November 26, 1343, which has been compared to Pliny the Younger's the letter to Tacitus describing the 79 CE eruption of Vesuvius, Petrarch wrote to his patron, Cardinal Giovanni Colonna, describing a storm on the Bay of Naples.

This selection is excerpted from *Familares* V.5, Bernardo, 1:243–47.

A certain bishop from a nearby island and interested in astrology had announced the danger several days earlier. But since such people almost never get to the truth, he predicted that Naples would be destroyed on November 25, 1343, not by a sea storm but by an earthquake. Furthermore he surrounded everything he said with such extraordinary terrors that a large portion of the population, under the threat of death and thus desirous of changing their manner of life, were intent on doing penance for their sins and abandoned all other kinds of activity.

Many others made fun of such idle fears especially because of the considerable number of bad storms that had occurred at that time. Therefore, they considered the prophecy wrong as to date and gave many good reasons for having no confidence in it. I myself was neither hopeful nor fearful, and, though favoring neither side, I inclined somewhat toward fear, for the fact seems to be that things that are hoped for come less readily than those that are feared. I had also heard and seen at that time many threatening signs in the skies which for one accustomed to living in northern climes resembled the supernatural events that occur in the cold of winter and make one prone to turn to fear and indeed to religion. What more need I say? It was the night before the predicted day. An anxious crowd of women, more concerned with the danger at hand than with modesty, ran to and fro through the alleys and streets, and holding their children to their breasts they tearfully and humbly crowded the doorways of churches. Worried by the public alarm, I returned home in the early evening....

I had scarcely fallen asleep when not only the windows but the walls themselves, though built of stone, were shaken from their very foundations and the night light, which I am accustomed to keep lit while I sleep, went out. We threw off our blankets, and in place of sleep the fear of imminent death overcame us.... What a downpour! what winds! what lightning! what deep thunder! what frightening tremors! what roaring of the sea! what shrieking of the populace!... We threw ourselves prostrate on the moist and naked floors.... When no doubt remained that it was daylight... we mounted our horses and descended to the port determined to see for ourselves or to perish if necessary....

The port was filled with frightening and dismal wreckage. The unfortunate victims, who had been scattered by the water and had been trying to grasp the nearby land with their hands, were dashed against the reefs and were like so many tender eggs. The entire shore line was covered with torn and still living bodies: someone's brains floated by here, someone else's bowels floated there. In the midst of such sights the yelling of men and wailing of women were so loud that they overcame the sounds of the sea and the heavens. To all this was added the destruction of buildings, many of whose foundations were overturned by the violent waves against which that day respected no bounds and respected no work of man or nature. They overflowed their natural limits, the familiar shoreline, as well as that huge breakwater which had been constructed by the zealous men and which, with its outstretched arms, as Maro says, constitutes the port and all that portion of the region which borders on the sea. And where there had been a path for strolling here was now something dangerous even for sailing.

A thousand or more Neapolitan horsemen had gathered there as if to assist at the funeral of their homeland. Having joined this group, I had begun to feel somewhat less frightened of perishing amidst so many. But suddenly a new clamor could be heard. The very place on which we stood, weakened by the waves that had penetrated beneath, began to give way. We hurried to a higher elevation. No one raised his eyes to the heavens, for the band of men could not bear to look at the angry faces of Jove and of Neptune. Thousands of mountainous waves flowed between Capri and Naples. The channel appeared not dark, or, as is usual in great storms, black, but greyish with the frightening whiteness of sea foam. Meanwhile the younger queen [Giovanna I], barefooted and uncombed, and accompanied by a large group of women, departed from the royal palace [Castel Nuovo] unconcerned about modesty in the face of such danger, and they all hastened to the Church of the Virgin Queen [Sta. Maria de Montevergine?] praying for her grace amidst such dangers.... and we could scarcely find an escape, and neither on the deep nor in port could a ship be found to equal those waves.

Three long ships from Marseilles, called galleys, which had returned from Cyprus after crossing the wide expanses of the sea and were anchored there ready to depart in the morning, we saw overcome by the waves with a universal outcry and without anyone being able to offer assistance and without a single sailor or passenger saved. In the same manner other, even larger, ships of all kinds, which had taken refuge in the port as if in a fortress, were destroyed. Only one of so many survived. It was loaded with robbers who had been spared their rightful punishment so that they could be sent on an expedition to Sicily, and who, having been spared the sword of the executioner, were to be exposed to the sword of battle. This huge and powerful ship, armed with the hides of bulls, although it had suffered the blows of the sea until sundown, also began to be overpowered. The exhausted prisoners hastened from all sides to the keel because of the threatening dangers. It is said that there were four hundred in number, a group large enough for a fleet, let alone a single ship. Furthermore they were powerful persons who, freed from death, feared nothing more obstinately and boldly. In postponing the outcome by slowing down the sinking of the ship, they prolonged the disaster well into the following night. When they were finally overcome, they abandoned their tools and dashed to the upper portions of the ship. Suddenly beyond all hope the skies began to clear and the exhausted sea began to slacken its roughness....

71. THE *CRONACA DI PARTENOPE* DESCRIBES THE SAME

This reading describes the same disaster, without Petrarch's classical references and literary skill, and adds a few details Petrarch omitted. It is taken from the *Cronaca*, book III, Altamura, 144. Translated by R.G. Musto.

22. On the twenty-fifth day of November in the twelfth indiction [1343], on Tuesday, the feast of St. Catherine [of Alexandria], there arrived a great tempest both in the sky and on the sea. It began on the previous night, and by divine will it lasted all day. It destroyed many buildings in the city of Naples adjacent to the harbor. It destroyed a great part of the Molo Grande and the Molo Piccolo, and many ships were lost, a total of fifty, in both the Molo Grande and Piccolo, along with much merchandise of great value.

72. PETRARCH DESCRIBES NAPLES UNDER GIOVANNA I, DECEMBER 1, 1343

Following the failure of his mission to Naples on behalf of Cardinal Giovanni Colonna to free the brigand Giovanni Pipino from prison, Petrarch expressed his disappointment and frustration by offering a stark new assessment of Naples and the state of life in the city after the death

of King Robert. Where previously the rituals of chivalry
and the joust were performed in the Largo delle Corregge
to renown throughout Christendom and had marked
Naples as the apogee of the courteous life, now they took
on the sinful nature of the gladiatorial games detested by
Petrarch's hero, St. Augustine, in his *Confessions* (VI.7–8).
From Naples being the center of high learning and cultural
rebirth, in a few short months it has become sinister and
dangerous, an archetype of the urban "jungle." The letter
would become an important document in the "black legend" of Queen Giovanna I and of the Angevin dynasty.[146]

This selection is taken from his *Familiares* V.6, Bernardo
1:249–50.

I was hoping to be free of the heavy fetters of business, and I
believe would have been if the poisonous serpent[147] had not
overcome the minds of the judges who had been restrained by
pity. One of the Psylli would not have been more capable of
recognizing poison with his mouth than I was in recognizing
it with my ear. I continue my opposition, but now I fear that
the damage is fatal. However, I shall continue trying as long
as any shred of hope remains. Perhaps last night I might have
obtained the courtesy even of rejection had the council not
adjourned because of the approaching darkness and had not
the incurable disease of the city compelled everyone to return
home early. Though very famous for many reasons, the city
possesses one particularly dark, repulsive and inveterate evil:
to travel in it by night, as in a jungle, is dangerous and full of
hazards because the streets are beset by armed young nobles
whose dissoluteness cannot be controlled by the discipline
of their parents, by the authority of their teachers or by the
majesty and command of kings. But is it any wonder that they
act brazenly under the cover of darkness without witnesses,
when in this Italian city in broad daylight with royalty and
the populace as spectators infamous gladiatorial games are

---

146. See introduction above, pp. lvi–lxi.

147. Most likely a reference to Roberto da Mileto. Petrarch's serpentine imagery
would be used again by the contemporary historian Domenico da Gravina in his
condemnation of Giovanna I's reign.

permitted of a wildness that is greater than we associate with barbarians? Here human blood flows like the blood of cattle, and often amidst the applause of the insane spectators unfortunate sons are killed under the very eyes of their wretched parents. It is indeed the ultimate infamy to hesitate having one's throat pierced by the sword as if one were battling for the republic or for the rewards of eternal life.

Fig. 53. Jousting on the Largo delle Corregge. Attributed to Cristoforo Orimina, c.1350. London, British Library, MS Add. 12228, fol. 213r.

I was taken unknowingly the day before yesterday to such a place not far from the city, which is called appropriately "The Furnace" where indeed a workshop full of soot and of inhuman fierceness darkens the bloody blacksmiths at the anvil of death. The queen [Giovanna I] was present as was Prince Andrew, a boy of lofty mind, if ever he were to assume the long-deferred crown. All the militia of Naples was also present in all their elegance and propriety. All the rabble had eagerly flocked to that place. And so I, curious about so great a crowd and about the passionate interest of well known people, thinking that I was about to view something great, focused my attention on the spectacle. Suddenly, as if something very delightful had occurred, thunderous applause resounded. I looked around and to my surprise I saw a most handsome young man lying at my feet transfixed by a sharp pointed sword, which emerged from his body. I stood there astounded, and my whole body shuddering. I spurred my horse and fled from the infernal spectacle, angry at my friends' deceit, at the cruelty of the spectators and the continued madness of the participants. This twin plague, dear father, as if inherited from our ancestors has reached subsequent generations in an ever increasing tempo, and the reason for it is that the license for committing crime has now acquired the name of dignity and freedom. Let this suffice, for it is a tragic matter and I have already wasted many words speaking of it with the obstinate citizens. Indeed you should hardly be astonished that your friends,[148] offering as they do such a prize for greed, should be prisoners in that city where killing men is considered a game, a city which Virgil indeed does call the most delightful of all, but as it stands now would not be considered unequal to Thrace in infamy: "Alas flee the cruel lands, flee the greedy shore." I certainly accept those words as relating to this city; and unless you hear otherwise, expect me to leave within three days to flee, even if my business remains unfinished, first to Cisalpine Gaul, and then to Transalpine Gaul and to you who always cause all my trips to be delightful unless they are by sea. Farewell.

Naples, calends of December [December 1, 1343]

73. Boccaccio's Naples, c.1343

Without overstating the case, if Petrarch laid out the "tragic" view of Naples under Giovanna I, Boccaccio might be said to lay out the "comic." Boccaccio had returned to Florence in 1340/41, and in 1348 he began work on his most successful work, *The Decameron*, using Naples as one setting and reflecting life during the early years of Giovanna's reign.

The novella of Andreuccio da Perugia (*Dec.* 2.5), describes the locals, the police and the cathedral in recounting the story of an unsuspecting northerner who had come to Naples to trade in horses — for which Naples was long well-known

---

148. The Pipini, accused of brigandage and treason. See Musto, *Apocalypse*, 245–51; and Boccaccio, *Life of Giovanna I*, below, Reading 81, at p. 297.

— and settled into an inn by the waterfront. As with many a later traveler, he arrived with plenty of money in his pocket, but he was soon bamboozled out of it by a beautiful young Neapolitan woman, who pretends to be his long-lost half-sister from Palermo forced into exile for her family's Guelf loyalties. After various adventures, including falling into a cesspool, he decides to bathe on the seashore. Obviously lost, he turns left and up *(su)* the steep incline of rua Catalana.[149] On his way he meets a pair of local swindlers who offer to cut him in on a special deal.

Our text is excerpted from Boccaccio, *The Decameron*, trans. Frances Winwar (New York: Modern Library, 1955), 73–76.

That day Messer Filippo Minutolo, an archbishop of Naples, had been entombed,[150] and with him some of his richest ornaments, including a ruby ring on his finger that was alone worth more than five hundred florins in gold. It was these gentlemen's intention to go and rob the archbishop, and they imparted their proposal to Andreuccio, who was more greedy for gain than he was wise. Accordingly, he started out with them. On their way to the cathedral Andreuccio stunk more than they could bear, and one of them suggested: "Can't we manage to have this stink-pot wash himself, somehow, so he won't smell so awful?"

"I guess so," replied the other. "We're near a spot where there's a well, with a rope and pulley and a great big bucket always ready. Let's go there and clean him up in a jiffy."

They got to the well and found the rope, as they had expected, but the bucket had been taken away. They considered what was to be done and decided to tie Andreuccio himself to the rope and lower him into the well to wash himself. Then, after he was good and clean, he was to tug at the rope and they would pull him up.

---

149. His inn must, therefore, have been between the Angevin walls and toward the Castel Nuovo, around the present Piazza Municipio.

150. Died 24 October 1301. On the Minutolo Chapel, see Stefania Paone, "La cappella Minutolo nel duomo di Napoli: Le storie apostoliche e i miti di fondazione dell'episcopio," in *Medioevo: Immagine e memoria* (Milan: Electa, 2009), 423–35; Bruzelius & Tronzo, 92–94; and Italica web gallery: http://www.flickr.com/photos/80499896@N05/sets/72157630152316564, images 25–28.

As fate would have it, they had barely lowered him into the well, when a couple of members of the police, overheated and thirsty from pursuing some mischief-maker, came to the well for a drink. No sooner did the two rascals catch sight of them than they took to their heels, before the policemen could see them.

Andreuccio had already performed his ablutions at the bottom of the well, and tugged at the rope to be hauled up. The officers, who were dying of thirst, putting down their shields, arms and coats, began to pull at it, thinking to find the bucket attached to the other end full of water, and the moment Andreuccio saw himself nearing the brink of the well, he dropped the rope and clutched at the edge with both hands. The policemen were stricken with such dread at the apparition, that they released their grasp without more ado and made off as fast as their legs could carry them.

Andreuccio was agape with astonishment, and but for the fact that he was holding on to the ledge for dear life, he might have fallen to the bottom and crippled or even killed himself. But when he came across such arms as his companions surely had not brought, he was more astonished. He could not get his wits together, and was afraid of falling into another trap, so leaving everything as it was and bemoaning his fate, he thought it best to be off and walked on aimlessly.

He had not gone very far when he stumbled upon his two companions on their way back to haul him out of the well. They were amazed when they recognized him, and asked who had got him out. Andreuccio answered that he was no wiser than they, told them how it had all happened, and described what he had found beside the well. Putting two and two together, they understood and laughing, told him in turn why they had run away and who had done him the service of drawing him up.

It was midnight by now. Without further words they went to the cathedral, entered it without any trouble, and made for the archbishop's tomb. Its ark[151] was of marble, and very

---

151. Boccaccio's Italian is *arca*, that is, the "ark" floating in the midst of duecento and trecento funerary monuments in Naples. To at least Boccaccio's eyes, the entire tomb was a canopied setting for the sarcophagus that seemed to float midway in its space, flanked by angels with outspread wings, much like representations of the Ark of the Covenant. See n. 152.

large. They pried open the massive lid with the help of their crowbars, raising it just enough to let a man slip through, and propped it up in place.

"Who's going to get in?" asked one.

"Not me," said the other.

"Nor me, either," answered the first. "Let Andreuccio do it."

"Not on your life," he said.

"What!" cried both of them, turning upon him. "You won't enter? By God, if you don't, we'll play such a tune on your skull that we'll make you fall down dead."

Andreuccio crept in out of fear, but once there, he reflected: "Those two scoundrels want me in here so that they can fleece me. Just as soon as I've handed them everything and I'm struggling to get out, they'll go their sweet way, and I'll be stung!"

He determined, therefore, to secure his own portion beforehand. As soon as he was down in the ark,[152] he suddenly remembered the valuable ring he had heard them talking about. It was the matter of a moment for him to slip it off the archbishop's finger and slide it onto his own. Then taking the dead man's crosier, mitre and gloves, and stripping him to the shift, he reached everything over to his partners and said there was nothing more. No, they insisted, the ring must be there; he was not to leave a single spot unsearched. He kept on answering that he could not find it, and making believe he was looking for it everywhere kept them guessing for a good long while. But they, on their side, were no less cunning than himself. They continued urging him to look, and at last, taking advantage of the delay, pulled out the prop that supported the lid, and took to their heels, leaving Andreuccio shut up in the ark.

What his sensations were on finding himself closed in with the dead, you may imagine. Again and again he attempted to raise the lid, by dint of working with his head and shoulders, but it was all lost labor. At last, overcome by despair, he fainted and fell upon the body of the archbishop. Had anybody seen both of them together, he would have found it difficult to determine which was more of a corpse, the archbishop or Andreuccio.

---

152. Winwar's translation of *arca* as "crypt" is misleading. Angevin noble tombs resembled descriptions of the Ark of the Covenant in Exodus 25:10–22, the ark chamber flanked by two golden Cherubim, wings extended inward (25:19–21).

Some time later, when he regained his senses, he broke into a desperate fit of weeping at his certain doom to one of two fates. If nobody came to let him out, either he must die of hunger and the stench of corruption, among the worms of the body, or if anyone did come and discover him there, he must be strung up for a thief on the gallows. While entertaining himself with such thoughts in the agony of his deep chagrin, he heard footsteps in the church and the voices of many people, who, as he was soon aware, were coming on the very errand he and his comrades had already accomplished. His terror knew no bounds.

As soon as the new visitors had pried open the ark and propped up the lid, a dispute arose among them as to which of them should enter. Nobody was willing.

"What are you afraid of?" cried one of the priests, after a long debate. "Do you think he'll eat you up? The dead don't eat the living. I'll go in myself."

No sooner had he spoken, than he lay flat on his stomach at the edge of the ark, turned his head toward the outside and thrust his legs down, ready to let himself drop to the bottom.

Andreuccio at this opportunity jumped up, seized the priest by a leg and made believe he wanted to pull him in. At that the man let out a yell fit to bring down the heavens and leapt madly out of the ark, putting the others into such a panic that leaving the lid propped up as it was, they all fled as though a hundred thousand devils were hot upon their trail.

Now that the way was clear, Andreuccio immediately clambered out of the ark, happier than he had ever hoped to be, and retraced his steps out of the church. Dawn was breaking. Aimlessly, he walked through the streets, wearing the ring on his finger.

At last, coming to the seashore, he was able to find his way back to the inn, where his friends and the host had waited up all night, wondering what could have happened to him. After he had related his many adventures, the host offered the opinion that Naples was not a healthy place for Andreuccio, and said he'd better leave it, and the sooner, the better. And Andreuccio did, readily enough, returning to Perugia, after having invested his money in a ring, when he had set out to buy horses.

74. Prince Andrew of Hungary is murdered at Aversa, September 18, 1345

The following text is taken from the *Cronaca di Partenope*, book III, Altamura, 146. Translated by R.G. Musto.

26. How the said Lord Andrew was strangled

In the same year of our Lord 1345, on Sunday night, September 18, in the fourteenth indiction, the said Lord Andrew, duke of Calabria, was strangled and stabbed in the city of Aversa, where Queen Giovanna was living with all her family and officials. The perpetrators of this murder — according to what was said — were Carlo Artus the grand chamberlain, Lord Roberto de' Cabanni the count of Eboli and grand seneschal,[153] and many other men and women.

On the following day the body of the said Lord Andrew, duke of Calabria, was carried to Naples and was buried in the cathedral of Naples in the chapel of St. Louis, which is next to the cathedral. The funeral was attended with the greatest honors and great mourning by the citizens of Naples and the Hungarians.

Subsequently many people were punished by the said count of Montescaglione [Bertram des Baux or de Balzo], the justiciar. They included the count of Terlizzi [Gace de Denisy],[154] who had been grand seneschal; Lord Raimondo de' Cabanni; the Magistressa [Filippa de' Cabanni]; and Sancia de' Cabanni, countess of Morcone. They were carried through the city of Naples in carts and torn by iron hooks all the way to the Piazza del Mercato. All the others who had conspired in the said murder with such great turpitude and great blame were all executed in due time through the judgment of God.

75. Giovanna I on the murder of Andrew of Hungary, September 21, 1345

In an official Latin letter to the government of Florence dated September 21, 1345, Queen Giovanna I offers a

---

153. On the de' Cabanni see above, p. 237 and n. 104.

154. On Terlizzi, see above, p. 255 n. 140.

brief account of the assassination of her husband, Prince Andrew of Hungary. Andrew was strangled, stabbed, hung and apparently sexually mutilated. The text is taken from the *Storia di Napoli* 3:238. Translation by R.G. Musto.

On the 18th of this month, when bedtime had come, our husband went down into the park adjacent to the loggia of the bedroom of our residence at Aversa. He did this imprudently and without any precautions, rather like an adolescent who was used to going out at any hour he chose. Without listening to anyone's advice, he followed only the impetuous impulses of his youth. He went without a companion, even closing the door behind him.

We awaited his return, but because he delayed too long, we were lulled back to sleep. But then his nurse, set out to look for him, found him at last, strangled against the wall of the park.... The wicked author of the crime, before inflicting the final punishment, added to the crime by inflicting the wounds that have so defiled our marriage.

76. DOMENICO DA GRAVINA DESCRIBES THE EXECUTION OF GIOVANNA I'S COURT OFFICIALS, LATE MARCH 1346

Queen Giovanna's closest female friends, associates and high officials — the last remnants of Robert of Anjou's administration and regency council[155] — were falsely accused,[156] arrested and summarily executed in an effort to isolate the queen and strengthen the faction of her royal cousins in Naples. In this Giovanna's cousins had the secret alliance of Pope Clement VI in Avignon. This selection is taken from Domenico da Gravina's *Chronicon*.

Gravina was a notary from the border region between Lucania (Basilicata) and Apulia, who provided an unofficial history, away from the centers of power in Naples, from the perspective of the provincial elite. Gravina was an adherent of the house of Durazzo, and he painted a picture

---

155. See Readings 65–66 above.

156. As Lewis of Hungary later believed (Reading 82), the papal inquest determined (Reading 77, p. 285) and Boccaccio attested (Reading 81).

of corruption and misrule under Giovanna I, which he contrasts to the reign of Robert the Wise as one of peace and justice. The *Chronicon* covers in detail the years between Andrew of Hungary and Giovanna I's wedding in 1333 to the second invasion of Lewis of Hungary. It relates the struggle in Apulia between the house of Durazzo and Giovanna's partisans. Gravina also takes the side of Lewis of Hungary and is generally a calumnious opponent of Giovanna I. Gravina's narrative of the execution of Giovanna's closest friends and advisors certainly matches what recent studies of medieval punishment have called a "theater of cruelty."[157]

Gravina's descriptions match the ferocity of the Villani's depiction (XIII, 17) of the mob's execution and ritual cannibalism on the supporters of the deposed duke of Athens in Florence following the overthrow of his tyranny there on July 26, 1343[158] or the Anonimo Romano's account of Cola di Rienzo's grisly murder in 1354.[159] Yet are they reliable narratives? Or have they borrowed elements from set

---

157. Since the late 1990s, medieval rituals of violence and punishment and the theater of cruelty have been examined fruitfully and at great length by historians using a variety of anthropological, literary, theater, art-historical and liturgical frames. Among the more compelling works are Enders, *Medieval Theater of Cruelty*; Merback, *Thief*; Daniel Baraz, *Medieval Cruelty: Changing Perceptions, Antiquity to the Early Modern Period. Conjunctions of Religion and Power in the Medieval Past* (Ithaca: Cornell University Press, 2003); Caroline Bynum, *Fragmentation and Redemption: Essays on Gender and the Human Body in Medieval Religion* (New York: Zone Books, 1992); and idem, "Violent Imagery in Late Medieval Piety," *Bulletin of the German Historical Institute* (2002): 3–36. Ester Cohen, "The Animated Pain of the Body," *American Historical Review* 105.1 (Feb. 2000): 36–68, offers valuable insights into medieval perceptions and descriptions of physical pain and torture. Samuel Edgerton, Jr., *Pictures and Punishment: Art and Criminal Prosecution during the Florentine Renaissance* (Ithaca: Cornell University Press, 1985) is of fundamental importance; as is Valentin Groebner, *Defaced: The Visual Culture of Violence in the Late Middle Ages*, trans. Pamela Selwyn (New York: Zone Books, 2004). The essays in Mark D. Meyerson, Daniel Thiery and Oren Falk, eds., "A Great Effusion of Blood"? Interpreting Medieval Violence (Toronto: University of Toronto Press, 2004) offer worthwhile variations on the theme.

158. Villani, *Nuova cronica*, book X.

159. Musto, *Apocalypse*, 341–47.

pieces: the medieval stage or the lives of the martyrs, for example? Art and life are surely in dialog here, but to what extent has still to be determined.

The selections are from the *Chronicon de rebus in Apulia gestis ab anno 1333 ad annum 1350*, A. Sorbelli, ed., RIS 12 (Citta di Castello: RIS, 1903), 567A–B. Translation by R.G. Musto.

Then the justiciar Bertrand des Baux gave orders to his retainers: the carts were prepared and irons were put in the forges and the instruments of torture were placed aboard. The grand justiciar ordered the count of Terlizzi put in one cart, bound by iron chains, and the grand seneschal Roberto de' Cabanni in the other. But he ordered that Lord Raimondo da Catania be stripped of his clothes and his flesh sliced off piece by piece all the way to Piazza Sant'Eligio.[160] Then he ordered him to be burned alive, along with the two counts. The grand justiciar condemned Lady Filippa to a similar punishment.

Listen to this: the condemned were led to their punishment, and the executioners mercilessly sliced their flesh repeatedly with burning meat hooks. While others lashed their bodies with whips, they were led through each and every street corner of Naples. At each stop, from the smallest to the largest intersection, the executioners cried out: "Each and every one of you traitors should suffer this and worse!" Some people spat right into their faces, others struck them with rocks.

When they reached the place of execution, where the fire was prepared, even though the burning hooks had left precious little of the flesh on their bodies, Lord Roberto de' Cabanni quickly gave up the ghost. But the count of Terlizzi was still alive. They were therefore pulled off the carts, and there they were hacked to pieces. Then as much of them as could be gathered up was thrown onto the fire. But the Neapolitans watching the execution were moved to frenzy. Pulling the bodies — dead or alive — from the fire, they fell on them with swords and axes and then threw them back into

---

160. About 1 km. to the present Piazza del Mercato. See Musto, Interactive Map: http://www.italicapress.com/index287.html.

the flames. Many took home their bones to make lasting souvenirs of the event: some made dice, some knife handles.

But because Lady Sancia was pregnant, the laws mandated that her sentence be deferred until she gave birth, nevertheless she was kept in jail under tight security.

77. GIOVANNA'S EXILE TO AVIGNON AND HER RETURN, 1348–52

The events surrounding King Lewis of Hungary's invasion of the Regno, seeking revenge for his brother Andrew's murder and the Angevin crown of Naples for himself, are among the most exciting of late medieval narratives. Forced to flee Naples as the nobility of the kingdom went over to the Hungarians en masse, and exhorting her subjects not to resist Lewis, Giovanna took a small flotilla of galleys to Provence, where she intended both to plead her innocence in Andrew's murder before the papal court at Avignon and to seek the financial and moral support of her liege lord, Pope Clement VI.

Joined by Louis of Taranto there, Giovanna exonerated herself, obtained recognition of Louis as her new consort and received substantial funding from the pope (largely through her sale of Avignon to him) and from her Provençal subjects. She and Louis returned to Naples in August 1348 and fought their way back to power over the next several years: Giovanna in Naples itself, and Louis in the south. They were able to formally celebrate their marriage and coronation in Naples in May 1352.

The narrative of Giovanna's exile and return is quite the opposite of the black legend of the Angevins[161] and the historiography that grew up after it: here she demonstrates herself to be energetic, resourceful and courageous in the face of almost overwhelming odds and vitriolic propaganda.

Yet the sources for Giovanna's journey are sometimes contradictory and sometimes so close to contemporary literary tales of accused queens: *Constance, the Empress of*

---

161. See above, pp. lvi–lxi.

Rome, the *Manekine*, *Griselda*[162] — tales full of faulted last wills, incestuous predators, false accusations and debasements, murderous pursuits, mysterious sea journeys, imprisonment, the intervention of high priests, exoneration and restoration — that one must wonder about the impact of literary modes upon the constructs offered in our surviving historical sources: do Villani, Gravina and others use such literary motifs to "fill in the gaps" for the queen's psychology, or for her travels during this period of confused events and unreliable witnesses?

One of the most popular empress of Rome tales, the *Roman du Comte d'Anjou* of Jehan Maillart (†1323), was a thinly disguised retelling of the fate of Philip IV's daughters-in-law and Giovanna's Capetian cousins Margaret,

---

162. The relationship between the literary tropes of the accused and exiled queen and the actual history of Giovanna I are not explicit or clear-cut; yet the apparent parallels between the existential situation of powerful women in the Middle Ages and the literature of the accused queen are strong. The works here offer valuable insights into the genre, the interrelationship between fiction and reality and the possible causal relationship between literary form and historical narrative. The bibliography is large and now well established. See for example, Nancy B. Black, *Medieval Narratives of Accused Queens* (Gainesville: University Press of Florida, 2003); János M. Bak, "Queens as Scapegoats in Medieval Hungary," in *Queens and Queenship in Medieval Europe: Proceedings of a Conference Held at King's College London, April 1995*, Anne J. Duggan, ed. (Woodbridge, UK: Boydell, 1997), 223–33; Alcuin Blamires, *The Case for Women in Medieval Culture* (Oxford: Clarendon Press, 1997); idem, ed., *Woman Defamed and Woman Defended: An Anthology of Medieval Texts* (Oxford: Clarendon Press, 1992); Steven Swann Jones, "The Innocent Persecuted Heroine Genre: An Analysis of Its Structure and Themes," *Western Folklore* 52 (1993): 13–41; and Peggy McCracken, *The Romance of Adultery: Queenship and Sexual Transgression in Old French Literature* (Philadelphia: University of Pennsylvania Press, 1998). For an English edition of *La Manequine* see Barbara Nelson Sargent-Baur, ed. and trans., *Philippe de Remi Beaumanoir, Manekine, John and Blonde, and "Foolish Generosity"* (University Park: Pennsylvania State University Press, 2010). For a recent discussion, see Linda Marie Rouillard, review of "Jean Wauquelin, *La Manequine*, Maria Colombo Timelli, ed. Textes Littéraires du Moyen Âge 13; Séries Mises en Prose 1 (Paris: Éditions Classiques Garnier, 2010)," *Speculum* 87.1 (January 2012): 288–89.

Blanche and Jeanne of Burgundy (d.1330, queen of Philip V) in the Tour de Nesle Affair.

Given the great popularity of such romance tales and their motifs at the Angevin court of Naples[163] and throughout Italy, could the actual actions of historical agents have been influenced by the fictions they read? After all, the twentieth century was not the first time that life imitated art.

Our texts are excerpted from book XIII of the *Nuova cronica* of Giovanni Villani and books I–III in Giuseppe Porta. ed., *Nuova cronica* (Parma: Guanda, 1990) and the *Cronica* of Matteo Villani in Matteo Villani and Filippo Villani, *Cronica*, Giuseppe Porta., ed. (Milan: Fondazione Pietro Bembo, 1995). Both selections have been translated by R.G. Musto.

1348, January 15. Queen Giovanna I flees to Avignon

Book I. XIII.111. Queen Giovanna, who had been reduced and forced into the Castel [Nuovo] of Naples, hearing that King Lewis [of Hungary] was coming toward Naples with such a large force, secretly and at night, on the 15th of January, departed from the castle with her private household staff and with whatever treasure she was able to take away from the castle. There was little of this left, since it had been badly safeguarded after the death of King Robert.

By way of Piedigrotta, the queen embarked in three armed galleys of Provence that she had reserved in a secret place, and she arrived at Nice on the 20th of January.[164] What she accomplished in Provence we shall discuss soon enough in another chapter.

Lord Louis, hearing that the queen had departed from Naples and that the king of Hungary was happily prospering [in his

---

163. See, for example, Alessandra Perriccioli Saggese, *I romanzi cavallereschi miniati a Napoli* (Naples: Società Editrice Napoletana, 1979); Francesco Sabatini, "Lingue e letterature volgari in competizione," in Carratelli, 401–31; and Dunbabin, *French in the Kingdom of Naples*, 269–74. Kelly, *New Solomon*, 22–72, discusses "Patronage" but does not explore the impact of French and Italian romance literature on the court. Nor, from Kelly's analysis of its sources (55–78), does this genre appear to have any impact on the *Cronaca di Partenope*. Its medieval sources appear to be purely historiographical.

164. A fortuitously short time. It took Charles of Salerno four weeks to make the same voyage in 1278. See Dunbabin, *French in the Kingdom of Naples*, 32–35.

invasion], at nightfall, along with Signore Niccolò Acciaiuoli, his trusted companion and advisor, realizing that things were not going well for them and that they had been abandoned by the other royals and by the barons, departed from Capua [where they had been holding the crossing of the Volturno River against the Hungarian advance] and came to Naples.

But not finding an armed galley, with great haste and fear they embarked with their personal households on a small yacht since they could not find a galley they could trust themselves to. And on that yacht, with great pain and difficulty, they arrived at Porto Ercole in the Maremma.[165] They left there on the 20th of January and arrived incognito at Siena on the 23rd of January. From there they went to the district of Florence....

115. How Lord Louis of Taranto and Queen Giovanna arrived in Provence

...Among the queen's company was Lord Maruccio Caracciolo of Naples, whom she had made her count chamberlain, and about whose relationship with the queen there was infamous and malicious gossip. As soon as they had reached port at Nice, they went on to Aix-en-Provence, and they were joined there in Aix by the count of Avellino from the lords of Balzo[166] and the lord of Salto who, with other great barons of Provence, presently seized the said Lord Maruccio along with six of his companions and imprisoned them at Nuva.[167]

They conducted the queen with a courteous escort to Chateau Arnauld,[168] and there no one could have a private conversation without the presence of the said barons of Provence. But the royal party fell under jealous suspicion that they were about to flee Provence for another county in the kingdom of France along with Monsieur Jean,[169] the son of the king of France, Giovanna's cousin, who had come at that time to the pope in Avignon along with the count of Armagnac and who

---

165. On the southwest coast of Tuscany.

166. Hugues des Baux, the hereditary seneschal of Provence.

167. Unidentified.

168. Roches-des-Arnaud, near Sisteron.

169. Probably Jean, duc de Berry (1340–1416).

was engaged in discussions with the pope. The Provençals were greatly scandalized by this since they did not wish to be subjected to the king of France and therefore planned the rebellion of Provence along with the dauphin of Vienne both for that reason and at the request of the king of Hungary.

For this reason the pope was afraid that Lord Jean would return to France and offered him a great sum of money, saying that he would pay him 20,000 florins plus the papal tithes from the entire kingdom of France for the next five years over the next two: an enormous treasure. And so the pope spent the treasure of the Church intended for the conquest of the Holy Land....

The rest of Giovanni Villani's discussion focuses on Louis of Taranto's and Niccolò Acciaiuoli's stay in Tuscany and attempts to gather support. Matteo Villani's continuation picks up the narrative at the end of May 1348 with Lewis of Hungary's departure from the Regno, most likely to escape the Black Death then raging in Italy, leaving behind a substantial force of Hungarians.

The following selections are excerpted from the *Cronica* of Matteo Villani, book I, and translated by R.G. Musto.

XX. How Lord Louis [of Taranto] had himself entitled "king" to the pope and returned to the Regno

Lord Louis, finding himself now at the papal court and married to Queen Giovanna and not himself the king, deliberated about returning to the Regno. It appeared to him necessary that he have the title of king in order to govern the kingdom's affairs along with the queen and to sign letters from himself and the queen and not to render his own title contemptible. And although Holy Church had still not decided to make him king of Jerusalem and of Sicily, he gave himself these titles, which he did not have, nor could he have. And so they began to write letters entitled in this manner: "Louis and Giovanna, by the grace of God king and queen of Jerusalem and Sicily, etc." And from that point Lord Louis was called king.

The said King Louis and Queen Giovanna, taking comfort in [the thought of] returning to the Regno, as we've said, began to plan how to do so without delay. Finding themselves cash poor, they requested aid from the pope and cardinals, which they did not provide. Therefore out of necessity they sold to the Church the jurisdiction that the queen held over the city of Avignon for 30,000 gold florins.[170] With no less insistence because of their dire need, they also asked at every hand the barons, communes and prelates.

With great effort they managed to arm ten Genoese galleys and to hire them on for four months. In the midst of all this, Louis sent on ahead Lord Niccolò Acciaiuoli of Florence as his bailo with full mandate to procure [materials, arms and men for the expedition]....

XXI. How the king and queen returned to the Regno

[Having news of conditions in the Regno], bringing together the barons of Provence and their own households, they embarked from Marseilles[171] in those ten Genoese galleys. After a propitious voyage, in a few days they arrived safe and sound at Naples at the end of August in that year [1348].

But the Castel Nuovo, Castel dell'Ovo, Castel Sant'Erasmo, the port and the Tenzana[172] were all under the control of, and guarded, by the troops of the king of Hungary. They could not therefore put into port anywhere in that area, and so they arrived outside Naples at Sta. Maria del Carmine, opposite the Ponte Guicciardi,[173] and there they landed. The king and the queen entered the church of Our Lady to await the barons and commune of Naples, who would conduct them into the city.

XXII. How the king and queen entered Naples amid great festivity

The barons had gathered in Naples awaiting the arrival of the king and the queen with their cavalry. Chief among them were the Sanseverino, the house of del Balzo, the admiral count of Montescheggioso, the Stendards, the count of Sant'Agnolo, those of the houses of Raonessa and of Catanzano, and many others.

---

170. June 9, 1348. The price was actually 80,000 florins. The *Cronica di Partenope* III.37 states it as 240,000.

171. July 28, 1348.

172. Unidentifed.

173. The newly constructed Ponte Guizzardo or Maddelena.

They were furnished with many horses and with rich trappings and noble robes and accoutrements, and with their shields covered with their standard arms. The gentlemen of Naples and the *popolo*, attired in great pomp, on foot and on horse, with great festivity and with great joy set out to the Carmine to conduct the king and the queen into Naples. For their part, the merchants of Florence, Siena and Lucca who were in Naples, as well as the Genoese, Provençals and other foreigners who were also there, joined in with all the other people, dressed in rich robes of velvet and in fabrics of silk and linen, with all kinds of musical instruments that heightened the festive feeling. They all went out to welcome the king and the queen, and meeting them, each company made its act of reverence....

Fig. 54. *Louis of Taranto and Giovanna I. Cristoforo Orimina, detail of the* Statutes of the Order of the Knot. *Paris, BNF, MS 4274, fol. 2v.*

Matteo Villani backtracks to record this account of the trial of Queen Giovanna before the pope and cardinals in Avignon. One notes that the two males — neither of them the legitimate heir to the throne — decide the fate of the legitimate (female) ruler of Naples. Translation by R.G. Musto.

2.XXIV. How Queen Giovanna exonerated herself at the Roman court

As we have already narrated, when the accord was reached between the king [Lewis] of Hungary and King Louis [of

Taranto], part of the agreement on each side was to entrust the decision to the pope and cardinals: if Queen Giovanna were to be found guilty of the murder of her husband Andrew, the brother of the king of Hungary, she was to be deprived of her kingdom, and if she were not found guilty, she would remain queen. The king of Hungary agreed to this pact, more out of a desire to return to his country than through any good will that he may have had in this matter.

Nevertheless, the commission developed beyond the order set out and the actual judicial document. The pastors of the Church, seeing no way in which they could honestly deliberate on this case, began to temporize. As things stretched on, the ambassadors of each side remained at court without any results for the commissions given to them by the said kings in regards to the Church. Seeing that if unresolved these charges could produce both infamy and danger for the queen, the [Neapolitans] strove with every effort to terminate the proceedings.

Although even the absolute truth of the matter could not have absolved the queen [of rumors and suspicions], to lift these lingering doubts and rumors they proposed that if anyone who suspected her imperfect matrimonial love could neither suggest nor prove that this event came about through the corrupt intent or will of the queen, but rather [came about] through the force of malice or the deeds of others [then it must be attributed to motives] that her fragile feminine nature could neither understand not repair.[174]

It was proven through several testimonies that this was indeed true, and after discreet and well-disposed hearings, the queen was judged innocent of such evil intent and absolved of every charge that might be levelled against her for whatever reason. The sentence was announced declaring her innocence. Faith joined with exculpation.

3.VIII. How King Louis and Queen Giovanna were crowned by the Church

When Pope Clement VI and his cardinals had sent legates to the Regno, on the 27th of May of the year [May 23, 1352,

---

174. The modern editor notes that the original Italian text here is corrupt.

Pentecost day], in the city of Naples a solemn mass was celebrated. With the customary solemnities there were anointed and crowned in the name of Holy Church, first King Louis and then Queen Giovanna, for the kingdoms of Jerusalem and of Sicily.

This was carried out with great festivity by the barons and the knights of the Regno and by the Neapolitans and foreigners, all of whom exerted themselves to honor the king and the queen by this feast.

At the palaces of the princes of Taranto on the Largo delle Corregge they held many jousts and great displays of arms. The king and the queen, dressed and adorned in clothes of royal majesty, received the homage of all the barons who had not been enemies in the [Hungarian invasion and civil war]. They equally received it from those who had sided with the king of Hungary against them, all of whom they pardoned, demonstrating their good spirit and will. And for those who had not come to the coronation to offer their homage, they set a just time limit within which they could come to offer their obedience in peace and in love....

78. BOCCACCIO'S LITERARY GEOGRAPHY, C.1355

Boccaccio was also interested in elucidating classical literary references to geography, and undertook his *De montibus...* where he provides another description of Vesuvius. His account was based, in part, on Pliny the Younger's letter to Tacitus describing the eruption of 79 CE that destroyed Pompeii and other cities. See also Reading 70 for Petrarch's use of that text.

Our selection is taken from Giovanni Boccaccio, *De montibus, silvis, de fontibus, lacubus et fluminibus* (Basil: Apud Io. Hervagium, 1532), 426. http://www.uni-mannheim.de/mateo/itali/boccaccio1/jpg/s426.html. Accessed 12/1/2012. Translated by Eileen Gardiner.

Vesuvius is a mountain in Campania, not connected with any other mountain, teeming everywhere with vineyards and orchards. At the base of its Sirocco (southeast) side lies Pompeii, and almost Sirocco (more east), lies Sarno, and further away, Benevento. On the Grecale side (northeast) lies

Capua and on the Mistral side (northwest) is Naples of the Chalcedons, called Parthenope.

From the middle of Vesuvius, near the summit, so much smoke used to pour out that it covered the region and instilled great fear in the local people. It did not quickly disappear, and for several days it was so dense that it blocked the rays of the sun, bringing night to the area. Finally, after covering all the houses in ashes, ending in the sea, which bathes its base in the west, it was possible to see a huge flame from the top of the burning mountain. After erupting burning stones for several centuries, today neither smoke nor flames arise from the summit.

There is still a large crater in the mountain, a clear testimony to past eruptions. At the foot of Vesuvius was a famous battle between the Romans and Latins. To win this battle[175] Consul Publius Decius dedicated himself to the gods of the underworld and immediately died.

The country folk today often call this mountain "La Somma."

79. GIOVANNA I FOUNDS STA. MARIA INCORONATA AND RENOVATES CASTEL DELL'OVO, 1363

The church of Sta. Maria Incoronata,[176] on today's via Medina, was long thought to be founded by Giovanna I in the 1350s on the site of a former court of justice founded by her father Charles of Calabria. It has now been dated to the 1360s. Over the centuries the church, like Giovanna's own memory, was buried and dismembered, and only in the 1980s was a full restoration begun.

The Castel dell'Ovo was built atop the site of the pleasure villa of Lucullus and of the oldest settlement in Naples. Here the *Cronaca di Partenope* repeats part of the ancient legend of the "egg," the *ovo* in Castel dell'Ovo already recounted by Conrad of Querfurt in Reading 37. The excavated hill and the arch under the castle described by the *Cronaca* are clearly visible in Fig. 55.

---

175. The Battle of Vesuvius in 340 BCE. See Livy, *De urbe condita* 8.9–10.

176. For the most recent analysis and summary of research see Vitolo, *La chiesa della Regina*.

This excerpt is taken from *Cronaca*, book III, Altamura, 166–67, and is translated by R.G. Musto.

Fig. 55. *Castel dell'Ovo c.1350. Cristoforo Orimina, detail of the* Statutes of the Order of the Knot. *Paris, BNF, MS 4274, fol. 5r.*

50. HOW THE INCORONATA AND CASTEL DELL'OVO WERE BUILT

At the time of her marriage [to Jaime IV of Majorca in September 1363], Queen Giovanna had constructed in the Largo delle Corregge in the city of Naples the church of Sta. Maria Incoronata, and she had repaired the Castel dell'Ovo.

According to an ancient prophesy it is said that in this castle there was an egg placed inside a carafe. If this carafe with the egg inside were to break, the castle itself would collapse. And this is so, because when Lord Ambrogio, natural son of the duke of Milan, was held prisoner in the Castel dell'Ovo, he broke the said egg while escaping and all the ancient buildings of the castle collapsed.

The queen had it rebuilt more beautiful and strong than before, and so that the castle would not lose its name, she had the egg encased in a vessel of glass more beautiful and subtle, better than ever before. The work was done by Giovanni de Gilo, of Piazza Sta. Caterina, called Jurice di Napoli. He was a Neapolitan and was full of virtue and subtle skill. And so that access to the castle would be easier, Giovanna had torn down a hill that stood before it below Sta. Lucia and the castle. She caused the waters that were in the garden of Castel Nuovo to be carried over arches, pillars and canals all the way to under the arch of Castel dell'Ovo. She had placed there a very beautiful basin of marble, which this Giovanni had carried there by ten pairs of oxen, with great effort, from S. Gennaro fuori le Mura.

80. Giovanna I requests relics for Sta. Maria Incoronata, 1364/67

In addition to the narrative and financial sources already cited above, a major source for the history of Naples remains its vast archives. Over the centuries many of the royal archives for the Angevin period have been lost, first during the riots against Giovanna I in March 1346 when the palace of Carlo Artus, the royal chamberlain, was destroyed; then again during the revolt of Masaniello in July 1647, when many tax and court records were burnt; and finally on September 30, 1943, when retreating Nazis deliberately firebombed the depository. Many of the archives have been painstakingly reconstructed over the years from copies held in Barcelona, Marseilles and other sites, as well as through modern transcriptions completed before World War II.[177] Other archives, such as that of Giovanna's secretary Niccolò Alunno d'Alife, compiled between 1347 and 1367, also survive.

The following letter was written in Latin and sent by Giovanna I to Charles V of Valois, king of France. It requests relics from the Crown of Thorns in the Sainte-Chapelle in Paris (consecrated in 1248 to house this Crown of Thorns) for inclusion in her new church of Sta. Maria Incoronata. It contains no internal dating element except for being written in Naples. However, we can date it from three indicators. The first is from the reigning dates of the addressee, Charles V, who became king on May 19, 1364. The second is the date of Charles's reply, which also lacks dating elements but which has been dated to 1367, and the third is a letter of Giovanna to Pope Urban V, which is included in Niccolò d'Alife's archive and is dated no later than 1367, the date of d'Alife's death.[178] Thus it is most likely that the letter was written no earlier than May 19, 1364 and no later than 1367.

The "incoronata" refers not to Giovanna's coronation of 1352,[179] as long believed, but to this crown of thorns.

---

177. The progress of this reconstruction has been documented by Filangieri et al., *I registri della cancelleria angioina*. See Introduction, pp. xvii–xviii.

178. See Vitolo, *La chiesa della Regina*, 21–22. For d'Alife, see Reading 65 at p. 239 n. 107.

179. See above, Reading 79 at pp. 287–88.

This letter is preserved in a copy from the d'Alife archive in the Biblioteca della Società Napoletana di Storia Patria, MS XXX C 2 bis, fol. 115. It has been edited by Vitolo, pp. 112–14; and is translated by R.G. Musto.

Fig. 56. Crown of Thorns. Main portal, Sta. Maria Incoronata. Photo: Italica Press..

To the most excellent prince, reverend and honored brother, pleasing greetings.

We have frequently considered having a chapel built in Naples to the praise and glory of our Redeemer and endowing it with the appropriate grants and emoluments for the clergy who will live there to celebrate the divine offices of the Lord. Our mind has often been prodded for the name by which this project ought to be distinguished as an acceptable gift to God and as a result of our devotion. At last and most recently the grace of divine mercy touched our devotion and, mercifully for us, it has generously decided that this chapel should be named for the saving Crown of our Redeemer following the example of that venerable chapel in the royal palace in Paris [the Sainte-Chapelle]. This should be done so that the Christian people might come together more devoutly to cross its threshold and so that this people might feel worthy in its devotion to His miraculous Crown of Thorns.

We therefore implore your royal excellence most earnestly that at least two thorns from the said crown of our Lord, which is preserved in that royal chapel in Paris along with other precious relics, as we have indicated, be granted to us and sent here through that venerable and religious man [Brother Petrus de Villiers] our chaplain and devoted member of our royal household, the visitor general of the Cistercian Order in our kingdom of Sicily; and that your sublimity agree to send this as our chapel's singular ornament and as our great consolation and satisfaction. For through this gift you will share in the divine intercessions that will take place in this our chapel for the increase of your merits, as well as for other spiritual benefits and pious works for God's clemency not yet experienced.

We remain in perpetual obligation to your exalted royalty. Dated Naples, etc.

81. GIOVANNI BOCCACCIO'S *LIFE OF GIOVANNA I*, c.1375

Some time between 1362 and his death in 1375, Giovanni Boccaccio concluded his *On Famous Women (De claris mulieribus)* with a life of Giovanna I. Boccaccio wrote this collection as a counterpart to Petrarch's work on famous men *(De viris illustribus)*, and he returned to his mentor's Latin to create a series of biographies in the classical style. He began the work in 1361 and worked toward its completed first draft in 1362 when he was invited to Naples by Niccolò Acciaiuoli, Giovanna's grand seneschal. He dedicated it to Andrea Acciaiuoli, countess of Altavilla, sister of Niccolò. The 106 biographies of both good and evil women mirror Petrarch's combination of mythological, semi-historical and classical figures and, like Petrarch's assemblage of famous men, brings the collection up to his own time with a handful of ancient and medieval women, including the legendary Pope Joan, Empress Constance, the Sienese widow Camiola; concluding with a biography of Giovanna.

Boccaccio's vision of women is complex and contested. His *Corbaccio* is seen by Alcuin Blamires as "a mordant experiment in unalloyed contempt" for women.[180]

---

180. *Woman Defamed*, 166. For the larger context, see also Thomas C. Stillinger and Regina Psaki, eds., *Boccaccio and Feminist Criticism* (Chapel Hill, NC: Annali d'Italianistica, 2006).

Renaissance scholar Constance Jordan[181] likewise reflects a feminist critique of a misogyny Boccaccio shared with his age. Yet, as one might expect from the author of the *Decameron*, Boccaccio's Neapolitan women are graceful, dynamic, courtly, courageous and virtuous even as the poet veils only slightly their real-life intrigues and love affairs at court. In his *Amorosa Visione* 42, he calls Giovanna *"gaia e leggiadretta,"* the image of grace and lightness, while he records the remarkable beauty of Agnes de Perigord.[182] His *Fiammetta* is reportedly based on Maria d'Aquino, King Robert's mistress; while Niccolò Acciaiuoli's affair with Catherine de Courtenay[183] forms the basis of his *Eclogue* 8. Sancia de' Cabanni, Giovanna's intimate friend and lady in waiting, is also described in favorable terms, as "noble and

---

181. "Boccaccio's In-Famous Women: Gender and Civic Virtue in the *De mulieribus claris,"* In *Ambiguous Realities: Women in the Middle Ages and Renaissance,* C. Levin and J. Watson, eds. (Detroit: Wayne State University Press, 1987), 25–47.

182. Agnes (1305–45) was only 30 when she became the widow of King Robert's youngest brother John of Gravina. She thus became the head of the house of Durazzo and chief rival to the house of Taranto on behalf of her sons, Charles and Louis of Durazzo. She was the daughter of Brunissenda of Foix, who was rumored to have been Pope Clement V's mistress. She might therefore have been a pope's daughter. Whatever her official lineage, Agnes was the sister of Cardinal Talleyrand de Perigord, a leading figure in Avignon and a close advisor and political ally of Pope Clement VI.

183. Catherine de Courtenay (de Valois) (1303–46) was the daughter of Charles de Valois and the granddaughter of Baldwin II, last Latin emperor of Constantinople and hence titular empress of Constantinople. She married King Robert's brother, Prince Philip of Taranto, c.1313. On Philip's death in 1331, Catherine tried to annul Giovanna's inheritance in favor of her sons, Robert, Louis and Philip II. Catherine was reportedly extremely ambitious, volatile and more than highly attractive; and she had reportedly taken several lovers. According to Boccaccio's *Eclogue* 8 and Giovanni Villani (XIII.75), among them was Niccolò Acciaiouli (1310–65), one of the most famous of the Florentine bankers, to whom the Angevins were long indebted, and later Giovanna's grand seneschal. To press Philip's claims as prince of Morea (the Latin Peloponnese) on his death she moved her court and family to Greece. She was accompanied by Acciaiouli, to whom she granted numerous fiefs in the Morea. The house of Taranto remained there from 1338 to 1341, defending Angevin claims from Greeks, Catalans and Turks.

gentle" (*Caccia di Diana* I.19).[184] Court life at Naples was "full of the most light-hearted feasts" (*Fiammetta* V).

While Jordan calls the collection "devious" and "pervasively critical" of women, Boccaccio's literary strategy for Giovanna's biography is ultimately more nuanced, as coy as it is elegant. Boccaccio introduces us to a queen, "more renowned than other women of our time for her nobility, power and goodness." After discussing her parentage, Boccaccio does not hesitate to place her firmly within the dynastic context of her Angevin forbearers without the least hint of discontinuity or decline: "Thus, in our days and in those of our fathers no family in the whole world has been more famous than this for its nobility." He then moves on to Giovanna's youth and proceeds to describe the queen's possessions in Naples, Provence and Forcalquier, their natural riches, their peoples and cities in such lengthy and glowing terms that the reader is tempted to think that Boccaccio has nothing positive to say about Giovanna herself. But then, with some knowledge of the growing chorus of condemnation that surrounded the queen, he continues: "If we examine this kingdom closely, our amazement will be as great as its fame, for it is a mighty kingdom and not usually ruled by women." Boccaccio then reverses his reader's anticipation once again: "And what is even more surprising, Joanna's spirit is equal to ruling it, so that she has preserved the noble character of her ancestors." "Ruling" or "governance" [*imperium*], "spirit" [*animus*], "character" [*indoles*] and "ancestor" [*avus*] would soon all become contested terms in the black legend of the Angevins.

Following the genre for such classically inspired biographies, Boccaccio offers examples of Giovanna's virtues that match the medieval ideal of *Buon Governo* spelled out in Lorenzetti's Sienese fresco cycle and by contemporary political thinkers such as Bartolo da Sassoferrato or Remigio de' Girolamo: she has cleared the realm of brigands, capturing and executing their leaders, such as Janni Pipino. "None of the previous kings had wanted or been able

184. On Sancia and the other de' Cabanni, see above Readings 65, 74, 76.

to do this." People and goods may now travel the realm without harm, the barons have been brought under control. The fact that Boccaccio had dedicated the work to the Acciaiuoli, first and foremost the ally of Louis of Taranto, makes his omission of Louis' role in all this the more apparent. That Boccaccio could concentrate on Giovanna's own accomplishments as ruler without fear of contradiction from those who were in the best possible position to know better makes his praise even more convincing.

Giovanna's personal virtues show her to be "the legitimate heir" of Robert the Wise. She is astute, generous, loyal and rewarding of service, patient, steadfast and "cannot be deflected from her righteous path." Boccaccio does not shy away from the stuff of the black legend, but meets it head on: "Through the fault of others, she has had to endure flight, exile, marriage, the grim ways of her husbands,[185] the envy of noblemen, undeserved ill-repute, the threats of popes and other things, all of which she has borne bravely. Finally, her indomitable soul has conquered everything; this would have been a great deed for a strong, powerful king, and not only for a woman."

Boccaccio concludes by extolling Giovanna's "charming appearance," grace and eloquence, her majesty and inflexibility when the occasion demands. He adds that "equally she can be affable, compassionate, gentle and kind, so that one could describe her as her people's ally rather than their queen." Then in a clear comparison to her grandfather Robert, he asks: "What greater qualities would one seek in a most wise king? And if someone wanted to express completely the integrity of her character, his speech would be very long. For these reasons, I not only think that she is noble and of splendid fame, but an eminent glory of Italy such as has never before been seen by any nation."

How accurate is Boccaccio's characterization, how closely related to the facts? He was, after all, writing in a venerable genre in which rulers from antiquity and through the Middle

---

185. From Virginia Brown, ed. and trans., *Famous Women*. The I Tatti Renaissance Library 1 (Cambridge: Harvard University Press, 2001), 466–75, at 471, l. 15.

Ages were described in stock literary tropes with a standard set of virtues, character traits, deeds and positive (or negative) effects on their realms. Rodney Lokaj[186] has assembled enough material from Boccaccio's other works, including his letters and the *Corbaccio*, to cast serious doubt on his admiring portrait of the queen. Boccaccio was clearly attempting to curry favor both with the Acciaiuoli and also with the queen herself, and a favorable review of the most powerful woman in Europe at the time could not hurt his chances.

Acciaiuoli invited Boccaccio to Naples almost immediately after the death of Louis of Taranto on June 5, 1362, and so it might then appear natural to omit the prince consort's role in the restoration of the kingdom. On the other hand, it was Niccolò Acciaiuoli himself who was held responsible for the second wave of slander against Giovanna during her conflict with Louis. Was not Boccaccio equally risking another potential patron's scorn in his positive assessment? Again, Boccaccio is the author of one of the most enduring "accused queen" stories. The patient Griselda appears for the first time in his *Decameron* (X.10), before it was incorporated into Petrarch's *Seniles* XVII.3[187] and then made its way into Chaucer's "Clerk's Tale." He was not above using fable and myth to stock his literary shelves.

Whatever its motives, Boccaccio's biography did record a popular affection for the queen, which seems to be borne out by her own use of the Neapolitan language as a means of expanding her base among the city's people.[188] According to Patrick Gilli,[189] Boccaccio's placing the queen at the head of a list of contemporary Italian women affirmed this "native" identity in the most positive light.

This selection is taken from Guido A. Guarino's translation of *Concerning Famous Women* (New Brunswick: Rutgers

---

186. "La Cleopatra neapoletana: Giovanna d'Angiò nelle 'Familiares' di Petrarca," *Giornale storico della Letteratura Italiana* 177 (2000): 481–521.

187. *Letters of Old Age*, 2:655–68.

188. For Boccaccio's own affectionate use of Neapolitan, see above Reading 62.

189. "L'intégration manquée des Angevins en Italie: Le témoignage des historiens," in *L'état Angevin*, 11–33, at 25–26.

University Press, 1963), rev. ed. as *On Famous Women* (New York: Italica Press, 2011), 248–50.

CHAPTER 104. JOANNA [GIOVANNA], QUEEN OF SICILY AND JERUSALEM

Joanna, the queen of Sicily and Jerusalem, is more renowned than other women of our time for her nobility, power and goodness. It would have seemed hateful not to speak of this woman, and yet it would have been better to remain silent than to write little about her. She was the first child of Prince Charles, the glorious duke of Calabria and first born of Robert, king of Sicily and Jerusalem of illustrious memory. Her mother was Marie [de Valois], the sister of King Philip [VI] of France. If we seek her parents' ancestors, we will not stop until, through many kings, we reach Dardanus, the founder of Troy, whose father the ancients said was Jupiter. From this family, so noble and ancient, so many famous princes have been born on both sides that there is no Christian king who is not related to it by blood or marriage. Thus, in our days and in those of our fathers no family in the whole world has been more famous than this for its nobility.

While Joanna was still a child, her father died in his youth [in 1328]. Since her grandfather Robert had no children of the better sex, at his orders she lawfully inherited the kingdom at his death [in 1343]. Her inheritance did not extend beyond the torrid zone, or to the North Pole among the Sarmatians, but was between the Tyrrhenian Sea and the Adriatic, from Umbria, Piceno and the old country of the Volscians to the Strait of Sicily under mild skies. Within these borders, her rule is obeyed by the ancient Campanians, Lucani, Bruttii, Salentines, Calabrians, Daunians, Vestuali [Vestini], Samnites, Peligni and Marsi, and by the people of many other lands such as, to mention the largest, the kingdom of Jerusalem, the island of Sicily, and Piedmont in Cisalpine Gaul, which have been usurped from her. In the same manner she is obeyed by those who dwell in the Seventh Province [Provence] between Narbonian Gaul, the Rhone and the Alps, and the county of Folcacherius [Forcalquier], and they recognize her as their mistress and queen. How many famous cities are in these provinces, how many remarkable towns, bays, refuges for sailors, shipyards, lakes, mineral springs, groves, forests, pastures, pleasant shelters and fruitful fields! How many people there are and great nobles, what great wealth, and what an abundance of things needed for life! Certainly, it is not easy to describe all this.

If we examine this kingdom closely, our amazement will be as great as its fame, for it is a mighty kingdom and not usually ruled by women. And what is even more surprising, Joanna's spirit is equal to ruling it, so that she has preserved the noble character of her ancestors. For, after she assumed the royal diadem, she very bravely attacked and cleaned out bands of wicked men, not only in the cities and inhabited places, but also in the Alps and out-of-the-way places, in forests, and in the dens of wild beasts, so that they all fled in fear or withdrew to strong fortresses. They were besieged by soldiers under a noble leader, and the siege of such places was not abandoned until the fortresses had been captured and these abominable men executed. None of the previous kings had wanted or been able to do this. She has so subjected the lands which she possesses that not only the poor but the rich as well can go safely and without care wherever they please, by night or by day. And no less beneficial, she has drawn the great men and nobles of the kingdom from their dissolute ways and has curbed them with such discretion that they have discarded their former arrogance, and those who earlier scorned kings now fear to see the face of this woman when she is angry.[190]

Moreover, she is so prudent that she can be deceived more easily by treachery than through shrewdness. She is so steadfast and constant that she will not be easily swayed in her just purposes without reason. This has already been shown clearly enough not long ago by the blows of Fortune which have often struck and buffeted her from every direction. For she has endured the internal struggles of petty fellow-princes and foreign wars which at times were waged within her kingdom. Through the fault of others, she has had to endure flight, exile, the grim ways of her husbands,[191] the envy of noblemen, undeserved ill-repute, the

---

190. Giovanna's accomplishments here clearly closely resemble the ideal of trecento government, as portrayed in Lorenzetti's *Buon Governo* or as reported for Cola di Rienzo's *buono stato*. See Musto, *Apocalypse*, 143–59.

191. We have substituted this phrase from Brown's translation, p. 471. Guarino reads, "marriage, strict conduct."

threats of popes, and other things, all of which she has borne bravely. Finally, her indomitable soul has conquered everything; this would have been a great deed for a strong, powerful king, and not only for a woman.

She has a marvelous, charming appearance; her speech is gentle, and her eloquence pleases everyone. Just as she is majestic and inflexible when the occasion demands, she is affable, merciful, gentle and friendly, so that one would say that she is her people's companion rather than their queen. What greater qualities would one seek in a most wise king? And if someone wanted to express completely the integrity of her character, his speech would be very long. For these reasons, I not only think that she is noble and of splendid fame, but an eminent glory of Italy such as has never before been seen by any nation.

Fig. 57. The murder of Charles III. From Eberhard Windecke, Das Buch von Kaiser Sigismund, c. 1440–50. Workshop of Diebold Lauber.

CHARLES III

King Charles III, or Charles III of Durazzo, was the son of Duke Charles of Durazzo, the cousin of Giovanna I and an Angevin rival for the throne against her. In 1346, following the murder of Giovanna I's husband Andrew at Aversa and in alliance with Robert of Taranto and Pope Clement VI, Duke Charles worked to destroy Giovanna's governing council. Charles of Durazzo aligned himself with Lewis of Hungary during Lewis' invasion of the Regno in 1347/48. But when all the royal cousins came to Aversa in 1348 to render homage to Lewis, in an act of vendetta — and as a clear indication of whom he suspected — the Hungarian king had Charles arrested for treason and

298

decapitated on the same spot where Lewis' brother Andrew had been murdered over two years earlier. Lewis then arrested the remaining Angevin cousins and — along with Giovanna's newborn son Charles Martel then in Charles of Durazzo's custody — had them brought back to Hungary. The infant Charles Martel died under mysterious circumstances some time after, but Charles of Durazzo's son Charles was raised in Hungary as a loyal follower of Lewis.

In 1381 Pope Urban VI declared Giovanna deposed and, at Lewis' urging, anointed the younger Charles of Durazzo king of Naples.[192] Now Charles III, Durazzo reached Naples in July 1381, despite the best efforts of Giovanna's fourth husband, Otto of Brunswick, to defend the capital and the queen. Charles had Giovanna strangled to death in 1382 and became the founder of the Angevin-Durazzo dynasty of Naples.

On the death of King Lewis of Hungary on September 11, 1382, his daughter Maria assumed the throne. But the barons of the kingdom summoned Charles III of Durazzo, one of the last surviving male Angevins, to take the crown from her in September 1385. On February 7, 1386 he was seriously wounded by an assassin. Poison, probably administered by the women attendants of Lewis' second wife Elizabeth of Bosnia, finally finished off Charles III of Durazzo on February 24, 1386.

82. CHARLES III OF DURAZZO CONQUERS NAPLES, 1381

The following selection not only follows Charles' conquest of Naples, but provides useful topographical details of the city of Naples on the verge of the quattrocento.[193] The Neapolitans' selling provisions to both sides of the conflict is not a sign of the southern perfidy but a standard practice right up through the Napoleonic era. It became outlawed only in the age of total war in the nineteenth and twentieth centuries when civilian populations themselves became direct and explicit targets of war. Charles III's use of projectile

---

192. For background, see Margarete Rothbarth, *Urban VI. und Neapel* (Berlin: Oldenbourg, 1913).

193. See Musto, Interactive Map: http://www.italicapress.com/index287.html.

weapons against Queen Giovanna in Castel Nuovo was also typical of the time but may reveal the special venom then widespread against this female ruler.

This text selection is taken from the *Cronaca di Partenope*, book III, Altamura, 167–70, and translated by R.G. Musto.

52. How King Charles III arrived at Ponte Maddalena in Naples

Fig. 58. Charles III enters Naples from the Ponte della Maddalena. Detail from cassone painting, c.1382. Master of Charles of Durazzo. New York, Metropolitan Museum of Art. Rogers Fund, 1906. Accession 07.120.1.

The said King Charles, after he took various advice as to how to please the divine majesty, on the sixteenth day of July, in the fourth indiction [1381], with the papal legate and all his army, departed the city of Nola and arrived via the Somma road at the Ponte Guizzardo, which crosses the river [Sebeto] at the city of Naples at the church of Sta. Maria Maddalena. He then arranged his army around the hour of vespers [in the evening] and had the army take refreshment. Then many people came out of the city of Naples with wine and fruit to refresh the king.

When Lord Otto [of Brunswick] heard of this, he set off directly with his army against King Charles along the Acerra road to the plain of Casanova di Napoli, to the borgo of Formello di Napoli. Between the two armies there was no more than a quarter mile distance. Once Lord Otto arrived there, King Charles remained for the duration of two hours outside the city of Naples, and then he entered it. No one stood in his way except the regent of Naples and the captain of Naples with a few men, who offered little resistance and then fled. King Charles passed through the [Piazza del] Mercato of Naples and through Porta Sant'Agostino [alla Zecca], then straight along the vie di Forcella and Nido all the way to the monastery of Sto. Corpo di Cristo [Sta. Chiara]. In this monastery he remained with his domestic staff.

The said Lord Otto remained outside the city and did not dare enter it. He kept the Porta Capuana free and retained the greater part of the city and all the fortresses in the city. Consequently on the following day, the seventh of July, King Charles barricaded all the streets that led to Castel Nuovo, in which Queen Giovanna remained with her council and certain men at arms of the royal family or of her husband's forces. Besieging the queen in the castle, Charles placed men at arms in the Largo delle Corregge and in the palace of the duchess of Durazzo and had one trebuchet set up at S. Pietro a Castello and another on the Molo. With these he hurled marble slabs and barrels full of excrement and loaded with other filthy matter against the castle. He quickly also ordered a tunnel dug from the palace of Lord Raimondo di Laimo, the count chamberlain, all the way to the wall of the tower of the great hall of Castel Nuovo.

The queen, doubting that the castle would stand without collapsing, as she was led to believe, began to negotiate a truce with King Charles through the mediation of Lord Ugo di S. Severino and Lord Iacobo de Capri, the count chamberlain of the kingdom of Sicily. These negotiations were relayed to Lord Otto, who was positioned with all his army, some posted in the city of Aversa and some in the city of Acerra, overrunning and despoiling the territory of Naples and the country estates of the city, setting them ablaze. This truce did not please Lord Otto. So, with his army of Germans and with the aforesaid Lord Robert d'Artois, the husband of the duchess of Durazzo who was besieged in Castel Nuovo along with the queen and the barons, on Saturday the twenty-fourth of August, Otto moved to Castel Sant'Erasmo,[194] which was outside the city of Naples, with the intention of forcefully aiding the said queen and duchess.

The following dawn, the twenty-fifth of the month, on the feast of St. Bartholomew the Apostle, every armed man descended from Monte Sant'Erasmo to the level ground in Piazza Sto. Spirito to attack the forces of King Charles and the people of Naples. These were on foot, armed with crossbows and lances, and so Lord Otto dismounted along with the marquis

---

194. See Musto, Interactive Map: http://www.italicapress.com/index287.html.

of Monferrato. Lord Otto and the brother of the marquis were wounded by the infantry, but because the marquis did not want to surrender he was killed by the infantry. The rest of the said army, struck by God's wrath, out of fear and the rush of wind and dust that rose up at sunrise against them, surrendered to anyone in King Charles's army who wanted to take them, to such an extent that every man in King Charles's army took prisoners.

As a result, the queen was terrified, and concluding that God's wrath was against her, she handed herself into the king's hands along with the duchess and everyone else who was in Castel Nuovo. After this King Charles's army besieged Castel Sant'Erasmo, in which Lord Robert d'Artois and Lord Otto's brother Lord Balthazar count of Ariano, Lord Nicola di Napoli and many others had taken refuge. Many people were taken to King Charles's quarters in the monastery of Sta. Chiara, and Queen Giovanna was put in Castel dell'Ovo.[195]

■

195. Our collection ends where it began: at Castel dell'Ovo.

CHAPTER 6: LITERATE CULTURES

Fig. 59. Fragment of an epitaph, 7th c., of an unknown priest, probably the dispensator of a diocese. Unknown provenance. Naples, Museo Archeologico Nazionale. Source: SN 2.2:547.

Fig 60. Inscription on a sepulchral tombstone from the ducal period, 10th c., which was reused in the Angevin period as a covering of the tomb of Robert d'Artois with the epigraph turned toward the inside. Church of S. Lorenzo Maggiore, Naples. Source: SN 2.1:117.

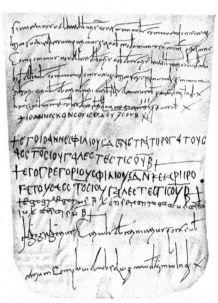

Fig. 61. The end of an instrument of 951 with the signature of Duke Giovanni III and of other witnesses, some in Greek and some in Latin. Source: SN 2.1:119. See above, Reading 23.

Fig. 62. The end of an instrument of 991 with the signatures of the monks of the monastery of S. Salvatore in insula maris, some signed in Greek and some in Latin. Source: SN 2.1:167.

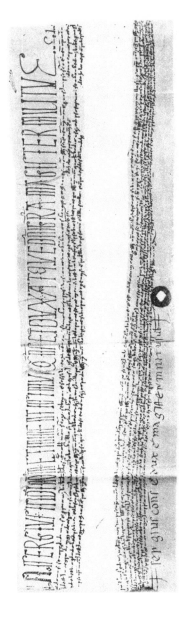

Fig. 63. The beginning and end of a document of 1131. The last duke of Naples, Sergius VII, grants various benefices and immunities to the monastery of SS. Severino e Sossio. This act has the distinction of being the only one of those surviving from the duchy to be drawn up in Beneventan script instead of a curial hand. Source: SN 2.1:349.

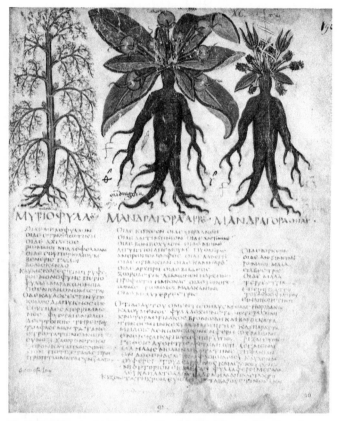

Fig. 64. Page from the Greek herbarium Discoride Neapolitanus. *Late 6th–early 7th c. Naples, BN, MS Vind. Graec. 1, fol. 90r. Provenance: Library of the Convent of S. Giovanni a Carbonara. Source: Fiorella Romana,* Biblioteca Nazionale Vittorio Emanuele III Napoli *(Florence: Nardini Editore, 1993), 44–45.*

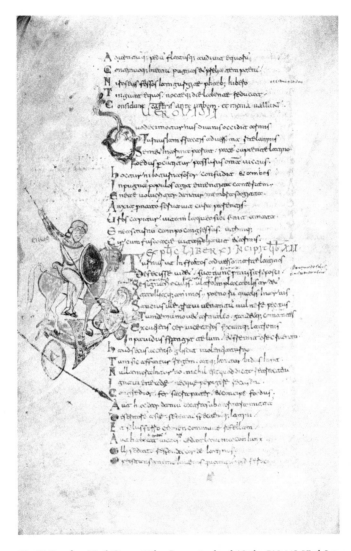

Fig. 65. Page from Virgil, Opera. 10th c. Beneventan hand. Naples, BN, MS. Vind. Lat. 6, f. 168v. Provenance: Library of S. Giovanni a Carbonara. Source: Romana, Biblioteca Nazionale Vittorio Emanuele III, 48–49.

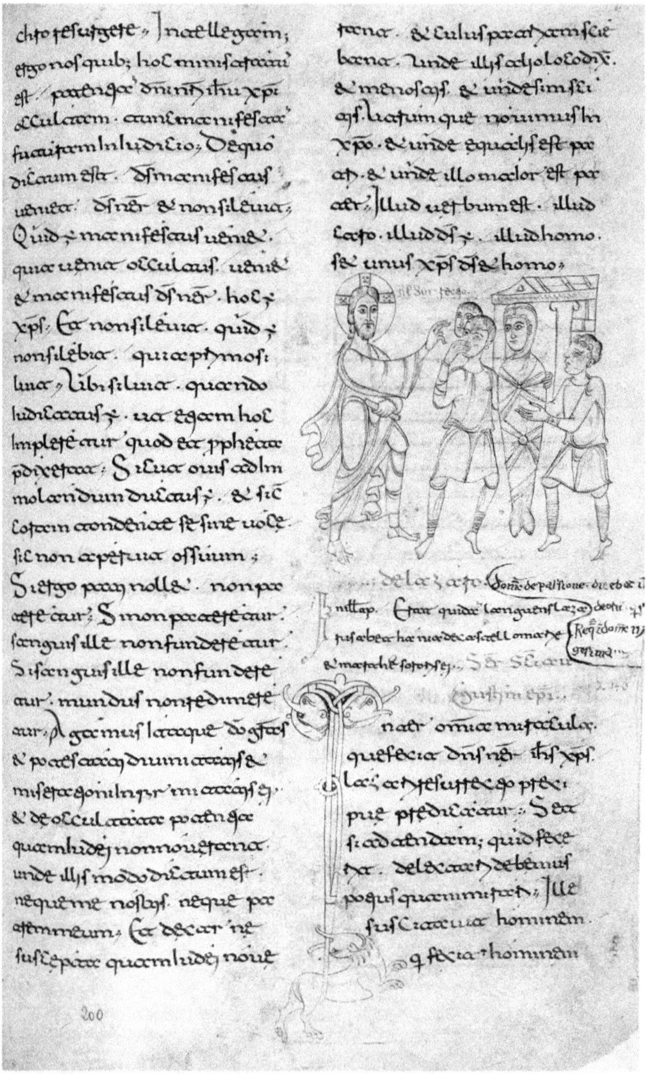

Fig. 66. Page from a book of homilies with illustration of the Resurrection of Lazarus. 11th c. Beneventan hand. Naples, BN, MS VI.B.2, fol. 200r. Provenance: Troia, Apulia. Source: Romana, Biblioteca Nazionale Vittorio Emanuele III, 50–51.

Fig 67. Page from a Greek Bible (New Testament). 11th c. Greek miniscule. Naples, BN, MS. Vind. Graec. 3, fol. 5v. Provenance: S. Giovanni a Carbonara. Source: Romana, Biblioteca Nazionale Vittorio Emanuele III, 52–53.

309

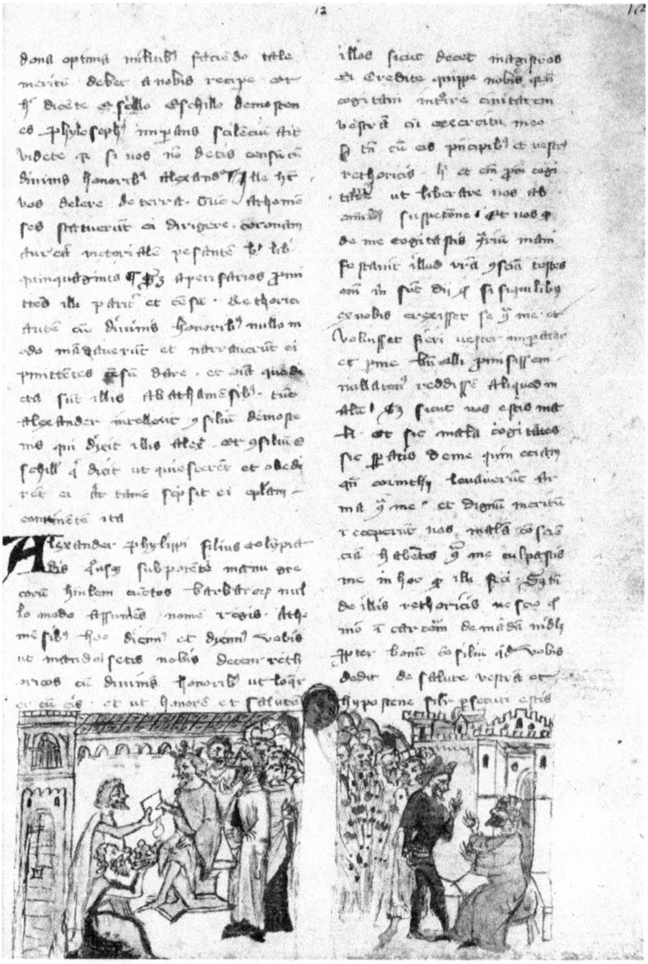

Fig. 68. Page of the translation by the Archipriest Leo of Il romanzo d'Alessandro. End of the 13th c. Gothic miniscule of Campanian School. Vatican City, BAV, Cod. Vat. Lat. 7190, fol. 12r. Source: SN 2.2:571. See above, Reading 21.

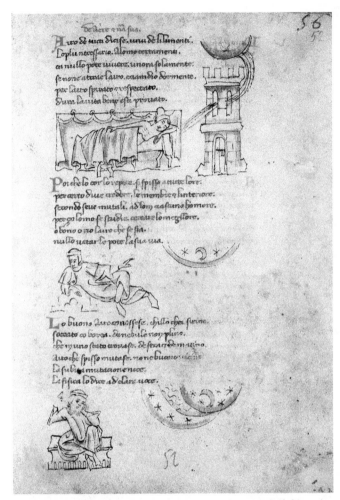

Fig. 69. From De balneis terrae laboris; de Regimine sanitatis. *First half of the 14th c. Italian Gothic script. Naples, BN, MS XIII.C.37, fol. 52r. Source: Romana, Biblioteca Nazionale Vittorio Emanuele III, 82–83.*

Fig. 70. From the Roman du roi Meliadus. *14th c. Italian Gothic book hand. London, British Library, MS Add. 12228, fol. 229v. Source: Alessandra Perriccioli Saggese, I* romanzi cavallereschi miniati a Napoli *(Naples: Società editrice Napoletana, 1979), Tav. LV.*

Fig. 71. From ibn Zakariya ar-Razi's Opera, translated from Arabic into Latin by Gerard of Cremona at the request of Charles I of Anjou. 14th c. French Gothic book hand. Naples, BN, MS VIII.D.22, fol. 101v. Provenance: S. Giovanni a Carbonara. Source: Romana, Biblioteca Nazionale Vittorio Emanuele III, 92.

313

Fig. 72. From Boethius' De arythmetica, De musica. *First half of the 14th c. Italian Gothic script. Naples, BN, MS V.A.14, fol. 47r. Source: Romana,* Biblioteca Nazionale Vittorio Emanuele III, *86–87.*

BIBLIOGRAPHY

This bibliography is arranged first into primary sources, then by secondary works by period, and then by author and publication date. For more specialized studies in the history of Naples' art and architecture, see Caroline Bruzelius and William Tronzo. Medieval Naples: An Architectural & Urban History 400–1400 (New York: Italica Press, 2011), 115–23. For complete bibliographies, with ongoing supplements, see http://www.italicapress.com/index346.html.

BIBLIOGRAPHY OF TEXTS
Texts are arranged alphabetically by author or title. Reading numbers follow in brackets.

Abû 'Abdallâh al-Idrîsî. *The Book of Roger.* Henri Bresc and Annliese Nef, trans. and eds. *Idrîsî: La première géographie de l'Occident.* Paris: Flammarion, 1999. Trans. in G.A. Loud, *Roger II and the Creation of the Kingdom of Sicily.* Manchester: Manchester University Press, 2012, 362–63. [32]

Adam de la Halle. *Jeu de Robin et Marion.* In *Théatre français au moyen age.* L.J.N. Monmerqué and Francisque Michel, eds. Paris: Firmin Didot Frères, 1842, 102–11. [47]

Alexander Neckham. *Anecdota de Vergilio (The Secret History of Virgil).* Joannes Opsopoeus Brettanus, trans. http://web.eecs.utk.edu/~mclennan/BA/AV/praefatio.html. [29]

Alexander of Telese. *The Deeds Done by King Roger of Sicily.* In Loud, *Roger II,* 77–122. [28]

Anacletus II. *Privilege to Roger II.* In Loud, *Roger II,* 304–6. [27]

Annali delle Due Sicilie dall'origine e fondazione della monarchia fino a tutto il regno dell'augusto sovrano Carlo III Borbone. 2 vols. Matteo Camera, ed. Naples: Fibreno, 1841–60, 2:225-26. [16, 25, 51]

Aquinas, Thomas. "Treatise on Law," *Summa Theologiae* II.90.4. Trans. David Burr and used on *The Medieval Sourcebook.* Fordham University www.fordham.edu/halsall/source/aquinas2.asp. [44]

Benjamin of Tudela. *The Itinerary: Critical Text, Translation and Commentary.* Marcus Nathan Adler, ed. New York: Philipp Feldheim, 1907; rev. ed. Michael A. Signer. Malibu, CA: Joseph Simon Publishers, 1983, 64–66. [33]

Boccaccio, Giovanni. *The Decameron.* Frances Winwar, trans. New York: Modern Library, 1955. [73]

—. *De montibus, silvis, de fontibus, lacubus et fluminibus.* Basel: Apud Io.

Hervagium, 1532, 426. http://www.uni-mannheim.de/mateo/itali/boccaccio1/jpg/s426.html. Accessed 12/1/2012. [78]

—. *Life of Giovanna I.* In *Concerning Famous Women.* Guido A. Guarino trans. New Brunswick: Rutgers University Press, 1963; rev. ed. as *On Famous Women.* New York: Italica Press, 2011, 248–50. [81]

—. also in Giovanni Boccaccio. *Famous Women.* Virginia Brown, ed. and trans. The I Tatti Renaissance Library 1. Cambrdige, MA: Harvard Univcersity Press, 2001, 466–75.

—. Neapolitan Letter, 1339. In Francesco Sabatini, "Prospettive sul parlato nella storia linguistica italiana (con una lettera dell' Epistola napoletana)." In *Italia linguistica delle origini: Saggi editi dal 1956 al 1996.* Francesco Sabatini and Vittorio Coletti, eds. Lecce: Argo, 1996, 2: 425–66; *Testi Napoletani dei secoli XIII e XIV.* Antonio Altamura, ed. Naples: Libreria Perrella, 1949, 143–45. [62]

The Book of Pontiffs (Liber Pontificalis): The Ancient Biographies of the First Ninety Roman Bishops to AD 715. Raymond David, ed., rev. 3rd ed. Liverpool: Liverpool University Press, 2010. [3, 8, 12]

—. *Lives of the Eighth-Century Popes.* Raymond David, ed. Liverpool: Liverpool University Press, 1992. [15]

—. *Lives of the Ninth-Century Popes.* Raymond David, ed. Liverpool: Liverpool University Press, 1995. [19]

Cassiodorus. *The Letters of Cassiodorus: Being a Condensed Translation of the* Variae Epistolae *of Magnus Aurelius Cassiodorus Senator.* Thomas Hodgkin, trans. London: H. Frowde, 1886; repr. 2006. [4, 6]

Cronaca di Partenope. Antonio Altamura, ed. Naples: Società Editrice Napoletana, 1974. [48, 54, 58, 60, 66, 67, 71, 74, 79, 82]

—. *The Cronaca di Partenope: An Introduction to and Critical Edition of the First Vernacular History of Naples (c.1350).* Samantha Kelly, ed. Leiden: Brill, 2011. [48, 66]

Chronicle of Morea. In *Crusaders as Conquerors: The Chronicle of Morea.* Harold E. Lurier, ed. and trans. New York: Columbia University Press, 1964, 191–94. [45]

Chronicon Siculum incerti authoris de rebus siculis. Giuseppe de Blasiis, ed. Naples: F. Giannini & fil., 1887. [59]

Commercial insurance contracts, 1261. In *Medieval Trade in the Mediterranean World: Illustrative Documents.* Robert S. Lopez and Irving W. Raymond, eds. New York: Columbia University Press, 1967, 257–58. [41]

Conrad of Querfurt. Letter to Hartbert, prior of Hildesheim. In Arnold of Lübeck, *Chronica Slavorum.* I.M. Lappenberg, ed. In *Scriptores Rerum*

Germanicarum 14. Hannover: Hahn, 1868, 174–83. [37]

Eugippius. *Memorandum [Life] of St. Severinus*. From http://www.tertullian. org/fathers/severinus_02_text.htm. Accessed 11/30/2012. [2, 5]

Florio e Biancofiore. In Antonio Altamura, "Un' ignota redazione del cantaro di Florio e Biancofiore (contribuito all storia del Filocolo)." *Biblion* 1 (1946–47): 92–133. [31]

Frederick II. *Licterae Generales*. Mario Spagnuolo, trans. *Medieval Sourcebook*. Fordham University. http://www.fordham.edu/halsall/ source/1224fred2-lictgen.asp. [39]

Giacomo da Lentini. *Sonnets*. In Dante Gabriel Rosetti, *The Early Italian Poets: From Ciullo D'Alcamo to Dante Alighieri (1100–1300)*. London: Smith, Elder and Co., 1861. Online at http://www.rossettiarchive.org/ docs/1-1861.yale.rad.html. [40]

Giovanna I. Letter on the murder of her husband, Andrew of Hungary, September 21, 1345. In SN 3:238. [75]

—. Letter to King Charles V of France, 1364/67. Niccolò d'Alife archive in the Biblioteca della Società Napoletana di Storia Patria, MS XXX C 2 bis, fol. 115. Edited by Paola Vitolo in *La chiesa della regina: L'Incoronata di Napoli, Giovanni I d'Angiò e Roberto di Oderisio*. Rome: Viella, 2008, 112–14. [80]

— Licence to Maria Incarnata to practice medicine. Monica H. Green, trans. In *Medieval Italy: Texts in Translation*. Katherine L. Jansen, Joanna Drell and Frances Andrews, eds. Philadelphia: University of Pensylvania Press, 2009, 324–25. [68]

Gravina, Domenico da. *Chronicon de rebus in Apulia gestis ab anno 1333 ad annum 1350*. A. Sorbelli, ed. RIS 12. Città di Castello: RIS, 1903. [76]

Gregory the Great, Letters. In *Nicene and Post-Nicene Fathers*. 2nd ser. 12– 13. Philip Schaff and Henry Wace, eds. James Barmby, trans. Buffalo, NY: Christian Literature Publishing, 1895. Selections on the website of Greek Orthodox Christian Church of Greater Omaha Nebraska at http://www.synaxis.org/cf/volume35; and http://www.synaxis.org/cf/ volume36. Accessed 10/30/12. [11]

John the Deacon. *Vita S. Athanasii in the Chronicon Episcoporum S. Neapolitanae Ecclesiae*. Bartolomeo Capasso, ed. *Monumenta ad neapolitani ducatus historiam pertinentia* 1. Naples: Francesco Giannini, 1881, reprint Salerno: Carlone, 2008, 213–20. [20]

Jordanes. *Getica sive De origine actibusque Gothorum (The Origin and Deeds of the Goths)*. Charles C. Mierow, trans. Princeton: Princeton University Press, 1908. Curated online by J. Vanderspoel at http://

www.harbornet.com/folks/theedrich/Goths/Goths1.htm. Accessed 12/16.12. [1]

Monumenta ad neapolitani ducatus historiam pertinentia. Bartolomeo Capasso, ed. Naples: Francesco Giannini, 1881; repr., Salerno: Carlone, 2008. [23]

Notitia quaedam de Johanne et Marino ducibus, et de Theodora Iohannis ipsius uxore (Ex Perzii Archiv, etc. t. IX, p. 692). In Capasso, *Monumenta,* app. I:339-40. [21]

Orsini, Giovanni, archbishop of Naples. "Cum in hac nostra Neapolitana ecclesia certi ritus modi et consuetudines ab antiquo fuerint et debeant observari." In Thomas Forest Kelly, *The Exultet in Southern Italy.* New York: Oxford University Press, 1996, 140-41. [30]

Pactum Sicardi. From Lopez and Raymond, 33-35. Trans. from Guido Padelletti, *Fontes iuris italici medii aevi.* Turin: E. Loescher, 1877, 318-24. [18]

Paul the Deacon. *History of the Langobards (Historia Langobardorum).* William Dudley Foulke, trans. Philadelphia: University of Pennsylvania Press, 1907, 31-32. [2, 13, 14]

Pegolotti, Francesco Balducci. *La pratica della mercatura.* Allan Evans, ed. Cambridge: Mediaeval Academy of America, 1936. [61]

Peter Damian, *De Iohanne III Neapoli duce et Pandulpho principe in infernum damnatis, ex S. Petri Damiani Opuscolis,* XIX, c. 9 et 10. In Capasso, *Monumenta,* app. I:346-47. [24]

Peter of Eboli. *De balneis Puteolanis.* In Erasmo Pèrcopo, *I bagni di Pozzuoli.* Naples: F. Furchheim, 1887. [36]

Petrarch, Francesco. *Itinerarium ad sepulchrum domini nostri Yeshu Christi.* Trans. by Theodore J. Cachey, Jr. as *Petrarch's Guide to the Holy Land.* Notre Dame: University of Notre Dame Press, 2002. [63]

—. *Letters on Familiar Matters.* Aldo S. Bernardo, trans. Albany: State University of New York Press, 1975; repr. New York: Italica Press, 2005. [69, 70, 72]

Pietro della Vigna. *Canzone amore, in cui disio ed ho speranza.* From *Lyrics of the Middle Ages: An Anthology.* James J. Wilhelm, ed. New York: Garland Publishing, 1990, 130. [40]

Procopius. *History of the Wars.* 3, Books V–VI.15. H.B. Dewing, trans., Loeb Classical Library. Cambridge: Harvard University Press, 1919. [7, 9, 10]

Pseudo-Callisthenes. *The Greek Romance of Alexander.* Richard Stoneman, trans. London: Penguin Books, 1991, 119–21. [22]

Ratio thesauriarum of Robert of Anjou. In Camera, *Annali,* 2:507. [55]

Rinaldo d'Aquino. Complaint against the Crusade. From *The Crusades:*

A Reader. S.J. Allen and Emilie Amt, eds. Peterborough: Broadview Press, 2003. [40]

Robert of Anjou. Edict on youth fashion, January 15, 1335. In Camara, *Annali* 2:411–12. [57]

—. Last Will and Testament, January 16, 1343. In Johann Christian Lünig, *Codex Italiae diplomaticus.* Frankfurt: Lanckisianorum, 1725–35, 2:LXXXII, cols. 1101–10. [65]

—. Sermons. In Darlen Pyrds, "The Politics of Preaching in Fourteenth-Century Naples: Robert d'Anjou (1309–1343) and His Sermons." Ph.D. diss., University of Wisconsin-Madison, 1994. [52]

Ryccardi di Sancto Germano Notarii. *Chronicon.* C.A. Garufi, ed. 2nd. ed. Bologna: RIS, 1938, 3–25; G.A. Loud, trans. *The Chronicle of Richard of S. Germano,* 1189–1207. [35]

Sancia of Naples (Majorca). Letter to the Chapter General of Assisi, July 25, 1334. In Ronald G. Musto, "Queen Sancia of Naples (1286–1345) and the Spiritual Franciscans." In *Women of the Medieval World.* Julius Kirshner and Suzanne F. Wemple, eds. Oxford: Basil Blackwell, 1985, 207–14. [56]

Sephronous. *Metrical Life of St. Mary of Egypt.* Trans. by Paul the Deacon. PL 73:671–90. Also available at http://www.fordham.edu/halsall/basis/maryegypt.html. Accessed 11/30/2012. [17]

Sergius VII. *Pactum* or *Promissio.* In Capasso, *Monumenta,* 2.2:157–58. [26]

The Song of Aspremont: Chanson d'Aspremont. Michael A. Newth, trans. and ed. New York: Garland, 1989, ll. 10890–11003, pp. 258–60. [34]

Villani, Giovanni. *Selections from The First Nine Books of the Croniche Fiorentine.* Rose E. Selfe, trans. Philip H. Wicksteed, ed. London: Archibald Constable, 1906. [38, 42, 43, 46, 49, 50]

—. *Nuova cronica.* Giuseppe Porta, ed. Parma: Guanda, 1990. [77]

Villani, Matteo. *Cronica.* In Matteo Villani and Filippo Villani, *Cronica.* Giuseppe Porta, ed. Milan: Fondazione Pietro Bembo, 1995. [77]

—. Tax revenue agreement. In Lopez and Raymond, 102–3. [53]

—. Tax revenue agreement. In William Edward Lunt, *Papal Revenues in the Middle Ages.* New York: Columbia University Press, 1934, 1:316–17, translating the original Latin from Göller, *Die Einnahmen der apostolischen Kammer unter Benedikt XII,* 179, 186. [64]

OTHER PRIMARY SOURCES CITED

Adam de la Halle. *Oeuvres complètes du trouvère Adam de la Halle (poésies et musique).* Charles Edmond Henri de Coussemaker, ed. Paris: Durand & Pédone-Lauriel, 1872.

ALIM: Archivio della latinità italiana del medioevo. Rome: Unione Accademica Nazionale, 1996–. (http://www.uan.it/notarili/alimnot. nsf).

Benedict of St. Peter's. *The Marvels of Rome (Mirabilia Urbis Romae)*. Francis Morgan Nichols, ed.; rev. ed., Eileen Gardiner. New York: Italica Press, 1986.

Boccaccio, Giovanni. *Amorosa Visione*. Vittore Branca, ed. Florence: G.C. Sansoni, 1944. English trans. Robert Hollander, Timothy Hampton, and Margherita Frankel. *Amorosa Visione*. Hanover, NH: University Press of New England, 1986.

—. *Elegia di Madonna Fiammetta*. In *Tutte le opere* 5.2. Carlo Delcorno, ed. Milan: A. Mondadori, 1994. English trans. Mariangela Causa-Steindler and Thomas Mauch. *The Elegy of Lady Fiammetta*. Chicago: University of Chicago Press, 1990.

Bowen, Marjorie. *The Sword Decides: A Chronicle of a Queen in the Dark Ages, Founded on the Story of Giovanna of Naples*. New York: McClure, 1908.

Cerasoli, F. "Clemente VI e Giovanna I di Napoli: Documenti inediti dell'Archivio Vaticano (1343–1352)." ASPN 21–22 (1896–97) 21:3–41, 227–64, 427–75, 667–707; 22:3–46.

Cologny, Fondation Martin Bodmer, Cod. Bodmer 135 at http://www.e-codices.unifr.ch/en/list/one/cb/0135.

Dean, Trevor, trans. and ed. *The Towns of Italy in the Later Middle Ages: Selected Sources Translated and Annotated*. Manchester: Manchester University Press, 2000.

Dumas, Alexandre. *Joan of Naples. Celebrated Crimes*. First published 1843, English trans. 1910, Etext #2750, David Widger, ed. Oxford, MS: Project Gutenberg, 2001 at http://www.gutenberg.org/files/2760/2760-pdf.pdf at dccclxviii. Accessed 11/8/12.

Ferrante, Joan M., trans. *Guillaume d'Orange: Four Twelfth-Century Epics*. New York: Columbia University Press, 1974.

Gregorius, Magister. *The Marvels of Rome*. John Osborne, ed. and trans. Toronto: Pontifical Institute of Mediaeval Studies, 1987.

Gregory the Great, *Letters*. In John R.C. Martyn, ed. *The Letters of Gregory the Great*. Toronto: Pontifical Institute of Mediaeval Studies, 2004.

Justinian I. *The Institutes of Justinian*. J.B. Moyle, trans. 5th ed. Oxford: Clarendon Press, 1913.

—, and Fred H. Blume. *Annotated Justinian Code*. Timothy Kearley, ed. http://uwacadweb.uwyo.edu/blume%26justinian. Accessed 11/11/12.

Newth, Michael A.H., trans. *Fierabras and Floripas: A French Epic Allegory.* New York: Italica Press, 2010.

Petrarch, Francesco. *Petrarch's Africa.* Thomas Goddard Bergin and Alice S. Wilson, trans. and ed. New Haven: Yale University Press, 1977.

Radcliffe, Ann. *The Italian, or the Confessional* [1797]. Robert Miles, ed. New York: Penguin Books, 2000.

Staël, Anne-Louise-Germanine, Madame de. *Corinnne, or Italy* [1807]. Sylvia Raphael, trans. New York: Oxford University Press, 1998.

Vuolo, Antonio, ed. *"Vita" et "Translatio" S. Athanasii Neapolitani episcopi. BHL 735, 737, Sec. IX.* Rome: Istituto Storico Italiano per il Medio Evo, 2001.

Walpole, Horace. *The Castle of Otranto* [1764]. E.F. Bleiler, ed. New York: Dover Books, 1966.

Webster, John. *The Duchess of Malfi* [1612/13]. In D.C. Gunby, ed. *The Works of John Webster* 1. Cambridge: Cambridge University Press, 2007, 379–713.

Ziolkowski Jan M., and Michael C.J. Putnam, eds. *The Virgilian Tradition: The First Fifteen Hundred Years.* New Haven: Yale University Press, 2008.

SECONDARY WORKS

GENERAL AND MULTIPERIOD

Akbari, Suzanne Conklin. *Idols in the East: European Representations of Islam and the Orient, 1100–1450.* Ithaca: Cornell University Press, 2009.

Bacco, Enrico, C. d'Engenio Caracciolo, Eileen Gardiner, Caroline A. Bruzelius, and Ronald G. Musto. *Naples: An Early Guide.* New York: Italica Press, 1991.

Benjamin, Walter. "Naples." In *Reflections: Essays, Aphorisms, Autobiographical Writings.* Peter Demetz, ed. New York: Harcourt Brace Jovanovich, 1978, 163–73.

Bologna, Ferdinando. "Momenti della cultura figurata nella Campania medievale." In Carratelli, 171–275.

Braudel, Fernand. *The Mediterranean and the Mediterranean World in the Age of Philip II.* Siân Reynold, trans. 2 vols. New York: Harper & Row, 1972–73.

Bruzelius, Caroline, and William Tronzo. *Medieval Naples: An Architectural & Urban History, 400–1400.* New York: Italica Press, 2011.

Capasso, Bartolommeo. *Topografia della città di Napoli nell'XI secolo.* Naples: Arte Tipografica di A.R. San Biagio dei Librai, 1895; reprint Naples: Arnaldo Forni Editore, 2005.

Carratelli, Giovanni Pugliese, ed. *Storia e civiltà della Campania: Il medioevo*. Naples: Electa, 1992.

Cavallo, Guglielmo. "La cultura greca: Itinerari e segni." In Carratelli, 277–92.

Comparetti, Domenico, E.F.M Benecke, and Jan M. Ziolkowski. *Vergil in the Middle Ages*. Princeton: Princeton University Press, 1997.

Davis, John A. "Casting off the 'Southern Problem': Or the Peculiarities of the South Reconsidered." In Schneider, 205–24.

—. "The South, the Risorgimento, and the Origins of the 'Southern Problem'." In *Gramsci and Italy's Passive Revolution*. John A. Davis, ed. London: Croom Helm, 1979.

Davis-Weyer, Caecilia. *Early Medieval Art, 300–1150: Sources and Documents*. Toronto: University of Toronto Press in association with the Medieval Academy of America, 1986.

De Leo, Pietro. *Mezzogiorno medioevale: Istituzioni, società, mentalità*. Soveria: Rubbettino, 1984.

Del Treppo, Mario. *Storiografia nel Mezzogiorno*. Naples: Guida, 2006.

De Seta, Cesare. *Cartografia della città di Napoli: Lineamenti dell'evoluzione urbana*. Naples: Edizioni scientifiche italiane, 1969.

—. *Storia della città di Napoli dalle origini al settecento*. Rome: Laterza, 1973.

—. *Napoli fra Rinascimento e Illuminismo: Storia della città*. Naples: Electa Napoli, 1997.

—. *Napoli (Le città nella storia d'Italia)*. Rome: Laterza, 2004.

Di Mauro, Leonardo. *La Tavola Strozzi*. Le bussole 1. Naples: E. De Rosa, 1992.

Di Stefano, Roberto, and Silvana Di Stefano. *La cattedrale di Napoli: Storia, restauro, scoperte, ritrovamenti*. Naples: Edizione Scientifica, 1975.

Esch, Arnold. "Spolien: Zur Wiederverwendung antiker Baustücke und Skulpturen im mittelalterlichen Italien." *Archiv für Kulturgeschichte* 51 (1969): 1–64.

Favro, Diane. "Naples." In *The Dictionary of Art*. Jane Turner, ed. 34 vols. New York: Grove, 1996, 22:469–87.

Ferraro, Italo, ed. *Napoli: Atlante della città storica*. 6 vols. to date. Naples: CLEAN, Oikos, 2000–.

Filangieri, Riccardo. "Report on the Destruction by the Germans, September 30, 1943, of the Depository of Priceless Historical Records of the Naples State Archives." *American Archivist* (1944): 252–55.

—, Stefano Palmieri, Maria L. Storch, et al. *I registri della cancelleria angioina*. Naples: Accademia Pontaniana, 1950–.

Frugoni, Chiara. *A Distant City: Images of Urban Experience in the Medieval World.* Princeton: Princeton University Press, 1991.

Galasso, Giuseppe. *Medioevo Euro-Mediterraneo e Mezzogiorno d'Italia: Da Giustiniano a Federico II.* Rome: Laterza, 2009.

—. *Napoli capitale: Identità politica e identità cittadina. Studi e ricerche 1266–1860.* Naples: Electa, 1998.

—. *Storia del regno di Napoli.* Turin: UTET, 2006.

Giampaola, Daniela, Vittoria Carsana, and Beatrice Roncella, eds. *Napoli, la città e il mare. Piazza Bovio: Tra Romani e Bizantini.* Milan: Electa, 2010.

Gregorovius, Ferdinand. *History of the City of Rome in the Middle Ages.* Annie Hamilton, trans. 8 vols. in 13. London: George Bell & Sons, 1909–12; new edition, with intro. by David S. Chambers, New York: Italica Press, 2000–2004.

Grierson, Philip, Mark A.S. Blackburn, Lucia Travaini, Fitzwilliam Museum. *Medieval European Coinage: With a Catalogue of the Coins in the Fitzwilliam Museum,* Cambridge. Cambridge: Cambridge University Press, 1998, 3. Italy, 406–29.

Guillon, André, ed. *Il Mezzogiorno dai Bizantini a Federico II.* Turin: UTET, 1983.

Horden, Peregrine, and Nicholas Purcell. *The Corrupting Sea: A Study of Mediterranean History.* Oxford: Blackwell, 2000.

Hyde, John K. *Society and Politics in Medieval Italy: The Evolution of the Civil Life, 1000–1350.* New York: St. Martin's Press, 1973.

La Rocca, Cristina. *Italy in the Early Middle Ages 476–1000.* Oxford: Oxford University Press, 2002.

Larner, John. *Italy in the Age of Dante and Petrarch, 1216–1380.* Longman History of Italy 2. New York: Longman, 1980.

Lewis, Norman. *Naples '44.* New York: Pantheon, 1978.

Little, Lester K. "Review Article: Plague Historians in Lab Coats." *Past & Present* 213 (Nov. 2012): 267–90.

Lucherini, Vinni. *La cattedrale di Napoli: Storia, architettura, storiografia di un monumento medievale.* Rome: École Française de Rome, 2009.

—. "Saggi: L'invenzione di una tradizione storiografica: Le due cattedrali di Napoli." *Prospettiva* (2004): 2.

Lumley, Robert, and Jonathan Morris, eds. *The New History of the Italian South: The Mezzogiorno Revisited.* Exeter: University of Exeter Press, 1997.

Martin, Jean-Marie. "Les bains dans l'Italie méridionale au Moyen Âge (VIIe–XIIIe siècle)," In *Bains curatifs et bains hygeniques en Italie de l'Antiquité au Moyen Âge.* Marie Guérin-Beauvois and Jean-Marie

Martin, eds. Collection de École Française de Rome 383. Rome: École Française de Rome, 2007, 53–78.

Mazzoleni, I(J)ole. *Le fonti documentarie e bibliografiche dal secolo x al secolo xx conservate presso l'Archivio di Stato di Napoli.* Naples: ASN, 1974, 31–52.

—. *I registri della cancelleria angioina, ricostruiti da Riccardo Filangieri 4 (1266–1270).* Naples: Accademia Pontaniana, 1952.

Metcalfe, Alex. *The Muslims of Medieval Italy.* Edinburgh: Edinburgh University Press, 2009.

Moe, Nelson. *The View from Vesuvius: Italian Culture and the Southern Question.* Studies in the History of Society and Culture 46. Berkeley: University of California Press, 2002.

Mundy John H., and Peter Riesenberg. *The Medieval Town.* New York: Van Nostrand, 1958.

Musto, Ronald G. "Google Books Mutilates the Printed Past." The Chronicle Review. *The Chronicle of Higher Education.* June 12, 2009, B4–5.

—. "Naples: Art Life and Organization." In *Encyclopedia of Italian Renaissance and Mannerist Art.* Jane Turner, ed. 2 vols. New York: Macmillan–Grove, 2000, 2:1130–31.

Napoli, Mario. "La città." SN 2.2 (1969): "La cinta urbana," 739–52.

Nicholas, David. *Urban Europe, 1100–1700.* New York: Palgrave Macmillan, 2003.

Oldoni, Massimo. "La cultura latina." In Carratelli, 295–400.

Peduto, P. "Archeologia medievale in Campania." *La voce della Campania: Cultura materiale, arti e territorio in Campania* 7.10 (1979): 247–62.

Pohl, Walter. "Introduction: Ego Trouble?" In *Ego Trouble: Authors and Their Identities in the Early Middle Ages.* Richard Corradini et al., eds. Vienna: Verlag der Österreichischen Akademie der Wissenschaften, 2010.

Romano, Serena. *Le chiese di San Lorenzo e San Domenico: Gli ordini mendicanti a Napoli.* Naples: Electa, 2005.

—, and Nicolas Bock, eds. *Il duomo di Napoli dal paleocristiano all'età angioina.* Naples: Electa, 2002.

Rörig, Fritz. *The Medieval Town.* Berkeley: University of California Press, 1967.

Russell, Josiah. *Medieval Regions and Their Cities.* Bloomington: Indiana University Press, 1972.

Santore, John. *Modern Naples: A Documentary History, 1799–1999.* New York: Italica Press, 2001.

Santoro, Lucio. *Le mura di Napoli*. Rome: Istituto italiano dei castelli, 1984.

Schneider, Jane. *Italy's "Southern Question": Orientalism in One Country*. Berkeley: University of California Press, 1998.

Spargo, John W. *Virgil the Necromancer: Studies in Virgilian Legends*. Cambridge: Harvard University Press, 1934.

Storia di Napoli. 11 vols. Ernesto Pontieri, ed. Naples: Società Editrice Storia di Napoli, 1967–78.

Tabacco, Giovanni. *The Struggle for Power in Medieval Italy: Structures of Political Rule*. Cambridge: Cambridge University Press, 1989.

Takayama, Hiroshi. "Law and Monarchy in the South." In *Italy in the Central Middle Ages, 1000–1300*. David Abulafia, ed. The Short Oxford History of Italy. Oxford: Oxford University Press, 2010, 58–81.

Taylor, Julie. "Muslim–Christian Relations in Medieval Southern Italy." *The Muslim World* 97.2 (2007): 190–99.

—. *Muslims in Medieval Italy: The Colony at Lucera*. Lanham, MD: Lexington Books, 2005.

Tolan, John V. *Saracens: Islam in the Medieval European Imagination*. New York: Columbia University Press, 2002.

Tramontana, Salvatore. *Il Mezzogiorno medievale: Normanni, Svevi, Angioini, Aragonesi nei secoli XI–XV*. Rome: Carocci, 2000.

Waley, Daniel. *The Italian City Republics*. 4th ed., with Trevor Dean. Harlow: Longman, 2010.

Wickham, Chris. *Early Medieval Italy: Central Power and Local Society 400–1000*. Ann Arbor: University of Michigan Press, 1989.

—. *The Inheritance of Rome: A History of Europe from 400 to 1000*. New York: Viking, 2009.

Wray, Shona Kelly, and Roisin Cossar. "Wills as Primary Sources." In *Understanding Medieval Primary Sources*. Joel T. Rosenthal, ed. New York: Routledge, 2012, 59–71.

LATE ANTIQUITY

Achelis, Hans. *Die Katakomben von Neapel*. Leipzig: n.p., 1935–36.

Arthur, Paul. *Naples: From Roman Town to City-State. An Archaeological Perspective*. Archaeological Monographs of the British School at Rome 12. London: British School at Rome, with the Dipartimento di Beni Culturali, Università degli Studi di Lecce, 2002.

Azzara, Claudio. "Ecclesiastical Institutions." In La Rocca, 85–101.

Borrelli, Gennaro. *La basilica di S. Giovanni Maggiore.* Naples: Officine Grafiche "Glaux," 1967.

Brun, Jean-Pierre and Priscilla Munzi. "La città di Cuma tra Tardoantichità e Altomedioevo: Le ricerche del Centre Jean Bérard." In Amedeo Feniello, ed. *Napoli nel Medioevo 2: Territorio e isole.* Galatina: Congedo, 2009, 1-34.

Cameron, Averil. *Procopius and the Sixth Century.* Berkeley: University of California Press, 1985.

Capasso, Bartolommeo. *Napoli greco–romana.* Naples: Arte Tipografica di A.R. San Biagio dei Librai, 1905; repr. Naples: Arturo Berisio Editore, 1978.

Cortese, Nino. *Cultura e politica à Napoli del cinque al settecento.* L'Acropoli 14. Naples: Edizioni scientifiche italiane, 1965.

Cavalieri Manasse, Giuliana, and Henner von Hesberg. "Dalle decorazioni architettoniche ai monumenti romani." In *Napoli: La città e il mare,* 27–50.

Christie, Neil. *The Lombards: The Ancient Longobards.* Oxford: Blackwell, 1995.

D'Arms, John H. *Romans on the Bay of Naples: A Social and Cultural Study of the Villas and Their Owners from 150 B.C. to A.D. 400.* Loeb Classical Monographs. Cambridge: Harvard University Press, 1970.

Döpp, Wolfram. *Die Altstadt Neapels: Entwicklung und Struktur.* Marburg: Geographisches Institut, 1968.

Duckett, Eleanor Shipley. *Gateway to the Middle Ages: Italy.* Ann Arbor: University of Michigan Press, 1961.

Etherington, Norman. "Barbarians Ancient and Modern." *American Historical Review* 116.1 (Feb. 2011): 31–57.

Evans, J.A.S. *Procopius.* New York: Twayne, 1972.

Fasola, Umberto M. *Le catacombe di S. Gennaro a Capodimonte.* Rome: Editalia, 1975.

Fiaccadori, Gianfranco. "Il Cristianesimo: Dalle origini alle invasioni barbariche." In Carratelli, 145–70.

Francovich, Riccardo. "Changing Structures of Settlements." In La Rocca, 144–67.

Fuiano, Michele. *La cultura a Napoli nell'alto medioevo.* Naples: Giannini, 1961.

Galasso, Giuseppe. "La città campane nell'alto medioevo." In *Mezzogiorno medievale e moderno.* Giuseppe Galasso, ed. Turin: Einaudi 1965.

Gelichi, Sauro. "The Cities." In La Rocca, 168–88.

Gentile, Mariella. "La fortificazione bizantina." In Giampaola, *Napoli: La città e il mare*, 51–56.

Giampaola, Daniela. "Il paesaggio costiero di Neapolis tra Greci e Bizantini." In Giampaola, *Napoli: La città e il mare*, 17–26.

—. "Introduzione allo scavo e alla mostra." In *Napoli: La città e il mare*, 11–16.

—, Vittoria Carsana, and Beatrice Roncella, eds. *Napoli: La città e il mare. Piazza Bovio: Tra Romani e Bizantini*. Naples: Electa, 2010.

Gillett, Andrew. Review of recent historiography on the Migrations/ Barbarian Invasions. In *The Medieval Review* 07.10.12 (https:// scholarworks.iu.edu/dspace/bitstream/handle/2022/6332/07.10.12. html).

Goffart, Walter. Review of Peter Heather, *Empires and Barbarians: The Fall of Rome and the Birth of Europe* (New York: Oxford University Press, 2010) in *The Medieval Review* 10.08.06 (https://scholarworks. iu.edu/dspace/bitstream/handle/ 2022/9050/10.08.06.html).

Greco, Emanuele. "L'Urbanistica." In *Neapolis: Atti del XXV Convegno di Studi sulla Magna Grecia 1985*. Taranto: n.p., 1986, 187–302.

Heather, Peter. *Empires and Barbarians: The Fall of Rome and the Birth of Europe*. New York: Oxford University Press, 2010.

Kaldellis, Anthony. *Procopius of Caesarea: Tyranny, History, and Philosophy at the End of Antiquity*. Philadelphia: University of Pennsylvania Press, 2004.

Little, Lester K., ed. *Plague and the End of Antiquity: The Pandemic of 541–750*. New York: Cambridge University Press, 2007.

Maier, Jean L. *Le Baptistère de Naples et ses mosaïques: Étude historique et iconographique*. Fribourg: Éditions universitaires, 1964.

Mathisen, Ralph W., and Danuta Shanzer. "Introduction." In *Romans, Barbarians, and the Transformation of the Roman World: Cultural Interaction and the Creation of Identity in Late Antiquity*. Farnham, Surrey: Ashgate, 2011, 1–11.

Ministero per i Beni e le Attività Culturali. Soprintendenza Archeologica di Roma. *Museo Nazionale Romano: Crypta Balbi*. Rome: Electa, 2000.

Napoli, Mario. "Topografia e archeologia." SN 1:373–508.

O'Donnell, James J. *Cassiodorus*. Berkeley: University of California Press, 1979.

Pohl, Walter. "Invasions and Ethnic Identity." In La Rocca, 11–33.

Reece, Richard. "Coins and the Late Roman Economy." In *Theory and Practice in Late Antique Archaeology*. Luke Lavan and William Bowden, eds. Leiden: Brill, 2003, 139–70.

Sogliani, Francesca. "I metalli: Testimonianze dell'officina tardoantica e altomedievale." In Giampaola, *Napoli: La città e il mare*, 87–89.

Vitolo, Giovanni. *Le città campane fra tarda antichità e alto medioevo*. Salerno: Laveglia, 2005.

von Falkenhausen, Vera. "La Campania tra Goti e Bizantini." In Carratelli, 7–35.

Wickham, Chris. "Rural Economy and Society." In La Rocca, 118–43.

THE DUCAL PERIOD

Berto, Luigi Andrea. "*Utilius est veritatem proferre*. A Difficult Memory to Manage: Narrating the Relationships between Bishops and Dukes in Early Medieval Naples." *Viator* 39.2 (2008): 49–63.

Capasso, Bartolomeo. *Topografia della città di Napoli nell' XI secolo*. Naples: Giannini, 1895; repr., Bologna: Arnaldo Forni, 2005.

Carsana, Vittoria, and Valeria d'Amico. "Piazza Bovio: Produzioni e consumi in età bizantina. La ceramica dalla metà del VI al X secolo." In Giampaola, *Napoli: La città e il mare*, 69–80.

Cassandro, Giovanni. "Il ducato bizantino." In SN 2.1:1–408.

—. "La 'promissio' del duca Sergio e la 'societas napoletana'." *Archivio Storico Italiano* 1.3–4 (1942): 135ff.

Cavallo, Guglielmo. "La cultura greca: Itinerari e segni." In Carratelli, 277–92.

Cilento, Nicola. "La chiesa di Napoli nell'alto medioevo." SN 2.2:641–736.

—. *Civiltà napoletana del medioevo nel secolo VI–XII*. Naples: Edizioni scientifiche italiane, 1969.

Colletta, T. *Napoli città portuale e mercantile: La città bassa, il porto e il mercato dall'VIII al XVII secolo*. Rome: Kappa, 2006.

D'Angelo, Edoardo. "Petrus Neapolitanus Subdiac." In Paolo Chiesa and Lucia Castaldi, eds. *La trasmissione dei testi Latini del Medioevo. Medieval Latin Texts and Their Transmisson*. TE.TRA. 1 (Florence: SISMEL, 2004), 349–63.

Del Treppo, Mario. "La marina napoletana nel medioevo: Porti, navi, equipaggi." In *La fabbrica delle navi: Storia della cantieristica nel Mezzogiorno d'Italia*. A. Fratta, ed. Naples: Electa, 1990.

del Vecchio, Franca. "I vetri: Il ciclo della produzione e i manufatti." In Giampaola, *Napoli: La città e il mare*, 81–85.

Febbraro, Stefania. "Il quartiere artigianale e la necropoli." In Giampaola, *Napoli: La città e il mare*, 57–61.

Feniello, Amedeo. "Contributo alla storia della 'Iunctura civitatis' (secc. X–XIII)." In *Ricerche sul medioevo napoletano: Aspetti e momenti della vita economica e sociale a Napoli tra X e XV secolo*. A. Leone, ed. Naples: Athena, 1996.

—. "Mercato della terra a Napoli nel XII secolo." In *Puer Apuliae: Mélanges offerts à Jean-Marie Martin*. E. Cuozzo, V. Déroche, A. Peters-Custot, V. Prigent, eds. Centre de Recherche d'Histoire et Civilisation de Byzance. Monographies 30. Paris: CRHCB, 2008.

—. *Napoli nel medioevo*. 2: Territorio e isole. Galatina: Congedo, 2009.

—. *Napoli: Società ed economia (902–1137)*. Rome: Istituto Storico Italiano per il Medio Evo, 2011.

Ferraro, Eleonora. "I mulini ad acqua del monastero del SS. Sergio e Bacco tra X e XIII secolo." *Schola Salernitana* 7–8 (2003): 27–38.

Figliuolo, Bruno. "Longobardi e Normanni." In Carratelli, 37–86.

Focillon, Henri. *The Year 1000*. New York: Harper & Row, 1969.

Foglia, Orsola. La basilica di S. Giovanni Maggiore. CD-ROM. Naples: Soprintendenza per i Beni Architettonici, n.d.

Frugoni, Arsenio. "La biblioteca di Giovanni III duca di Napoli (dal prologo dall'arciprete Leone al "Romanzo di Alesandro." *Annali della Scuola speciale per archivisti e bibliotecari dell'Universita di Roma* 9 (1969): 161–71.

Guillou, André, and F. Burgarella. *L'Italia bizantina: Dall'esarcato di Ravenna al tema di Sicilia*. Turin: UTET, 1988.

Hodges, Richard, and Brian Hobley. *The Rebirth of Towns in the West, AD 700–1050*. London: Council for British Archaeology, 1988.

Holmes, Catherine. "Treaties between Byzantium and the Islamic World." In *War and Peace in Ancient and Medieval History*. Philip de Souza and John France, eds. Cambridge: Cambridge University Press, 2008, 141–57.

Huddleston, Gilbert. "Pope St. Gregory I ('the Great')." *The Catholic Encyclopedia*. New York: Robert Appleton Company. *New Advent*, http://www.newadvent.org/cathen/06780a.htm. Accessed 10/30/12.

Kreutz, Barbara M. *Before the Normans: Southern Italy in the Ninth and Tenth Centuries*. Philadelphia: University of Pennsylvania Press, 1991.

Liccardo, Giovanni. *Vita quotidiana a Napoli prima del medioevo*. Naples: Edizioni Scientifiche Cuzzolin, 1999.

Markus, R.A. *Gregory the Great and His World*. Cambridge: Cambridge University Press, 1997.

Martin, Jean-Marie. "Economia naturale ed economia monetaria nell'Italia meridionale longobarda e bizantina (secoli VI–XI)." In *Storia d'Italia*.

Annali 6: *Economia naturale, economia monetaria.* Ruggiero Romano and Ugo Tucci, eds. Turin: G. Einaudi, 1983, 181–219.

—. "Les documents de Naples, Amalfi, Gaète (IXe–XIIe siècles): Ecriture, diplomatique, notariat." In *L'heritage Byzantine en Italie (VIIIe–XIIe siècle).* 1: *La frabrique documentaire.* Jean-Marie Martin, Annick Peters-Custot and Vivien Prigent, eds. Collection de L'École Française de Rome 449. Rome: École Française de Rome, 2011, 51–85.

—. "Les fortifications de Naples (Ve–XIIIe siècle)." In *Castrum* 8. *Le château et la ville: Espaces et réseaux (VIe–XIIIe siècle).* Patrice Cressier, ed. Madrid: Velásquez, 2008, 299–310.

—. "Grégoire le Grand et l'Italie." In *Histoire et culture dans l'Italie byzantine: Acquis et nouvelles recherches.* A. Jacob, J.-M. Martin and G. Noyé, eds. Collection de l'École Française de Rome 363. Rome: l'École Française de Rome, 2006, 239–78.

Moorhead, John. *Gregory the Great.* London: Routledge, 2005.

Peters-Custot, Annick. *Les Grecs de l'Italie mèridionale post-byzantine (IXe–XIVe siècle): Une acculturation en douceur.* Rome: École Française de Rome, 2009.

Roncella, Beatrice. "I magazini." In Giampaola, *Napoli: La città e il mare,* 63–68.

Rotili, Mario. *L'arte a Napoli dal VI al XIII secolo.* Rome: Unione accademica nazionale, 1978.

Rovelli, Alessia. "Coins and Trade in Early Medieval Italy." *Early Medieval Europe* 17 (2009): 45–76.

Straw, Carole Ellen. *Gregory the Great.* Berkeley: University of California Press, 1988.

Venditti, Arnaldo. "L'architettura dell'alto medioevo." SN 2.2:773–876.

THE NORMANS

Avery, Myrtilla. *The Exultet Rolls of South Italy.* 2 vols. Princeton: Princeton University Press, 1936.

Bresc, Henri and Annliese Nef, trans. and eds. *Idrîsî: La première géographie de l'Occident.* Paris: Flammarion, 1999.

Capasso, Bartolommeo. "La Vicaria vecchia." ASPN 15 (1889): 97–139, 685–749; 16 (1890): 388–433, 583–635.

Cavallo, Guglielmo, Giulia Orofino, and Oronzo Pecere, eds. *Exultet: Rotoli liturgici del medioevo meridionale.* Rome: Istituto Poligrafico e Zecca dello Stato, 1994; CD-ROM. Cassino: Università degli studi di Cassino. Ministero per i beni e le attività culturali, 1999.

D'Onofrio, Mario, and Valentino Pace. *Italia romanica: La Campania*. Milan: Jaca Book, 1981.

Fuiano, Michele. *Napoli nel medioevo (secoli XI–XIII)*. Biblioteca napoletana 8. Naples: Libreria Scientifica, 1972.

—. "Napoli normanna e sveva." SN 2.1:409–518.

Glass, Dorothy F. *Romanesque Sculpture in Campania: Patrons, Programs, and Style*. University Park: Pennsylvania State University Press, 1991.

—. "Sicily and Campania: The Twelfth Century Renaissance." *ACTA* 2 (1975): 131–46.

Haskins, Charles Homer. *The Normans in European History*. Boston: Houghton Mifflin, 1915.

Houben, Hubert. *Roger II of Sicily: A Ruler Between East and West*. Graham A. Loud and D. Milburn, trans. Cambridge: Cambridge University Press, 2002.

Jamison, E.M. "The Norman Administration of Apulia and Capua." Papers of the British School at Rome 6 (1913): 211–481.

Kelly, Thomas Forrest. *The Exultet in Southern Italy*. New York: Oxford University Press, 1996.

Kristeller, Paul Oskar. "La scuola medica di Salerno secondo ricerche e scoperte recenti." *Quaderni del Centro studi e documentazione della Scuola Medica Salernitana* 5. Salerno: Scuola Medica Salernitane 1980, 138–94.

Lavarra, C. *Mezzogiorno normanno: Potere, spazio urbano, ritualità*. Lecce: Congedo, 2005.

Loud, Graham A. *The Age of Robert Guiscard: Southern Italy and the Norman Conquest*. New York: Longman, 2000.

—. *Church and Society in the Norman Principality of Capua, 1058–1197*. Oxford: Clarendon Press, 1985.

—. *Conquerors and Churchmen in Norman Italy*. Aldershot: Ashgate, 1999.

—. "How 'Norman' Was the Norman Conquest of Southern Italy?" *Nottingham Medieval Studies* 25 (1981): 13–35.

—. *The Latin Church in Norman Italy*. Cambridge: Cambridge University Press, 2007.

—. *Montecassino and Benevento in the Middle Ages: Essays in South Italian Church History*. Aldershot: Ashgate, 2000.

—. "The Papacy and the Rulers of Southern Italy, 1058–1198." In Loud and Metcalfe, *The Society of Norman Italy*, 151–84.

—. *Roger II and the Creation of the Kingdom of Sicily*. Manchester: Manchster University Press, 2012.

—, and A. Metcalfe, eds. *The Society of Norman Italy.* The Medieval Mediterranean 38. Leiden: Brill, 2002.

Matthew, Donald. *The Norman Kingdom of Sicily.* Cambridge: Cambridge University Press, 1992.

Musca, Giosuè., ed. *Le eredità normanno-sveve nell'età angioina: Persistenze e mutamenti nel Mezzogiorno. Atti delle quindicesime giornate normanno-sveve, Bari, 22–25 ottobre 2002.* Bari: Dedalo, 2004.

Norwich, John Julius. *The Kingdom in the Sun, 1130–1194.* London: Longman, 1970.

Oldfield, Paul. *City and Community in Norman Italy.* Cambridge: Cambridge University Press, 2009.

Pasca, Maria, ed. *La Scuola Medica Salernitana: Storia, immagini, manoscritti dall'XI al XIII secolo.* Soprintendenza per I Beni Ambienti Architettonici, Artistici e Storici di Salerno e Avellino. Naples: Electa, 2005.

Predelli, Maria Bendinelli. "The Textualization of Early Italian *cantari.* In *Textual Cultures of Medieval Italy.* William Randolph Robins, ed. Toronto: University of Toronto Press, 2011, 145-66.

Shatzmiller, Joseph. "Jews, Pilgrimage, and the Christian Cult of Saints: Benjamin of Tudela and His Contemporaries." In *After Rome's Fall: Narrators and Sources of Early Medieval History.* Walter A. Goffart and Alexander C. Murray, eds. Toronto: University of Toronto Press, 1998, 337–47.

Siraisi, Nancy G. Medieval and Early Renaissance Medicine: An Introduction to Knowledge and Practice. Chicago: University of Chicago Press, 1990.

Skinner, Patricia. "The Tyrrhenian Coastal Cities under the Normans." In Loud and Metcalfe, *Society of Norman Italy,* 75–96.

Takayama, Hiroshi. *The Administration of the Norman Kingdom of Sicily.* The Medieval Mediterranean 3. Leiden: Brill, 1993.

Tronzo, William. *The Cultures of His Kingdom: Roger II and the Cappella Palatina in Palermo.* Princeton: Princeton University Press 1997.

von Falkenhausen, Vera. "The South Italian Sources." *Proceedings of the British Academy* 132 (2007): 95–121.

THE HOHENSTAUFEN

Abulafia, David. *Frederick II: A Medieval Emperor.* New York: Oxford University Press, 1988.

—. *Italy in the Central Middle Ages, 1000–1300.* Oxford: Oxford University Press, 2004.

—. "The Kingdom of Sicily under Hohenstaufen and Angevin Rule." *New Cambridge Medieval History.* Vol. 5, c.1198–c.1300. David Abulafia, ed. Cambridge: Cambridge University Press, 1999, 497–524.

Cilento, Nicola. "La cultura e gli inizi dello studio." In SN 2.1:521–640.

Hunt, Richard William, and Margaret T. Gibson. *The Schools and the Cloister: The Life and Writings of Alexander Nequam (1157–1217).* Oxford: Clarendon Press, 1984.

Kauffmann, Claus Michael. *The Baths of Pozzuoli: A Study of the Medieval Illuminations of Peter of Eboli's Poem.* Oxford: B. Cassirer, 1959.

Kintzinger, Martin. "Macht des Wissens: Die Universitäten Bologna und Neapel." In *Die Staufer und Italien: Drei Innovationsregionen im mittelalterlichen Europa.* Alfried Wieczorek, Bernd Schneidmüller and Stefan Weinfurter, eds. 2 vols. Stuttgart: Konrad Theiss Verlag, 2010, 395-402.

Napoli, Mario. "La città." SN 2.2:737–72.

Oldfield, Paul. "The Kingdom of Sicily and the Early University Movement." *Viator* 40.2 (2009): 135–50.

Pispisa, Enrico. *Il regno di Manfredi: Proposte di interpretazione.* Messina: Sicania, 1991.

Powell, James M. *The Liber Augustalis: Or, Constitutions of Melfi, Promulgated by the Emperor Frederick II for the Kingdom of Sicily in 1231.* Syracuse, NY: Syracuse University Press, 1971.

Rotili, Mario. "Arti figurativi e arti minori: Nell'età normanna e sveva." SN 2.2: 877–986.

Tronzo, William, ed. *Intellectual Life at the Court of Frederick II Hohenstaufen.* Washington, DC: National Gallery of Art, 1994.

Vitolo, Giovanni. "L'età svevo-angioina." In Carratelli, 87–144.

Zampino, Giuseppe Filomena Sardella, et al. *Le terme puteolane e Salerno nei codici miniati di Petro da Eboli.* Naples: Casa Editrice Fausto Fiorentino, 1995.

THE ANGEVINS

Abbate, Francesco. *Storia dell'arte nell'Italia meridionale: Il Sud angioino e aragonese.* Rome: Donzelli Editore, 1998.

Abulafia, David. *The Western Mediterranean Kingdoms 1200–1500: The Struggle for Dominion.* London: Longman, 1997, 57–171.

Aceto, Francesco. "'Status' e immagine nella scultura funeraria del trecento a Napoli: Le sepolture dei nobili." In Arturo Carlo Quintavalle, ed. *Medioevo: Immagini e ideologie.* Milan: Electa, 2005, 597–607.

Alabiso, Annachiara, Mario De Cunzo, Daniela Giampaola, Adele Pezzullo, eds. *Il monastero di Santa Chiara*. Naples: Electa, 1995.

Ambrasi, Domenico. "La vita religiosa." SN 3:437–574.

Asperti, Stefano. *Carlo I d'Angiò e i trovatori: Componenti "provenzali" e angioine nella tradizione manoscritta della lirica trobadorica*. Ravenna: Longo, 1995.

Bak, János M. "Queens as Scapegoats in Medieval Hungary." In *Queens and Queenship in Medieval Europe*. Anne J. Duggan, ed. Woodbridge, UK: Boydell, 1997, 223–33.

Baraz, Daniel. *Medieval Cruelty: Changing Perceptions, Antiquity to the Early Modern Period*. Conjunctions of Religion and Power in the Medieval Past. Ithaca: Cornell University Press, 2003.

Barbero, Alessandro. "Il mito angioino nella cultura italiana e provenzale fra duecento e trecento." In *Robert d'Angio fra guelfismo e umanesimo*. Biblioteca Storica Subalpina. Deputazione Subalpina di Storia Patria 201.80. Turin: Palazzo Carignano, 1983, 389–450.

Bentley, Jerry H. *Politics and Culture in Renaissance Naples*. Princeton: Princeton University Press, 1987.

Beyer, Andreas. "Napoli." In *Storia dell'architettura italiana: Il quattrocento*. Francesco Paolo Fiore, ed. Milan: Electa, 1998, 434–59.

Black, Nancy B. *Medieval Narratives of Accused Queens*. Gainesville: University Press of Florida, 2003.

Blamires, Alcuin. *The Case for Women in Medieval Culture*. Oxford: Clarendon Press, 1997.

—. *Woman Defamed and Woman Defended: An Anthology of Medieval Texts*. Oxford: Clarendon Press, 1992.

Bologna, Ferdinando. *I pittori alla corte angioina di Napoli, 1266–1414, e un riesame dell'arte nell'età fridericiana*. Saggi e studi di storia dell'arte 2. Rome: Ugo Bozzi, 1969.

Bonnot, Isabelle, ed. *Marseille et ses rois de Naples: La diagonale angevine, 1265–1382*. Marseille: Archives municipales, EdSud, 1988.

Borghese, Gian Luca. *Carlo I d'Angiò e il Mediterraneo: Politica, diplomazia e commercio internazionale prima dei Vespri*. Rome: Ecole Française de Rome, 2008.

Boyer, Jean-Paul. "La prédication de Robert de Sicile (1306–1343) et les communes d'Italie: Le cas de Gênes." In *Prêcher la paix et discipliner la société: Italie, France, Angleterre (XIIIe–XVe siècle)*. Rosa Maria Dessi, ed. Turnhout: Brepols, 2005, 383–411.

Bräm, Andreas. *Neapolitanische Bilderbibeln des Trecento: Anjou-Buchmalerei von Robert dem Weisen bis zu Johanna I*. 1: *Bilderbibeln,*

Buchmaler und Auftraggebar; 2: *Abbildungen.* Wiesbaden: Reichert, 2007.

Brown, Elizabeth A.R. "Moral Imperatives and Conundrums of Conscience: Reflections on Philip the Fair of France." *Speculum* 87.1 (January 2012): 1–36.

Bruzelius, Caroline. "Charles I, Charles II, and the Development of an Angevin Style in the Kingdom of Sicily. " In *L'état angevin,* 99–114.

—. "Queen Sancia of Mallorca and the Convent Church of Sta. Chiara in Naples." *Memoirs of the American Academy in Rome* 40. Ann Arbor: University of Michigan Press 1995, 69–100.

—. *The Stones of Naples: Church Building in Angevin Italy, 1266–1343.* New Haven: Yale University Press, 2004.

Burckhardt, Jacob. *The Civilization of the Renaissance in Italy.* S.G.C. Middlemore, trans. Benjamin Nelson and Charkles Trinkaus, eds. 2 vols. New York: Harper & Row, 1958.

Bynum, Caroline. *Fragmentation and Redemption: Essays on Gender and the Human Body in Medieval Religion.* New York: Zone Books, 1992.

—. "Violent Imagery in Late Medieval Piety." *Bulletin of the German Historical Institute* (2002): 3–36.

Caggese, Romolo. *Roberto d'Angiò e i suoi tempi.* 2 vols. Florence: Bemporad e Figlu, 1922–30; repr. Bologna: Il Mulino, 2001.

Carozzi, Claude. "La victoire de Bénévent et la légitimité de Charles d'Anjou." In *Guerre, pouvoir et noblesse au Moyen Âge: Mélanges en l'honneur de Philippe Contamine.* Jacques Paviot and Jacques Verger, eds. Paris: Presses de l'Université de Paris, 2000, 139–45.

Casteen, Elizabeth. "Sex and Politics in Naples: The Regnant Queenship of Johanna I of Naples, 1343–1382." *Journal of the Historical Society* 11 (June 2011): 183–210.

Catto, Jeremy. "Ideas and Experience in the Political Thought of Aquinas." *Past & Present* 71 (1975): 3–21.

Clarke, Paula. "The Villani Chronicles." In *Chronicling History: Chroniclers and Historians in Medieval and Renaissance Italy.* Sharon Dale, Alison Williams Lewin, and Duane J. Osheim, eds. University Park: Pennsylvania State University Press, 2007.

Clogan, Paul M. "Italian Humanism in the Court of King Robert of Anjou." In *Acta Conventus Neo-Latini Bariensis.* Medieval & Renaissance Texts & Studies 184. Rhoda Schnur, et al., eds. Tempe, AZ: MRTS, 1998, 189–98.

Cohen, Ester. "The Animated Pain of the Body." *American Historical Review* 105.1 (Feb. 2000): 36–68.

De Frede, Carlo. "Da Carlo I d'Angio à Giovanna I (1263–1382)." In SN 3:1–333.

de Rosa, Luigi. "Land and Sea Transport and Economic Depression in the Kingdom of Naples from the Fourteenth to the Eighteenth Century." *The Journal of European Economic History* 25.2 (1996): 339–68.

Dunbabin, Jean. *Charles I of Anjou: Power, Kingship and State-Making in Thirteenth-Century Europe.* London: Longman, 1998.

—. *The French in the Kingdom of Sicily, 1266–1305.* Cambridge: Cambridge University Press, 2011.

Duran, Michelle. "The Politics of Art: Imaging Sovereignty in the Anjou Bible," in Watteeuw and Van der Stock, *The Anjou Bible,* 73–93.

Edgerton, Samuel, Jr. *Pictures and Punishment: Art and Criminal Prosecution during the Florentine Renaissance.* Ithaca: Cornell University Press, 1985.

Egidi, P. "Ricerche sulla populazione dell'Italia meridionale nei secoli XIII e XIV." In *Miscellanea di studi storici in onore di Giovanni Sforza.* Paolo Boselli, ed. Turin: Baroni, 1920, 731–50.

Elliott, Janis, and Cordelia Warr, eds. *The Church of Santa Maria Donna Regina: Art, Iconography, and Patronage in Fourteenth-Century Naples.* Burlington, VT: Ashgate, 2004.

Enderlein, Lorenz. *Die Grablegen des Hauses Anjou in Unteritalien: Totenkult und Monumente 1266–1343.* Römische Studien der Bibliotheca Hertziana, Bd. 12. Worms-am-Rhein: Wernersche Verlagsgesellschaft, 1997.

Enders, Jody. *The Medieval Theater of Cruelty: Rhetoric, Memory, Violence.* Ithaca: Cornell University Press, 1999.

Epstein, Steven. *Wills and Wealth in Medieval Genoa, 1150–1250.* Cambridge: Harvard University Press, 1984.

L'état angevin: Pouvoir, culture et société entre XIIIe et XIVe siècle. Collection de l'École Française de Rome 245; Nuovi studi storici 45. Rome: École Française de Rome & ISIME, 1998.

Feniello, Amedeo. "Gli interventi sanitari dei secoli XIV e XV." In *Napoli nel Medioevo. La Città del Mezzogiorno Medievale* 4 (2007): 123–35.

—. "Napoli al tempo di Renato d'Angiò," BISEAMI 112 (2010): 273–95

Fleck Cathleen A. *The Clement Bible at the Medieval Courts of Naples and Avignon: A Story of Papal Power, Royal Prestige, and Patronage.* Farnham, Surrey, UK: Ashgate, 2010.

—. "Patronage, Art, and the Anjou Bible in Angevin Naples (1266–1352)." In Lieve Watteeuw and Jan Ven der Stock, eds., *The Anjou Bible: A Royal Manuscript Revealed, Naples 1340.* Leuven: Peeters, 2010, 37–51.

Forcellini, Vincenzo. "'L'horrendum tripes animal' della lettera 3 del libro V delle *Familiari* di Petrarca." In *Studi di storia napoletana in onore di Michelangelo Schipa*. Naples: I.T.E.A., 1926, 167–99.

Fuiano, Michele. *Carlo I d'Angiò in Italia: Studi e ricerche*. Naples: Liguori, 1974.

Gaglione, Mario. "La basilica ed il monastero doppio di S. Chiara a Napoli in studi recenti." *Archivio per la storia della donna* 4 (2007): 127–209.

—. *Donne e potere a Napoli: Le sovrane angioine. Consorti, vicarie e regnanti (1266–1442)*. Catanzaro: Rubbertino Editore for l'Alto Patrocinio dell'Università degli Studi di Napoli Federico II, 2009.

Gardner, Julian. "Saint Louis of Toulouse, Robert of Anjou, and Simone Martini." *Zeitschrift für Kunstgeschichte* 39 (1976): 12–33.

Gilli, Patrick. "L'intégration manquée des Angevins en Italie: Le témoignage des historiens." In *L'état Angevin*, 11–33.

Goldstone, Nancy. *The Lady Queen: The Notorious Reign of Joanna I*. New York: Walker & Company, 2009.

Greenblatt, Stephen. *Renaissance Self-Fashioning: From More to Shakespeare*. Chicago: University of Chicago Press, 1980.

Groebner, Valentin. *Defaced: The Visual Culture of Violence in the Late Middle Ages*. Pamela Selwyn, trans. New York: Zone Books, 2004.

Guerri dall'Oro, Guido. "Les mercenaires dans les campagnes napolitaines de Louis le Grand, roi de Hongrie, 1347–1350." In *Mercenaries and Paid Men: The Mercenary Identity in the Middle Ages*. John France, ed. Leiden, Brill, 2008, 61–88.

Guidarelli, Gianmario. "La costruzione del Duomo di Napoli e l'invenzione di una falsa tradizione." In *Storia e narrazione: Retorica, memoria, immagini*. Gianmario Guidarelli and Carmelo G. Malacrino, eds. Milan: Mondadori, 2005, 35–44.

—. "La ricostruzione angioina della cattedrale di Napoli, 1294–1333." In *I luoghi del sacro: Il sacro e la città fra medioevo ed età moderna*. Fabrizio Ricciardelli, ed. Florence: Mauro Pagliai Editore, 2008, 187–206.

Hamburger, Jeffrey F. "Medieval Self-Fashioning: Authorship, Authority, and Autobiography in Suso's Exemplar." In *The Visual and the Visionary: Art and Female Spirituality in Late Medieval Germany*. New York: Zone Books, 1998, 233–78.

Hay, Denys, and John Law. *Italy in the Age of the Renaissance, 1380–1530*. New York: Longman, 1989.

Herde, Peter. *Karl I von Anjou*. Stuttgart: Kohlhammer, 1979.

—, and Stefano Tiraboschi. *Cölestin V. (1294): Peter vom Morrone, der Engelpapst. Mit einem Urkundenanhang und Edition zweier Viten.*

Stuttgart: Hiersemann, 1981.

Hersey, George L. *The Aragonese Arch at Naples 1443–1475*. New Haven: Yale University Press, 1973.

Heullant-Donat, Isabelle. "Quelques réflexions autour de la cour angevine comme milieu culturel au XIVe siècle." In *L'état angevin*, 173–91.

Hinch, Jim. "On The Swerve: Why Stephen Greenblat Is Wrong — and Why it Matters." *Los Angeles Review of Books* (Dec. 1, 2012), http://lareviewofbooks.org/article.php?type&id=1217&fulltext=1&media#article-text-cutpoint. Accessed 12/1/12.

Hoch, Adrian S. "*Beata Stirps*, Royal Patronage and the Identification of the Sainted Rulers in the St. Elizabeth Chapel at Assisi." *Art History* 15.3 (1992): 279–95.

Horrox, Rosemary, ed. *The Black Death*. Manchester: Manchester University Press, 1994.

Housley, Norman. *The Italian Crusades: The Papal–Angevin Alliance and the Crusades against Christian Lay Powers, 1254–1343*. New York: Oxford University Press, 1982.

Irblich, Eva, and Gabriel Bise. *The Illuminated Naples Bible: Old Testament, 14th-Century Manuscript*. G. Ivans and D. MacRae, trans. New York: Crescent Books, 1979.

Jamison, E.M. "Documents from the Angevin Registers of Naples: Charles I." *Papers of the British School at Rome* 17 (1949): 87–89.

Jones, Michael. "The Last Capetians and Early Valois Kings, 1314–1364." In *The New Cambridge Medieval History* 6, c.1300–c.1415. Michael Jones et al., eds. Cambridge: Cambridge University Press, 2000, 388–421.

Jordan, Constance. "Boccaccio's In–Famous Women: Gender and Civic Virtue in the *De mulieribus claris*." In *Ambiguous Realities: Women in the Middle Ages and Renaissance*. C. Levin and J. Watson, eds. Detroit: Wayne State University Press, 1987, 25–47.

Jordan, William C. *The Great Famine: Northern Europe in the Early Fourteenth Century*. Princeton: Princeton University Press, 1996.

Kekewich, Margaret Lucille. *The Good King: René of Anjou and Fifteenth Century Europe*. Basingstoke, UK: Palgrave Macmillan, 2008.

Kelly, Samantha, ed. *The Cronaca di Partenope: An Introduction to and Critical Edition of the First Vernacular History of Naples (c.1350)*. Leiden: Brill, 2011.

—. *The New Solomon: Robert of Naples (1309–1343) and Fourteenth-Century Kingship*. Leiden: Brill, 2003.

—. "Royal Patronage and Royal Propaganda in Angevin Naples: Santa Maria Donna Regina in Context." In Elliott and Warr, *The Church of Santa Maria Donna Regina*, 27–43.

Kiesewetter, Andreas. "La cancelleria angioina." In *L'état Angevin*, 360–415.

Killerby, Catherine K. *Sumptuary Law in Italy, 1200–1500*. Oxford: Clarendon Press, 2002.

Lecoy de la Marche, Richard Albert. *Le roi René: Sa vie, son administration, ses travaux artistiques et littéraires d'après les documents inédits des archives de France et d'Italie*. Paris: Firmin-Didot, 1875.

Léonard, Emile G. *Les Angevins de Naples*. Paris: Presses Universitaires de France, 1954.

—. *Histoire de Jeanne I, reine de Naples, comtesse de Provence (1343–1382): Mémoires et documents historiques*. 3 vols. Monaco: Imprimerie de Monaco, 1932–37.

Leone de Castris, Pierluigi. *Arte di corte nella Napoli angioina*. Florence: Cantini, 1986.

—, ed. *Castel Nuovo: Il Museo Civico*. Naples: E. de Rosa, 1990.

—. "Napoli, capitale del Mezzogiorno angioina: L'arte e la corte." In Musca, 127–99.

Lewis, Andrew W. *Royal Succession in Capetian France: Studies on Familial Order and the State*. Cambridge: Harvard University Press, 1981.

Lokaj, Rodney. "La Cleopatra neapoletana: Giovanna d'Angiò nelle 'Familiares' di Petrarca." *Giornale storico della Letteratura Italiana* 177 (2000): 481–521.

Maillard, Jean. *Adam de La Halle: Perspective musicale*. Paris: H. Champion, 1982.

Martin, Jean-Marie. "Fiscalité et économie étatique dans le royaume angevin de Sicile à la fin du XIIIe siècle." In *L'état Angevin*, 601–48.

Mazzoleni, Jole. "Les archives des Angevins de Naples." In Bonnot, 25–29.

McCracken, Peggy. *The Romance of Adultery: Queenship and Sexual Transgression in Old French Literature*. Philadelphia: University of Pennsylvania Press, 1998.

Merback, Mitchell B. *The Thief, the Cross, and the Wheel: Pain and the Spectacle of Punishment in Medieval and Renaissance Europe*. Chicago: University of Chicago Press, 1999.

Meyerson, Mark D., Daniel Thiery, and Oren Falk, eds. *"A Great Effusion of Blood"? Interpreting Medieval Violence*. Toronto: University of Toronto Press, 2004.

Michalsky, Tanja "Die Repräsentation einer *Beata Stirps*: Darstellung und Ausdruck an den Grabmonumenten der Anjous." In *Die*

Repräsentation der Gruppen. Texte – Bilder – Objekte. Andrea von Huelsen Esch, Otto Gerhard Oexle, eds. Göttingen: Vandenhoeck & Ruprecht, 1998, 187–224.

Minieri-Riccio, "Geneaologia," ASPN 7 (1882): 254.

Miskimin, Harry A. *The Economy of Early Renaissance Europe, 1300–1460.* Cambridge: Cambridge University Press, 1975.

Morisani, Ottavio. *Pittura del trecento in Napoli.* Naples: Libreria scientifica editrice, 1947.

—. "L'Arte di Napoli nell'età angioina." SN 3:575–664.

—. "Monumenti trecenteschi dei Angioini a Napoli." In *Gli Angioini di Napoli e Ungheria: Atti del colloquio italo–ungherese.* Rome: Accademia Nazionale dei Lincei, 1972, 159–73.

Mott, Lawrence V. *Sea Power in the Medieval Mediterranean: The Catalan–Aragonese Fleet in the War of the Sicilian Vespers.* New Perspectives on Maritime History and Nautical Archaeology. Gainesville: University Press of Florida, 2003.

Musca, Giosuè, Francesco Tateo, Enrico Annoscia, and Pierluigi Leone de Castris, eds. *La Cultura angioina: Civiltà del Mezzogiorno.* Milan: Silvano Editoriale, 1985.

Musto, Ronald G. *Apocalypse in Rome: Cola di Rienzo and the Politics of the New Age.* Berkeley: University of California Press, 2003.

—. "Franciscan Joachimism at the Court of Naples, 1309–1345: A New Appraisal," *Archivum Franciscanum Historicum* 90.3–4 (1997): 419–86.

—. "Queen Sancia of Naples (1286–1345) and the Spiritual Franciscans." In *Women of the Medieval World.* Julius Kirshner and Suzanne F. Wemple, eds. Oxford: Basil Blackwell, 1985, 179–214.

—. "Review of Paolo Vitolo, *La chiesa della Regina: L'Incoronata di Napoli, Giovanna I d'Angiò e Roberto di Oderisio.* Rome: Viella, 2008." *Renaissance Quarterly* 62 (Spring 2009): 200–201.

—. "Review of Samantha Kelly, *The New Solomon: Robert of Naples (1309–1343) and Fourteenth-Century Kingship.*" *Renaissance Quarterly* 57.3 (Autumn 2004): 984–85.

—. "Review of *The Anjou Bible: A Royal Manuscript Revealed. Naples 1340,* ed. Lieve Watteeuw and Jan Van der Stock; *The Clement Bible at the Medieval Courts of Naples and Avignon: A Story of Papal Power, Royal Prestige, and Patronage,* by Cathleen A. Fleck." *Renaissance Quarterly* 64.2 (Summer 2011): 587–90.

Nelson Sargent-Baur, Barbara ed. and trans. *Philippe de Remi Beaumanoir, Manekine, John and Blonde, and "Foolish Generosity."* University Park:

Pennsylvania State University Press, 2010.

Orefice, Marcello. *Il vecchio Maschio degli Angioini: Tra fantasie e storiche realtà. La rivisitazione di un castello definitivamente perduto*. Naples: Edizioni scientifiche italiane, 2008.

Paciocco, Roberto. "Angioini e 'spirituali': I differenti piani cronologici e tematici di un problema." In *L'état Angevin*, 253–87.

Pade, Marianne, Hannemarie Ragn Jensen, and Lene Waage Petersen, eds. *Avignon and Naples: Italy in France–France in Italy in the Fourteenth Century*. Rome: L'Erma di Bretschneider, 1997.

Palmieri, Stefano. *La cancelleria del regno di Sicilia in età angioina*. Naples: Accademia Pontaniana, 2006.

—. "Il Castelnuovo di Napoli: Reggia e fortezza angioina." *Atti della Accademia Pontiniana* n.s. 47 (1999): 501–19.

Pane, Giulio. *La Tavola Strozzi tra Napoli e Firenze: Un'immagine della città nel quattrocento*. Naples: Grimaldi & C. Editori, 2009.

Paone, Stefania. "La cappella Minutolo nel duomo di Napoli: Le storie apostoliche e i miti di fondazione dell'episcopio." In *Medioevo: Immagine e memoria*. Milan: Electa, 2009, 423–35.

Perriccioli Saggese, Alessandra. *I romanzi cavallereschi miniati a Napoli*. Naples: Società Editrice Napoletana, 1979.

Peyronnet, George. "I Durazzo e Renato d'Angiò, 1381–1442." SN 3:335–436.

Pryds, Darleen. *The King Embodies the Word: Robert d'Anjou and the Politics of Preaching*. Studies in the History of Christian Thought 93. Leiden: Brill, 2000.

—. "The Politics of Preaching in Fourteenth-Century Naples: Robert d'Anjou (1309–1343) and His Sermons." Ph.D. diss., University of Wisconsin-Madison, 1994.

Rothbarth, Margarete. *Urban VI. und Neapel*. Berlin: Oldenbourg, 1913.

Rotili, Mario. *Miniatura francese a Napoli*. Benevento: Museo del Sannio, 1968.

Rouillard, Linda Marie. "Review of Jean Wauquelin, *La Manequine*. Maria Colombo Timelli, ed. Textes Littéraires du Moyen Âge, 13; Séries Mises en Prose 1 (Paris: Éditions Classiques Garnier, 2010)." *Speculum* 87.1 (January 2012): 288–89.

Runciman, Steven. *The Sicilian Vespers: A History of the Mediterranean World in the Thirteenth Century*. Cambridge: Cambridge University Press, 1958.

Sabatini, Francesco. "Lingue e letterature volgari in competizione." In Carratelli, 401–31.

—. *Napoli angioìna: Cultura e società*. Naples: Edizioni scientifiche italiene, 1975.

Samaran, C.S. "Les registres angevins de Naples." *Bibliothèque de l'Ecole de Chartes* 115 (1957):192–93.

Senatore, Francesco. "The Kingdom of Naples." In *The Italian Renaissance State*. Andrea Gamberini and Isabella Lazzarini, eds. New York: Cambridge University Press, 2012, 30–49.

St. Claire Baddeley, Welbore. *Robert the Wise and His Heirs 1278–1352*. London: W. Heinemann, 1897.

Starn, Randolph. *Ambrogio Lorenzetti: The Palazzo Pubblico, Siena*. New York: George Braziller, 1994.

Stillinger, Thomas C., and Regina Psaki, eds. *Boccaccio and Feminist Criticism*. Chapel Hill, NC: Annali d'Italianistica, 2006.

Swann Jones, Steven. "The Innocent Persecuted Heroine Genre: An Analysis of Its Structure and Themes." *Western Folklore* 52 (1993): 13–41.

Thomas, Chantal. *The Wicked Queen: The Origins of the Myth of Marie-Antoinette*. New York: Zone Books, 2001.

Torraca, Francesco. "Giovanni Boccaccio a Napoli (1326–1339)." ASPN 39 (1914): 25–80, 229–67, 409–58, 605–96.

Toynbee, Margaret R.S. *Louis of Toulouse and the Process of Canonisation in the Fourteenth Century*. Manchester: University Press, 1929.

Unterkircher, Franz, ed. *King René's Book of Love: Le Cueur d'Amours Espris*. New York: G. Braziller, 1975.

Vagnoni, Mirko. "Una nota sulla regalità sacra di Roberto d'Angiò alla luce della ricerca iconografica." *Archivio Storico Italiano* 167.620 (2009): 253–67.

Venditti, Arnaldo. "Urbanistica e architettura angioina." SN 3:665–888.

Vitale, Giuliana. *Élite burocratica e famiglia: Dinamiche nobiliari e processi di costruzione statale nella Napoli angioino-aragonese*. Naples: Liguori, 2003.

Vitolo, Giovanni. "Il regno angioino." In *Storia del Mezzogiorno* 4.1. *Il Regno dagli Angioini ai Borboni*. Giuseppe Galasso and R. Romeo, eds. Rome: Edizioni del Sole-Rizzoli, 1986; Editalia, 1994, 9–86.

—. "L'età svevo–angioina." In Carratelli, 87–144.

—, and Rosalba Di Meglio. *Napoli angioino–aragonese: Confraternite, ospedali, dinamiche politico–sociali*. Salerno: Carlone, 2003.

Vitolo, Paola. *La chiesa della regina: L'Incoronata di Napoli, Giovanni I d'Angiò e Roberto di Oderisio*. Rome: Viella, 2008.

Warr, Cordelia, and Janis Elliott, eds. *Art and Architecture in Naples, 1266–*

1713: New Approaches. Malden, MA: Wiley-Blackwell, 2010.

Watteeuw, Lieve, and Jan Van der Stock, eds. *The Anjou Bible: A Royal Manuscript Revealed. Naples 1340.* Leuven: Peeters, 2010.

Weisheipl, James A. *Friar Thomas d'Aquino: His Life, Thought and Works.* Oxford: Blackwell, 1974.

Wilkins, Ernest Hatch. *Life of Petrarch.* Chicago: University of Chicago Press, 1961.

Ziegler, Philip. *The Black Death.* Harmondsworth: Penguin Books, 1970.

■

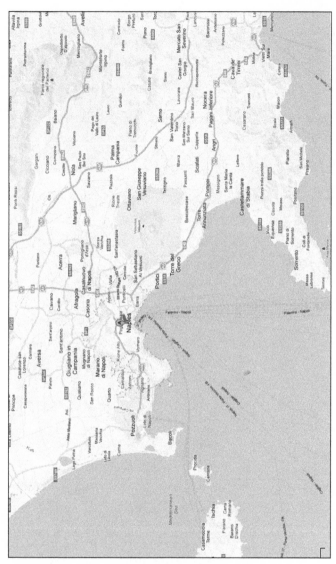

Map of Naples and Campania. Source: Google Map

APPENDICES

ONLINE RESOURCES

INTERACTIVE MAP: http://www.italicapress.com/index287.html

ONLINE BIBLIOGRAPHY: http://www.italicapress.com/index346.html

KINDLE EDITIONS
Bruzelius & Tronzo, *Medieval Naples: An Architectural & Urban History:*
    http://www.amazon.com/dp/B0091Y5WZO
Musto, *Medieval Naples: A Documentary History:* http://www.amazon.
    comMedieval-Documentary-History-400-1400-ebook/dp/B0064P03ZC

IMAGE GALLERIES
The URL for each site is derived from taking tURL (http://www.flickr.com/photos/80499896@N05/sets/72157630) and adding the specific site number. The numbers of images in each gallery is the total uploaded as of January 1, 2013.

Site	Gallery #	Images
Castel Capuano	808244632	10
Castel dell'Ovo	153362290	33
Castel Nuovo	165392752	26
Castel Sant'Elmo (Belforte)	808796440	7
Catacomb of San Gennaro	152526498	11
Certosa di San Martino	152166968	5
Duomo (Cathedral)	152316564	30
S. Domenico Maggiore	148664544	37
S. Giorgio Maggiore	150173448	12
S. Giovanni a Carbonara	164220128	26
S. Giovanni a Mare	169072410	13
S. Giovanni a Pappacoda	151046570	16
S. Giovanni in Fonte (Baptistery)	149953976	13
S. Giovanni Maggiore	159535292	29
S. Lorenzo Maggiore	149709946	22
S. Paolo Maggiore	150918068	11
S. Pietro a Maiella	168803908	11
Sant'Eligio	166265640	15
Sta. Chiara	151262510	39
Sta. Chiara, Campanile	168472374	10
Sta. Maria Donnaregina	164795244	25
Sta. Maria Incoronata	165725336	35
Sta. Maria Maggiore (Pietrasanta)	150746808	19
Sta. Restituta	149817080	11
Total images as of 12/29/2010		**466**

∎

Castelluccio di Pizzofalcone   Castel Nuovo (5)   Castel Belforte (1

Castel dell'Ovo (4)   Sta. Croce (51)   Torre dell'Oro   Certosa di S.Martino (9)

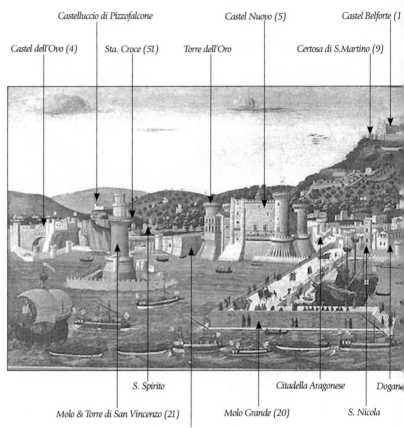

S. Spirito   Citadella Aragonese   Dogan

Molo & Torre di San Vincenzo (21)   Molo Grande (20)   S. Nicola

Palace of the Angevin Princes

THE TAVOLA STROZZI

The *Tavola Strozzi* is a panoramic panel painting of the bay, city and environs of Naples. It was discovered by Corrado Ricci in 1901 in the Palazzo Strozzi in Florence. The scholarly consensus now identifies it as the celebration of the Aragonese defeat of Jean d'Anjou on 7 July 1465 at the naval battle of Ischia. The painting is tempera on wood, 82 x 245 cm., now in the Museo di San Martino. It was most likely a cassone panel, or perhaps the headboard of a bed, designed by Benedetto da Maiano. It has been convincingly dated now to between 1465 and 1478, most likely to 1472/73. The crispness of its detail provides a remarkably accurate visual source for the Aragonese and medieval city.

S. Domenico Maggiore
(28)

S. Giovanni a Carbonara
(30)

Castel Capuano
(2)

S. Pietro ad Aram
(39)

Monteoliveto
(43)

Sta. Chiara (48)

S. Lorenzo Maggiore
(35)

Duomo (18)

SS. Annunziata
(45)

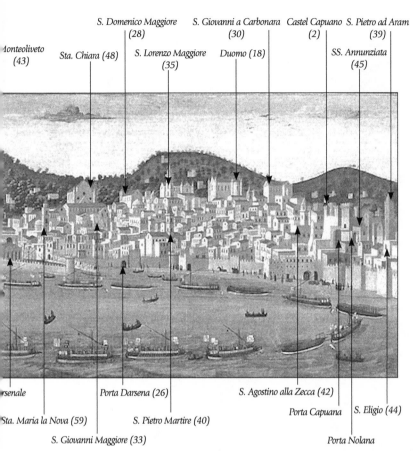

senale

Sta. Maria la Nova (59)

Porta Darsena (26)

S. Pietro Martire (40)

S. Giovanni Maggiore (33)

S. Agostino alla Zecca (42)

Porta Capuana

S. Eligio (44)

Porta Nolana

The perspective point of the *Tavola* is either from a ship off the Molo Grande or from the tower on the Molo itself, as argued in a recent analysis by Roberto Taito (http://www.tavolastrozzi.it/studio.htm). Scholarly consensus had settled on Francesco Rosselli or Francesco Pagano as its painter, but this has been cast into doubt by Pane (2009), 94–119, 141–67, who cites the lack of documentary evidence and attributes it to an unknown Tuscan painter, perhaps in Florence or Siena (141), who executed it from perspective drawings carried out in Naples. The image has been discussed and analyzed at length. See, for example, Di Mauro (1992); De Seta (1997), 11–53; and most recently in Pane (2009).

Labels are to identifiable sites and many are also keyed to the map below, pp. 348–49.

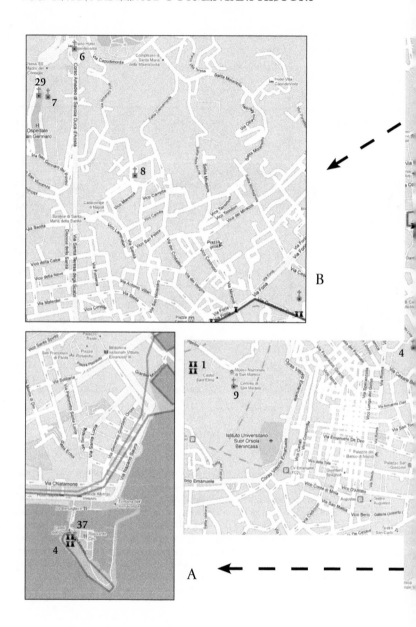

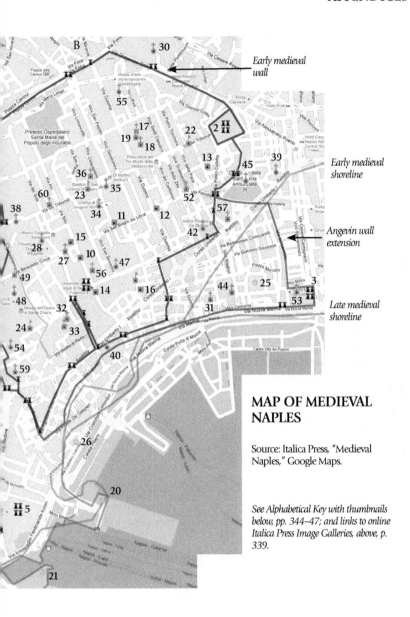

Early medieval
wall

Early medieval
shoreline

Angevin wall
extension

Late medieval
shoreline

MAP OF MEDIEVAL NAPLES

Source: Italica Press, "Medieval Naples," Google Maps.

See Alphabetical Key with thumbnails below, pp. 344–47; and links to online Italica Press Image Galleries, above, p. 339.

ALPHABETICAL KEY TO MAP

1. Castel Belforte (Sant'Elmo, Sant'Erasmo)

9. Certosa di S. Martino

2. Castel Capuano

10. Diaconia of S. Andrea ad Nilum

3. Castel del Carmine

11. Diaconia of S. Gennaro all'Olmo

4. Castel dell'Ovo

12. Diaconia of S. Giorgio Maggiore

5. Castel Nuovo

13. Diaconia of S. Pietro

6. Catacomb of S. Gaudioso

14. Diaconia of SS. Giovanni e Paolo

7. Catacomb of S. Gennaro

15. Diaconia of Sta. Maria ad Presepem

8. Catacomb of S. Severo

16. Diaconia of Sta. Maria in Cosmedin (in Portanova)

17. Duomo: Baptistery (San Giovanni in Fonte)

 18. Duomo: Cathedral of Sta. Maria Assunta

 19. Duomo: Sta. Restituta

 20. Molo Grande

 21. Torre & Molo S. Vincenzo

 22. Palazzo of Gianni Caracciolo

 23. Palace of Philip of Taranto

 24. Palazzo Penna

 25. Piazza del Mercato

 26. Portus de Arcina

 27. S. Angelo a Nilo

 28. S. Domenico Maggiore

 29. S. Gennaro extra Moenia

 30. S. Giovanni a Carbonara

 31. S. Giovanni a Mare

 32. S. Giovanni a Pappacoda

33. S. Giovanni Maggiore

 34. S. Gregorio Armeno

 35. S. Lorenzo Maggiore

 36. S. Paolo Maggiore

 37. S. Pietro a Castello

 38. S. Pietro a Maiella

 39. S. Pietro ad Aram

 40. S. Pietro Martire

 41. S. Trinità al Palazzo

 42. Sant'Agostino alla Zecca

 43. Sant' Anna dei Lombardi (Monteoliveto)

 44. Sant'Eligio

 45. SS. Annunziata

 46. SS. Sergio, Bacco e Sebastiano

 47. SS. Severino e Sossio

 48. Sta. Chiara

49. Sta. Chiara: Campanile

 57. Sta. Maria Egiziaca

 50. Sta. Chiara: Friars' Church

 58. Sta. Maria Incoronata

 51. Sta. Croce

 59. Sta. Maria la Nova

 52. Sta. Maria in Piazza

 60. Sta. Maria Maggiore (Pietrasanta)

 53. Sta. Maria del Carmine

 54. Sta. Maria Donnalbina

 55. Sta. Maria Donnaregina

 56. Sta. Maria Donnaromita

Fig. 74. S. Giovanni Maggiore. Apse, triumphal arch, northwest column with monogram of Bishop Vincentius (r.558–81). Photo: Italica Press.

INDEX

■

This Book Was Completed on January 19, 2013
At Italica Press in New York, NY. It Was Set in
ITC Giovanni and Adobe Charlemagne.
This Print Edition Was Produced
On 60-lb Natural Paper
in the USA, UK
and EU
■

CPSIA information can be obtained
at www.ICGtesting.com
Printed in the USA
FSHW012029131218
54469FS